Recognition in the Arabic Narrative Tradition

Edinburgh Studies in Classical Arabic Literature
Series Editors: Wen-chin Ouyang and Julia Bray

This series departs from conventional writing on Classical Arabic Literature. It integrates into its terms of enquiry both cultural and literary theory and the historical contexts and conceptual categories that shaped individual writers or works of literature. Its approach provides a forum for path-breaking research which has yet to exert an impact on the scholarship. The purpose of the series is to open up new vistas on an intellectual and imaginative tradition that has repeatedly contributed to world cultures and has the continued capacity to stimulate new thinking.

Books in the series include:

The Reader in al-Jāḥiẓ
Thomas Hefter

Recognition in the Arabic Narrative Tradition: Discovery, Deliverance and Delusion
Philip F. Kennedy

Counsel for Kings: Wisdom and Politics in Tenth-Century Iran
Volume I: *The* Naṣīḥat al-mulūk *of Pseudo-Māwardī: Contexts and Themes*
Louise Marlow

Counsel for Kings: Wisdom and Politics in Tenth-Century Iran
Volume II: *The* Naṣīḥat al-mulūk *of Pseudo-Māwardī: Texts, Sources and Authorities*
Louise Marlow

Al- Jāḥiẓ: In Praise of Books
James E. Montgomery

Al- Jāḥiẓ: In Censure of Books
James E. Montgomery

Hikayat Abi al-Qasim*: A Literary Banquet*
Emily Selove

The Qur'an: Literary Perspectives
Shawkat M. Toorawa

edinburghuniversitypress.com/series/escal

Recognition in the Arabic Narrative Tradition

Discovery, Deliverance and Delusion

Philip F. Kennedy

EDINBURGH
University Press

For
Alan Jones
res ipsa loquitur

Edinburgh University Press is one of the leading university presses in the UK. We publish academic books and journals in our selected subject areas across the humanities and social sciences, combining cutting-edge scholarship with high editorial and production values to produce academic works of lasting importance. For more information visit our website: edinburghuniversitypress.com

Edinburgh University Press Ltd
The Tun – Holyrood Road
12 (2f) Jackson's Entry
Edinburgh EH8 8PJ

First published in hardback by Edinburgh University Press 2016

Typeset in 11/15 Adobe Garamond by
Servis Filmsetting Ltd, Stockport, Cheshire,
and printed and bound in Great Britain by
CPI Group (UK) Ltd, Croydon CR0 4YY

A CIP record for this book is available from the British Library

ISBN 978 1 4744 1372 5 (hardback)
ISBN 978 1 4744 3217 7 (paperback)
ISBN 978 1 4744 1373 2 (webready PDF)
ISBN 978 1 4744 1374 9 (epub)

Contents

Preface and Acknowledgements

In the early 1990s, when I was a Junior Research Fellow at St John's College, Oxford, I read closely the picaresque narratives of Badī^{c} al-Zamān al-Hamadhānī (d. 1008 AD), known as the *maqāmāt*. I was particularly interested in their allusive, intertextual aspects and was puzzled by the consistency of the recognition scenes that are a mainstay of the *maqāmah* genre. Terence Cave was a tutor and fellow in French literature at St John's and had just published *Recognitions: A Study in Poetics* (1988), a masterpiece of literary analysis raised from a detailed reading of Aristotle's *Poetics*. In conversations with Professor Cave I realised quickly the importance of his study to my understanding of the *maqāmāt* as a genre, but also to literary studies in general – his work surely deserves no less the renown and influence of Erich Auerbach's *Mimesis*.

Since the mid-1990s an interest in recognition generally has resulted in my compiling a series of case studies that probe its nature in pre-modern Arabic literature. By 2005 I progressed as far as an examination of recognition in the development of Naguib Mahfouz's *oeuvre*: the results are enlightening regarding the growth of the author's discrete literary dispositions. The need to publish some of this work became ever more pressing, but the effort to finish the typescript would lead each summer to amassing ever more materials and case studies; the pressure I put on myself to finish I mixed up, mistakenly, with the desire to be exhaustive.

I owe the solution to my dilemma to the brilliance and engaged editorial guidance of friends: my series editors, Wen-chin Ouyang and Julia Bray; my pals, Shawkat Toorawa and James Montgomery; and my professional editor, Gemma Juan-Simó. All counselled me the same way: 'publish your earliest materials first: they constitute an organic study on their own'. More than I could perceive, they saw the centrality of Joseph in these first forays into my examination of anagnorisis and so in recent months I gave up the idea of producing a book that would exhaust two decades' worth of readings. I have left to mature further for another day my studies of the *Arabian Nights*, of *adab* micro- and macro-narratives, of Isma^{c}ili biographies and autobiographies, of the Arab Oedipus, of the contemporary Arab novel, and of the insights that world literature and film can shed on the cognitive nature of Arabic literature. The chapters that follow, then, are the earliest harvests of my study and hold together in broadest terms and organically – or so I hope – as a single study of recognition and providence and recognition and delusion. It has been a strange experience to follow my tracks into the past, unearth and reread early drafts of materials, guided by my colleagues and mentors, to revive for present purposes something worth publishing. Retrospection yields insight – that is certainly something one learns from anagnorisis.

Over the years I have included anagnorisis among the subjects that I teach at New York University and NYU Abu Dhabi. My first classes focused more on Arabic materials but with time I have tried to place recognition in Arabic literature within the narrative context more broadly across cultures. All courses I have taught have featured films that illustrate various aspects of Aristotle's figure. *Babette's Feast*, *The Third Man*, *Fiore delle Mille e una Notte* and *Angel Heart* have been among my favourites, but there is scarcely a film or a book that I come across that does not advance my sense of the importance, variety – and inexhaustibility – of anagnorisis in creative narrative expression. I thank the undergraduates who sat through my courses. Among my graduate students, now scholars and teachers in their own right, I acknowledge fondly the insights over the years of Chris Stone, Jeannie Miller, Kristin Sands, Lara Harb, Mark Wagner, Rebecca Johnson, Robyn Creswell, Shareah Taleghani, Waiel Abdelwahed and the late Walter Oller.

Among the scholars from whom I have received help and much insight are Andras Hamori, Dan Beaumont, Geert Jan van Gelder, Marilyn Lawrence, Marlé Hammond, Piero Boitani, Richard Allen, Richard Sieburth, Robert Irwin, Wendy Doniger, the members of the Columbia Arabic Studies Seminar and the members of the School of Abbasid Studies. Marina Warner has consistently been most kind in assuring me the book was well worth the effort of finishing. To Michael Gilsenan I owe the memories of many conversations. Opera has often been the meeting point of our shared interest in recognition. But more than all else, Michael has always encouraged a faltering young colleague to 'get on with it'. It is a role of cajoling, kindly but firmly, he took over with aplomb from Professor Alan Jones, my first teacher and mentor. I am grateful to Zvi Ben Dor, the encumbent 'chair' of my department in New York, for invaluable encouragement over the last 18 months.

Over the years, my family – in French and in English – have been sweetly baffled by my obsession with recognition. But after much experience, they can see a recognition scene coming a mile off and while not wishing to probe every aspect of the figure (they prefer to enjoy their films and their books) they have helped me gather a corpus that stretches far beyond this volume, indeed, beyond Arabic literature. I thank them with all the emotional force and vigour I can muster for their love and their patience, especially for forgiving my travails with excess luggage during the itinerant summer months and during my absences over the years in sundry corners of adopted, and invariably messy, study retreats. *Du fond du coeur, merci Marianne, India, Gabriel, Isabelle, Agnès, Nicole, Philippe et 'Philou'.* I thank my mother with love and earnest for convincing me that a life spent studying Arabic, if done seriously, would not be one wasted; and my father, just as deeply, for the support he provided me with when I spent an academic year at the American University in Cairo. They both, in different ways, shaped my life. I thank my sister and brother, Florence and Edward, for looking after my diasporic family meanwhile.

I thank the Faculty of Arts and Science, NYU, and the NYU Abu Dhabi Institute for two generous study leaves that were spent in part writing the materials within these pages. Most recently my wonderful and inspiring colleagues at the NYU Abu Dhabi Institute have been clement with me during the months this past autumn when I finalised this typescript. Antoine, Gila, Lisa, Manal, Nahed, Nils, Nora, Reindert, Sharon, Tarek: I am grateful and indebted to you all. I am grateful also to Nicola Ramsey and Ellie Bush at Edinburgh University Press for their gracious correspondence seeing this typescript through the process that would end up in a contract to publish. I have been lucky in the person of Sue Dalgleish who performed a painstaking task of copy editing, and who was patient with me far beyond the call of duty:

I thank her profusely. Last and by no means least, I thank Samia Meziane and Gemma Juan-Simó for their meticulous work on the final proofs.

I dedicate this book to Alan Jones. He first cured me of the irksome effect of *Joseph and the Amazing Technicolor Dreamcoat* and led me to dream about Joseph more critically.

Philip F. Kennedy
Abu Dhabi, 26 December 2015

Time shall unfold what plighted cunning hides

Shakespeare, *King Lear*, Act I, Scene 1

I came back to the houseboat with my head in a whirl: when Jodu's eyes met mine, in the Consoo House, it was as if our lives had changed. A strange and powerful thing is recognition!

Amitav Ghosh, *Flood of Fire*

Introduction

> I'm going out of my mind. You must say something. She is my daughter, Riri. Tell me . . . I'm going crazy. I realize I've been despicable . . . Tell me the girl's my daughter!
>
> Naguib Mahfouz, *Autumn Quail*

The recognition scene is a feature of narrative that has shown extraordinary resilience in literary history and transformative power in works of literature. The evidence lies in its robust survival and reinventions from antiquity to the present time. It thrives in most traditions of storytelling, and across all narrative media, from primitive oral folklore to the most sophisticated contemporary novels and films. In quality it ranges from the artistically sublime to rude cliché. The recognition scene has several key features: in its commonest form, it gives resolving shape to the plot of a story, very often providing 'the sense of an ending', and stands for narrative knowledge and enlightenment. It can carry – within a relatively circumscribed moment – the signature of an entire narrative. It is the part of a story that is emblematic of the whole and can thus act as the very token and sterling stamp of fiction, even though it exists in tales that are both imagined and real. In its most classic form, the recognition scene is clearly both a theme and a structuring device – what we learn from and through it – can bring closure to a narrative.

The importance of recognition in narrative poetics and literary hermeneutics (or interpretation) is enormous. Moreover, recognition, or anagnorisis, is fundamental to a range of narrative traditions outside the Western canon. In this book I track, trace and analyse anagnorisis in Arabic narrative literature from pre-Islamic Arabia to the present – a literature, like most, suffused with tensions between transcendental truth and material incertitude.[1]

By and large, in Arabic literary history, anagnorisis has been associated principally with the *maqāmah* genre of which it is one of the defining features;[2] these picaresque adventures shore up the argument that anagnorisis can be understood to be the signature feature of fiction (as a result of which it is liable to be parodied in all traditions), and also that it can be an important tool in the hermeneutics of narrative, that is, in the process of determining what meaning is conveyed in unfolding events or what facetious literary game is afoot. But I do not confine myself to the *maqāmah*. I look at anagnorisis in the Qur᾿an and *tafsīr*;[3] in the biography (*Sīrah*) of the Prophet Muḥammad; in the Hadith corpus; in religious stories of initiation (especially in the Sufi, Shiᶜi and Ismaᶜili milieux); in belletristic (*adab*) collections, particularly romances and tales of providential deliverance after distress; in popular Arabic storytelling, such as the *Arabian Nights*;[4] and in the modern Arabic novel, which has developed in the last sixty years to show both classical (or clichéd) and post-modern (or fractured) tendencies.

The following *khabar*, or medieval story,[5] illustrates a few of recognition's characteristics in the medieval Arabic corpus.[6] It is set in early ninth-century Baghdad. The narrative is recounted by the caliph al-Ma᾿mūn's (d. 833 AD) chief of police who was summoned to the palace one evening and ordered by the caliph to supervise the detention of a prisoner until the following morning. Aware of the acute importance of his charge, the police chief decides to take the prisoner home, the more assiduously to keep a watchful eye upon him. There he learns that the man was from Damascus. Showing evident delight at this fact, the chief exclaims: 'God reward the people of Damascus with ample goodness!' He then asks the prisoner: 'To which family do you belong?' The man replies – indirectly, evasively and manipulatively – 'Whom do you have in mind?' The chief explains that he was in fact angling to find out about a certain 'So-and-so'. The prisoner insists that he first be told of the police chief's dealings with this other man ('So-and-so') before he will explain his current plight. And so the chief tells the story of a charged encounter that had taken place years before.

He had been posted to Damascus when the people rioted against the Abbasid authorities. Escaping from the governor's palace, he took refuge from the angry crowd in the backstreets and found himself standing before a man who sat calmly at his front door. The fugitive pleaded: 'Save me! May God reward you equitably!' (The reciprocity invoked in this standard pious formula is not empty of meaning, as events transpire.) The Damascene quickly ushered in the fugitive who was then shown into the private quarters by the man's wife. When the crowd giving chase arrived and insisted they search all parts of the house they were rudely sent packing by the feisty woman who barred them from the female sanctum by appealing to their sense of shame. Thereafter, the police chief spent four months in this safe haven,[7] treated with great honour and hospitality by his discreet and anonymous hosts.[8] 'All this time,' the chief adds in his account, 'the man did not know who I was; he neither pried into my affairs nor asked my name, and only ever addressed me by my *kunyah*.'[9] Eventually the hosts prepared a mount and provisions for their guest, allowing him to join a caravan that was headed for Baghdad. He took leave of them, pledging to return in kind the extraordinary benevolence they had shown him.

When al-Maʾmūn's shackled prisoner hears the police chief's detailed account of his erstwhile saviour, he says: 'God has finally made it possible for you to keep faith with your promise to your former host . . . for I am that man. The harm I have suffered has simply ravaged me physically and rendered me unrecognisable.' He then explains that an insurrection had recently, again, taken place in Damascus. This time he himself was accused of being one of the instigators and was brought in chains to Baghdad. His punishment at the hands of the caliph looks likely to be severe, so he asks the police chief for an opportunity to put his worldly affairs in order before his inevitable demise. Without hesitation the police chief cuts loose his chains and allows him to go free, pledging to take responsibility for his actions before the caliph. The Damascene, for his part, refuses to leave the capital before learning the consequences of the police chief's merciful intercession.

When the caliph hears the whole story the following day, his initial rage quickly abates and he claims to be vexed only by the Damascene's apparent absence, for it means the latter cannot be rewarded for the generous act of rescue he had once so selflessly performed years before. Knowing the Damascene's identity adds urgency, in keeping with the caliph's attitude, to the obligation of keeping faith with an old pledge and offering hospitality. Here the recognition story plays detectably on the semantics of *maʿrifah* – of knowing, of giving, of recognising, of offering *maʿrūf*. One might even argue that this story illustrates the act of a sovereign performing *al-amr bi-l-maᶜrūf wa-l-nahy ᶜan al-munkar*, 'Ordering what is right [lit. recognised] and forbidding what is wrong [lit. unrecognised]',[10] and that, in its narrative intrigue, it hints at the important original cognitive substrate of meaning contained in the phrase. Ultimately, we learn that the Damascene did remain behind, was rewarded by the caliph with honours and high office in Damascus, and offered praise to God, in words which echo the initial plea of the once fugitive police chief. This underlying providential theme is the ultimate object – or predicate – of recognition for the anecdote's pious audience.

Several of the story's elements depend on the recognition scene that is focalised in the words: 'I am that man!' It is the central turning point of the story, condensing what comes before and motivating all that comes after. It provides, in this instance, the axial point across which both halves are arranged to form a symmetry of narrative construction. The backdrop of each half is rebellion in Damascus, and upon this shared subject across time the providential story is assembled. In fact, in general recognition is the moment in which the recursive structure of storytelling is felt most palpably; it reprises the past, and restores memory through the act of narration.

In this narrative, recognition also has a distinct ethical sense. Recognition of identity crystallises unquestioned acceptance of the stranger; it entails reciprocity, has restorative effect, and delivers the deepest sense of reunion and return. The recognition scene is real and concrete, but it feels uncanny and gives coincidence a miraculous sheen by virtue of its reversal of action and expectation.[11] In the moment of recognition, any of the values that the story carries in its latent and figurative DNA come to the fore with clarity. Conversely, the recognition scene provides a portal from which one can contemplate the surrounding parts of a narrative and glean the symbolic meaning of the whole.

The act of telling and retrieving the original story restores the balance of justice. The end of the entire cycle takes us to the beginning and back again into the present with a sense of sovereign justice established in a God-given realm. In this respect, it is important to note that the first and principal recognition scene is paired with another or part of another, though in the second instance the meaning of recognition is broadened: al-Maʾmūn listens to the story as it has already unfolded before us and, against the current of expectation, recognises the integrity of the actions of his two subjects. The caliph receives the chief of police and then the Damascene in his palace, just as the chief of police had received the shackled prisoner in his own house. Recognition, succour and hospitality to the stranger, which in Arabic are all semantic cousins of each other rooted in the radicals -*ᶜ-r-f*, thus lie at the heart of the anecdote: recognition is the thematic substrate of the story, its focal turning point, and its most conspicuous structural device. As Terence Cave has noted in *Recognitions: A Study in Poetics*, 'recognition represents the most quintessentially fictional type of plot: it is the signature of a fiction, the local detail that stands for the whole.'[12]

According to Aristotle, a well-crafted recognition scene is one of the basic constituents of a successful narrative. It is the moment when hidden facts and identities come to light: for instance, a son discovers in horror that his wife is his mother and his children are his siblings. Aristotle coined the term anagnorisis for this concept.[13] Although it is as important as mimesis and catharsis, which are generally familiar, the study of anagnorisis in the Arabic narrative tradition – and, indeed, most traditions – has tended to languish in the dark, despite the fact that the recognition scene is the point in a narrative when truth comes to light, with all the distinct connotations it can have in different genres, periods and cultures of literary history. For truth – because it is never absolute or unassailable, and may be comic as well as tragic, dispiriting as well as sublime – lends itself to interpretation. Thus anagnorisis becomes the key to a hermeneutics of narrative, to an understanding of how one reads values and meaning into or out of a story.

This book has been written in the long shadow of Aristotle,[14] whose definition of anagnorisis – variously translatable as 'recognition', 'discovery' or 'disclosure', depending on the context and how broad a view one takes of its instantiations – is literally and irrefutably invested with the idea of knowledge:[15]

> *Recognition* [*anagnorisis*], as in fact the term indicates, is a change from ignorance to knowledge, disclosing either a close relationship or enmity, on the part of people marked out for good or bad fortune.[16]

If we borrow this as a helpful – but not prescriptive – conceptual tool to consider narrative across all media and cultures from antiquity to the present, recognition becomes key to the way we make meaning and the way we read.[17] Because anagnorisis itself is about disclosure, focus upon it in any given work or text lends itself to disclosures of various social and disciplinary kinds of knowledge: issues of gender, identity, class, truth and morality are all made to come to the fore. According to Aristotle's particular coinage, the study of it can open up portals upon the general and social epistemology, both cognitive and moral, of any narrative.

The movement from ignorance to knowledge implied in anagnorisis is a simple paradigm of narrative that operates in a palette of literary categories: tragedy, of course, but also comedy, epic, scripture, romance, the picaresque, and the novel.[18] Furthermore, recognition exists both in 'high' and 'low' literature, which is to say, in works of differing and unequal literary status. 'High' literature delights in – or cannot escape – the influence of a device that some circles esteem proper to low literature, such as the modern soap opera.[19] This prejudice has its roots in the fact that, in certain commentaries on the *Poetics*, the recognition scene acquired a bad name. It became the black sheep – a stale, implausible and unsightly way of resolving a plot in which the author has simply lost his way or entirely lost control. It contravenes Aristotle's basic desire that the optimal story should unfold according to rational lineaments of cause and effect.

And yet we encounter it still – surprising us even when we can 'see it coming' – in the most well-wrought contemporary novels. Julian Barnes's (b. 1946) acclaimed novel, *The Sense of an Ending* (2011), testifies to the surviving efficacy and relevance of anagnorisis. Any prejudice against it is therefore rash. In this respect, we should underline that some, perhaps a majority, of the founding texts of the Western canon are steeped in the use and significance of recognition: Genesis, the life of Jesus (the Gospels), the Greek tragedies, the Hellenistic novels, the plays of Shakespeare, and the whole romance tradition up to the eighteenth century - as well as picaresque texts that choose in part to undermine romance – are often themselves recognition stories.[20] It has been like an unshakable, 'selfish gene' of literature.

A recognition scene – a point in a narrative's plot when someone's true or full identity is disclosed – is commonly simply the symptom of a text.[21] As such, it is curious how anagnorisis can trace either a movement of moral ascent or decline. Simplistically, scripture (and, to a large extent, romance following scripture) would seem predisposed to enunciate moral principles, while the picaresque can trace their breakdown. But the ambiguities of complex narratives do not allow these two divergent tendencies to be so clearly discrete and dichotomous. In a genre like the Arabic *maqāmah*, there is a taut symbiosis between literary dispositions that are either edifying and revelatory or subversively picaresque. Certainly, it can be said of the most accomplished examples of the *maqāmah*, as it can be said of Surah 12 in the Qurʾan and of *Autumn Quail* (1962), to cite just one modern novelistic example by Naguib Mahfouz (1911–2006), that the recognition scene is quintessentially a symptom of the textual structure and thematic weave of the works in question. Judging anagnorisis to be both thematic and structural is on some level – where there is erosion of the distinctive semantics of the terms used – another way of viewing the relationship between anagnorisis and a given narrative as synecdochal. This is the case *a fortiori* when there can be deemed to be a correlation between a structural (turning) point and a developing theme.

Synecdoche by its very definition has a subordinate connotation; it may well be deemed to obey the 'hermeneutical principle that the whole is more than the sum of its parts, and brings this insight to bear'.[22] Meaning – some of which may be doctrinal – is ultimately determined by context. However, there is a view of synecdoche that tends in the opposite direction, privileging the particular over the general. According to Cave, there are three ways of understanding synecdoche:

1. as an identifying scar or a handkerchief that may stand for an entire fiction (or a handbag, as in *The Importance of Being Earnest*);
2. whereby the moment of recognition effectively contains the entire narrative in condensed form: it may be the encapsulation of a narrative's movement towards disclosure, repeating in some instances the details of the narrative that betoken the identity of the players (as in Shakespeare's *Pericles* where, in Act V, Marina alludes to the entire family drama in the recognition scene with her father);
3. as that feature of narrative in which a story is told within a story such that the embedded story alludes to the epistemology of the larger enframing text (as in the *Arabian Nights*, or, to give a contemporary example, in Thomas Pynchon's *The Crying of Lot 49*).

Wherever one places the emphasis, if one accepts the basic premise, recognition becomes a rhetorical figure standing in for both narrative and narrative poetics, at the heart of both of which it must – by such definitions – lie.

Cave does not just highlight synechdoche when analysing recognition; he identifies six theoretical issues, all of which are relevant and, I would argue, often essential, to explorations of anagnorisis in Arabic narrative literature. These relate to (1) recognition and parody, (2) the hunting ('cynegetic') model of reading, (3) the relationship that recognition can establish between the text and the reader, (4) the inextricable relationship between theme and structure, or ethos and muthos, (5) the synecdochal function of recognition already mentioned, and (6) recognition as a problem moment.

There is also a central question born from the fact that, in the texts we will treat, recognition is fairly consistently inflected with its opposite – misrecognition:[23] to what extent can recognition in a narrative, especially when it is more or less coterminous with that narrative's climax, purvey a sense of cognitive certainty? In scripture, for example, God's hand can be recognised in the pattern of lives, but to what degree are materially-bound readers allowed to depart from any reading of a given narrative with a sense of having acquired certain and unshakeable knowledge? The omniscience this entails is solely a divine attribute. Mortals can only be required to have faith, which is a much more restricted and, at the same time, open-ended way of reading narrative conclusions that recede into cognitive ellipses, implicitly or otherwise. Cave develops his own argument and his own corpus of recognition in both theory and practice around one dominant notion: that recognition is a 'problem moment'; that narratives seldom, if at all, allow one to slip into any kind of epistemological complacency.[24]

This needs to be understood in a variety of ways, however. In classical Arabic narrative literature, certain religious narratives and their romance derivatives are anathema to tales of picaresque disposition. Recognition in religious texts may give one, or emerge in parallel with, truth, deliverance (*faraj*), reunion and faith; the *maqāmāt* and other related texts of imposture, by contrast, deliver one to the uncomfortable realisation that language is invariably the vehicle of, by turns, facetious or grotesque fraud and deceit. If such a theoretical claim has only faint force when rendered in abstraction, it gains weight when we can posit a concrete connection between a more restricted corpus of texts existing in some parodical and dynamic relationship. Indeed, it would not be reckless to argue that the *maqāmāt* of al-Hamadhānī owe something to the intriguing culture of tenth- and eleventh-century Isma^{c}ili clandestine missionaries (*dā^{c}īs*) functioning in their far-flung fields of operation,[25] especially to the manner in which their lives were transcribed in patterned narratives of travel, secret knowledge and disclosure. Elements of the *maqāmāt* may indeed suggest a caricature of the initiatory practice of the *dā^{c}īs*, who certainly led picaresque lives, and excelled at disguise and imposture in the cause of their own greater, and soon to be made manifest, truth.[26]

That the recognition scene may indeed be a problem moment is only elusively grasped as an issue. It presupposes that narrative knowledge and anagnorisis are quite unstable, and that recognition scenes can have all the permanence, before and after the fact, of mushrooms that sprout after rain. But because knowledge is always implicated, and because some meaning, however subjective, may be at stake it is desirable to see how artists, writers and scholars of various narrative traditions, especially those outside the Western tradition, navigate the reefs and shoals of recognition's knowledge and uncertainties.

The recognition scene in Arabic-Islamic narrative literature is in some respects simply a mechanism. It does not determine or predetermine the knowledge and relationships it reveals; the subjects that unfold, while often similar, can vary, sometimes at tangents that are poles apart. This variance is a question of distinct literary moods and, at times, a question of discrete genres. Illustrating this point, the two following stories share subjects but produce, on the one hand, tragedy and, on the other, a sense of deliverance. Salma Jayyusi, evoking the corpus of pre-Islamic tribal battle lore (the *Ayyām al-^{c}Arab*), sketches the first, tragic, story as follows:

> The elaborate story woven around Kulaib, head of the tribe of Taghlib, depicting his arrogance and megalomania, his confiscation of people's rights and property, and finally his punitive death at the hands of his brother-in-law, Jassas, of the tribe of Bakr, sister tribe of Taghlib, is interwoven with the agonized experience of Jalila, Kulaib's wife, also the sister of Jassas. Caught in the clutches of a treacherous fate that made her a pawn between husband and brother, she experienced great suffering, especially

> felt in the story's tragic end: Jalila was pregnant with Kulaib's child when he was killed. Having been sent back to her tribe after her husband's demise, Kulaib's son is born in the Bakr tribe and grows up unaware that the uncle bringing him up was the killer of his father. According to the old Arabian tribal laws, it was the duty of the son to kill his father's killer, and therefore, when he eventually learns the truth, he has no alternative but to kill the man who has loved and raised him.[27]

There are elements that are plainly universal about the structure and subject of this tragedy: the discovery of complicated parentage, the momentous realisation of what has happened, and the inexorable consequence. The ultimate lesson here is uncompromising and unforgiving: a murdered parent cries out for revenge. But, even while the principle of such retribution subsisted into Islamic times in another story, that takes place two centuries later, one duty locks horns with another highly cherished obligation: the sacred pledge of life-giving succour, whence an ambiguous surplus of didactic reflection comes into view. Jayyusi labels it 'The Strangest Story';[28] its backdrop is the sanguinary transition from Umayyad to Abbasid times. In terror for his life, the narrator, the Umayyad Ibrahim ibn Sulayman ibn ᶜAbd al-Malik,[29] seeks refuge in Kufa in the house of a total stranger. He is given food and shelter. Safely ensconced, he begins to notice his rescuer's regular excursions from his home:

> 'Why is it,' I asked him one day, 'that you always ride out?'
>
> 'Ibrahim ibn Sulayman ibn ᶜAbd al-Malik killed my father,' he told me, 'and I have been told he's hiding in al-Hira. I go out each day to seek my revenge on him.'

Mortified and thrown upon the horns of a dilemma, Ibrahim risks his life by dutifully confessing his identity, but is spared by his host who will not betray the pledge of safety he has promised his now unwelcome guest.

By providing a comparative perspective on all these materials, this study addresses students of narrative literature across linguistic, regional and cultural traditions, particularly Arabic-Islamic and European. It highlights the importance of intertextuality in classical Arabic texts, showing the various ways in which literature and other genres of writing must be read together as manifestations of one complex cultural narrative. It offers detailed analyses of stories, both fictional and non-fictional, that demonstrate the productivity of interdisciplinarity in literary studies. It argues that anagnorisis, together with its attendant epistemology, embodies the ideological and ethical concerns underpinning other forms of classical Arabic writings, and also that what may be called the 'non-literary' has in common with the 'literary' an abiding preoccupation with aesthetics. This approach offers new vistas for reading, understanding and interpreting classical Arabic literature, as well as the culture in which it was produced.

This volume comprises five studies of the ways in which knowledge is unfolded in Arabic narratives, namely close readings of: (1) Qurʾanic narrative; (2) the life of Muḥammad as told in the most famous vulgate Sunni version (the redaction of Ibn Hishām); (3) the iconic image of Joseph as a loaded trope within narratives of recognition, across a broad range of texts and registers; (4) anecdotes of deliverance after evil, in which the archetype or mythic structure of anagnorisis plays a conspicuous and recurring role; and (5) picaresque stories, the *maqāmāt*, which facetiously undermine the truth-conveying complacencies of storytelling before the twelfth century AD and have much to say about narrative poetics in both the fashioning and parodying of stories, tendencies that are both contrary and complementary.

Writ large, the progression is from the narratives of providential deliverance that we find in Chapters 1 and 2 to ones of parody and satire, disabusing the delusion that one can trust in the truth of dutiful, virtuous, even godly language. In this movement or scheme, Chapter 3 is transitional in showing how religious material can be deftly reused – rewritten intertextually, or simply alluded to – in less religious (and certainly non-liturgical) writing; Chapter 4 treats an essentially non-religious genre of writing that can appeal to the pious, for these are providential stories of deliverance after distress. The *maqāmāt* discussed in the final chapter undermine, for the duration that one reads them, any trust one can have in providence and show the dispiriting nature of discovery for those exposed to the cheating veil of eloquent, conning verbal and narrative displays.

The thread of this book is provided in varying degrees and variegated ways by the figure of Joseph (and to a lesser extent, the figure of Joseph as

Muḥammad), giving linear and progressive coherence to the ensemble of texts. The broad generic arc of selected materials moves from religious to quasi-religious and ultimately secular texts; this reflects a progress of dispositions: from the edifying, in the first four chapters, to the dispiriting and facetious, in the last. The key feature of analysis is the privileging of the integrity of the work or narrative in question – for example, Surah 12 (Yusuf), the *Sīrah* of Ibn Hishām, complete anecdotes from *al-Faraj ba*ᶜ*d al-Shiddah*, the *Maqāmah* – over, the pursuit of thematic coherence; the 'dream', for example, could have been used as one organising principle, but the emphasis has been rather to show how the sundry effects of a recognition story – variously, the figure of synecdoche and related structural implications; its (ethical) hermeneutics; anagnorisis as a problem moment; the play of intertextuality; the rich and motley tissue of epistemology – rely to a significant degree on seeing the fullness of the work in question.

Notes

1. Anagnorisis does also exist in some examples of classical Arabic poetry that exhibit features of narrative. As a theme, the difficulty of recognition is quintessential to one of the founding images of the pre-Islamic tradition: the struggle to discern and recognise the traces of the beloved's former encampment. But it is, in fact, the anecdotes that support these poems that tend to emphasise the fact and highlight the dramatic feature of anagnorisis.
2. The *maqāmah*, treated in detail in Chapter 5, is a picaresque anecdotal genre which features a wandering rogue hero who treats – and cheats – his audience with eloquent games of deception reified in his very persona.
3. *Tafsīr* is Qurᵓanic exegesis which began maturing as a genre of religious writing in the ninth century AD. It developed first within the Sunni traditionist milieu, then later, among Shiᶜi and Sufi commentators. One of the most theosophical of *mufassirīn* (exegetes) in the Islamic tradition may be argued to be Fakhr al-Dīn al-Rāzī (d. 1209) whose *Mafātīḥ al-ghayb* informs much of the supplementary commentary provided by the endnotes in Chapter 1.
4. For an idea of how scholars treat recognition as it occurs in Arab folklore (and according to a folkloric scheme reminiscent, say, of the 'functions' of Vladimir Propp), see Hasan El-Shamy's *Folk Traditions of the Arab World: A Guide to Motif Classification* (Bloomington: Indiana University Press, 1995), vol. I, pp. 150ff.: 'H. Tests: H0–H199, Identity tests: recognition'.

5. A *khabar* (pl. *akhbār*) is an individual anecdote, usually with an accompanying chain of transmission, relaying events and stories about real people; but their authenticity varies enormously across works of historiography and *adab* or belletristic collections.
6. The story can be found in Ibn ᶜAbd Rabbih, *al-ᶜIqd al-Farīd*, vol. 3 (Beirut: Dār al-Kitāb al-ᶜArabī, 1983), p. 81, and al-Ibshīhī, *al-Mustaṭraf fī kull fann mustaẓraf*, vol. 1 (Cairo: Muṣṭafā al-Bābī al-Ḥalabī, 1952), p. 240. Recently the anecdote was published in full in Muḥammad Abū l-Faḍl Ibrāhīm *et al.* (eds), *Qiṣaṣ al-ᶜarab*, vol. 1 (Beirut: al-Maktabah al-ᶜAṣriyyah, 2011/1432), pp. 211–14.
7. The word *arghad* that describes this time in hiding alludes to the Qurᵓanic paradise; cf. the use of the adverbial form *raghadan* in Q Baqarah 2:35, 58; and Q an-Naḥl 16:112.
8. The anonymity of the two principal characters in the narrative is compensated for by the salient details of their stories.
9. A *kunyah* is a person's cognomen, such as Abū Zayd, meaning the 'Father of Zayd'; it usually refers to the person's eldest son but can also convey a characteristic of the person, such as in the name 'Abū Nuwās' – the 'Father [i.e. possessor of] hanging locks'. The point being here is that his given name and family name were never divulged.
10. In Michael Cook's study of the phrase and concept of *al-amr bi-l-maᶜrūf wa-l-nahy ᶜan al-munkar* and its application in Islamic governance throughout history, he does not probe the original cognitive substrate of the phrase.
11. We are used to the phrase 'tragic reversal', but reversal is tragic in tragedy only.
12. Terence Cave, *Recognitions: A Study in Poetics* (Oxford: Clarendon Press, 1988), p. 492.
13. A striking detail that emerges from the work of Terence Cave and also Piero Boitani is that the ancient Greek terms for 'recognition', 'reader' and 'reading' (respectively *anagnôrisis*, *anagnôstês*, and *anagignôskein* or *anagnôsis*) are closely phonetically and conceptually related. The study of anagnorisis, when its definition stretches out beyond the clichéd sense we have of the classic (jaded even) recognition scene, provides important insight into how to read, in every possible sense. If we accept the last proposition, anagnorisis can be understood to furnish part of the essential humanism of art and literature. See Cave, *Recognitions*, p. 260, and Boitani, *The Tragic and the Sublime in Medieval Literature* (Cambridge: Cambridge University Press, 1989), p. 161.

14. Aristotle discusses anagnorisis in chapters 6, 11, 14 and 16 of his *Poetics*.
15. Some of the following analysis appeared in the 'Introduction' to Philip F. Kennedy and Marilyn Lawrence (eds), *Recognition: The Poetics of Narrative. Interdisciplinary Studies of Anagnorisis* (New York: Peter Lang, 2008).
16. Aristotle, *Poetics*, trans. Malcolm Heath (London: Penguin, 1996), p. 18.
17. Examples of works that illustrate that there is indeed a thematic payoff that accrues through the mechanism of anagnorisis can be observed variously in different traditions and eras and across artistic media, ranging from, e.g. the Indian film *Chaudvin ka Chand* (which explores socio-cultural aspects of purdah in post Moghul India); Surah 12, the epitome of Islamic providential narrative; the recent Egyptian novel *Ajniḥat al-Farrāshah* by Muḥammad Salmāwī in which a son's discovery of a lost mother is a metonym for the Mother Nation's awakening in incipient revolution; and Rabī^{c} Jābir's *al-I^{c}tirāfāt* in which the hero's troubled recognitions reflect the fractured psyche produced by the Lebanese civil war. There are countless (and highly variegated) examples in contemporary culture. To cite just one, the payoff of recognition in the novella, and especially the film, *Babette's Feast* is quite extraordinary. We have written elsewhere, 'It is . . . essential to discern consistently the difference between a simple structural point in the highly determined morphology of a Russian folktale (*pace* Vladimir Propp) and the extraordinary potential for humanistic interpretation that inheres, for example, in the long, drawn-out recognition scene in *Babette's Feast* (the Oscar winning-film based on the novella by Karen Blixen) in which anagnorisis is layered, cognitive, affective, spiritual, and forgiving, but also preserves its surplus of doubt and the inevitable potential that humans have for not understanding things fully.' See Kennedy and Lawrence (eds), *Recognition: The Poetics of Narrative*, p. 5.
18. Most of these genres are represented in the repertories of opera and film, as well as in narrative literature. See Jessica Waldoff, 'Recognition: a Challenge for Opera Studies', in Kennedy and Lawrence (eds), *Recognition: The Poetics of Narrative*. From the repertory of cinema – and for the sake of example – *The Third Man* (dir. Carol Reid, 1949) surrenders its humanistic preoccupations best of all when viewed from the perspective of recognition.
19. Or the demagogic chat show. In the gory voyeurism of *The Jerry Springer Show*, for instance, disclosures within families, and between families and supposed friends seem designed to cater to the same human impulse for lurid and destructive entertainment that drew crowds to the Coliseum in ancient Rome.
20. The question of whether Henry Fielding's (1707–54) *Tom Jones* (1749) is a

romance or a picaresque novel depends to some extent on how one reads the elements of recognition in the work.

21. Thus, for example, when Pip recognises Magwitch (and the fact that he, not Miss Havisham, has been his benefactor throughout the years), we are encountering the crystallisation of a theme that saturates Charles Dickens' (1812–70) *Great Expectations* (1860–1) as a whole.
22. Robert Alter and Frank Kermode (eds), *The Literary Guide to the Bible* (Cambridge, MA: Harvard University Press, 1987), p. 44.
23. What in French Vladimir Jankélévitch has termed 'la méconnaissance' (in *Le je-ne-sais-quoi et le presque-rien*, vol. 2: *La méconnaissance, Le malentendu* (Paris: Seuil, 1980)).
24. Cf. especially Cave, *Recognitions*, p. 489.
25. See Heinz Halm, *The Empire of the Mahdi: The Rise of the Fatimids*, trans. M. Bonner (Leiden: Brill, 1991), p. 42.
26. James T. Monroe posited a connection between Hamadhānī and Isma^{c}ilism three decades ago; as others have done, I reverse the proposition about al-Hamadhānī's Isma^{c}ili allegiance.
27. Salma Jayyusi (ed.), *Classical Arabic Stories* (New York: Columbia University Press), p. 11; she cites from Ibrāhīm *et al.* (eds), *Qiṣaṣ al-^{c}Arab*, vol. 1, pp. 225–6; in turn cited from Abū Isḥāq Ibrāhīm ibn ^{c}Alī al-Ḥuṣrī, *Zahr al-ādāb wa-thamar al-albāb* (Beirut: Dar al-Jīl, n.d.), vol. 3, p. 52.
28. Jayyusi cites from Ibrāhīm *et al.* (eds), *Qiṣaṣ al-^{c}Arab*, vol. 1, pp. 225–6.
29. Son of the Umayyad caliph, Sulayman ibn ^{c}Abd al-Malik, who ruled from 715–17 AD; along with his other siblings he was too young to succeed to power when his father sought an heir and was passed over for his cousin ^{c}Umar ibn ^{c}Abd al-^{c}Azīz (682–720 AD).

I

A Cognitive Reading of the Qurʾanic Story of Joseph

We find in the Qurʾan and the life of Muḥammad one of the most fascinating relationship constructs between a text and its contextual psychology in literature; at its crux is the fundamental question: is anagnorisis commensurate with the disclosure of certain truth, which would seem a natural Islamic reflex given that this is revelation, or can a surplus of doubt be sustained with, and after, anagnorisis? At first glance, the recognition scenes in the Qurʾanic version of the Joseph story are untrammelled moments of divine reassurance. They convey the providential deliverance that is a staple of uncomplicated romance. But placing the surah in the context of the life of Muḥammad may prise open the narrative to a degree of uncertainty that pervades the Qurʾan and, to a large extent, other Islamic literatures. In general, the Qurʾanic prophets were modelled on the life of Muḥammad (this is especially apparent from a reading of Surah 26 – al-Shuʿāraʾ). Surah 12 (Yusuf) straddles the Meccan and Medinese period, internalising the former and anticipating the latter, especially Surah 2 (al-Baqarah) in which the animosity of the Jewish community of Medina is recognised for what it is, viz. the denial of the scripture that prophesied the coming of Muḥammad. Epistemology, and the struggle against uncertainty, has a determinative role in all these materials.

This chapter, inspired by in-depth readings of various medieval *tafsīr* (or exegetical) works, is written following the incremental method of Islamic exegesis; this allows us to explore the cognitive nuances and details of the narrative as they develop through the surah – they are the constitutive elements of what, epistemologically speaking, is tantamount to a complex organic whole.

Surah 12 (Yusuf) of the Qurʾan, devoted entirely to an account of the story of Joseph, is a succinct and stylistically distinct version of events told in detail in Genesis 37[1] and 39–45.[2] It has spawned numerous studies to such a degree that one might label a separate branch of Qur᾿anic studies as 'Josephologie'.[3] While most of these will contribute some helpful detail to our appreciation of how the text works as a narrative of recognition, only focused analysis of anagnorisis will allow us to temper the hermeneutic bareness of these predominantly structural examinations of the surah.

It is, in particular, the cognitive saturation of the narrative that begs proper analysis. The typology of knowledge in Surah 12 is both vertical and horizontal. To wit, knowledge is differentiated paradigmatically on a verticle axis, with divine omniscience at its apex, but develops according to the most fundamental dynamic of plot on a linear axis, informed by cycles of unfolding time. In this horizontal movement, the progression from ignorance to knowledge subtends an essential part of the syntax of the story. Knowledge, acquired through moments of discovery, disclosure and recognition, is the predication of both the 'disastrous ignorance and imperfect knowledge' that suffuse the plot in its earliest parts.[4] Anagnorisis crystallises out of this cognitive saturation.

The predication of plot – the full resolution of the syntax of narrative – takes, in this particular tale, the form of a compound anagnorisis. Recognition not only marks a progression from ignorance to knowledge but also, in the process, conjoins two types of knowledge, that is, omniscient-cum-divine and contingent-cum-experiential. As intimated, this allows one to understand divine knowledge paradigmatically and human knowledge syntagmatically, but showing the two to be organically imbricated within each other as events unfold. In other Qur᾿anic surahs, the more paradigmatic the narrative(s) the more the determining agency of God becomes transparent. In a compelling study of Qur᾿anic poetics, Michael Zwettler has shown how this feature works distinctly in Surah 26 in which historical detail and human-cum-prophetic individuality is reduced progressively, pericope by pericope, in order to offer up the essence of the divine plan with incrementally greater force. Surah 26 is quite forcefully polemical. There is a polemical aspect to Surah 12, certainly, but the surah's overture stresses its individual beauty and this feature requires its human detail to be considered and underlined. This does not diminish the theology of the story. It may even enhance it. Surah 12 is a perfect encapsulation of the paradoxes that subsist when one tries to square the conceptual circle of God's coexisting omniscience, omnipotence and justice.[5] One is most able to glean this by tracing the way knowledge unfolds through the story.

That this is the most beautiful story suggests strongly that it is built upon a tacit poetics; this is what leads us to propose that elements of Qurʾanic poetics, at least where *this* narrative is concerned, may be shared with any system of poetics that describe narrative, across genres, but principally that of romance. Of the three all-important concepts in Aristotle's *Poetics*, only anagnorisis comes close to being a synonym for revelation (with its attendant peripety and catharsis, both moral and cultural). The following reading explores the hypothesis that anagnorisis is at the heart of the poetics of Surah 12 – of its doctrinal and revelatory beauty. Surah 12 contains an anagnorisis in the classic sense: the formerly hidden identity of a person is eventually disclosed and light is shed upon the multi-layered truth.

The Prologue[6]

> 12:1 *Alif, Lām, Rāʾ*. These are the signs of the clear Scripture.
> 2 We have sent it down as a Recitation in Arabic, so that you may understand.
> 3 We are recounting to you, [Muḥammad], the finest of stories, for We have inspired you with this Recitation, and you were one of those who were not aware [of the story] before it[s revelation].

This is a story about clarity and insight that emerge through a process of growth and becoming, like the Qurʾan itself. That the Islamic scripture at this point in its early pre-Medinese history had only been partially revealed is the most germane way of making the point. One might add, however: if knowledge is in part inspired by God's determination of events as they unfold, this never results in human, nor even prophetic, omniscience. Revelation is simply part of the process that keeps the believer learning and progressing on a path towards salvation; hence the staggered revelations of the Joseph narrative.

The open-ended implications of verse 3 are some of the most intriguing in the surah. Of what is the person addressed in the verse (that is, Muḥammad and by extension his community) heedless? The dominant aesthetic sense given to *qaṣaṣ* forces one to consider the poetics of the story and one is consequently obliged to appreciate the full implications of the remainder of the verse, in particular, 'Even though you were one of those who were not aware' (*wa-in kunta min qabli-hi la-mina l-ghāfilīn*).[7] Not aware of what: of the story itself, or rather of the very qualities of the story? To some extent we must allow these two possibilities to overlap and coexist with each other. We can reconcile the explicit meaning of the phrase, as interpreted by Jones,[8] with a sense of the aesthetics of narrative that may also be implied. This would suggest that the story might in fact have been familiar but that its aesthetic virtues – its poetics – went unnoticed. Its ability to move and transform a believer's awareness of providence and corollary features is contingent upon the exquisite fashioning of this most moving of family romances. On this view, the aesthetics of the narrative are inextricably linked with the very process of revelation; indeed, the story becomes a finely wrought humanistic metonym for revelation itself. Divine knowledge is abstractable and paradigmatic, because it is transcendent, while human knowledge is conveyed most efficiently when it is translated through the vagaries of mundane lives. In this story – not exceptionally – at least two kinds of knowledge converge, and the success of this enunciatory epistemology owes much to the very human qualities of the narrative.

What verse 3 may be asking us to grasp is the fact that one should muffle prior knowledge of the tale the better to appreciate this, its most enhanced rendering. The tale is one of moral transfiguration. One understands this fact best of all when moved progressively by the vagaries of the plot, held in suspense of its complex denouement. One should muse on this story at every recitation with renewed innocence, each time remaining sensitive to the various layers of discovery that it promises and delivers. In this way the Scripture is itself aware, in the first instance of its unfolding, of its dramatic and transformative potential. One of the significant features of this surah is Joseph's subordination to the play (and plying) of knowledge and ignorance that God determines for him. Reading figuratively, Muḥammad too is subjugated to knowledge revealed to him from on high; this is surely part of the intent of *wa-in kunta min qabli-hi la-mina l-ghāfilīn*: the drama unfolds before Muḥammad for the first time with all of its dramatic impact, and he can identify with the figural representations of Jacob and Joseph whose knowledge in the narrative of Surah 12 is acquired progressively and cumulatively.[9]

Only if one affects a responsive sensibility to the discoveries that emerge from the plot does one internalise the teaching it is calculated to deliver. Verse 3 encourages its audience to ponder in what way this is the acme of storytelling. However, one feature we have not yet broached is the narrative's integrity. Does the fact that the story of Joseph is told in its entirety have a role to play in an aesthetic view of the text? In this regard, it is pertinent to evaluate whether or not *aḥsan al-qaṣaṣ* is dependent in any way on the fact that this story is told from beginning to end without interruption or lacuna, a fact unique in the Qur᾽an.[10] Recognition requires a full story from which to emerge the better to work its transformative magic and enchantment.

Joseph's Dream and Jacob's Response

> 12:4 When Joseph said to his father, 'O my father, I have seen [*ra᾽aytu*] eleven stars and the sun and the moon – I have seen them bowing down to me.'
> 5 He said, 'O my son, do not recount your dream [*ru᾽yā-ka*] to your brothers lest they devise some piece of guile against you. Satan is a very clear enemy to man.
> 6 In this way your Lord is choosing you; And He will teach you something of the interpretation of what you are told, And He will perfect His blessing on you and on the family of Jacob, just as He perfected it before, on your forefathers, Abraham and Isaac.'

The story begins, though not quite *in medias res*, abruptly. The dream which Joseph recounts to his father – the second of the two biblical dreams (Genesis 37:9) – is described as a vision, for 'I have seen'/*ra᾽aytu* here is associated with the noun *ru᾽yā* ('dream-vision') not the verbal noun *ru᾽yatun* ('seeing'). Its importance is thus heightened. The Hebrew *ḥalūm* does not here yield its Arabic cognate *ḥulm*; this root occurs later in the surah with less positive meaning when Pharaoh's soothsayers describe his dreams, playing down their divine aspect, as *aḍ῾āf aḥlām* ('tangled nightmares') – subordinating themselves by their erring judgement, and unwittingly, to the prophetic gifts of Joseph.

The point is that Jacob from the very outset behaves in a way that will characterise his attitude and comportment throughout: he recognises the mantic quality of the dream, ackowledging that it is a *ru᾿yā* ('a vision'); however, he tries to suppress it ('do not recount your dream to your brothers').[11] In Genesis, Jacob hears this dream and berates the arrogance of his son, quashing the dream in another way, refusing to acknowledge the meaning it so clearly contains:

> 37:10 And he told it to his father, and to his brethren: and his father rebuked him, and said unto him, What is this dream that thou hast dreamed? Shall I and thy mother and thy brethren indeed come to bow down ourselves to thee to the earth?

Yet significantly, showing us the paradox of his situation, he keeps the words in mind (37:11): 'But his father observed the saying.'[12]

Both versions, and perhaps the Qur᾿anic one most clearly, betray Jacob's inchoate knowledge of future events and their significance.[13] For the way events unfold linearly and temporally holds part of their intrinsic meaning. Jacob does not at this stage recognise that these events *will* happen; he merely acquiesces in what they would mean *were* they to happen. This notwithstanding, the fact is also that he is fearful, and fear, which stems from uncertainy about the final outcome of events, feeds off ignorance, of which it is by turns both a corollary and a manifestation.

When one reads the Qur᾿an comparatively against Genesis, one gleans an irony that links verses 5 and 6. It is an irony that escapes Jacob, for as the story unfolds it is the very fact of Joseph apparently recounting this dream to his brothers that sets in motion events that will ultimately fulfil the premonitions of verse 6. The brothers are in some sense playthings of this narrative irony, no more clearly than in Genesis when, upon seeing Joseph approaching their camp in the fields of Dothan, they remark caustically (37:19–20): 'Behold, this dreamer cometh. Come now therefore, and let us slay him, and cast him into some pit, and we will say, Some evil beast hath devoured him: and we shall see what will become of his dreams.'

Particularly effective in 12:6 is the use of the *muḍāri*ᶜ ('imperfect') tense. It lends itself to ambivalence: Jacob is both able with these words to tell his son what his Lord is doing and what he will do in the future. The verse is one of annunciation: the Lord is (1) choosing you to carry on the prophetic lineage of your forefathers, and by this act (2) he will make more fully apparent to you what He has only begun now to teach you.[14] We should accept a temporally ambiguous reading of this verse. This is especially felicitous for fathoming the inconsistencies in the subsequent conduct of Jacob whose fear for Joseph betrays imperfect knowledge despite his own prophetic gifts. Jacob never mourns Joseph as he does in Genesis, but he feels his young son's loss and one can conjecture that the consolatory force of his words '*yutimmmu ni^{c}mata-hu ^{c}alay-ka*' is for a time lost on the old patriarch in his moments of greatest despair.

An element of verse 6 wants further commentary; it relates to one of the most significant details in the theology of the Genesis narrative. A number of Jewish commentators have stressed how divine providence is made manifest in 45:5 when Joseph addresses his penitent brothers: 'Now therefore be not grieved, nor angry with yourselves, that ye sold me hither: for God did send me before you to preserve life.' Here Joseph's declaration to his brothers is first of all revelatory before it is consolatory. The brothers have been responsible for their actions and this fact allows one to understand why Joseph has staged their redemption by trying them and testing the sincerity of their moral transfiguration since the time they threw him into the pit. That he should have tried them and inflicted an ordeal upon them establishes that their guilt needed to be expunged – it was indeed their guilt. Yet God had willed events to unfold in this way and ultimately their responsibility is annulled. The contradiction is mitigated by viewing actions along the temporal axis that defines the humanism of the deeds and events of the story. Only once we have acted in time and place, according to the naturalistically temporal, principally linear, shape of existence, can we be forgiven our actions.

A similar ambiguity is inscribed in Surah 12, but it hinges on the role given to Satan – a role that is entirely absent from Genesis. The locution *inna l-shayṭāna li-l-insāni ^{c}aduwwun mubīn* (verse 6) is temporally open-ended; it can be read as a general statement, as indeed can a large number of the Qur$^{\circ}$anic phrases that mark the verse endings in the surah: the Devil, in general, is a manifest enemy to mankind. The locution of verse 100, by contrast, is unambiguous and specific: it was Satan who 'caused strife between' Joseph and his brothers (*nazagha l-shayṭānu baynī wa-bayna ikhwatī*). It is significant that the semantic ambiguity of verse 6 should somehow give way to a clear predication in the manner of the narrative itself as it unfurls. In this way, the phrase *inna l-shayṭāna li-l-insāni ᶜaduwwun mubīn* is suggestive of the entire narrative scheme: a semi-epiphanic statement yields further along in the storyline to a limpid and specific epiphany. Overall, the Devil's role is not so much clear as it *becomes* clear. Only the epithets that describe God do not hew to this developmental ontology. The Devil's role, by contrast, is subject to time and space. This evokes an important contingency in verse 6: the temporally ambiguous *yuᶜallimu-ka* ('[God] will teach you') is dependent upon the divine omniscience with which the verse ends (*inna rabba-ka ᶜalīmun ḥakīm*). Knowledge in this narrative is a temporally, and to some extent spatially, contingent emanation of divine omniscience. What the text leads one to expect is a nexus – in so far as one is possible – between human and acquisitive knowledge, on the one hand, and transcendent divine knowledge, on the other. This conjunction is achieved not so much at the first recognition scene, when Joseph first recognises his brothers who remain ignorant of his identity, but in the final act of recognition at 12:100–1, which is both recognition and epiphany combined, as we shall see.

Jacob's Fears and the Brothers' Jealous Crime

> 12:7 In the story of Joseph and his brothers are signs for those who ask questions:
> 8 When they [the brothers] said, 'Joseph and his brother are dearer to our father than we are, though there is a group of us. Our father is clearly in manifest error.
> 9 Kill Joseph or cast him into some land, And your father's face will focus only you. Thereafter you can be a righteous people.'

Verse 8 introduces ignorance of a kind. It is a verse that is linked lexically and thematically in a significant structural and interpretive way with verse 95. Jacob's unequal – and inequitable – love for his sons cannot be ignored, however much Muslim commentaries expatiate on the infallibility of the patriarchs. His foible is slightly exacerbated in the Qur᾿anic version of the story by verse 5 in which, instead of chiding his young son (as in Genesis 37:10), he is effectively complicitous with him in his dream. But is the father in any true moral sense in manifest error (*ḍalālin mubīn*), as the brothers claim? His partial knowledge will be discussed forthwith, together with the way verse 95 allows one to understand the full force – and irony – of verse 8. For now, we should simply note that *ḍalāl* ('error') is used just three times in this surah, and only once is it associated with someone other than Jacob (to wit, Potiphar's wife in 12:30). The two disjunctive references to Jacob coming at the beginning and close to the end of events bookend the story; in the final accusation the initial one is evoked and shown to have been erroneous. Such a coherent, cross-textual reading surfaces distinctly from a progressive reading of the storyline as a whole and is itself characteristic of the narrative, as we have begun to intimate.

A prior disjunction subsists more immediately in the transition from verse 8 to 9. The brothers have accused their father of *ḍalāl* only to juxtapose to this their own dark imperatives: 'Kill Joseph or cast him out into some land.' In the same way that *ḍalālin mubīn* looks forward to 12:94 (where the patriarch is accused of suffering senile delusion for imagining Joseph to be still alive), so the continuation of verse 12:9 must be understood fully in the light of developments in the story. It is of course an act of mammoth hypocrisy for the brothers, having just accused their father of error and at the very moment of plotting a heinous crime, to imagine that they will be able subsequently to join the ranks of the righteous. To act with such deluded premeditation makes a mockery of contrition (*tawbah*).

Any reading of the surah must allow for two contrary facts: the effects of the narrative unfolding without any prior knowledge of its audience, and the clear or possible allusions in the text to detailed aspects of the fuller biblical version and Midrashic accretions.[15] That the brothers should expect to become *qawmun ṣāliḥūn* after their wrongdoing is perhaps simply metatextual: it can be taken as an allusion to the destiny of the Children of Israel as detailed in Genesis (cf. especially Genesis 49).[16] If the Qurʾanic phrase is unlikely to be as historically proleptic as this, it looks forward nevertheless to the succour the brothers are given by Joseph in their time of need and the forgiveness with which they are ultimately embraced. What is especially fascinating is the syntactical contingency of this utterance; their righteousness is conditional upon their dark imperative: they can only in a sense become righteous if or once they have committed their nefarious act. There is of course an element of determinism here, and it is an aspect governing their lives of which they are themselves at this stage unaware. We are forced to aver as an upshot that their galling desire to kill in order only afterwards to join the ranks of the righteous is analogous with their father's vague knowledge that his son will learn – only in the future – to interpret the meaning of related events (*aḥādīth*) and of dreams of events such as these. When Jacob addresses Joseph's dream in 12:6, he does not in fact explain it but merely tells Joseph that he will one day be able to interpret the details of the vision – of the events of the vision after they have happened (hence *aḥādīth*). This is semi-interpretation that works by prolepsis suggesting that the meaning of the present is contingent upon future events; Jacob provides a partial interpretation, Joseph will provide its complement only when the time is self-evidently right.

A tension subsists in Surah 12 between human action and transcendent knowledge: between God's omniscience and the inevitability that man will act before a preordained ending in varying degrees of ignorance of the outcome of events. Human actions determine the truth that God alludes to but of which He will disclose the full meaning only when those deeds have run their course. It is deeds such as these that are stressed in the final phrase of 12:10, albeit cast in vagueness:

> 12:10 One of them said, 'Do not kill Joseph. Just throw him into the bottom of a pit, And some caravan will pick him out – if you must do something (*in kuntum fāʿilīn*).'

Of course they must. The Qur'anic construction, 'One of them said', refuses to fix the identity of the speaker, but those familiar with Genesis will detect the presence of both Reuben and Judah here (Genesis 37:20–7):

> 37:20 Come now therefore, and let us slay him, and cast him into some pit, and we will say, Some evil beast hath devoured him: and we shall see what will become of his dreams.
> 21 And Reuben heard it, and he delivered him out of their hands; and said, Let us not kill him.
> 22 And Reuben said unto them, Shed no blood, but cast him into this pit that is in the wilderness, and lay no hand upon him; that he might rid him out of their hands, to deliver him to his father again.

> 23 And it came to pass, when Joseph was come unto his brethren, that they stript Joseph out of his coat, his coat of many colours that was on him;
> 24 And they took him, and cast him into a pit: and the pit was empty, there was no water in it.
> 25 And they sat down to eat bread: and they lifted up their eyes and looked, and, behold, a company of Ishmeelites came from Gilead with their camels bearing spicery and balm and myrrh, going to carry it down to Egypt.
> 26 And Judah said unto his brethren, What profit is it if we slay our brother, and conceal his blood?
> 27 Come, and let us sell him to the Ishmeelites, and let not our hand be upon him; for he is our brother and our flesh. And his brethren were content.

The sequence of events is different in the separate traditions. In Genesis there is no foreshadowing of the passing of the caravan before its appearance on the scene. By contrast, in the Qurʾan we observe the contingency in the syntax of verse 12:10; it is a feature of the way the narrative unfolds deterministically: *if* you throw him into the pit *then* a caravan will pass and take him off. According to one view of the text, they will never be aware of the caravan that does indeed take Joseph down into Egypt; they have simply unknowingly been a pawn of this eventuality, the occurrence of which they, or one in their number, voices oblivious of the fact that this is just one of a series of cause-and-effect sequences in which they are themselves enmeshed and which will come to haunt them. The way that verse 10 unfolds in verse 19 ('A caravan came'/*wa-jāʾat sayyāratun*) is similar to the way elements of 12:13 are echoed in 12:17. In verse 13, Jacob expresses his fear that if Joseph is dispatched with his brothers 'a wolf may eat him'; in verse 17, the brothers explain Joseph's disappearance to Jacob thus: 'Father, we were racing against one another, and we left Joseph with our things; and *the wolf ate him* . . .' The closely identical statements mark fear in one instance and mendacity in the other, both impulses reflect that persistent ignorance writ varied and large.

Ignorance is woven into this passage of Surah 12 (verses 11–18) in a variety of ways:

> 12:11 They said, 'Father, how is it that you do not trust us with Joseph? We really are his sincere well-wishers.

> 12 Send him with us tomorrow, And he can enjoy himself and play, we shall watch over him.'
> 13 He said, 'It grieves me that you should take him out. I fear that a wolf may eat him whilst you are paying no attention.'
> 14 They said, 'If a wolf can eat him when there is a group of us, in that case we are losers.'
> 15 So when they had taken him off and agreed to put him in the bottom of a pit; We revealed to him, 'You will tell them about this affair of theirs when they are unaware [of who you are].'
> 16 And when they came to their father in the evening, weeping,
> 17 They said, 'Father, we were racing against one another, and we left Joseph with our things; and a wolf ate him. But you will not believe us, even though we are telling the truth.'
> 18 They brought his shirt with false blood on it. He said, 'No! Your souls have enticed you to do something wrong. [May I have] fair patience. God is one to whom I must turn for help against what you describe.'

Jacob knows that Joseph has been chosen by God to be a prophet, why therefore should he fear that he be mauled to death by a wolf?[17] This is the fearful rendering of the inchoate knowledge that he will have to part with his son before being reunited with him subsequently. Separation will be a death of sorts, though never so unequivocally as in Genesis 37 (31–4):

> 31 And they took Joseph's coat, and killed a kid of the goats, and dipped the coat in the blood;
> 32 And they sent the coat of many colours, and they brought it to their father; and said, This have we found: know now whether it be thy son's coat or no.
> 33 And he knew it, and said, It is my son's coat; an evil beast hath devoured him; Joseph is without doubt rent in pieces.
> 34 And Jacob rent his clothes, and put sackcloth upon his loins, and mourned for his son many days.

This passage is central to the way recognition is woven into the biblical version of the narrative.[18] In the Qur᾽an we observe that there is a complex psychology governing 13 and 17. Since he is a prophet we might surmise that Jacob's concern about the wolf foretells the deceit his sons will soon perpetrate on him; and yet he only partially realises the nature of this deceit. His imperfect knowledge cannot displace his fear and console him.[19] This is of course circular, and part of the essential theological tension of the narrative. Conversely we might understand that the brothers latch onto the theme of the wolf precisely to play on their father's fear, as the best way of drawing a veil over their actions. The manipulation of fear, augmenting ignorance, clouds the truth.

We should now consider 12:13 in its entirety:

> [Jacob] said, 'It grieves me that you should take him out. I fear that a wolf may eat him whilst you are paying him no attention.'

The Arabic for the last phrase beginning at 'whilst you' is *wa-antum ᶜan-hu ghāfilūn*. This is the second occurrence of the root *ghafala* in this surah: we have encountered it before at 12:3. Already, there, it was suggested that the meaning is polyvalent, carrying both the sense that the surah's audience *did not know* the story of Joseph before its revelation in the Qurᵓan and also that they were *previously oblivious* of its didactic significance. The two readings sit felicitously together. It is clear that in 12:13 the overt meaning is the one given in the above translation; but Jacob may also be subliminally suggesting that if the brothers were to neglect their younger sibling it would reflect their ignorance of his destiny. Support for this polyvalent reading comes almost immediately afterwards in 12:15, a verse which succinctly describes discrepant levels of knowledge:

> 15 So when they had taken him off and agreed to put him in the bottom of a well; and We revealed to him [the message], 'You will tell them about this affair of theirs when they are unaware [of who you are].'

No such divine encouragement is offered to Joseph in Genesis. In Surah 12 it shows to what degree the parts of the narrative work sequentially in terms of each other, that is, propleptically. Joseph is the recipient of revelation, a mantic gift that is exclusive to him (with the exception of his father, Jacob). In the exegetical tradition (e.g. in Bayḍāwī's commentary) the phrase 'when they are unaware' is said also to mean that when Joseph was being consoled with the knowledge that he would eventually bring his brothers to account, they were unaware that he was receiving revelation.[20] Both readings are grammatically correct. In both cases the verse provides a succinct nexus of ignorance and inspired knowledge, already a developing leitmotif of the narrative. Inevitably the preferred meaning in exegesis is the former, which accords with Jones' translation. This being the case, we should draw attention to a curious inversion in the full narrative. At 12:15 the brothers' ignorance is projected into the future. At 12:89, at the point when Joseph actually discloses his identity to his brothers, their ignorance is projected back into the past: 'Do you remember what you did to Joseph and his brother when you acted with ignorance?'

This brings us to one of the most fundamental semantic nuances of the particular epistemology of this narrative: the Arabic for 'when you acted with ignorance' in 12:89 is *wa-antum jāhilūn*. It is not therefore the same shade or nuance of ignorance that the narrative highlights at these two separate points. The *jahl* that attaches to the brothers when they commit their crime is more profoundly moral than cognitive. In early Arabic, cognitive ignorance is one of several facets of *jahl*. The latter traces a broad semantic spectrum: it connotes the inability to perceive the ethical virtues that constitute the social and communal fabric, as well as a cognitive deficit of things in general. We should underscore here, therefore, that the full epistemology of this narrative as a whole sketches more than the development of a straight dichotomy between human and divine knowledge. Divine knowledge embraces all, but human knowledge is both cognitive, on the one hand, and moral-ethical, on the other.

The circular movement of prolepsis followed by analepsis we have just described in part substantiates the symmetry of the narrative which others have described at length.[21] In this study we are more concerned with subordinating any structural view to a hermeneutics and the perfect enunciation of a theme, to see how the future unfolds from the past – and how the past is understood in the future.

When Joseph's brothers come to their father in the evening weeping (12:14) and lie, they add an interesting gloss about the scepticism they quite expect to be met with: 'But you will not believe us, even though we are telling the truth' (*wa-mā anta bi-muʾminin la-nā wa-law kunnā ṣādiqīn*). Jones adds to his translation a footnote: 'The use of *wa-law* meaning "although" does not imply a hypothetical situation. For another good example of *wa-law* with a "real" meaning, see 40:14 *wa-law kariha l-kāfirūn* "although the unbelievers are averse".' This rendering of *wa-law* restricts the meaning of the phrase. But working on the principle of semantic polyvalence in the Qurʾan we might recast 'does not' as 'need not'. For there is a certain felicity in understanding *wa-law* here as referring both to the brothers' situation at the time of their speech and more hypothetically to their speech generally, with an implicit glance forward to the future.

In a sense, the brothers' phrase *wa-law kunnā ṣādiqīn* ('even if we were telling the truth') is analogous with the phrase in 12:9 that states that they will be among the righteous only *after* they have committed their crime. They may be unaware of the callous irony with which they speak, but we have come to expect this, it is after all of them that it is said: *wa-hum lā yashʿurūn* (12:15 – 'while they were unaware'). The proleptic aspect of *wa-law kunnā ṣādiqīn* emerges when we compare how 12:17 leads into 12:18 and how this transition, together with certain details of the dialogue it depicts, are repeated verbatim in the transition from 12:82 to 12:83. These will be discussed in due course; they are the surest sign that structural symmetries of the text work in tandem with the development of its broad cognitive themes.

Two further aspects of 12:17–18 warrant attention. First, the use of the word *muʾmin* in the straightforward sense of 'to believe' reminds us that religious faith – *īmān* – is a matter of belief, of ascribing truth to that which we cannot know.[22] Belief is not grounded in positivistic knowledge, though the faithful can acquire this retrospectively. Secondly, the two verses carry the lexical and thematic inflection of much of the wider surah: the word *nastabiqu* foreshadows the race to the door between Joseph and Zulaykha (12:25 *wa-stabaqā l-bāb*), another contest that is stained by nefarious intent, though the first race is itself a fiction concocted by the brothers. We have already seen how the brothers' lie, *fa-akala-hu l-dhiʾbu* ('the wolf ate him') capitalises on Jacob's voicing of his fears (12:13 *akhāfu an yaʾkula-hu l-dhiʾbu*, 'I fear that the wolf will eat him').[23] A shirt belonging to Joseph appears on three occasions in the events of the text (the word *qamīṣ* itself actually occurs six times).[24] It is an important element of the narrative's thematic development. Its role in conjoining the physical and spiritual layers of the story is significant. In this first instance the shirt is set between the evocations of truth (the last word of 12:17 being *ṣādiqīn*) and lies, for the brothers 'brought his shirt (Genesis's tunic) with false blood on it' (*jā᾿ū ᶜalā qamīṣi-hi bi-damin kadhibin*); the associations of *ṣidq* and *kidhb* are sustained and evident in 12:27: *in kāna qamīṣu-hu qudda min qubuli fa-ṣadaqat wa-hum mina l-kādhibīn*. In the first instance (12:18), the shirt is coated in blood and veils a temporarily suppressed truth; in the second instance, the shirt itself allows a truth to emerge (12:28 *fa-lammā ra᾿ā l-qamīṣa qudda min duburin qāla inna-hu min kaydi-kunna*). In the third instance, the shirt brings about an epiphanic moment: it restores Jacob's sight, both his spiritual intuition and his physical faculty. Joseph's shirt thus illustrates, in contrived and measured fashion, the different mental processes explored and developed in sequence by the narrative: perjury, rational conjecture and inspired intuition. The shirt cast upon Jacob's face at 12:93 was not a shirt he could have actually physically recognised. Another significant inversion inheres in this fact, for in the first instance Jacob refuses to recognise his son's shirt[25] and in the third instance he recognises the deeper significance of a shirt that he has physically never actually seen; to make his recognition of his still distant son dependent solely on another physical faculty – smelling his son's fragrance upon the article – is too reductionist (too obtusely pragmatic even for the purposes of this narrative). It is certainly only a part of the truth, part of that same nexus of the physical and spiritual layers of the story to which we have alluded intermittently.

One of the most cited phrases from Surah 12 is Jacob's initial answer to his sons at 12:18 – 'Your souls have enticed you to [do] something [wrong]. [May I have] fair patience. God is the one to whom I must turn for help against what you describe' (*bal sawwalat la-kum anfusu-kum amran fa-ṣabrun jamīlun wa-llāhu l-mustaᶜānu ᶜalā mā taṣifūna*).[26] Of this full citation the particular phrase *fa-ṣabrun jamīlun* is certainly the most striking, due both to the syntactical ellipsis which makes it semantically ambiguous and to its recurrence at 12:83.[27] Grammatically the phrase is a subject without a predicate or, conversely, a predicate without a subject. A flight of interpretive fancy would suggest that the story – the on-going narrative – is the phrase's predicate. That is to say, the abstraction of the quality of patience in this open-ended construction allows *qaṣaṣ* to be the predicate of *ṣabr*, and vice versa. The point of this turn of interpretation (indeed any interpretation of this anomalous construction) is simply to emphasise the theme: the beauty of patience (*ṣabr*). It is a quality illustrated most pointedly in the narrative by the comportments of Joseph and Jacob; and the most essential related idea in the epistemology of the surah is that *ṣabr* is a sub-facet of *ḥilm* (forebearance) in the classical panoply of *muruwwah,* ethical qualities and societal values inherited by Islam with nuanced shifts of emphasis from the *jāhiliyyah. Ḥilm* itself is an antonym of *jahl* which is 'ignorance' in its broadest sense.

What is clear in 12:18 about the word *amran*, in this indeterminate form, is that while Jacob is aware that his sons have done *something* wrong, he simply does not know *exactly what* that thing is. The locution as a whole is thus a subtle and succinct way of expressing the fact of knowing and not knowing.[28] Both the sentiment and the attitude, we should note, are quite missing from the biblical version (cf. 37:35) and, in a new context, it repeats the tension of 12:6.

Going Down into Egypt

> 12:19 A caravan came, and they sent their water-carrier, and he let down his bucket. He said, 'Good news. Here is a young man.' They hid him away as something to sell – but God was aware of what they were doing.
> 20 And they sold him for a paltry price, some *dirhams* counted out, [for] they were indifferent about him.
> 21 The Egyptian who bought him said to his wife, 'Give him good lodging. It may be that he will be of benefit to us or that we adopt him as a son.' In this way we made a place for Joseph in the land. [This was] so that We might teach him something of the interpretation of tales. God was master of his affairs, but most of the people do not know [that].
> 22 When he reached his prime we gave him judgement and knowledge. Thus We reward those who do good.

Joseph's descent into Egypt in the biblical version contains some confusion on the matter of who conveys him there. It is not altogether clear whether the Midianites were the same people as the Ishmaelites.[29] In the Qur'anic version, in which the *sayyārah* – the caravan – remains without ethnic association, the ambiguity discussed by the commentators (the *mufassirūn*) revolves more around the role of the brothers. Was it they who sold Joseph to the Ishmaelites once they had arrived on the scene, or was it the latter who simply secreted the youth (*asarrū-hu*) in their baggage and then sold him on for a paltry sum in Egypt?

That the men of the *sayyārah* should have attached little value to the adolescent boy upon selling him is curious given the auspicious way he is announced to them initially (in Dothan) by their forager (or scout): 12:19 *yā bushrā hādhā ghulāmun* ('Good news! Here is a young man'). And why, if not as a token showing their appreciation of their human chattel, did they hide him among their goods? It would accord more with the wider text that it should have been the brothers who valued him little in selling him. But this fact is hard to reconcile with the logic of the following ayah in which we find ourselves abruptly in Egypt, reference there being made to the sale of Joseph to Potiphar.

In any event, the point of the description *wa-kānū min-hu mina l-zāhidīn* is that whoever[30] sold Joseph into slavery could not and did not recognise his true worth: denuded, cast into a pit, huddled into baggage as so much grain, he cannot have offered much of a spectacle.[31] Even before his vicious man-handling, his brothers clearly were incapable of divining beyond the outer carapace of his aspect the future in store for him. It was the requisite *firāsah*, or gift of physiognomy, that they lacked.[32] In the architecture of this passage of the surah, this lack of discernment works in parallel with the suppression of truth that marks the actions of the merchant caravan in the previous verse – actions that remained unhidden from God's eyes. We should simply remark that the phrase *wa-asarrū-hu biḍāᶜatan wa-llāhu ᶜalīmun bi-mā yaᶜmalūn* sustains the cognitive tension that runs throughout the narrative, modulated in different ways that are often particular to the Qur᾿anic version, as is the case here.

It is recognition that provides a transition into Egypt. Although Potiphar paid a 'paltry sum' for his slave, yet we suspect he would have spent much more, for he saw in him a good deal more than a mere servant.[33] Verse 12:21 is indeed fundamentally in tune with the overarching cognitive-cum-theological theme of the whole narrative. Here is the full verse in translation:

> 12:21 The Egyptian who bought him said to his wife, 'Give him good lodging. It may be that he will profit us or we may adopt him as a son.' In this way We made a place for Joseph in the land. [This was] so that We might

> teach him something of the interpretation of tales. God was predominant over his affair, But most of the people do not know [that].

God knows everything. He also determines everything that He wills. What is clear here is that people's deeds are corollaries of their knowledge; God contrives the actions of men according to a design that He knows and they do not yet. The prophets catch glimpses of – recognise – God's design before the full unfolding and retrospective evaluation (*taʾwīl*) of events. *Taʾwīl* indeed has both a prospective and retrospective sense; *taʾwīl al-aḥādīth* connotes as much knowing the upshot of matters as interpreting their meaning once they have transpired. Joseph is given notice in dreams of the events that happen in this surah; it is unlikely therefore that *aḥādīth* should be taken literally to mean dreams, given the absence of any other instance of such usage in Arabic. Rather they are the mantic events prefigured and related in dreams; as such the word comes to be translated as dreams by a process of synecdoche.[34]

The outcome of events is very much influenced by Potiphar. Potiphar favours Joseph's presence in his household because God wills it so (*ka-dhālika makkannā li-yūsufa fī l-arḍ . . . wa-llāhu ghālibun ʿalā amri-hā*), but there must be some glimpse of a subjective, affective and intellectual experience that Potiphar has of this overarching deterministic design, and this is clear in his words to his wife: 'It may be that he will profit us or we adopt him as a son.'[35] Potiphar must have been either consciously or subconsciously cognisant of the qualities of the youth in order to desire him as a son, or to anticipate the benefit he would gift his own household, Pharaoh and Egypt as a whole.[36] In echoing, or possibly prefiguring, a Qurʾanic phrase used of Moses in Surah 29:9, Potiphar's instructions to his wife are clearly intended to herald the prophetic role that his newly acquired slave will have.[37]

It follows that knowledge accrues from events determined by God; while God can impart knowledge and determine events independently of each other, for this is the ultimate logic of divine omnipotence and omniscience, the providential design of the story requires that knowledge be closely contingent upon unfolding events. Here then is the crux of the paradox that provides this surah's theological dynamic: God determines events in order to impart knowledge; yet by the same token He imparts knowledge in order to determine events – a chronologically measured give-and-take, where at any given point in the narrative one or other side of this providential equation (determined event or inspired understanding) has greater relief. An arresting by-product of this is that God is bound by mankind's humanity to the same degree that mankind is bound by God's divinity (and somewhere within the interstices lies the cloudy matter of mankind's responsibility for his actions).

We should clarify the semantic influence that *li-nuᶜallima-hu min taʾwīli l-aḥādīth* exerts within the same verse (12:21) upon *wa-aktharu l-nāsi lā yaᶜlamūn*: one implication of this is that most people are not given the sort of knowledge that Joseph acquires in the course of the narrative. Is it not also implied here that Potiphar has known more than most? That is, 12:21 carries implicitly much of the attitude and insight attributed to Potiphar in Genesis 39:2–6 (esp. 39:3).

> 2 And the LORD was with Joseph, and he was a prosperous man; and he was in the house of his master the Egyptian.
> 3 *And his master saw that the LORD was with him, and that the LORD made all that he did to prosper in his hand.* [emphasis added]
> 4 And Joseph found grace in his sight, and he served him: and he made him overseer over his house, and all that he had he put into his hand.
> 5 And it came to pass from the time that he had made him overseer in his house, and over all that he had, that the LORD blessed the Egyptian's house for Joseph's sake; and the blessing of the LORD was upon all that he had in the house, and in the field.
> 6 And he left all that he had in Joseph's hand; and he knew not ought he had, save the bread which he did eat. And Joseph was a goodly person, and well favoured.

12:22 is reiterative insofar as a verse from another surah, to wit 29:14, which refers to Moses, is repeated thus sharing the scheme of prophetic history into which Joseph's life has been written. The knowledge and judgement that are bestowed upon Joseph are also preliminary and incremental and allow him to stand firm when faced with the temptations of his master's wife. Two very different instances of *ᶜilm* are illustrated in what ensues immediately upon 12:22.

Wiles and Seduction

12:23 The woman in whose house he was tried to seduce him. She shut the doors and said, 'Come on.' He replied, 'God is my refuge. [Your husband] is my master. He has given me good lodging.'
24 She had designs on him; and he would have had designs on her, had he not seen the proof of his Lord. So it was that he might turn evil and immorality from him.
25 The two of them raced to the door, and she tore his shirt from behind. They met her lord and master at the door. She said, 'What is to be the recompense of a man who has had evil designs against your folk, other than that he should be imprisoned or a painful punishment.'
26 He said, 'She it was who tried to seduce me.' Then one of her folk bore witness, 'If his shirt is torn from in front, she is telling the truth, and he is a liar.
27 But if his shirt has been torn from behind, she is lying, and he is telling the truth.'
28 When he saw that his shirt was torn from behind, he said, '[This] is one of your women's tricks. The trickery of you women is immense.
29 Jospeh, turn away from this; and you, [my wife], seek forgiveness for your sin. You are one of the sinners.'
30 Some of the women in the city said, 'The ruler's wife is trying to seduce her young man. He has smitten her heart with love. We think her clearly in the wrong.'
31 When she heard their sly talk, she invited them and prepared for them a couch and gave to each of them a knife. Then she said to Joseph, 'Go into their presence.' When they saw him, they admired him, and they cut their hands, and said, 'God is wonderful. This is not a mortal. This is nothing but a gracious angel.'
32 She said, 'This is the one about whom you blamed me. I did try to seduce him, but he remained chaste; but if he does not do what I tell him to do, he shall be imprisoned and shall be one of those who are humbled.'
33 He said, 'My Lord, I prefer prison rather than that to which these women call me; but if You do not turn their tricks from me, I shall incline to them in youthful folly and I shall become one of the heedless.'

34 So His Lord answered him and turned their tricks from him; He is the Hearer and Knower.
35 Then it seemed good to them after they had seen the signs to imprison him for a time.

In 12:23 Joseph's initial response to Zulaykha is ambiguous; it appears to echo Potiphar's foregoing instructions to his wife (*akrimī mathwā-hu*) and refers to God's providential steering of Joseph's life (*ka-dhālika makkannā li-yūsufa fī l-arḍ*): Joseph has *both* his earthly and heavenly masters in mind, it would appear, when he resists the advances of the mistress of the household. That *rabb* can refer to either of the subjects described, that is, that he may be referring to God here in addition to his master,[38] is supported by the fact that the word is used in the adjacent and following ayah – in the latter case clearly referring to God. (A similar ambiguity in meaning/referent obtains in 12:52 where it is not clear whom Joseph is stating that he did not betray.)

12:24 has caused the exegetes to be much exercised. In *Mafātīḥ al-Ghayb*, Fakhr al-Dīn al-Rāzī (d. 1209 AD) discusses this passage in particular detail in order to show that no sin attached to Joseph – that his resolve never weakened before the advances of Zulaykha. Yet there is a grammatical duplicity about the construction *hamma bi-hā law-lā ra᾽ā burhāna rabbi-hi*. Clearly it is possible, indeed necessary, with Rāzī, to stress that *hamma bi-hā* ('he had designs on her') is governed by the conditional *law-lā*, indicating that '*he would have – if*' but that he in fact *did not*. The implications, however, are tantalising and the phrase is nicely inflected with both the humanity of Joseph – his human weakness (some influence is exerted on the critical phrase and unconditional *hamma bi-hā* by its juxtaposition with the determined *hammat bi-hi*) – and the providential hand that has made him a prophet and therefore rendered him invulnerable to sin. He is made to recognise the signs of his Lord. This could simply be the moral insight that he intuits. Yet it is striking that this fact is rendered as a seeing – a corporal recognition of sorts – for in the Muslim tradition, as in the Judaic tradition, it was the appearance of the figure of his father before him (in some instances Gabriel)[39] – the recognition of a person or figure – that enables him to recognise a moral principle. A physical human presence is made to mediate in the apprehension of a fact, allowing us some broad insight into the way recognition scenes function and the role that they can have in carrying and making manifest the underlying epistemology of a narrative. Human recognition becomes the synecdoche for the theme of moral recognition as a whole, a fact that is far more apparent later in the surah.[40] (The figure of Jacob may be a populist exegetical brushstroke, one borrowed from the Jewish tradition, but we should note that it is in all the principal and mainstream *tafāsīr*.)[41]

What is clear in verse 12:24 is that moral insight/knowledge (*raʾā burhāna rabbi-hi*) is divinely determined (*ka-dhālika li-naṣrifa ᶜan-hu l-sūʾa wa-l-faḥshāʾ*). But if according to the foregoing discussion Man is divested of agency, in the ensuing sordid entanglement (12:25–9) human agency (and responsibility) is restored, both in action and reflection. It is syllogistic reasoning that establishes the truth of Joseph's innocence and Zulaykha's guilt, respectively; the scene has the flavour of a trial, and the imagined jury is asked to follow the simple and unassailable logic of circumstantial deduction: it is the shirt that provides the focus of this important passage. In the course of four verses (25–8) the fact of the shirt having been torn from behind is mentioned three times; in the first instance we find a statement of fact: Joseph fled his temptress and his shirt was torn from behind (the passive form, *qudda*, suggests that the agency is unknown (*majhūl*) and also, perhaps, that an ulterior/higher agency than that of Zulaykha is involved). In the second instance an anonymous witness proposes that the external evidence be considered. It is cast as a syllogistic contingency: if the shirt is torn from behind then Joseph is telling the truth and she is lying, and vice versa. In the last instance the clear physical evidence that Potiphar beheld is reported (12:27): 'So when he saw that the shirt was torn from behind . . .' The truth (*ṣidq*) is now established. And yet justice, real truth – *Ḥaqq* – is suppressed for a time: Potiphar asks Joseph not to speak publicly of this scandal (*aᶜriḍ ᶜan hādhā*);[42] this last is a detail absent from the biblical version as is, correspondingly, the scene before Pharaoh's court in which the truth of Zulaykha's seduction is finally disclosed.

Prison, the Catechism and the Two Prisoners' Dreams

Even as it obeys the providential contours and detours of romance, Joseph's subsequent imprisonment stands as a metonym for suppressed truth. Yet according to the ironic staging of the story it is here, in prison, that the deeper truths of the surah begin properly to emerge: the evidence for this is the central, doctrinal sermon that he – the Hebrew slave[43] – delivers to his fellow inmates, the butler and the baker.[44]

Now, for the truth to be suppressed it must of necessity first be known. Interesting in this particular case is what it is precisely that is known and perceived. Potiphar is cognisant of Joseph's innocence yet asks him to keep quiet (*aᶜriḍ ᶜan hādhā*). The women of Memphis, now aware that the youth will not give in to the 'wiles of women' (cf. 12:33) and that he is innocent of Zulaykha's advances, nevertheless have him thrown into prison. Potiphar, we recall, has remarked the special qualities of the youth; the women too have observed his innocent aspect and comportment. For it is the hint of a numinous mission that seems to underlie the phrase (12:35): 'Then it seemed good to them, *after they had seen the signs* (*raʾaw al-āyāt*), to imprison him for a while.'[45] We should argue the point further: *raʾaw āyāt* is an extremely loaded phrase in the context of this surah, which is (1) a chapter in the book of inspired signs (2) to be understood by mankind (3) as to their deeper meaning (4) with the benefit of hindsight (such is the force of verses 1–3). Perception, use of the verb *raʾā*, is both straightforwardly optical (as in 12:27, when Potiphar sees that Joseph's tunic has been torn from behind) and oneiric, imaginal and mantic (12:6). The women can see that Joseph is innocent and get a glimpse of what lies behind his outward beauty. But this deeper knowledge is still inchoate; it troubles them and they decide not to kill the youth but to cover up the problem for a time – *ḥattā ḥīn*. *Ḥattā ḥīn* is a subconscious acquiescence in the fact the real truth is bound to be disclosed with time. This is a natural reading of the phrase if we take incarceration as a metonym for suppression. *Ḥattā ḥīn* is, indeed, another deterministic detail in the text; for it is not the women's desire that their moral failure should be veiled from view for a fixed period only, but God's determination of events. In this view, *ḥattā ḥīn* is an invisible leitmotif of the way the story is patterned in time according to providential design. It is the barest abstraction of the scheme of a temporal and cognitive development that gives the story its shape.

> 12:36 Two young men entered the prison with him. One of them said, 'I see myself pressing wine'; the other said, 'I see myself carrying on my head

some bread, from which the birds are eating. Tell us the interpretation, for we see that you are one of those who do good.'
37 He said, 'No food from which you have your sustenance will come to you except that I shall have told you its interpretation before it comes to you. This is from what my Lord has taught me. I have forsaken the religion of a people who do not believe in God and are unbelievers about the world to come.
38 I have followed the religion of my fathers Abraham and Isaac and Jacob. It was not for us to associate anything with God. This is part of God's bounty to us and to the people; but most of the people are ungrateful.
39 O two fellow-prisoners, are various Lords better or God, the One, the Victorious?
40 Apart from Him you worship only names given by you and your fathers. God has sent down no authority for them. Judgement belongs only to God. He has ordered you to serve Him alone. That is the true religion; but most people do not know.
41 O two fellow-prisoners, one of you will pour wine for his master; the other will be crucified, and the birds will eat from his head. The matter about which you seek my opinion has been determined.'
42 He said to the one of the two he thought would be saved, 'Mention me in the presence of your master.' But Satan caused him to forget to mention him to his master, and so he lingered in prison for several years.

The two young men imprisoned with Joseph are described with stark and effective economy; their dreams are sketched in scant detail: the one presses wine, the other carries on his head a basket from which the birds eat (none of the numerical and mantic contrivances of the biblical dreams survive here; cf. Genesis 40:9–17). The details in the biblical version are essential to the details of the interpretation. In Genesis the tense dynamic between the auspicious and ominous dreams is carried in the striking dialogue between the prisoners, who are down-in-the-mouth and are questioned by Joseph. It is the latter who initiates the exchange, though he divests himself of responsibility for the interpretation of the dreams. Particularly memorable is the fact of the baker's misprision, that he misreads his own dream in the light of the favourable interpretation given to the butler's dream. Discernment is a quality that is distressingly deficient in this man.

It is recognition, indeed, which comes through most strongly in the economy of the Qurʾanic text; it is expressed differently, however.

> 12:36 Two young men entered the prison with him. One of them said, 'I see myself pressing wine'; the other said, 'I see myself carrying on my head some bread, from which the birds are eating. Tell us its interpretation, for we see that you are one of those who do good [*al-muḥsinīn*].'

We have commented before on the root *raʾā* ad locum 12:35. Here, the verb occurs three times within the space of a single verse. What are we to make of these repetitions? The semantics of 'seeing visions in dreams', the mantic aspect of these particular visions in the unfolding story, exert an influence on the nature of the 'sighting' of the qualities of Joseph. There is a further iterative detail in this verse: *al-muḥsinīn* – 'the righteous' – is used six times in the narrative, five of which, spread evenly throughout the text, refer to Joseph. Although there is vagueness about the quality being extolled, we should observe its consistency: Joseph has the quality before he enters prison and it survives with him when he leaves, right up to the point when he reveals himself to his brothers. It is that same quality that marks him as a prophet, for it is linked with the knowledge and judgement that God gives to the young man on the eve of his entanglement with Zulaykha (cf. 12:22 *wa-lammā balagha ashudda-hu ātaynā-hu ḥukman wa-ᶜilman wa-kādhālika najzī l-muḥsinīn*).[46]

We should consider the frayed logic of the prisoners' terse eulogies; they support an interpretation that differentiates between categories and echelons of knowledge. Simple syllogistic logic would suggest that since Joseph has been imprisoned, he must be a base criminal. But why, then, do they 'see' him as 'one of those who do good'? Precisely, comes the answer, because they perceive in him those numinous qualities that give shape and meaning to the whole story, though they do not know this fully (and nor, as yet, does he). There is, then, a significant hierarchy of knowledge: the butler and the baker are blind to the semiotics of their own dreams, and are ignorant in this sense, but they are given mantic hints to the qualities of Joseph and, concomitantly, to the precious knowledge[47] he is privy to.[48] To link the prisoners' phrase *innā narā-ka mina l-muḥsinīn* with recognition is ironical in the full context of the story given that his brothers utter the same words later in the storyline when, having still failed to recognise their lost sibling, they plead with him to detain someone other than young Benjamin (cf. 12:78 *inna la-hu aban shaykhan kabīran fa-khudh aḥada-nā makāna-hu innā narā-ka mina l-muḥsinīn*). The rich contextual implications of this verse are manifold and will be considered duly.

Ayah 12:36, in the meantime, begs further scrutiny as a thread in the epistemological tissue of events. It is a verse of transition in the architecture of the surah; it is the first instance in which Joseph is given to explain the meaning of things. Jacob's initial prognostication in 12:6 refers only to Joseph's prophetic potential. Here he is invited to realise his potential by his fellow inmates (*nabbiʾ-nā bi-taʾwīli-hi*) and he accedes to the request in the following verse: 'No food from which you have your sustenance will come to you except I shall have told you its interpretation before it comes to you.' The ensuing phrase signifies the essential transition: 'This is of what my Lord has taught me' (*dhālikumā mimmā ᶜallama-nī rabbī*). Jacob's earlier divination (12:6 *rabbu-ka . . . yuᶜallimu-ka min taʾwīli l-aḥādīth*) has begun now to bear fruit, the distinction of verbal tenses marking the development: *yuᶜallimu-ka* → *ᶜallama-nā* (future → preterit).

The phrase *dhālikumā mimmā ᶜallama-nī rabbī*[49] is transitional as much within the arc of the surah as within the verse itself. This is important, for it allows one to integrate the following sermon (12:37–40) within Surah 12's overarching structure and architecture. It has been suggested that the sermon marks the doctrinal centre of the whole surah. Here the monotheism of Joseph is cast in the style of Meccan polemical Islam. It is the most intensely Qurʾanic passage, one might say. Conversely, it has also been indicated in recent scholarship that the sermon does not sit well with the symmetries and parallelisms of micro-structure within the section.[50] However, the latter view – essentially, that the sermon is interpolated – can be resisted by gauging the transitional aspect of the phrase in question. *Dhālikumā* clearly must refer to some antecedent – the fact of interpreting the dreams – but the further connection of the phrase with what follows is confirmed by a certain lexical harmony between parts of 12:36–7 and the earlier verse, 12:6. To wit: (12:6) *yuᶜallimu-ka* → *yutimmu niᶜmata-hu ᶜalay-ka wa-ᶜalā āli* *yaqūba ka-mā atamma-hā ʿalā abaway-ka min qablu ibrāhīma wa-isḥāqa* → 12:36–7 *ʿallama-nī rabbī* → *wa-ttabaʿtu millata ābāʾī ibrāhīma wa-isḥāqa wa-yaʿqūba.* In the distended cognitive fabric of the surah the ability to interpret dreams is rendered contingent upon the practice of true religion, though they are not always overtly related; this is almost as, if not more, important than the details of the sermon itself, for they have little in common with the broad cognitive themes we have been enucleating.[51] The resonances of this overt religiosity are sustained through to the completion of the narrative.

It is in the catechism that the Qurʾanic version of the Joseph story most essentially parts company with the biblical version and its Midrashic accretions. In Genesis no issue is made of the fact that Joseph's religion, the religion of his forefathers, was not the same as that of his first master, Potiphar, and of his second master, Pharaoh;[52] he was even rewarded in his success as an administrator with the hand of the daughter of an Egyptian highpriest (cf. Genesis 41:45).[53] When Joseph indicates to Pharaoh that 'interpretation comes from God', the two men seem to share articles of belief; their religion is, if only momentarily, marked more by commonality than by difference. There is, further, a certain quality of oblivion in Genesis, nowhere better expressed than in the naming of Joseph's two sons (cf. Genesis 41:51–2 '51 And Joseph called the name of the firstborn Manasseh: For God, said he, hath made me forget all my toil, and all my father's house. 52 And the name of the second called he Ephraim: For God hath caused me to be fruitful in the land of my affliction.')[54] Forgetfulness does, of course, play its part in the Qurʾanic narrative, but it does not, as in the Bible, act as an unguent for Joseph's losses. According to the dominant view of the commentaries it is the Devil who makes the butler forget to mention Joseph to his master/Pharaoh; he contrives that Joseph should languish in prison as punishment for having himself abandoned his Lord in a moment of human weakness.

To reiterate, the Qurʾanic catechism is exceptional but should not be viewed as being shoehorned into the surah. In the contours of nascent Islam that are so clearly recognisable from the sermon, especially aspects of *tawḥīd*, lies a further detail that relates to the theology of the narrative as a whole: *ini l-ḥukmu illā li-llāh. Ḥukm* – the *ḥukm* of which God imparts to Joseph – is the complement of God's knowledge in delineating the theological challenge of the text. It is significant that hard upon the phrase comes the qualifier *wa-lākinna akthara l-nāsi lā yaʿlamūn*. God is omniscient (*ʿalīm*) and He determines events according to His judgement (*ḥukm*); man acts and is responsible for his deeds and he comes to know, but his knowledge is relative and differentiated according to a hierarchy governing both man in society and man's relationship to God. Joseph provides a meeting point between the two, for when he pronounces the sentence *quḍiya l-amru lladhī fī-hi tastaftiyān*, he is telling us that the future – not all of which he is knowledgeable about – has already been determined in the past: the design of the story is not ultimately contrived in the unfolding moments (though it is experienced in this way for didactic effect and aesthetic diversion, and here we refer back to the point made above in respect of 12:3). No amount of personal and affective insight into the moral fabric of religion can or will change the course of divine decree; the irony is that the dream's fulfilment is functional, for it *must* come true in order for those other things to be realised about which Joseph is, if not in the dark, then at least uncertain of. This is clear effectively and by affect in the following verse (12:42) in which the strident confidence of *quḍiya l-amru lladhī fī-hi tastaftiyān* sets off the rash conjecture of Joseph's request to Pharaoh's butler.

> He [Joseph] said to the one he *thought* would be saved, 'Mention me in the presence of your master.'[55] But Satan caused him to forget[56] to mention him to his master, and so he lingered in prison for several years.

The root *ẓanna* has an important nuance in the Qurʾan (and in classical Arabic generally). If it can be translated as 'to conjecture', it is not entirely innocent conjecture; it has the hue of doubt and is often brought to play in the context of those who question the tenets of Islamic eschatological teaching.[57] It is, therefore, strange, that, after the initially compelling interpretation of the dream, Joseph should come to doubt it in its immediate application to his plight. It is perhaps this doubt, this abandonment of cognitive and moral certainty, that leads to condign retribution, even if Satan is the actual agent of Joseph's chastisement. The use of *ẓanna* here is paradigmatic rather than enunciatory; it simply evokes in Joseph the momentary rashness that will see him punished for a while.[58] It certainly further establishes the consistently nuanced epistemology of (Joseph's) religion. Here is the paradox: the punishment is providential, for the final timing of his exit will catapult him into the loftiest position of state power and influence.

Pharaoh's Dream

> 12:43 The king said, 'I see seven fat cows that are devoured by seven thin ones, and seven green ears of corn and others withered. You nobles, give me your opinions about my dream if you are able to interpret dreams.'
> 44 They replied, 'Tangled nightmares. We know nothing of the interpretation of dreams.'
> 45 The one of the two who had been saved [now] remembered after a time and said, 'I shall tell you its interpretation. Send me.'
> 46 'Joseph, you man of truth, give me your opinion about seven fat cows that are devoured by seven thin ones and seven green ears of corn and others that are withered, so that I may return to the people, so that they may know.'
> 47 He said, 'You will sow for seven years as is your custom. But what you harvest, leave it in the ear, except for a little which you may eat.
> 48 Then after that will come seven hard [years] which will devour what you have made ready for them, except for a little which you may store.
> 49 Then after that will come a year in which people will have rain and in which they will press.'
> 50 The king said, 'Bring him to me.' When the messengers came to him, his answer was, 'Return to your master and ask him, "What about the women who cut their hands?" My Lord has knowledge of their tricks.'
> 51 He said [to the women], 'What about that affair of yours when you tried to seduce Joseph?' They replied, 'God save him! We know no evil against him!' The wife of the ruler said, 'Now the truth has come to light. It was I who tried to seduce him. He was truthful.
> 52 That is so that he may know that I did not betray him in his absence and that God does not guide the manoeuvres of those who betray.
> 53 Yet I do not declare that my soul was innocent. The soul always enjoins wrong-doing, except so far as my Lord has mercy. My Lord is Forgiving, Merciful.'
> 54 The king said, 'Bring him to me, and I shall attach him to my person.'

> And when he talked to him, he said, 'To-day you are trusted and firmly established at our side.'
> 55 He replied, 'Set me over the store-houses of the land. I am a knowing guardian.'
> 56 Thus we gave Joseph a place in the land, for him to settle in it wherever he wished. We make Our mercy reach those whom We wish. We do not let the wage of those who do good go to waste.
> 57 Yet the wage[59] of the world to come is better for those who believe and are godfearing.

An aesthetic emerges: knowledge and ignorance are arranged in a contrastive chiaroscuro of varying intensities. The effect is felt markedly in the episode of Pharaoh's two-part dream. Pharaoh's magicians are stymied by his visions which they dismiss as 'tangled nightmares'; in this scornful verbal gesture, their ignorance is twofold: (1) they fail to recognise the mantic origins of the dream and (2) ignore its latent significance. Their failure prompts the butler to recall Joseph to mind and announce that he will solve the dark oneiric riddle.

The highly syncopated economy of scene changes in this part of the narrative is one of the most striking stylistic aspects of the Qurʾanic narrative.[60] We will concentrate on the connection between the semantic elements of the two scenes juxtaposed; a semiotic-cum-hermeneutic reading of the surah might suggest that the way Joseph is first addressed by the butler, *ayyu-hā l-ṣiddīq*, holds the answer to the puzzle of the Qurʾan's additional scene in which Joseph refuses to be released from prison before his innocence is established at court. As Alan Jones has noted, 'In the Haggada *ṣaddīq* is used as an epithet of Joseph.' Even in the Judaic tradition there is clearly an affinity between moral behaviour and truth. There is a correlation between chastity and honesty, especially when chastity signifies abstaining from taking the property of others, obviating the need for living a subsequent lie; glib as it might seem, there is a fundamental point to be salvaged from the fact that chastity is perceived from the moral perspective of religious truth. From a crosstextual perspective, *al-ṣiddīq* harks back to the earlier scene and looks forward to the court scene that Joseph insists on (12:50) in order to clear his name – to establish precisely that he was always telling the truth (12:51) despite the *de facto* public calumny of his imprisonment.[61]

Part of the economy of this section is the tacit recognition that Joseph's interpretation is authentic. We are allowed to gather that there is something self-evident about the truth.[62] The same psychology may operate here as that which frames the subsequent confession of Zulaykha and the other women. Are they coerced into giving evidence against themselves? This hardly seems to be the case. Pharaoh asks a question about their actions, mentioning their seduction of Joseph as a statement of fact (*idh rāwadtunna yūsufa ᶜan nafsi-hi*), and they give an answer not about themselves but about Joseph: 'We know no evil against him.' The truth has become ripe for harvest here; in this respect it is noticeable that *al-ḥaqq* is the subject of the verb of disclosure: 'Now the truth has come to light.' It has become self-evident, the aspect of becoming being stressed by the emphasis placed on the word *al-āna* – only now, at its proper and appointed time, has the truth emerged. The word *al-āna* resolves the tension generated by the imprisonment of Joseph – the suppression of truth – *ḥattā ḥīn. Ḥattā ḥīn* and *al-āna* can indeed be viewed as radically abstracted structuralist ingredients of the text: of the temporally contingent patterning of events and the resolution of plot.[63]

Regarding 12:52, Rāzī's commentary on Zulaykha's confession is of particular merit and typical of the psychological subtlety of motive he is given to analyse in depth. These subtleties are for the most part labelled *daqīqah*s:

> When Joseph asked, 'What about the women who cut their hands?' he was acting discreetly and showing consideration for his master's wife, for he mentioned the women without any specific mention of her at all. She, for her part, recognised (*fa-ᶜarafat*) that he omitted to mention her in order to protect her (*riᶜāyatan li-ḥaqqi-hā*) – out of respect for her and in order to hide the truth which stood against her (*ikhfāʾan li-l-amri ᶜalay-hā*). She therefore wished to reward him for this noble gesture and was thus obliged to divulge the truth of the affair (*fa-lā jarama azālati l-ghaṭāʾ*), confessing that the guilt was all hers and that Joseph was wholly innocent.[64]

In the moment of truth Joseph was concerned about discretion, a paradox emanating from courtesy; this to some degree illustrates the ethical layering of knowledge and truth. A well-chosen anecdote further related by Rāzī as analogue illustrates even more concisely the paradox of concealment/protection and confession/truth:

> I have read in a book that a woman took her husband to court claiming her dowry from him. The Qāḍī ordered her face to be uncovered so that the witnesses could properly testify [in her favour]. At this her husband said, 'There is no need for that, for I now acknowledge the truth of her claim (*innī muqirrun bi-ṣidqi-hā fī daᶜwā-hā*).' His wife's reply to this was, 'Since you have paid me this honour (*lammā akramta-nī ilā hādhā l-ḥadd*), then bear witness [all those that are present] that I discharge you of any debt you may owe me.'[65]

We note in this connection that Joseph never divulges his brothers' crime publicly (in Genesis, not even to his father).[66]

Zulaykha is of course rehabilitated in other ways, too: thus, in prophetic apocrypha, Zulaykha's marriage to Joseph and the discovery of her virginity as related in Rāzī.[67] This is recognition as moral restitution: a woman cast in the role of (evil) temptress was innocent *all along*; she was physically and hence spiritually pure and intact.

There is something particularly poignant and emblematic about the finely alliterative and assonanatal phrase, *al-āna ḥaṣḥaṣa l-ḥaqqu* (12:52 'Now the truth has come to light'). It is the most crystalline affirmation of disclosure as an essential theme in the whole surah and the words could be aptly borrowed to pass comment on the denouement of the entire narrative. In this passage of confession and disclosure (12:50–2), the root *ᶜilm* appears three times, attaching to diverse players: God (*inna rabbī bi-kaydi-hinna ᶜalīm*), the women of Memphis (who say *mā ᶜalimnā ᶜalay-hi min sūʾ*) and Potiphar (*dhālika li-yaᶜlama annī lam akhun-hu bi-l-ghayb*). Realisation is thus here collective but knowledge is still somewhat hierarchical: it is cast variously as divine omniscience, confession and reassurance, for Potiphar already knew from circumstantial evidence that Joseph was innocent. Knowledge is subsumed in *al-Ḥaqq*, which is a lexically discrete invocation of God. (God is referred to commonly simply as *al-Ḥaqq* in Sufi literature.)[68]

This passage adds weight to the gathering momentum of disclosure, which must be viewed as the symbolic code of the text, and offers an aesthetic-cum-semiotic view that redresses the excesses of seeing the narrative predominantly as a simple arabesque of symmetries: each disclosure looks proleptically to the next and is carried over into it, so that the text becomes progressively and increasingly informed by discovery and the stark ironies that become apparent as ignorance is shed.

The Brothers' Arrival: The First Recognition

> 12:58 And Joseph's brothers came and went to see him. He recognized them, but they did not recognize him.
> 59 When he provided them with their provision, he said, 'Bring me a brother of yours from your father. Do you not see that I give full measure? I am the best of hosts.
> 60 If you do not bring him to me, there will be no measure for you and you will not approach me.'
> 61 They replied, 'We shall ask his father to send him. We shall certainly do that.'
> 62 He said to his young men, 'Place their goods [back] in their baggage, so that they may recognize them when they go back to their people, so that they may return.'
> 63 When they returned to their father, they said, 'Father, [further] measure has been denied to us; so send our brother with us. We shall watch over him.'
> 64 He replied, 'Shall I entrust him to you in any other way than I entrusted his brother to you before? God is better as a guardian – He is the most merciful of the merciful.'
> 65 When they opened their belongings, they discovered their goods had been returned to them. They said, 'Father, what more can we desire? Here are our goods returned to us. We can get provision for our folk and guard our brother, and we shall get an extra camel-load. That is an easy measure.'
> 66 He said, 'I shall not send him with you until you give me an undertaking in God's name that you will bring him back to me unless you are overwhelmed.' When they gave him their undertaking, he said, 'God is the guardian of what we say.'
> 67 He said, 'My sons, do not enter by one gate. Enter by various gates. I can avail you nothing against God. Judgement belongs to God alone. I put my trust in Him. Let all the trusting put their trust in Him.'
> 68 And when they entered as their father had told them, it would have availed them nothing against God. It was simply a need in Jacob's soul

> which he satisfied. He had some knowledge because of what We had taught him; but most of the people do not know.

There is a poignancy that inheres in the transition into 12:58 where ignorance and knowledge are reconfigured – as recognition and *méconnaissance*. Joseph has been 'given a place in the land', providential strings of influence constantly pulling, when his brothers appear before him. He recognises them but they remain utterly ignorant of his identity: 12:58 *wa-jāʾa ikhwatu yūsufa fa-dakhalū ʿalay-hi fa-ʿarafa-hum wa-hum la-hu munkirūn*. The dramatic syncopation of the narrative is marked here: the seven years of famine having been passed over tacitly in the close succession of verses.[69] The verse is succinct and starkly bare of the emotions that the narrative might be steeped in at this point; Genesis gives fuller account of feelings and motives (Genesis 42:6–9):

> 6 And Joseph was the governor over the land, and he it was that sold to all the people of the land: and Joseph's brethren came, and bowed down themselves before him with their faces to the earth.
> 7 And Joseph saw his brethren, and he knew them, but made himself strange unto them, and spake roughly unto them; and he said unto them, Whence come ye? And they said, From the land of Canaan to buy food.
> 8 And Joseph knew his brethren, but they knew not him.
> 9 And Joseph remembered the dreams which he dreamed of them . . .

As they bow down before him, the biblical Joseph recognises his initial dream. This cognitive nexus is significantly forestalled in the Qurʾan, allowing other events – a complementary pattern of lives – to mediate and act as conduit for the final epiphany and Joseph's transfiguration. (The two versions of the story are also assembled and structured according to their discrete theologies and histories; Genesis cannot place so much literary and hence doctrinal emphasis on the final recognition scene, although recognition is certainly an enhanced and developed element of the narrative, for subsequent events are too important in delineating the later history of the tribes of Israel.)[70]

In 12:58, knowledge modulates also in another way: the cognitive root is changed from *ʿilm* to *maʿrifah*. Arabic does not have the equivalent of the Latin iterative prefix *re-*; *re*cognition cannot be rendered in precise equivalence to the English term. Nor can the complexity of anagnorisis ever be rendered in a single word. Arabic does, however, have an extremely nuanced semantics that is contextual: *ᶜarafa* is precisely the cognitive verb of preference for 'recognition'. Indeed, there may be cause for arguing that there is always *re*cognition in *maᶜrifah*, such that an iterative prefix (if such a thing could be crafted for the root) would be needlessly pleonastic.

However succint the verse, there are resonances of which we should be apprised; it is the evocation of a familiar doublet (*al-amr bi-l-maᶜrūf wa-l-nahy ᶜani l-munkar*) that will convey these implications. As a cornerstone of Islamic theology and a determining feature of Islamic political thought, *al-amr bi-l-maᶜrūf* emerged as one of the chief theoretical, and as far as possible practical, duties of the caliph. Right conduct and praxis is equated in Islam with known conduct, with that which is familiar and recognisable; nefarious practice is that which is unfamiliar, unknown, unrecognisable. The implications of this are important in a culture in which *sunnah* provides the paragon for correct behaviour. The stranger – if someone is allowed to be a stranger, which rarely happens except in texts that illustrate ignominious, avaricious behaviour[71] – is regarded with suspicion, as an outcast; there is something self-fulfilling here, for if one reacts to an 'other' as a stranger, refusing hospitality, one is committing a breach of a strict code of comportment. Rather one should receive the stranger precisely as if one knows him, acknowledge him by providing shelter, food and water, and ultimately recognise him, thus proferring *maᶜrūf* ('succour', 'generosity') according to the practice of *ᶜurf* (whose root – *ᶜ-r-f* – is of course shared with that of *maᶜrifah*).

When Joseph recognises his brothers (*ᶜarafa-hum*), there is affirmation that he occupies the moral and ethical high ground. By the same token, that his siblings should fail to recognise him casts them in a negative light and associates them with *munkar*, either reminding one of the egregious moral wrongdoing that lies in their past or suggesting that they have not yet been purged of their crime. *Wa-hum la-hu munkirūn* evokes a detail made manifest in the fuller details of the biblical *récit* (cf. Genesis 42:41 'And they said one to another, We are verily guilty concerning our brother, in that we saw the anguish of his soul, when he besought us, and we would not hear; therefore is this distress come upon us').[72] As when Joseph is cast into the pit in the Bible, so in the Qur᾽an we are not privy to the words he must have addressed to his brothers – we cannot imagine that he suffered their harsh treatment without at least some verbal struggle,[73] some appeal for clemency in whatever form. And they must equally have denied him, the Arabic for which would be rendered most succinctly as *ankarū-hu*. This moral failing tarnishes them still in their failure to recognise their brother. The Qur᾿an's *wa-hum la-hu munkirūn* – whose temporal signification is, like its semantics, open-ended, having the possibility of referring to all of the present, past and future – fulfils the function of Genesis' emotionally fraught 'and we would not hear' (42:41).

So, recognition and *méconnaissance*[74] are part of the moral epistemology of the narrative at its most salient structural moments. This proposition invites us to posit a meaningful connection beyond the plain unfolding of narrative sequence between 12:59 (*fa-ᶜarafa-hum*) and 12:60 (*wa-lammā jahhaza-hum bi-jahāzi-him*). That is to say, '[his] provid[-ing] them with their provision' is a gesture of kindness consistent with a paragon of moral-ethical comportment, the qualities implicit in the root *ᶜarafa-hum*, those very qualities which they denied him ingnominiously in their past.[75]

Joseph's initial recognition of his brothers is the first part of a compound and evolving anagnorisis in five parts: in the second part he discloses his identity, in seclusion, to his full brother Benjamin (12:69), forewarning him not to despair during the trials that will torment and test their brothers; the third part consists in Joseph revealing himself to all his brothers (12:89–90); the fourth part sees Jacob's recognition of Joseph's scent (12:96) and the highly charged recovery of his sight; the fifth and resolving recognition falls appropriately enough to Joseph when he finally realises fully the meaning of his dream (12:100–1). In the contrivance of this ending we should note the exquisite realisation of narrative deferment.[76] To this end the Qur᾿anic narrative parts company with Genesis, as already signalled: the brothers return three times to their father, not merely twice; in Genesis Joseph reveals himself at the most emotionally fraught point of the narrative, after framing and detaining Benjamin, and immediately after Judah's famously moving speech, the speech which enunciates resoundingly the moral reformation of the brothers. The Bible is concerned with vindicating the behaviour of the brothers, the forefathers of the tribes of Israel;[77] the Qur᾿an is concerned with the aesthetics of the story, for, as we have argued, the theology can emerge from these very qualities.

Within the orbit of the first recognition – the brothers' initial appearance in Egypt (12:58–68) – the narrative explores two types of knowledge: when Joseph secretes his brothers' wares back into their baggage he explains that it is so they might recognise it and hence return to him (*laᶜalla-hum yaᶜrifūna-hā idhā nqalabū ilā ahli-him laᶜalla-hum yarjiᶜūn*). These are not innocent words; they contain the second and only other instance of the root *ᶜarafa* in the text. Recognition here is a synecdoche for the fuller disclosures yet to come; it is recognition then that is made to exert some invisible influence over the brothers. This recognition that something has come back to them will initiate a process of cognitive growth.[78]

Jacob's warning to his sons not to re-enter Egypt from one gate lest they all perish together, is accompanied by a catechism that reiterates the essential theology of the narrative, some elements of which were explored in identical terms in Joseph's prison sermon.[79] Verses 12:67–9 trace the most conspicuous outline of the theology of determinism-omniscience, repeating the phrase *ini l-ḥukmu illā li-llāh*.[80] The theology of this is explained in verse 68: 'And when they entered as their father had told them, it would have availed them nothing against God. It was simply a need in Jacob's soul which he satisfied. He had some knowledge because of what We had taught him; but most of the people do not know.' Conclusions are not to be drawn unequivocally from this passage, but the text is deliberately suggestive of Islamic theology: human knowledge is relative and controlled by God, who controls events to the same degree; withal, man is reponsible for his actions and falls prey to fear of that which lies outside his circumscribed sphere of perception. In the end only a blind – unseeing, unknowing – faith in divine providence can avail him at all. The knowledge of which Jacob partakes (12:68 *inna-hu la-dhū ᶜilmin li-mā ᶜallamnā-hu*) is a realisation precisely of this theological crux,[81] one that is essential to providential design, and one that is essential to the genre of romance. It was partial knowledge that allowed Jacob to fear the wolf, ignorance then gnawing away at hesitant certainties.

The Second Recognition: Aside with Benjamin

> 12:69 When they went to see Joseph, he placed his brother at his side and said, 'I am your brother. So do not be distressed at what they have done.

70 When he provided them with their provisions, he put a drinking-cup into his brother's saddle-bag. Then a crier cried, 'O caravan, you are thieves.'
71 They said as they came towards them, 'What are you missing?'
72 They replied, 'We are missing the king's goblet. Whoever brings it will get a camel-load. I am its guarantor.'
73 They said, 'By God, you know that we have not come to do mischief in the land and that we are not thieves.'
74 They replied, 'What shall be recompense for it, if you are liars.'
75 They said, 'The recompense for it? The person in whose saddle-bag it is found – the recompense for it will be [with him]. Thus we pay back those who do evil.'
76 Then he began with their bags, before his brother's bag. Thus We contrived for Joseph's sake. He was not one to take his brother under the king's law had God not wished it. We raise by degrees those whom we wish; and above every man of knowledge is One who knows.
77 They said, 'If he steals, there was a brother of his who stole before him.' But Joseph kept the secret to himself and did not reveal it to them.
78 They said, 'O mighty one. He has a father who is a very old man indeed. Take one of us in his place. We think that you are one of those who do good.'
79 He replied, 'God forbid that we should seize anyone other than the one with whom we found our goods. If we did that, we should be doing wrong.'
80 When they despaired of him, they conferred together in private. The eldest of them said, 'Do you not know that your father took from you an undertaking in God's name? And before that you were remiss in the matter of Joseph. I shall not leave [this] land until my father gives me permission or God gives judgement in my favour. He is the best of judges.
81 Return to your father and say, "O father, your son stole. We testify only to that which we know. We could not guard against the Invisible.
82 Ask the settlement in which we were and the caravan in which we came. We are really speaking the truth".'
83 He said, 'No! Your souls have enticed you to [do] something [wrong]. [May I have] fair patience. It may be that God will bring them all to me. He is the Knowing, the Wise.'

> 84 He turned away from them and said, 'Oh, how I grieve for Joseph.' His eyes turned white from grief and he was choking with emotion.
> 85 They said, 'By God, you will never cease remembering Joseph until you are worn out or one of those who perish.'
> 86 He said, 'I complain of my anguish and sorrow only to God. I have some knowledge from God that you do not have.
> 87 My sons, go and search out news of Joseph and his brother. Do not despair of God's comfort. Only unbelievers despair of God's comfort.'
> 88 When they went to see [Joseph], they said, 'O mighty one, affliction has touched us and our folk. We bring goods of little value. But give us full measure and be charitable to us. God recompenses those who are charitable.'

When Joseph identifies himself to Benjamin (12:69) unctuous sentiment is banished from the text (as it is also at 12:58 and subsequently at 12:89–90): 'When they went to see Joseph, he placed his brother by his side and said, "I am your brother. So do not be distressed at what they have done."'[82] It is the interference of subjects in Joseph's forewarning that is significant: Joseph relieves Benjamin of past distress but allows him more importantly to stand steadfast in the trial – the charade of accusations against him – that will ensue. Only the brothers will remain ignorant of the cruel game afoot.

But events are begging them to recognise the repetitions that lie in the details of the narrative; hence the similarities of transition between 58–59 and 69–70 give pause for thought. This is a metatextual aspect of the verses but what we detect on this anagnostic level may be read back into the storyline: the brothers are being beckoned to recognise situations that repeat themselves uncannily. We, the readers, are in a position to perceive the parallelisms between disclosure (12:58 and 12:69) and the ensuing phrase *fa-lammā jahhaza-hum bi-jahāzi-him* (12:59 and 12:70), respectively; the brothers, who are caught up in the events themselves, not privy to garlanded words on a page, must recognise rather that the secretion of sundry items into their baggage is a pattern of manipulation; one may argue that both the audience, on one hand, and players in the surah, on the other, are subjected to a similar cognitive process of realisation. They (or we) must realise and be reminded that Joseph was once placed secretly as so much fodder among the bundles of a caravan of merchants.

Before Joseph reveals himself to his brothers (12:89–90) they are twice accused of lying. Both accusations come in the aftermath of the second recognition – Benjamin of Joseph. This section of the surah limns minutiae of dramatic delay and further explores the surah's now familiar theology; and knowledge is pointed up in mottled shades. When the brothers are accused collectively of theft (12:70 *inna-kum la-sāriqūn*), they answer (12:73) 'By God, you know that we have not come to do mischief in the land and that we are not thieves.'[83] This is comparable with Genesis 44:16 'And Judah said, What shall we say unto my lord? what shall we speak? or how shall we clear ourselves? God hath found out the iniquity of thy servants: behold, we are my lord's servants, both we, and he also with whom the cup is found.' However, the distinction between the Qurʾan and Genesis lies principally in the emotive and moving speech of Judah, one of the most memorable and rhetorically laden pleas in literature. It is the force of this speech, with its sincere admission of guilt, that moves Joseph to unveil himself in the Bible, *before* forcing a further return to his father Jacob with news of Benjamin's detainment (12:81); it is the proximity of Judah's speech to the resolving recognition of Joseph (44:16 – 45:1) that may be seen to exert an influence on Judah's coming clean: 'God hath found out the iniquity of thy servants' – or vice versa. Anagnorisis is part of the coda that leads organically and thematically into disclosure. In the Qurʾan disclosure is held at one further remove, giving the brothers the confidence of their claim (12:73 'you know . . . that we are not thieves!').[84] They still have to plead their innocence to their father in a scene fraught with the ironies of this version of the romance, a scene that is essential to the Qurʾan's particular structure.

12:76 contains the irony of controlled and choreographed deferment, in a detail of the Qurʾanic narrative that is strikingly similar to Genesis. Compare Genesis 44:12 'And he searched, and began at the eldest, and left at the youngest: and the cup was found in Benjamin's sack' with the Qurʾanic 'Then he began with their bags before his brother's bag' (*fa-badaʾa bi-awʿiyati-him qabla wiʿāʾi akhī-hi*). Disclosure – faked or real – is retarded; this small detail, part of the narrative suspense in general, dovetails with the more significant fact that the Qurʾan delays the final recognition and the ultimate resolution of the narrative (12:100) until after a third return to Canaan.

We have already intimated at an epistemological dichotomy at the two points that mark the boundaries of an intervening spectrum: (1) knowledge that impinges on the immediacy of events, and (2) knowledge that is part of and simultaneously articulates a theology that emanates from divine omniscience. The contrast between these two modes of cognisance – the extent to which epistemology imbues and pervades the text, turning shades with the merest glint of detail – is subtly conveyed in the movement from 12:76 to 12:77.

12:76, in which the discovery of the 'stolen cup' features, contains a deterministic gloss: 'He [Joseph] was not one to take his brother under the king's law had God not wished it. We raise by degrees those whom we wish; and above every man of knowledge is One who knows.'[85] By degrees of what? By degrees of worldly power and influence – Joseph wielding power over Egypt and over his brothers, subordinate only to Pharaoh himself? Or by degrees of knowledge?[86] The answer seems to be both, for *darajātin* is influenced in the meaning we ascribe to it by what comes immediately before (an action: *mā kāna li-yaʾkhudha . . . illā an yashāʾa llāhu*) and after (knowledge: *wa-fawqa dhī ʿilmin ʿalīm*). Nowhere is the theology of dynamic interplay between knowledge and action more evident than here.[87]

12:77 is steeped at first in sordid detail: are the brothers lying when they claim, referring to Benjamin, 'If he steals, there was a brother of his who stole'?[88] The *mufassirūn* explain this with anecdotes that take us back to the distant past of Joseph's childhood: he once appeared to have wilfully stolen a belt having been framed by his aunt who could not bear to part with him;[89] there are echoes here of Joseph and Zulaykha, and echoes of the law determining that Benjamin now belongs to the victim of the crime with which he has been framed. One view of the brothers' statement is then that Joseph did once steal; he acknowledges the wrongdoing but only inwardly, 'keep[-ing] the secret to himself' (*fa-asarra-hā yūsufu fī nafsi-hi . . .*). The antecedent noun for the pronoun in *asarra-hā* is not clear.[90] (What is clear is that the agent/subject of the verb is Joseph – victim and object of the only other instance of this verb in the narrative when in 12:19 he was hidden among the goods of the Midianites.)

It may also be that the brethren have consciously lied in their claim that 'there was a brother of his who stole before'; Joseph then angrily suppresses his knowledge of their persisting perjury.[91] There is yet a third possibility, one that is conditional on the syntax of their claim: '*If* he steals, there was a brother who stole before him . . .' Exgetes have argued along these lines in excusing Abraham from the force of one of his four lies.[92] Benjamin did not steal, nor therefore did Joseph; he was an innocent victim of their malice. What Joseph suppresses then is his innocence as well as his identity – innocence in his case being a metonymic aspect of his identity. The brothers, who for their part suffer in ignorance, are bound by the syntax of their statement, just as they are bound by the syntax of the larger narrative, whose predication – the release of meaning – comes only when the plot has run its full course. Joseph knows that they are effectively lying, though less gallingly than they had lied before, but they, on the other hand, do not. In 12:81 the brothers appear to state categorically to Jacob *inna bna-ka saraqa* ('your son stole'); but this too is only a contingent truth: *wa-mā shahidnā illā bi-mā ᶜalimnā* ('but we only bear witness to what we know') – a palindrome, for the logic of what they claim is equally *wa-mā ᶜalimnā illā bi-mā shahidnā* ('we only know what we bear witness to').

12:77 then is polyvalent and ambiguous; the point of the verse may simply be to sustain the palindromic themes of suppression and disclosure, etching further in the audience's mind the disparities of knowledge and the power that Joseph wields, both in general and immanently, as a result of their epistemological mismatch. The residual tension of this verse will be released only in subsequent revelation(s).

There is a further development we should enucleate in 12:77. When Joseph suppresses knowledge of his brothers' lie, he offers this admonition, 'You are in an evil plight, God is well aware of what you are describing.' Formulaically similar words were uttered by Jacob when the brothers lied more heinously before (12:18 *wa-llāhu l-mustaᶜānu ᶜalā mā taṣifūn*, the assonance of which is resolved in the following verse, *wa-llāhu ᶜalīmun bi-mā taᶜmalūn*). But there is a distinction between the two claims: then Jacob ascribed to God knowledge he could not himself have; now Joseph, by contrast, ascribes to God knowledge that he shares but dissembles. His collusion here marks a point in the echelons of knowledge we have described intermittently: Joseph is loftier even than Jacob; he has suffered more and risen higher – it is he who interprets dreams.

We have already intimated some of the ironies of 12:78. The verse marks a transition; no longer will the brothers' actions or thoughts be wretched. When they acknowledge Jacob's love of Benjamin ('He has a father who is a very old man indeed'), they come to terms with the jealous motives of their past[93] and, as a sign of their contrition, they glimpse the special qualities of the man whom they are importuning (we have already made the case above for the polysemous implications of *innā narā-ka mina l-muḥsinīn*).[94] The text will come full circle only when the well-calibrated anagnorisis of identity is hewn to the qualities they now perceive – to this incipient recognition.[95]

This deficiency of their knowledge will persist in another scene, one of the most carefully crafted in the entire narrative (12:81–7). The brothers return to Jacob in Canaan without Benjamin, explaining his absence by the fact that he apparently committed a theft. To their impotence they add the apologetic gloss: *wa-mā kunnā li-l-ghaybi ḥāfiẓīn* ('We could not guard against the Unseen World') – we could not foretell what would happen to Benjamin when we pleaded with you to send him down to Egypt with us. Their blindness here contrasts with Joseph's now tested oneiromantic gift. The phrase comments generally and vaguely on the human condition and in this respect, therefore, on certain aspects of the entire narrative. But its resonances are more precise, for the two key words (*ghayb* and *ḥāfiẓīn*) are used independently at different points in the surah according to their broader semantics: (1) *ghayb* has the overt physical meaning of 'absence' (Joseph did not betray Potiphar in the latter's absence), in addition to the more numinous sense it has here and later; (2) *ḥāfiẓīn,* too, has both a straightforwardly corporeal (cf. 12:12) as well as a mantic dimension. The narrative of this surah, we are reminded, has physical and metaphysical dimensions in equal measure. This nexus between physical and spiritual domains is even more clearly an aspect of the recurring motif of Joseph's shirt: human life, though inclined toward spirituality by degrees, is mediated through the mundane details of the tangible world. What the brothers tell their father here is a shade of the truth; yet he responds to their claim accusing them of malevolent connivance, as he did in 12:18 (*bal sawwalat la-kum anfusu-kum amran fa-ṣabrun jamīlun*). Their former complaint, that he would not believe them even if they spoke truthfully, has now been poignantly realised. There is a recognition here, and this may be the point of paradox in the Qur᾿anic version: Jacob perceives the plight and therefore presence of his long lost son; he recognises that in the iterative and patterned hue of events there lies a sign.[96] The brothers have not made the connection (between, for example, their utterance of the word *ḥāfiẓīn* now (12:81) and before (12:12 and 12:63)) and cannot grasp the significance of why Jacob responds to them now as he did before when Joseph first disappeared. It is Joseph – Benjamin's double – who is evoked in the father's mind, not just because the events are similar but because their likeness simultaneously veils and unveils a meaning;[97] providence manipulates events but allows Jacob to be beforehand with others in interpreting them.

Although the brothers have not lied this time, they are misguided – Benjamin did not steal – and though, Jacob is not yet comforted, he is now more certain that he is right: his son is still alive. Jacob is only ever blinded by sentiment not ignorance,[98] though of course uncontrolled sentiment is an ignorance of sorts, a loss of *ḥilm*. The paradox that operates here is that knowledge exacerbates his grief, requiring the great measure of patience he calls upon for the second time.

Jacob has sensed the survival of Joseph[99] and instructs his sons in 12:87 to search for him and his brother (*taḥassasū min yūsufa wa-akhī-hi*). One notes first of all that the plights of Benjamin and Joseph have been bracketed together; more significant even than this is the force of the verbal imperative, *taḥassasū*, that is, 'seek out with the senses' – it is the physical senses (the *ḥawāss*) that are conjured in this phrase, not any mantic faculty.[100] In delegating this task to his sons, and in the particular formulation of his instructions, lies yet another conjunction of the material and spiritual realms. The dynamic of this exchange (Jacob/intuition → the sons/bodily search) will be reversed when they return to their father for the last time with Joseph's tunic. Before this, a crucial point in the narrative supervenes: the disclosure of Joseph's identity (12:89–90).

Joseph Reveals Himself to his Brothers

> 12:89 He said, 'Do you remember what you did to Joseph and his brother when you acted with ignorance?'
> 90 They said, 'Are you really Joseph?' He replied, 'I am Joseph, and this is my brother. God has been gracious to us. If one is god-fearing and patient, God does not let the wage of those who do good go to waste.'

> 91 They said, 'By God, God has preferred you over us. In truth we were sinners.'
> 92 He said, 'To-day there will be no reproach against you. God will forgive you. He is the most merciful of the merciful.'

As in 12:58, where Joseph first recognises his brothers, verse 12:89 is astonishingly succinct – it is half the length of surrounding ayahs. From the perspective of anagnorisis it is obviously a crux in the narrative; it is further one of the most semantically laden verses in the surah[101] and one of the most brilliant examples of Qur᾿anic stylistic concision.[102] This wants analysis in order to appreciate the understated emotions of the scene, for the Qur᾿an has apparently excised the sentiments painted in detail in Genesis;[103] in the latter it is emotions that burst forth when Joseph finally divulges himself – he can no longer, literally and figuratively, contain himself.[104]

The Arabic of 12:89 is *qāla hal ᶜalimtum mā faᶜaltum bi-yūsufa wa-akhī-hi idh antum jāhilūn*. Arberry translates this as, 'He [J.] said, "Are you aware of what you did with Joseph, when you were ignorant?"' Alan Jones prefers, 'Do you remember what you did with Yūsuf and his brother when you acted with ignorance?' *ᶜAlimtum* permits, then, of various hues; and with 'awareness' and 'remembrance'[105] they are not yet exhausted. To arrive at the full resonances of the verb in this particular context we will work backward from its antonym. '*Idh antum jāhilūn*/when you were ignorant/when you acted with ignorance': it is not the varieties of temporal resonance here that need to be glossed further but the very nature of ignorance.

So, the force of Joseph's rhetorical question – which is his way of articulating recognition of his brothers – is: are you now morally purged, that is, morally and objectively capable of reflecting on what it was that you did to Joseph? It is a question about moral transformation[106] involving both memory and agnition, for it requires them, if they have not already done so, to recall, understand and only then repent[107] of what they did in the past. Recognition comes from meditating not in the first place on physical identity[108] but on the very nature of the deed – the crime – committed by the brothers.[109]

Our reading of 12:89 leans heavily on the doublet *ᶜilm/jahl*. Each word in this lexical antonymy influences the precise meaning of the other, according to context; that is, the words are not independent of each other and this mirrors the varying lexicon of recognition in the surah. We have seen in 12:58 that the use of *ᶜarafa* both influences and is influenced by its antonym, *ankara*.[110]

To the leading question that is posed in 12:89 the brothers themselves answer with a question: are you really Joseph (*a-inna-ka la-anta yūsuf*)? And the initial response to this is ever so terse: 'I am Joseph and this is my brother' – no welling of tears, no obvious sentiment. Both parties to the reunion simply acknowledge each other and then give voice, in marginally greater detail, to aspects of the theology of the story, annexing to these the gesture of forgiveness that will draw a sponge across the sins that have been committed.

It is the very skeletal aspect of the scene,[111] despite its crucial importance, that anticipates the pending fulfilment of the narrative, showing that the reunion of the brethren is not an end in itself but part of the process of a distended anagnorisis that will resolve itself in the revelation of 12:100–1. No reproach now attaches to the brothers (*lā tathrība ᶜalay-kumu l-yawm*),[112] though their knowledge and the realisation of the nature of their crime, is still contingent on unfolding events.

> 12:93 'Take this shirt of mine and throw it over my father's face, and he will see again. Then bring all your family to me.'
> 94 When the caravan set off, their father said, 'I would say that I perceive the scent of Joseph, but for the fact that you would think me completely wrong.'
> 95 They said, 'By God, you perist in your old error.'
> 96 When the bearer of good tidings came, he threw it over his face and he saw again. He said, 'Did I not tell you that I knew something from God that you did not know?'
> 97 They said, 'Father, ask forgiveness for us for our sins. We were sinners.'
> 98 He said, 'I shall ask my Lord to forgive you. He is Forgiving and Merciful.'
> 99 When they came to see Joseph, he placed his parents by his side and said, 'Enter Egypt in safety, if God wills.'

The brothers are dispatched to Canaan for the last time with the tunic[113] that will restore Jacob's sight[114] – a detail missing from Genesis, which we already know has a different narrative coda.[115] Upon announcing that the living fragrance of Joseph has reached him from an implausible distance, Jacob – whose blindness has been caused by his grief – is accused of being old and dithering by his spiritually myopic entourage (*inna-ka la-fī ḍalāli-ka l-qadīm*);[116] it is a brief moment laden with irony, for his restored sight will be the proof of the uncanny knowledge he has intimated all along (*a-lam aqul la-kum annī aᶜlamu mina llāhi mā lā taᶜlamūn*), and of his special relationship with Joseph. It is the divine grace, the miracle, of Joseph's effect on Jacob that prompts a further confession from them, a deeper realisation of what it was they themselves had been blind to before.[117]

Joseph Recognises his Vision

> 12:100 He placed his parents on the throne, and they [all] fell down before him, prostrating themselves. He said, 'Father, this is the interpretation of my vision long ago. My Lord has made it true. He was good to me when He brought me out of prison and then brought you from the desert, after Satan had caused strife between me and my brothers. My Lord is subtle in what He wills. He is the Knowing and the Wise.
> 101 My Lord, You have bestowed some power on me and taught me something of the interpretation of tales. O creator of the heavens and the earth, you are my protector in this world and the next. Take me as one who has submitted (*musliman*) and join me with the righteous.'

The play of retrospection in recognition is manifest in 12:100–1. It must still exert an influence on his brothers, for they bow down to Joseph enacting a scene that they had originally refused to acknowledge (the Arabic for this would, again, be *ankarū*). In this bodily gesture they recognise their brother more comprehensively and unequivocally than they have before, at the very moment in which he himself discerns the realisation of his dream and his father's vague prophecy. That it is a moment of divine epiphany,[118] is evidenced in the fact that having addressed his father (12:100),[119] he now turns, almost physically moved, to address God in 12:101. The beatific presence of God is felt: for He had not only determined this moment, like every other, but given notice of it so many years before.[120] It is this retrospective aspect that makes it plausible to forge a connection between the narrative itself and the discursive peroration: just as Joseph's status as a prophet is fully apprehended retrospectively, so we read Muḥammad back into the text – Joseph is a figura for Muḥammad offering the promise of recognition and deliverance in troubled times. It is fascinating and of course relevant to note that Joseph played a similar role in Christian literature, as we will see in Chapter 3.

The Peroration: Seeing Joseph in the Life of Muḥammad

Alan Jones notes about the final section that it is (p. 220) 'a passage of argument that arises from the narrative, and one may view the narrative as its preamble.' He adds in a footnote: 'The rest of the *sūra* is addressed to Muḥammad.' In italics below are elements that are about or resume themes and details of the Joseph narrative. In bold are related elements that are associated with Muḥammad, especially in the early to mid Meccan polemical revelations that delineated his role – and that of the Qur'ān – in the restoration of monotheism and its pristine prophetic lineage. If recognition is the all important theme in the story of Joseph then it must be seen to have a rhetorical or asseverative role in the early proselytising mission of Muḥammad.

> 12:102 That is from the tidings of *the Invisible*, with which *We inspire you. You were not with them when they agreed on their plan and were plotting.*
> 103 But **most of the people are not believers**, even if you are eager for that.
> 104 **You do not ask them for any wage for it. It is only a reminder to all beings.**
> 105 **How many a sign is there in the heavens and the earth that they pass by and turn their faces away!**
> 106 And *most of them do not believe in God unless they associate others with Him.*
> 107 **Do they feel secure that a covering of God's punishment will not come upon them and that the Hour will not come upon them suddenly** *when they are unaware.*
> 108 Say, 'This is my way. I call to God *with sure knowledge*, I and whoever follows me. Glory be to God,
> 109 **We have only sent before you men whom We inspired** from the people of the settlements. Have they not travelled in the land and seen how

was the punishment of those who were before them? The abode of the world to come is better for those who are god-fearing. *Do you not understand?*
110 Then, when the messengers despaired and thought that *they were deemed to be lying, Our help came to them,* **and those whom We wished were saved.** Our might cannot be turned away from the people who are sinners.
111 *In their stories there is a lesson for those of understanding.* **It is not a tale that is invented but a confirmation of what [has gone] before it and a setting forth of everything and a guidance and a mercy for people who believe.**

Disclosure, Determinism and Aesthetics: Qushayrī on *kashf* and *ma᾽āl* in Surah 12

Qushayrī's commentary (*Laṭā᾽if al-ishārāt*) is far shorter than Rāzī's expansive *Mafātīḥ al-ghayb* which has informed the annotations to our own commentary above. It is thus easier to characterise. On the whole, it yields an aesthetic sensibility far more than Rāzī's theologically driven and detailed tour de force. As in every other classical *tafsīr*, Qushayrī's method is piecemeal, verse-by-verse analysis and commentary. Yet more perceptibly than others he is given to observing logical and consequential thematic links between parts of the narrative, or to showing how a theme may thread its way through the whole; thus (p. 167): 'When Joseph mentioned his dream to his father, Jacob recognized the truth it contained (*ṣidqu taᶜbīri-hā*); it was for that reason that he was continually mindful of Joseph during his absence, such that after many years he was chided – *ta-llahi tafta᾽u tadhkuru yūsufa*, to which his response was *innī aᶜlamu mina llāhi mā lā taᶜlamūn*, for he was confident that the dream had spoken truthfully'; or (p. 187) 'The beginning of Joseph's tribulations were provoked by a dream that he had and then divulged; [in the same way] the cause of his salvation was a dream that Pharaoh had and which he then divulged; in this way we learn that God does what He wills.' The pattern of events is what betrays significance and the changing hue of events is what we are meant to interpret. We might also note that the observation is truncated, for in the end Joseph's dream is of course auspicious. A similar pattern of contrastive but meaningful developments is perceived in the fact that Jacob's cognisance of Joseph's plight is obscured when he is still relatively close at hand (still in Canaan), whereas he eventually senses his son's fragrance from the improbable, miraculous, distance of eighty parasangs.

But the literary touches of Qushayrī lie also in his sensibility – his sensitivity, for example, to the sentiments of the text, on occasion even forging connection between the Qurʾan and the canon of classical Arabic poetry. Thus his remarks on that sweet breeze (*nasīm al-rīḥ*) that brought his son's fragrance from Egypt (p. 206): '*hādhihi sunnatu l-aḥbābi: musāʾalatu l-diyāri wa-mukhāṭabatu l-aṭlāli wa-fī maʿnā-hu anshadū*' (here he cites two anonymous verses of poetry):

> *Innī la-astahdī l-riyāḥa nasīma-kum/ idhā hiya aqbalat naḥwa-kum bi-hubūbi*
> [I seek your fragrance in the breeze, it guides me when it gusts towards you]
> *Wa-asʾalu-hā ḥamla l-salāmi ilay-kumū/ fa-in hiya yawman balaghat-nī ujībū*
> [I ask it to greet you and if ever she reaches me I'll answer as I should]

Where poetry is quoted in *tafsīr* the impulse is usually philological. Here, in its nuancing of the theme of love, the quotation is clearly the fruit of Sufi sensibility.

Qushayrī also has a keen sense of the deferment of an ending (p. 205):

> *al-balāʾu idhā hajama hajama marratan wa-idhā zāla zāla bi-l-tadrīj: ḥalla bi-yaʿqūba marratan wāḥidatan ḥaythu qālū fa-akala-hu l-dhiʾbu wa-lammā zāla l-balāʾu fa-awwalan wajada rīḥa yūsufa ʿalay-hi l-salāmu thumma qamīṣa yūsufa thumma yawma l-wuṣūli bayna yaday yūsufa thumma ruʾyata yūsufa*
> [Disaster strikes in one go when it strikes but recedes by degrees: it afflicted Jacob in a fell swoop when the brethren lied to him . . . but it receded in three stages; when he found the fragrance of his son, and then his shirt and then saw him upon entering into Egypt.]

One could, with hindsight, expatiate on this observation and apply it further to other points in the narrative; it is this narrative technique in particular which characterises anagnorisis both in general and in the specific instance of Surah 12 where anagnorisis is certainly as much *ethos* as *muthos* and therefore a sustained phenomenon. However restricted the point Qushayrī makes may be, it is valuable in identifying the kind of analysis that can successfully showcase the qualities of the narrative. That is, a given *tafsīr* can suggest a manner of reading parts of the Qurʾan; no reading is ever exhaustive, least of all in Sufi circles where commentary is more idiosyncratic and *sui generis* than in the mainstream Sunni tradition. His commentary on 12:3 – on how the surah constitutes *aḥsan al-qaṣaṣ* – is a further product of such individuality. Qushayrī gives six brief accounts of the surah's self-vaunted beauty: notably, because it is devoid of the sort of prescriptive religious teaching that weighs heavily on the heart (*li-khuluwwi-hi ᶜani l-amri wa-nahy*); and because it is a romance – *fa-fī-hi dhikrun li-l-aḥbāb*. This is quite different to Rāzī, and the majority of commentators, for whom the aesthetic is linked to the surah's didacticism on the nature of providential determinism (cf. above, note 5).

But it is in particular Qushayrī's sense of unfolding events (*maʾāl*) that is of relevance to a study of recognition in so far as recognition is a facet and function of the way a narrative evolves, a function that cannot be understood as a localised phenomenon within a text; that is, it is not restricted structurally, thematically, temporally – even spatially – to a turning point, a brief moment (however loaded with consequence that point might be).

Maʾāl in Hava's Arabic-English dictionary, a dictionary which can give a good idea of the semantic range a word carries, is given as, 'End, result. Return to a place, retreat. Event. Meaning (of a writing).' None of these nuances should be abandoned in our consideration of what Qushayrī actually means by (p. 177) '*al-ᶜibratu lā turā mina l-ḥaqqi fī l-ḥāli wa-inna-mā l-iᶜtibāru bi-mā yaẓharu fī sirri taqdīri-hi fī l-maʾālī*' ('A lesson issuing from truth cannot be perceived on the spur of the moment, rather [proper] consideration of the secrets contained in events decreed come when [events have run their full course]'). 'End', 'return', 'event' and 'meaning' all provide glimpses of how this narrative works didactically: once events have followed their full course they then shed retrospective light on the events of the past; in the process the theological meaning of the narrative is conveyed.[121] Anagnorisis relates metonymically to this process; and a recognition scene in any particular instance is clearly, at the very least, a synecdoche of anagnorisis in the full sense of its implication in Qushayrī's *maʾāl*. The author must also have been influenced in the use of this term by the importance of another form of the root in Surah 12, viz. *taʾwīl* (which occurs eight times). That is, Qushayrī allows us to link *taʾwīl* ('interpretation') with the very process of narrative, a fact which influences also the way we understand *aḥādīth*; the latter cannot simply be taken to mean dreams, if indeed it means this at all, but events which shed meaning retrospectively in the fullness of their allotted time.[122]

Qushayrī's description of determinism is different from Rāzī's; this need hardly surprise us. Thus the Qurʾanic *ka-dhālika li-naṣrifa ʿan-hu l-sūʾa wa-l-faḥshāʾ* is not explained according to a theory of *tarjīḥ* (*pace* Rāzī, *Mafātīḥ*)[123] but as a *kashf*; it is evidently an anagnorisis of sorts (p. 179): '*al-ṣarfu ʿani l-ṭarīqi baʿda ḥuṣūli l-hammi kashfun wa-l-sūʾu l-maṣrūfu ʿan-hu huwa l-ʿazmu ʿalā l-zinā.*' It is this view of the text – which is certainly not incompatible with the view that privileges determinism-cum-providence – that needs to be emphasised more than it ordinarily is in a study of anagnorisis. An aspect of this view is reiterated in Qushayrī's discussion about the etiology of the phrase *al-āna ḥaṣḥaṣa l-ḥaqqu* (p. 183): '*yuqālu lammā ẓulima yūsufu bi-mā nusiba ilay-hi anṭaqa llāhu tilka l-marʾata ḥattā qālat fī ākhiri amri-hā bi-mā kāna fī-hi hatku sitri-hā fa-qālat "al-āna ḥaṣḥaṣa l-ḥaqq".*' Determinism is thus subordinated to *kashf*, or vice versa, for an element of that which is disclosed is the very determinism of the process of disclosure.

Notes

1. Chapter 38 of Genesis, devoted exclusively to the story of Judah and Tamar, is entirely absent from the Qurʾan. How Genesis 38 relates to the surrounding narrative of Joseph purely in terms of the abstract poetics of anagnorisis is in fact relevant to Chapter 3.
2. The arabisation of the story is worthy of remark: a symptom of this in *tafsīr* is the arabisation of every detail, especially those which can be culturally determined, such as names, e.g. Yūsuf; thus Ibn Isḥāq Aḥmad b. Muḥammad Ibrāhīm al-Thaʿlabī's (d. *c.*1035 AD) lives of the prophets/exegesis entitled the *ʿArāʾis al-majālis fī qiṣaṣ al-anbiyāʾ* (Egypt: Maktabat al-jumhūriyyah al-ʿarabiyyah, 1954), p. 108: *al-asafu fī l-lughati al-ḥuznu wa-l-asīfu al-ʿabdu wa-jtamaʿā fī-hi fa-li-dhālika summiya yūsufu* ('*al-asafu* means "sorrow" and *al-asīfu* means "the slave" both of which were conjoined in Joseph, hence his name in Arabic, Yūsuf'). For an English translation, see Thaʿlabī, *Lives of the Prophets*, trans. and annotated by William M. Brinner (Leiden: Brill, 2002).

3. Though this term usually applies to the study of St. Joseph, husband of Mary.
4. Robert Alter, *The Art of Biblical Narrative* (New York: Basic Books, 1981), p. 176.
5. Regarding the phrase *aḥsan al-qaṣaṣ* ('the finest of storytelling/stories') in 12:3, Fakhr al-Dīn al-Rāzī (d. 1209 AD) makes the point both at the beginning and end of his analysis of Surah 12 in *Mafātīḥ al-ghayb* ('The Keys to the Hidden World [of God]') (Beirut, 1980), that the narrative is the 'finest of stories' in so far as it is a sustained exemplum and provides a lesson about providential determinism; however, he offers no aesthetics or poetics outside this statement (cf. p. 228, *ḥusnu hādhihi l-qiṣṣati inna-mā kāna bi-sababi anna-hu yuḥṣalu min-hā l-ᶜibratu wa-maᶜrifatu l-ḥikamati wa-l-qudrati*: 'the beauty of this story lies simply in the fact that an exemplum and knowledge of sound judgement and power can be gleaned from it'). One could argue that a narrative aesthetic determines some of Rāzī's more finely tuned observations, such as the fact that there is effectively a chronological implication in the word order of 12:22, *ātaynā-hu ḥukman wa-ᶜilman* ('We gave him sound judgement and knowledge'), wherein *al-ḥukm* is practical wisdom (*al-ḥikmah al-ᶜamaliyyah*) and *al-ᶜilm* is theoretical wisdom (*al-ḥikmah al-naẓariyyah*). Theoretical knowledge issues from practical, experiential, empirical knowledge: that is, *ᶜilm* issues from and gives retrospective clarity to the unfolding events of a narrative. Abū ᶜAbd Al-Raḥmān Muḥammad b. al-Ḥusayn al-Sulamī (*Ziyādāt ḥaqā'iq al-tafsīr*, ed. Gerhard Böwering (Beirut: Dār al-Mashriq, 1995)) lends some weight to Rāzī's view; for him the *qiṣṣah* has a dual function (p. 62): to entertain the masses (*ᶜawāmm*) and to provide didactic sustenance for the elite (*khawāṣṣ*) – *ishtaghala l-ᶜawāmmu bi-samāᶜi l-qaṣaṣi wa-shtaghala l-khawāṣṣu bi-l-iᶜtibāri fi-hi ka-qawli-hi laqad kāna fi qaṣaṣi-him ᶜibratun li-ūlī l-albābi min-hā l-ᶜibratu wa-l-fikratu wa-li-l-ᶜawāmmi l-unsu bi-qaṣaṣ* ('the general public is preoccupied with listening to the stories, the special class of mystics with reflecting on its didacticism in key with the Qur'anic phrase "in their stories are lessons for those blessed with intelligence": they ponder and think about the narratives whereas the general public enjoys them as stories'). That is, it is the Sufis that are capable of understanding the deeper meaning of the story; whether the lesson they take from it in the end is the same as that gleaned by Rāzī is impossible to say – for Sulamī's commentary, which leans heavily on the teachings of Jaᶜfar al-Ṣādiq, is stenographic in the extreme, covering in total only a couple of printed pages; however, what Sulamī relates on *fa-ṣabrun jamīlun* ('decent patience', 12:18) coalesces with Rāzī's convictions about

providential determinism: (p. 63) *al-ṣabru l-jamīlu l-sukūnu ilā mawāridi l-qaḍāʾi sirran wa-ʿalanan* ('"decent patience" is the act of being tranquil and receptive to what fate deals out, both in secret and openly'). Thaʿlabī's view espoused in *ʿArāʾis al-majālis* for why it was labelled *aḥsan al-qaṣaṣ* somewhat focuses on the ethics of Joseph's comportment toward his brothers: (p. 107) *ṣabru-hu ʿalā adhā-hum . . . wa-karamu-hu fī l-ʿafwi ʿan-hum ḥaythu qāla 'lā tathrība ʿalay-kumu l-yawma yaghfiru llāhu la-kum'* ('His forbearance in enduring their harmful behavior towards him . . . and the nobility of his forgiveness when he told them, after revealing himself to them [Q Yūsuf 12:92]: "No blame attaches to you today"'), etc. Qushayrī (in *Laṭāʾif al-ishārāt*, ed. Ibrāhīm Basyūnī (Cairo: Dār al-Kutub al-ʿArabī, 1968–71)) has further views on the qualities of the narrative, coming closer to a literary sensibility. No commentator identifies the narrative construction of Surah 12 specifically, though elsewhere they were clearly cognisant of this aspect of the text (cf. the postscript to this chapter below entitled *Disclosure, Determinism and Aesthetics: Qushayrī on* kashf *and* maʾāl *in Surah 12*).

6. Below for the English rendering of the meaning of the Qurʾanic verses I am using Alan Jones' clear and elegant translation: *The Qurʾān* (Exeter: Gibb Memorial Trust, 2007).
7. De Prémare has preferred to understand the root *qaṣaṣ* not simply to convey storytelling, rather leaning on the root meaning of 'cutting', he proposes a layer of meaning that connotes 'decisively/conclusively didactic stories' (*Joseph et Muhammad. Le chapitre 12 du Coran* (Aix-en-Provence: Publications de l'Université de Provence, 1989), p. 41); *qaṣaṣ* in this sense shares the basic meaning of *ʿibrah* and evokes the Qurʾanic leitmotif of learning from lives of the past. In the stories of biblical prophets lies instruction for communities of the present. De Prémare is particularly forceful about reading reflections of Muḥammad's circumstances into the bulk of the narrative (Joseph as a figura for Muḥammad) thus explaining some of the ways the narrative parts company with its versions in Genesis and the apocrypha of the Midrash.
8. On this verse Alan Jones (*The Qurʾān*) has written: 'Most western scholars have assumed that the line of the narrative, which omits large sections of the biblical account, presupposes a general knowledge of the story amongst those who first heard it. I have never been able to convince myself of this: the phrase in verse 3, the full meaning of which is, "you were one of those who were not aware of the story before its revelation," is very much against this.' Jones adds: 'The phrase *wa-in kunta min qabli-hi mina l-ghāfilīn* is addressed to Muḥammad. It

is difficult to see how it can indicate anything other than that the story was not well known to Muḥammad and his audience, if indeed it was known at all.'

9. Cf. 12:102ff. (*anbāʾ al-ghayb* . . . etc.) 'That is from the tidings of the Invisible, / with which We Inspire you. / You were not with them / when they agreed on their plan and they were plotting.' Jones adds in a note: 'The rest of the *sūra* is addressed to Muḥammad.'
10. Elements of the story of Moses are recounted in single pericopes that are almost as long, e.g. in Surah 20, but the life of Moses is essentially broken up into numerous surahs from which a single biography would need to be reconstituted – and the Qurʾan does not appear to invite one to do this.
11. Jacob's anxious desire to suppress the dream is explained in the Sufi exegete Abū l-Qāsim al-Qushayrī's (b. 986 AD) *Laṭāʾif al-ishārāt*, p. 168. It is also told with didactic and misogynistic inflection in Thaʿlabī's *ʿArāʾis*, p. 111. That the Qurʾan implies that Joseph did indeed tell his brothers, or that his brothers were made aware of the dream(s), can be gauged from *qiṣaṣ/tafsīr* traditions; thus, for example, in Thaʿlabī, *ʿArāʾis*, p. 110, *fa-qaṣṣa ʿalay-hi ruʾyā-hu fa-balagha ikhwata-hu fa-qālū yā bna rāḥīla laqad raʾayta ʿajaban yūshiku an tudʿā anna-ka mawlā-nā wa-naḥnu ʿabīdu-ka fa-shaqqa ʿalay-him ruʾyā-hu wa-ḥasadū-hu baʿḍa l-ḥasad* ('He told his [father] his dream and it reached the brothers; they said to him, "Son of Rachel, you have seen a marvelous thing, it almost makes a claim that you are our master and we your servants." This irked them and they began to envy him').
12. Cf. also John MacDonald, 'Joseph in the Qurʾān and Muslim Commentary. I. A Comparative Study', *The Muslim World* 46:2 (April 1956), p. 17: 'Jewish tradition (e.g., Josephus: *Antiquities* II. 2–3) has it that Joseph told his father Jacob first by himself and Jacob was understanding. But again (Lekah Gen. Xxxvii 10) later Joseph told his brothers in the presence of Jacob who scolded him.'
13. Cf. W. Lee Humphreys, *Joseph and His Family: A Literary Study* (Columbia: University of South Carolina Press, 1988), p. 109: '[Jacob] could have found in these dreams, however disquieting and upsetting of domestic harmony they might have been, some important hints as to what the future had in store. Certainly this notice [Jacob 'kept the saying'] reinforces for the reader the suspicion that we have more here than simply reflections of a boy spoiled by special attention that feeds grandiose visions. This is more than telling tales on siblings.' Similarly, Claus Westermann (*Joseph: Studies of the Joseph Stories in Genesis* (London: Bloomsbury, 1996), p. 10): 'Even though Jacob is shocked

by Joseph's dream and reproaches him, he remembers it. He heeds his son, for he is well aware of what dreams can mean. *This becomes mute testimony to the further development of the story.*' [emphasis added].

14. Regarding 12:6, on the psychology of dream interpretation, Rāzī (*Mafātīḥ*, p. 87) offers a view that sits well with an analysis of the text focusing on anagnorisis. The deferment of an ending is often a feature of narratives that are resolved in recognition. Rāzī's view that the interpretation of auspicious dreams, as against ominous dreams, is delayed as long as possible for optimum effect is a statement to the same effect from a psychological rather than narratological perspective.
15. This is clear from the corpus of *tafsīr/qiṣaṣ* which draws substantially on Isrāʾīliyyāt material, e.g. Thaʿlabī (*ʿArāʾis*, p. 29) on Jacob rebuking his sons for the way they have divulged the existence of Benjamin to the Egyptian potentate – an account which accords almost exactly with the biblical version.
16. King James version (KJV), Genesis 49:1 And Jacob called unto his sons, and said, Gather yourselves together, that I may tell you that which shall befall you in the last days. 2 Gather yourselves together, and hear, ye sons of Jacob; and hearken unto Israel your father . . . 9 Judah is a lion's whelp: from the prey, my son, thou art gone up: he stooped down, he couched as a lion, and as an old lion; who shall rouse him up? 10 The sceptre shall not depart from Judah, nor a lawgiver from between his feet, until Shiloh come; and unto him shall the gathering of the people be.
17. On 12:13, see Rāzī, *Mafātīḥ*, p. 216: when Jacob, reunited with Joseph in Egypt, was shown the papyrus parchments piled up in Pharaoh's storehouses, he rebuked his son, 'With all these *qarāṭīs* why is it that you never wrote to me [to console me in your absence]?' Joseph answered that he had been forbidden from doing so by Gabriel upon the instructions of God 'Because you uttered the words "I fear the wolf will eat him".' Clearly one traditional view is that Jacob was himself punished for losing faith. Rāzī in fact deals with this quandary at length – the conundrum of the inconsistency between Jacob's knowledge and his fear (cf. *Mafātīḥ*, p. 91 and *passim*).
18. Cf. Robert Alter, *The Art of Biblical Narrative*, pp. 3–12, on the links between this passage and Genesis 38. In fact both Genesis and the Qurʾan treat essentially the instability or untrustworthiness of physical signs.
19. Cf. Rāzī, *Mafātīḥ*, p. 216; cf. also Qushayrī (*Laṭāʾif*, p. 171): *yuqālu l-ʿajabu min qubūli yaʿqūba mā abdā banū-hu la-hu min khaṭfi yūsufa wa-qad tafarrasa*

fī-him qalbu-hu fa-qāla li-yūsufa 'wa-yakīdū la-ka kaydā' wa-lākin idhā jā᾿a l-qaḍā᾿u fa-l-baṣīratu taṣīru masdūdatan ('It is said to be strange that Jacob accepted what the brothers divulged to him regarding Joseph's kidnapping since he could read their hearts and had warned Joseph "They will plot malevolently against you"; however, when fate strikes one's insight is [momentarily] blinded'); the choice of the word *baṣīrah* here is significant suggesting the restoration of Jacob's sight (*baṣīrah*) at 12:96 must be understood figuratively, as here, as well as simply visually.

20. Rāzī, somewhat relatedly, makes a philological note about the 'bottom of the well' into which Joseph was cast (*Mafātīḥ*, p. 95): *al-ghayābatu kullu mā ghayyaba shay᾿an wa-satara-hu fa-ghayābatu l-jubbi ghawru-hu wa-mā ghāba min-hu ᶜan ᶜayni l-nāẓiri wa-aẓlama min asfali-hi* ('The unseen place refers to all that which renders something absent and hidden; so the "unseen part of the pit" refers to its depths and to that part which lay beyond sight, towards its darkest recesses'). It is symbolic, therefore, and drolly ironic that it was here – out of physical sight – that Joseph received revelation from the *ᶜālam al-ghayb* ('the unseen world') while the brothers were kept unaware that he would one day inform them they had been spiritually blind. (Another complementary view of the pit, that functions narratively, does not render it so dark and deep, for Joseph was to be spotted visually by the Midianites.)
21. See Mustansir Mir, 'The Quranic Story of Joseph: Plot, Themes, and Characters', *The Muslim World* 76:1 (1986), pp. 1–15, and esp. Michel Cuypers, 'Structures rhétoriques dans le Coran. Une analyse structurelle de la sourate "Joseph" et de quelques sourates brèves', *Midéo* 22 (1995).
22. Cf. Rāzī, *Mafātīḥ*, p. 101, *al-īmānu fī aṣli l-lughati ᶜibāratun ᶜan taṣdīq*: 'Faith originally has the sense of belief'.
23. Cf. Rāzī, *Mafātīḥ*, p. 97; Qushayrī, *Laṭā᾿if*, p. 172; and Thaᶜlabī, *ᶜArā᾿is*, p. 112, who relates a tradition of the Prophet: *lā tulaqqinū l-nāsa l-kidhba fa-yakdhibū fa-inna banī yaᶜqūba lam yaᶜlamū anna l-dhi᾿ba ya᾿kulu l-insāna ḥattā laqqana-hum abū-hum* ('do not drill people in telling lies, for the sons of Jacob did not know that the wolf might eat a human until their father drilled them in that possibility').
24. Cf. Rāzī, *Mafātīḥ*, p. 102: *qāla l-shaᶜbī qiṣṣatu yūsufa kullu-hā fī qamīṣi-hi* ('al-Shaᶜbī said, "The story of Joseph is all in his shirt"').
25. For an important study on the symbolism of the shirt in the Genesis narrative, see Aldina da Silva, *La Symbolique des Rêves et des Vêtements* (Anjou: Fides, 1995). Cf. also de Prémare, *Joseph*, p. 35.

26. The liturgical importance of the phrase can be gathered from comments by Rāzī (in *Mafātīḥ*, p. 105).
27. The Egyptian dialect version of this, *iṣ-ṣabr gamīl*, renders the phrase in a more grammatically resolved construction.
28. Cf. Rāzī, *Mafātīḥ*, pp. 103–4 and Qushayrī, *Laṭāʾif*, p. 174.
29. See the relevant note in Alter's translation of Genesis.
30. Cf. Rāzī, *Mafātīḥ*, p. 107, for whom it was either the brothers or the Midianite merchants/the *sayyārah*. Genesis 37:28 'Then there passed by Midianite merchantmen; and they drew and lifted up Joseph out of the pit, and sold Joseph to the Ishmeelites for twenty pieces of silver and they brought Joseph into Egypt . . .' 37:36 'And the Midianites sold him into Egypt unto Potiphar, an officer of Pharaoh's, and captain of the guard.'
31. Cf. Jaᶜfar al-Ṣādiq, 'Le Tafsir Mystique attribué à Gaᶜfar Sadiq', ed. Paul Nwyia, *Mélanges de l'Université Saint Joseph* 43 (1968), p. 201. Qushayrī (*Laṭāʾif*, vol. 3, p. 175) relates a unique detail which has the merit both of clarifying a view that it was the brothers who sold Joseph and of attempting to relate this and subsequent parts of the narrative to each other: *yuqālu lammā kharrū la-hu sujjadan ᶜalimū anna dhālika jazāʾu man bāᶜa akhā-hu bi-thamanin bakhsin* ('It is said that when they prostrated themselves to him they recognized that this was punishment for selling their brother for such a paltry sum').
32. Cf. Thaᶜlabī, *ᶜArāʾis*, p. 117 for the signs that appeared to Mālik b. Duᶜr on the descent into Egypt – signs that are strikingly reminiscent of signs associated with Muḥammad's person, allowing him to be recognised by Christian monks before his mission as prophet (see below, Chapter 2). These are important elements in any argument that reads Joseph as a figura for Muḥammad.
33. Cf. Genesis 39:3 'And his master saw that the LORD was with him.' One should consider whether the material referred to by Toufiq Fahd on the role of *firāsah* in the purchase of slaves is at all analogous to the *firāsah* of Potiphar in the acquisition of Joseph; cf. Fahd, *La Divination arabe: études religieuses, sociologiques et folkloriques sur le milieu natif de l'Islam* (Paris: Sindbad, 1987), p. 387.
34. I am persuaded by the force of de Prémare's excellent analysis of *aḥādīth*, *Joseph*, pp. 45–8.
35. These words are reminiscent of what Ḥalīmah's husband says to her when she takes on the charge of wetnursing the Prophet Muḥammad, as recounted in the *Sīrah* of Ibn Hishām.
36. Cf. Thaᶜlabī, *ᶜArāʾis*, p. 118: '*ᶜan ᶜAbdullāhi bni Masᶜūdin qāla afrasu l-nāsi*

thalāthatun: al-ᶜazīzu ḥīna tafarrasa fī yūsufa wa-qāla li-mra᾿ati-hi akrimī mathwā-hu . . .' ('On the authority of Ibn Masᶜūd: the most gifted people in physiognomy were three: Potiphar when he saw the qualities of Joseph, thus telling his wife "Make good his stay among us". . .').

37. Muslim tradition tends to place Surah 28 shortly before the revelation of Surah 12 in the Meccan period; Noldeke places 12 before 28; however, both views are in unison in dating the surahs from the same basic period of revelation and this concord in the end may be what is most significant. Verses 12:21 and 28:9 clearly cast Joseph and Moses in analogous roles – prophets in Egypt.
38. Cf. Qushayrī, *Laṭā᾿if*, p. 178.
39. Cf. MacDonald, 'Joseph in the Qur᾿ān', p. 26: 'a voice called out and warned him to beware. Joseph paid no attention although the warning was given three times, so captivated was he by the woman's beauty and seductive words, until finally Gabriel himself (or according to another version, a vision of Potiphar) appeared. The more generally accepted version is that Jacob appeared as an apparition.' Nehama Leibowitz's commentary provides a Rabbinic/Midrashic account of this episode and its deep moral significance: *Studies in Bereshit (Genesis): in the context of ancient and modern Jewish Bible commentary* (Jerusalem: World Zionist Organization, 1976), p. 415. Louis Ginzberg's narrative rendering of this incident in *The Legends of the Jews*, vol. 2 (Philadelphia: Jewish Publication Society, 2003) conveys the moral and cognitive significance of this apparition (pp. 53–4): 'When he was on the point of complying with the wish of his mistress, the image of his mother Rachel appeared before him, and that of his aunt Leah, and the image of his father Jacob. The last addressed him thus: "In time to come the names of thy brethren will be graven upon the breastplate of the high priest . . . know, he that keepeth company with harlots wasteth his substance." . . . Astonished at his swift change in countenance, Zuleika said, "My friend and true-love, why art thou so affrighted that thou art near to swooning?" Joseph: "I see my father!" Zuleika: "Where is he? Why, there is none in the house." Joseph: "Thou belongeth to a people that is like unto the ass, *it perceiveth nothing. But I belong to those who can see things.*"' Clearly, to see and recognise Jacob is here a gift of moral perception.
40. Cf. Qushayrī (*Laṭā᾿if*, p. 178) who dislikes the anecdotes that tell of a physical apparition; they are too corporeal: '*kāna l-burhānu taᶜrīfan mina l-ḥaqqi iyyā-hu bi-āyatin min āyāti ṣanᶜi-hi qāla taᶜālā "saturī-him āyāti-nā fī l-āfāqi wa-fī anfusi-him ḥattā yatabayyana la-hum anna-hu l-ḥaqqu*' ('the proof came from God in the form of a sign He fashioned and He said, "You will show

them our signs on the horizons and within themselves such that the divine truth will become clear to them"').

41. Cf. MacDonald, 'Joseph in the Qur'ān', p. 26.
42. Cf. Rāzī, *Mafātīḥ*, p. 124. De Prémare (*Joseph*) offers an interesting discussion of this 'cover up', relating it thematically and lexically to Q at-Tahrim 66:1–5.
43. Cf. Genesis for reference to the Hebrew slave; al-Suddī was clearly aware of this detail in the biblical material: see de Prémare, *Joseph*, p. 88 (who cites from al-Ṭabarī's *tafsīr*).
44. On the importance of this passage, see especially the distinct discussions of Cuypers ('Structures rhétoriques') and Hämeen-Anttila ('"We will Tell You the Best of Stories": A Study of Surah XII', *Studia Orientalia* 67 (1991), pp. 7–32).
45. Cf. Rāzī, *Mafātīḥ*, p. 127, who offers a physical and spiritual level of interpretation; he prefers the spiritual, the fact that Joseph is *karīm* (which is not a physical attribute), and he adds pragmatically that angels don't look anything like humans! Sulamī is clear that the women detected some numinous aura in Joseph (*Ziyādāt*, p. 63): *akbarna-hu li-l-haybati llatī shāhadna fī-hi wa-min-hu* ('they expressed wonder on account of the aura they perceived to emanate from him') (cf. also Ja'far al-Ṣādiq, 'Le Tafsir Mystique', p. 201). Henry Fielding dealt with the issue of angelic good-looks in his masterpiece *Tom Jones* (which has other, romance, features in common with the Joseph story), see p. 401 of the Penguin edition, book 9, chapter 2, in which the Man of the Hill's housekeeper says of Jones: '"Nay . . . I could almost conceive you to be some good angel; and to say the truth, you look more like an angel than a man, in my eye." Indeed he was a charming figure, and if a very fine person, and a most comely set of features, adorned with youth, health, strength, freshness, spirit, and good nature, can make a man resemble an angel, he certainly had that resemblance.'
46. This interpretation is not endorsed by all the classical commentators; al-Bayḍāwī (d. 1286 AD) interprets the phrase as referring to a specific quality that became apparent whilst Joseph was in the prison, i.e. that the butler and the baker could see he was a gifted interpreter of other people's dreams. This seems to be just one level of intended meaning. See *Bayḍāwī's Commentary of Surah 12 of the Qur'ān*, trans. A. F. L. Beeston (Oxford: Oxford University Press, 1963), p. 84.
47. They replace the function of the gaoler in Genesis who, like Potiphar, is made to glimpse the virtues of his new charge; cf. 39:21–3:21 'But the LORD was with Joseph, and shewed him mercy, and gave him favour in the sight of the

keeper of the prison. 22 And the keeper of the prison committed to Joseph's hand all the prisoners that were in the prison; and whatsoever they did there, he was the doer of it. 23 The keeper of the prison looked not to any thing that was under his hand; because the LORD was with him, and that which he did, the LORD made it to prosper.'

48. Not all views of the prisoners are this positive; cf. for example, Rāzī, *Mafātīḥ*, p. 134, who relays the tradition that has it that they concocted their dreams cynically in order to test this Hebrew slave. *Either* recognition *or* dramatic irony (and not apparently both, since they are irreconcilable) is privileged in the literary operations that are read back into the narrative in the *tafsīr/qiṣaṣ* tradition.
49. Note also that *mimmā ᶜallama-nī rabbi* ('of what my Lord has taught me') comes closely before *innī taraktu millata qawmin lā yu᾿minūna bi-llāh* ('I have abandoned the creed of a community that does not believe in God'). It is virtually a causal connection that inheres here.
50. See Cuypers, 'Structures rhétoriques', *passim*.
51. For a different view of the function of the sermon (one which divorces it essentially from the underlying theme(s) and agenda of the surah), see Ṭabarī, *Jāmiᶜ al-bayān* (vii, 12/129, quoted in de Prémare, *Joseph*, p. 97): *inna yūsufa kariha an yujība-humā ᶜan ta᾿wīli ru᾿yā-humā li-mā ᶜalima min makrūhi dhālika ᶜalā aḥadi-himā fa-aᶜraḍa ᶜan dhikri-hi wa-akhadha fī ghayri-hi* ('Joseph was loath to answer them on account of the misfortune that would befall one of the two, so he refrained from mentioning this and began talking about something else').
52. Cf. elements of paganism/idol-worship among the peoples of the patriarchs, in particular those indicated in the earlier biography of Jacob. It is not until Moses (and Exodus) that idol-worship is breathed upon with the fire of God's wrath through his chosen prophet.
53. Genesis 41:45: 'And Pharaoh called Joseph's name Zaphnathpaaneah; and he gave him to wife Asenath the daughter of Potipherah priest of On.' J. H. Hertz (in *The Pentatuech and Haftorahs* (London: Soncino Press, 1960), p. 158) has observed the protective function of this acquired name.
54. Cf. the observations of Nahum M. Sarna in *Understanding Genesis* (New York: Jewish Theological Seminary of America, 1966), p. 222: '[Joseph] was . . ., apparently, so thoroughly satisfied with his situation that he preferred not to be reminded of his past. He expresses this most clearly in the names he gives to his sons . . . It is just when this point has been reached that [his] brothers appear once again on the scene.'

55. Genesis 40:14: 'But think on me when it shall be well with thee, and shew kindness, I pray thee, unto me, and make mention of me unto Pharaoh, and bring me out of this house.' Cf. Q 12:42: 'Remember me to your lord' (*udhkur-nī ʿinda rabbi-ka*). The phrase prompts a gloss by Rāzī (*Mafātīḥ*, p. 144) on the ambiguous use of the word *rabb.*
56. In the discussion of the hierarchy of knowledge which permeates the text we note Rāzī's contrary comments (*Mafātīḥ*, p. 146) to the effect that Satan cannot in fact truly make man forget, he can only distract/tempt him (*ilqāʾ al-waswasah*). Gnosis resides in the heart; it transcends Satan and emanates from God.
57. See other examples of the use of *ẓanna* in the Qurʾan: e.g. Q Al-Imran 3:154: *yaẓunnūna bi-llāhi ghayra l-ḥaqqi ẓanna l-jāhiliyyah* ('they conjecture about God in ways that are not true as in the Age of Ignorance').
58. Regarding 12:42 the classical commentators are not all comfortable with this understanding of the nuances of *ẓanna* in this verse. Rāzī (*Mafātīḥ*, p. 143) adduces examples from the Qurʾan of uses of *ẓanna* that exclude conjecture, uncertainty and equivocation. Further, he observes, it is not a given that the referent in *ẓanna*, the subject of the verb, is Joseph; it could also be the prisoner. Rāzī simply does not want the weak epistemology of *ẓanna* to stem from Joseph and thus to foreshadow his misguided request: 'Remember me to your lord.' However, we should note than the equivocation contained in the semantics of the root is sustained in other instances of its usage by Rāzī, for example (*Mafātīḥ*, p. 189), *fa-lammā shāhadū anna-hum akhrajū l-ṣuwāʿa min raḥli-hi ghalaba ʿalā ẓunūni-him anna-hu huwa lladhī akhadha l-ṣuwāʿ* ('when they witnessed [Joseph's men] taking the goblet from [Benjamin's] baggage they conjectured that he must be the one who had stolen it'). We note that in Thaʿlabī's paraphrastic and elaborative reconstruction of the Qurʾanic narrative he replaces *ẓanna* with *ʿalima*, thus: *fa-qāla yūsufu . . . li-lladhī ʿalima anna-hu nājin min-humā*; yet, *ẓanna* is more subtle, for it announces Joseph's mistake in the very moment and act of making his rash request.
59. Cf. this motif in the exordium, after the narrative proper (12:102–11).
60. It has been analysed limpidly by A. Johns; see Johns, 'Quranic Presentation of the Joseph Story', in G. R. Hawting and A.-K. A. Shareef (eds), *Approaches to the Qurʾān* (London: Routledge, 1993).
61. 12:50. Several *mufassirūn* (cf. Rāzī, *Mafātīḥ*, p. 151) relay Muḥammad's great admiration for Joseph's insistence on clearing his name *before* leaving the prison. Two points emerge from this: (1) emphasis is given to the theme of

innocence and the intertwining relationship between innocence and truth/disclosure, and (2) Muḥammad's association with Joseph, a fact which, largely on the basis of the peroration (12:102–11), supports a reading of the surah as a figural representation of Muḥammad.

62. For a related observation on the economy of this section, cf. de Prémare, *Joseph* p. 96.
63. That disclosure is part of a process, drawn out and developed with linear time, emerges from Qushayrī's Sufi observation on the growth and blossoming of Zulaykha's real-cum-mystical love for Joseph (*Laṭā᾿if*, p. 189): *thumma lammā tanāhat fī maḥabbati-hi aqarrat bi-l-dhanbi ᶜalā nafsi-hā fa-qālat 'al-āna ḥaṣḥaṣa l-ḥaqqu' fa-l-tanāhī fī l-ḥubbi yūjibu hatka l-sirri wa-qillata l-mubālāti bi-ẓuhūri l-amri wa-l-sirr* ('when she became excessively enamoured of him she confessed her guilt and said "Now the truth has been revealed", and this is because excessive love obliges one to rend the veil of secrecy oblivious to the [consequences of] divulging concealed matters').
64. Rāzī, *Mafātīḥ*, p. 153.
65. Loc. cit.
66. Cf. Qushayrī, *Laṭā᾿if*, p. 169: *wa-yuqālu min qaḍiyyati l-ijtibā᾿i isbālu-hu l-sitra ᶜalā fiᶜli ikhwati-hi ḥaythu qāla 'wa-qad aḥsana bī wa-akhraja-nī mina l-sijni' wa-lam yadhkur khalāṣa-hu mina l-bi᾿ri* ('it is said about the matter of [Joseph's] being [divinely] chosen [for his virtues] that he kept the deeds of his brothers covered up by saying "He treated me well and extracted me from prison" without mentioning his being saved from the well').
67. Rāzī, *Mafātīḥ*, p. 162.
68. The root *ḥaqq* is used one other time in the surah at 12:100 referring to the dream which God has made come *true*. The nuance is less lofty, though we might note here a link both between God and truth and God's determination of events.
69. In 12:58 the initial descent of the brothers into Egypt is given without prologue – the transition is abrupt. Genesis (42:1–20) we remember explains that it was Jacob who urged his sons to seek grain there, deriding them for their impotence ('Why do you look one upon another?'). This detail surfaces somewhat in *tafsīr*: Rāzī (*Mafātīḥ*, p. 165) relates of Jacob that he had news of the man in Egypt who was distributing grain among the people (cf. also de Prémare, *Joseph*, p. 116). We quite expect Jacob to know more than his sons. Joseph for his part is depicted as lying in wait for his brothers on the basis of the vision he received in 12:15 – since he knew that he would see them again he scrutinised

physically all those who arrived at his court. This detail may be seen to spoil the surprise – the shock – of recognition, but it is interesting to note a similar detail elaborated in Thomas Mann's *Joseph and his Brothers* (cf. Boitani, *The Bible and Its Rewritings*, trans. Anita Weston (Oxford: Oxford University Press, 1999), p. 38). Rāzī proceeds to give three reasons for the brothers' failure to recognise Joseph: (1) his *ḥājib* kept him at a distance and he spoke to them only by means of an intermediary; furthermore, they were in a state of fear, an attitude exacerbated by the majestic aura and surroundings of a foreign potentate; (2) when they threw him into the pit he was a young boy. They now attended his court, his physical-sartorial aspect markedly changed: he wore a beard, clothes of silk, a golden necklace and golden crown. Time had passed and they had simply forgotten [him]; (3) remembrance and gnosis (*ᶜirfān*) come from God alone – there follows a self-fulfilling, circular gloss: *wa-laᶜalla taᶜālā mā* [*sic*] *khalaqa dhālika l-ᶜirfāna wa-l-tadhakkura fī qulūbi-him taḥqīqan li-mā akhbara-hu ᶜan-hu bi-qawli-hi 'la-tunabbiʾanna-hum bi-amri-him hādhā wa-hum lā yashᶜurūn'* ('perhaps God created this knowledge and remembrance in their hearts [to realise the truth of] what [Jacob] had informed [Joseph], to wit: "You will inform them of this deed of theirs while they are unaware"'), i.e. there are discrete levels of human knowledge (all subject to divine decree). Here, in terms of the epistemological scheme of the narrative, there are clearly at the very least two levels of intelligence and recognition: tending toward the personal and particular, and tending toward the divine/the absolute. (Joseph's recognition of his brothers – this very particular and physical agnition – is in part divine epiphany, ever more so as the narrative unfolds in 12:100). Sulamī makes Joseph's recognition depend on his moral purity (*ṣafāʾ*) and the brothers' ignorance/inability to recognise him stem from their coarseness/former ill-treatment of their sibling: (*Ziyādāt*, p. 64) *jahalū-hu* [not *ankarū-hu,* we note] *li-mā taqaddama min jafwati-him* ('They did not know him on account of their earlier harsh treatment of him'). The force of this morality will be relevant again in discussion of 12:89–90.

70. Cf. especially Hugh White (*Narration and Discourse in the Book of Genesis* (Cambridge: Cambridge University Press, 1991)) on the teleological aspect of the narrative. For a fascinating commentary on the implications of Joseph remembering his dreams in the unfolding of subsequent events, see Nehama Leibowitz, *Studies in Bereshit*, pp. 458–9 and Eric Lowenthal, *The Joseph Narrative in Genesis* (New York: Ktav, 1973), p. 67.
71. Cf. al-Jāḥiẓ, *al-Bukhalāʾ*: the story of the Miser from Merv who refused to

recognise a man who had helped him often in the past. For the story in full see Chapter 4, p. 198.

72. Cf. also their refusal to exchange greetings with Joseph in Genesis 37:4 – their refusal to recognise/acknowledge him.
73. Cf. Thaᶜlabī, *ᶜArāᵓis*, p. 113.
74. Qushayrī is fascinating on the brothers' *méconnaissance*; he interprets on two levels: (1) pragmatic: like most other commentators he notes the discrepancy between the way they left Joseph and his later stature in Egypt; (2) he describes their moral ignorance. Thaᶜlabī, in his gloss on *wa-hum la-hu munkirūn* ('while they did not recognize him' which also gives 'while they treated him evilly'), also stresses the deterministic aspect of the event. Braiding these two elements together gives us the doctrinal essence of the surah – which revolves around anagnorisis (and its prior deferment).
75. One of the great aesthetic paradoxes of Qurᵓanic narrative succinctness – in the logical sequence of details that are actually given to the reader – is Joseph's request that they send/bring to him 'a brother of theirs born of their father' (*iᵓtū-nī bi-akhin la-kum min abī-kum*). That he should know this detail of their lives emphasises the nature of his recognition; they, however, do not question his knowledge, nor does the text try and explain it. In Genesis, by contrast, there is a quasi-syllogistic aspect to this disclosure – but Jacob senses that the details of the Egyptian potentate's discovery of Benjamin's existence do not square up with objective reason; he berates his sons for divulging this information unnecessarily; they answer that they were cornered, but the truth is in fact that they imagine retrospectively that they were cornered: fear (has) blinded them, and they remain insouciant of the extent to which they have been/are being manipulated. All this may be read implicitly into the Qurᵓanic narrative lacuna (here and at 12:83). Cf. the detailed reproduction of the episode in Genesis in Thaᶜlabī's *ᶜArāᵓis*, p. 129.
76. Further observations on the technique of literary deferment/dramatic retardation can be found in Qushayrī (*Laṭāᵓif*, p. 205).
77. This view of Genesis 37–50 is especially marked in the analysis of Hugh White (*Narration and Discourse*, p. 260).
78. Robert Alter has written brilliantly on the repetition of this discovery in the Genesis narrative, a fact which, though traditionally attributed to the clumsiness of editorial hands that brought together two distinct narrative recensions ('E' and 'J'), allows of deep psychological observation on the levels of meaning and the layers of recognition which the brothers experience – sequentially – as

a result of this (these) discoveries; see *The Art of Biblical Narrative* ('Composite Artistry'), pp. 137–9.

79. In his narrative reconstruction of midrash, Ginzberg (*Legends*, vol. 2, pp. 82–3) relates that Jacob warned his sons not to enter 'the city' all by a single gate *on the first occasion* of their descent into Egypt; it was this fact that lent support to Joseph's accusation that they were spies – they were not behaving normally: 'If it is true that ye came hither to buy corn, why is it that each one of you entered the city by a separate gate?'
80. This later became a Khārijī slogan.
81. 12:68. In a lengthy discussion of the nature of the knowledge imparted to Jacob, Rāzī sets out a broad relationship between *ᶜilm* ('knowledge') and *ᶜamal* ('action') (nouns/terms which clearly evoke the theology of omniscience-determinism): (*Mafātīḥ*, p. 177) Jacob is *dhū ᶜilmin li-fawāᵓidi mā ᶜallamnā-hu wa-ḥusna āthāri-hi wa-huwa ishāratun ilā kawni-hi ᶜāmilan bi-mā ᶜallama-hu* ('Jacob had knowledge of the benefits we taught him and this signals the fact that he acted according to the knowledge He imparted to him'). God imparts knowledge to determine events; that is, knowledge determines (is beforehand with) actions to the same degree that human empirical knowledge is a retrospective cognisance of actions/events. Recognition in this narrative is in the service of the realisation of this fact.
82. In Genesis Joseph reveals himself to his brothers on a single occasion. Cf. MacDonald ('Joseph in the Qurᵓān', p. 216), 'Does the Qurᵓān reflect the outline of a Jewish tradition . . . that whilst at table Joseph had his magic astrolabe brought to him and asked Benjamin to look on it. Thus Benjamin discovered Joseph and the latter acknowledged the relationship.'
83. Cf. Jaᶜfar al-Ṣādiq, 'Le Tafsir Mystique', p. 201: *aḍmara yūsufu fī amri-hi munādī-hi iyyā-hum bi-l-sirqati mā kāna min-hum fī qiṣṣati-hi maᶜa abī-him inna fiᶜla-kumu lladhī faᶜaltum maᶜa yūsufa yushbihu l-sirāq* ('when Joseph ordered his messenger to accuse them of theft he kept to himself, as he considered the story and [what they did to] his father, the thought that "this deed that you committed with Joseph was like a theft"').
84. Regarding 12:73, traditional accounts of motive and sentiment may be altogether too naive, yet they have the merit of clarity in interpreting events; Rāzī (*Mafātīḥ*, p. 180) relates one view of the brothers' moral transformation already before Joseph reveals himself to them in 12:89: *qāla l-mufassirūna ḥalafū ᶜalā amrayni aḥadu-humā ᶜalā anna-hum mā jāᵓū li-ajli l-fasādi fī l-arḍi li-anna-hu ẓahara min aḥwāli-him imtināᶜi-him mina l-taṣarrufi fī*

amwāli l-nāsi bi-l-kulliyyati lā bi-l-akli wa-lā bi-irsāli l-dawābbi fī mazāriᶜi l-nāsi ḥattā ruwiya anna-hum kānū qad saddū afwāha dawabbi-him li-allā taᶜbatha fī zarᶜin ('The exegetes have said that they swore oaths on two matters: first, that they had not come to wreak havoc in the land, as evidenced by their behavior and that they desisted from robbing people of their possessions and, secondly, that as a token of this they had muzzled their livestock so that they would not graze on the property of others'). Such a picture of their moral purity resists the calculation of de Prémare that the brothers in the Qur᾿an remain morally intransigent after their crime, giving in only to their material needs.

85. On the complication about which law is addressed here, see de Prémare, *Joseph*, p. 126.
86. Cf. Q al-Mujadilah 58:11: *yarfaᶜi llāhu lladhīna āmanū min-kum wa-lladhīna ūtū l-ᶜilma darajātin wa-llāhu bi-mā taᶜmalūna khabīrun* ('God will raise in rank those of you who have believed and have been given knowledge. God is informed of what you do.' Jones, *The Qur᾿ān*, p. 506).
87. On 12:76, that *darajāt* refers principally to levels of knowledge is clear in Rāzī (*Mafātīḥ*, p. 182): *al-murādu min narfaᶜu darajātin man nashā᾿u huwa anna-hu taᶜālā yurī-hi wujūha l-ṣawābi fī bulūghi l-murādi wa-yakhuṣṣu-hu bi-anwāᶜi l-ᶜulūmi . . . hādhihi l-āyatu tadullu ᶜalā anna l-ᶜilma ashrafu l-maqāmāti wa-ᶜalā l-darajāt* ('The meaning of "We raise in echelons those whom we will" is that God shows whom he wills aspects of right guidance in order to achieve the desired goal and he gives special gifts of knowledge to those [thus] concerned . . . This verse shows that knowledge is the most noble of stations and that it exists on various echelons'). The brothers are not by implication cast as ignorant, they simply occupy a lower epistemological rung than Joseph (it is a pious motive that rehabilitates the brothers in this way): (p. 183) *wa-fawqa kulli dhī ᶜilmin ᶜalīmun wa-l-maᶜnā anna ikhwata yūsufa kānū ᶜulamā᾿a fuḍalā᾿a illā anna yūsufa kāna zā᾿idan ᶜalay-him fī l-ᶜilm* ('Above each knowledgeable person is one with greater knowledge meaning that Joseph's brothers were indeed righteous and knowledgeable but that Joseph had greater knowledge than they'). Rāzī is prompted by this verse further to attack Muᶜtazilite epistemology; the latter argued on the basis of this verse that divine knowledge is essential not particular (*taᶜālā ᶜālimun bi-dhāti-hi lā bi-ᶜilmi-hi . . . law kāna ᶜāliman bi-ᶜilmi-hi la-kāna dhā ᶜilmin*). Rāzī's riposte to this theology adduces Qur᾿anic verses where God does seem to be portrayed as having knowledge of particulars, e.g. Q Fuṣṣilat 41:48 *wa-lā*

taḥmilu min unthā wa-lā taḍaʿu illā bi-ʿilmi-hi ('No woman becomes pregnant or gives birth without His knowledge').

88. Regarding 12:77, there is much ambiguity concerning the light in which the brothers are seen; they may have bountiful knowledge according to one view, always mindful that they are prophets (cf. Rāzī, *Mafātīḥ*, p. 89, who explains their original jealousy: *hādhā yadullu ʿalā anna-hu qad kāna la-hum ʿilmun bi-taʿbīri l-ruʾyā* ('this shows that they had foreknowledge of his interpretation of dreams')), but that does not eliminate the possibility of their persistent intemperance toward Joseph, and by extension his brother Benjamin, when the situation becomes thorny. Consider the following anecdote related by Rāzī: (p. 183) 'When the cup was extracted from Benjamin's baggage they lowered their heads and indited, "How amazing it is that Rachel should have given birth to two thieves! How much we are made to suffer because of you!" Benjamin replied to this, "And how much we are made to suffer because of *you*! You took my brother away and lost him in the wilderness, and now you have the nerve to make such an accusation!" They asked how then it was that the cup was found in his baggage, and he replied that the same person placed the cup there as had placed their wares back among their baggage after their first visit.' Benjamin is being indiscreet here; but what the anecdote really shows is that he is capable of reading and grasping the pattern of events.
89. Cf. Rāzī, *Mafātīḥ*, p. 184.
90. Ibid., pp. 184f.
91. Cf. Rāzī, *Mafātīḥ*, p. 191: *khayyala la-kum anfusu-kum anna-hu sariqa wa-mā sariqa* ('You imagined that he had stolen but he did not steal').
92. See the discussion of 12:24 above and the examination of Q al-Anʿām 6:74 in Norman Calder, '*Tafsīr* from Ṭabarī to Ibn Kathīr', in G. R. Hawting and A.-K. A. Shareef (eds), *Approaches to the Qurʾān* (London: Routledge, 1993).
93. When they castigate their father at 12:85 it need not be construed as being through malice of motive. They are simply genuinely concerned that their father will not accept the apparent death of Joseph.
94. Cf. Reuben to Joseph in Thomas Mann's *Joseph and his Brothers*: 'We recognize you in your greatness, but you recognize us not in our good faith' (quoted in Boitani, *The Bible and its Rewritings*, p. 41).
95. A symptom of the fact that recognition is perceived as a facet of rehabilitation (i.e. part of the moral growth and eventual repentance of the brothers) can be gauged from the anecdote often related to colour in the background of this point in the narrative (in Thaʿlabī, *ʿArāʾis*, p. 134; also in Rāzī, *Mafātīḥ*,

p. 188): when Joseph showed intransigence vis-à-vis Benjamin (i.e. when he refused to release him) Jacob's sons grew angry.

96. Rāzī offers four psychologically penetrating reasons to explain why Jacob cried out 'Joseph!' when informed of Benjamin's detainment (*Mafātīḥ*, p. 193): (1) *al-ḥuznu l-jadīdu yuqawwī l-ḥuzna l-qadīm* ('recent sadness compounds an old sadness' – in respect of which he cites an apt fragment of poetry by Mutammim b. Nuwayrah elegising his brother Mālik: *inna l-asā yabᶜathu l-asā*, 'grief revives grief'); (2) Benjamin and Joseph were born of the same mother and resembled each other strikingly, so that with the loss of Benjamin Jacob could no longer console himself by gazing upon his features as he was wont to do; (3) the disaster of Joseph's disappearance was the origin of all subsequent disasters; (4) he knew at least that Benjamin still lived whereas he could not be sure that Joseph was still alive (though he knew for sure that his sons had lied in respect of exactly how he had disappeared). The ambiguities of Jacob's role are apparent here, for there are other perspectives of his function that demand he knew all along that Joseph was alive – that is, he suffered the torment of emotion not ignorance (though we must ignore ourselves the fact that the two overlap in Islamic moral epistemology). The most affecting view of Jacob's ignorance is that, while he knew Joseph still lived, he feared he might have abandoned his religion; this is related in particular in Sufi exegeses.
97. On Benjamin as Joseph's double, see in particular de Prémare, *Joseph*.
98. Cf. Qushayrī, *Laṭā᾽if*, p. 200. Ginzberg (*Legends*, pp. 79–80) provides us with a similar view in his narrative synthesis of midrash: 'The famine: . . . the sons of Jacob were ignorant of what their old home-keeping father knew, that corn could be procured in Egypt. Jacob even suspected that Joseph was in Egypt. His prophetic spirit, which forsook him during his grief for his son, yet manifested itself now and again in dim visions, and he was resolved to send his sons down into Egypt.'
99. The Muslim tradition offers what it is and how it is that Jacob knew more than his sons (*aᶜlamu mina llāhi mā lā taᶜlamūn*); a patchwork of reasons is given in Rāzī: (1) (*Mafātīḥ*, pp. 198ff.) he was visited by the angel of Death and asked, Have you taken the soul of my son? No, came the reply, and he pointed toward Egypt explaining, Seek your son over there; (2) further, he knew that Joseph's vision (*ru᾽yā*) was truthful from the obvious signs of perfection in his son; (3) perhaps God (*laᶜalla-hu taᶜālā*) had informed him by revelation (*awḥā ilay-hi*) that he would unite him with his son, but He had simply not specified when (*mā ᶜayyana l-waqta*); (4) when his sons informed him about

the Egyptian potentate (*sīrat al-malik*) and how perfect he was in word and deed, Jacob hoped that this might be Joseph (i.e. he recognised his son in these descriptions) – for it was unlikely that a person of such quality should emerge among the unbelievers; (5) he knew for sure that Benjamin could not steal and further the potentate had not harmed Benjamin despite the accusation of theft; he conjectured therefore (*ghalaba ᶜalā ẓanni-hi*) that this must be Joseph. The sum of these imaginings can only leave us reeling. Do they spoil or enhance the final effect of recognition? They are at least clear in proffering a view of Jacob quite distinct from his biblical antecedent who was all along verily *mourning* his lost son (in Genesis 42:38 he declares categorically that Benjamin's brother 'is dead').

100. Cf. Rāzī, *Mafātīḥ*, p. 198 and Qushayrī, *Laṭāʾif*, p. 201.

101. Islamic exegesis comments in general more on the drama than the semantics of this recognition scene. Rāzī, for example, provides an account of the letter which the brethren relayed to Joseph from Jacob: it contains a brief history of the patriarchs – their trials and tribulations – and ends with a categorical denial of the possibility that Benjamin could have stolen until: *lammā qaraʾa yūsufu l-kitāba lam yatamālak wa-ᶜīla ṣabru-hu wa-ᶜarrafa-hum anna-hu yūsuf* ('[Joseph] read the letter and could control himself no longer, his patience exhausted he told them he was Joseph'). As in the case of Joseph's private disclosure to Benjamin, the *tafsīr* tradition/*qiṣaṣ* material provides a recognition scene fraught with emotion and rhetoric (Rāzī, *Mafātīḥ*, p. 203). When *tafsīr* satisfies popular hankerings and offers the physical circumstances of the recognition scene there is a tacit acknowledgement that the Qurʾan by contrast itself purveys rather the pregnant but unseen cognitive and moral implications of the event.

102. The dramatic enhancement of *qiṣaṣ* material shows that the succinctness of Qurʾanic narrative (a facet of Qurʾanic style) does not preclude vivid anecdotal accretions in the exegetical tradition: it is in this light that we should appreciate the characterisation of players in the romance; the depictions may often go off on a radical tangent that need not be reconcilable with other, doctrinally determined, views of the material, e.g. that the brothers of Joseph were prophets and therefore not innately evil; for such a view of their character is hard to grasp in the anecdote (Thaᶜlabī, *ᶜArāʾis*, p. 115) which relates their response to their father Jacob's refusal to believe their account of Joseph's demise at the hands of a fictitious wolf: 'Let us return to the pit and extract Joseph; let us then rip (*nufarriqu bayna*) his ribs from his flesh and return with him [to see

our father].' Of course this vivid (and macabre) flourish shows to what degree they are steeped in ignorance (of the fact that Joseph is still alive).

103. Genesis is distinct in this respect; for an excellent analysis of the patterning of Joseph's emotional responses to his brothers' in a tripartite crescendo leading to his final unveiling, see especially Alter, *The Art of Biblical Narrative*, p. 168.

104. Genesis 45:1 Then Joseph could not refrain himself before all them that stood by him; and he cried, Cause every man to go out from me. And there stood no man with him, while Joseph made himself known unto his brethren. 2 And he wept aloud: and the Egyptians and the house of Pharaoh heard. 3 And Joseph said unto his brethren, I am Joseph; doth my father yet live? And his brethren could not answer him; for they were troubled at his presence.

105. The best argument in support of translating *ᶜalimtum* as 'do you remember?' is the earlier question which Judah levels at his brothers at 12:80: *a-lam taᶜlamū anna abā-kum qad akhadha ᶜalay-kum mawthiqan mina llāhi wa-min qablu mā farraṭ-tum fī yūsuf* ('do you not remember how your father extracted a sacred oath from you and how you had acted grievously towards Joseph before that?'). What is interesting here indeed is precisely the semantic overlap which brings the two parts of the question together; Judah subconsciously has made a connection between the events that try the brothers now and their earlier treatment of Joseph (do you remember → do you recognise → do you realise → do you know?). As in Genesis, we are exposed to signs of the brothers' (sense of) guilt; we should stress that the exiguous and skeletal treatment of the subject should not downplay the force of the emotions that are implied in the Qur᾽anic version – a point which de Prémare has somewhat overlooked in suggesting that the brothers experience *no* profound moral regret.

106. Qurṭubī (*Al-Jāmiᶜ li-aḥkām al-Qur᾽ān* (Beirut: Dār al-Kutub al-ᶜArabī, 1980)) accords with this interpretation in essence, as does Qushayrī (*Laṭā᾽if*, p. 203).

107. The relationship between repentance and disclosure is emphasised in certain midrashic commentaries, e.g. Nehama Leibowitz (commenting on Midrash Rabbah, *Studies in Bereshit*, p. 468).

108. In much of the exegetical/*qiṣaṣ* material that gives account of the final recognition of Joseph and his brothers, the agnition is described according to the physical circumstances of the unveiling, that is the mental-cognitive – epiphanic – process is translated into visual effects (Rāzī, *Mafātīḥ*, p. 203). Cf. also Bayḍāwī, *Commentary*, p. 94.

109. Some influence on the scene of disclosure may be exerted by the request of the brothers in the immediately preceding verse, 12:88, in which the roots *awfi*

('give full measure, faithfully') and *taṣaddaq/al-mutaṣaddiqīn* ('to give charity, those who give charity') are conspicuous. At least we are reminded of the ethical use the lexicon of truth was put to in the Qurʾan/Islam.

110. De Prémare (*Joseph*, p. 133) relates material from midrash showing how recognition works in tandem with revelation: 'C'est au moment où Joseph se fait reconnaître par ses frères que les commentateurs juifs placent l'évocation du Jugement de Dieu. Le livre de Genèse, quant à lui, ne parlait pas de Jugement de Dieu, mais seulement de réconciliation entre les frères.'

111. The details that fill in the narrative in Genesis are part of a distinct programme; thus, for example, we learn (45:1) 'and not a man stood with him while Joseph revealed himself to his brothers'. Such a detail stresses that this scene is principally one that reunites the tribes of Israel; the Qurʾanic anagnorisis – with its fuller revelatory import – is for mankind as a whole.

112. In his commentary on 12:92, in which Joseph informs his brothers that they are free from reproach, Rāzī (*Mafātīḥ*, p. 206) relates an interesting detail to the effect that Joseph's identity, having been revealed fully to his brothers (and prophetic heritage/status), will now become clear to the people of Egypt at large, for they have considered him thus far as a slave made good. It is presented as an element in the psychology of his forgiveness of his brothers (cf. Genesis 45:5 which is quite different).

113. For the amorphous boundaries between the physical and spiritual spheres of the sub-lunar world, consider the implications of the following discussion (Rāzī, *Mafātīḥ*, p. 206 *re* the shirt which Joseph instructs his brothers to cast upon his father's face): *inna-mā ʿarafa anna ilqāʾa dhālika l-qamīṣi ʿalā wajhi-hi yūjibu quwwata l-baṣari bi-waḥyin mina llāhi taʿālā wa-law-lā l-waḥyu la-mā ʿarafa dhālika li-anna l-ʿaqla lā yadullu ʿalay-hi wa-yumkinu an yuqāla laʿalla yūsufa ʿalay-hi l-salāmu ʿalima anna abā-hu mā ṣāra aʿmā illā anna-hu min kathrati l-bukāʾi wa-ḍayqi l-qalbi ḍaʿufa baṣaru-hu fa-idhā ulqiya ʿalay-hi qamīṣu-hu fa-lā budda an yanshariḥa ṣadru-hu* ('It was only through divine inspiration that [Joseph] knew that casting the shirt upon [Jacob's] face would restore his power of sight; were it not for this inspiration he could not have known since it goes against reason; one may say that Joseph did not know that his father had gone blind rather [he surmised] that due to the intensity of his [father's] sobbing and heartache his sight would have weakened so if [Joseph's] shirt were cast upon [Jacob's] face he would inevitably feel uplifted'). Jacob's sight is understood only as a physical/visual faculty that has been hampered by excessive sentiment, whereas Joseph has been inspired with numinous

instruction on how he is to cure his father. This ignores the mantic ability that allows Jacob to detect the scent of Joseph from a distance, and the fact that his 'sight' – which is a patent symbol – must surely be understood more broadly. Both sides of the equation (father and son) should be redressed according to an even measure of the physical and numinous spheres in each case. This is a symptom of the narrative as a whole in which the two dimensions evolve in parallel.

114. We have said that there is an inverse relationship in the role given to Joseph's tunic. Jacob refuses to acknowledge Joseph's shirt when it is brought to him steeped in the perjuring blood of a kid; yet from an impossible distance he recognises the fragrance of his son on the shirt that is sent to him from Egypt. What shirt is this then? Is it a shirt newly acquired, an accoutrement of Egyptian origin, the symbolism simply being that it belongs to Joseph? Jacob recognises it for what it represents, miraculously, though he has never actually seen this shirt physically before – for Joseph was stripped of the clothes he wore when he last saw his father. The Muslim tradition solves the problem of recognition in a way that emphasises Joseph's prophetic heritage, and the connection between father and son (cf. Rāzī, *Mafātīḥ*, p. 208): 'when Nimrūd the Tyrant threw Abraham into the fire Gabriel (peace be upon him) came down to him with a shirt from heaven and a carpet; he clothed him in the shirt, set him on the carpet, then sat to speak with him. Abraham subsequently gave it to Isaac, who gave it to Jacob, who gave it to Joseph . . .' Here more than ever the shirt is the physical materialisation of the spirit world.

115. On Jacob's meeting with (recognition of) Joseph in Genesis, RamBan has some fascinating details (cited in Leibowitz, *Studies in Bereshit*, pp. 502–3): '"And Joseph made ready his chariot, and went up to meet Israel his father, to Goshen; and he appeared unto him . . ." I do not understand the implication of the phrase "and he appeared unto him" . . . But the true explanation is, in my opinion, that Israel's eyes were already dim with age or that Joseph came in his chariot with his face covered by the turban as is the custom of Egyptian kings and was not recognised by his father . . . Therefore the text reminds us that as soon as he appeared unto his father and he was able to look at him closely his father recognised him and fell on his neck and wept for him more, in continuance of the constant weeping for him till this day, during all the time that he had not seen him.' Cf. Lowenthal (*The Joseph Narrative*, p. 118): 'Joseph "appeared" to Jacob (RaShi) as God "appeared" to Abraham (cf. 12:7; 17:1; 18:1) to Isaac (cf. 26:2, 24) and to himself (cf. 35:9). He gazes up at his

son, who stands on the chariot. No other human being "appears" in Scriptures . . .'

116. There is an effective contrast that operates in the text at this point, from the accusation *ta-llāhi inna-ka fī ḍalāli-ka l-qadīm* ('by God!, you are still as misguided as you were years ago') to the resumption of Jacob's sight. If the brothers reprimand their father for loving Joseph with the same intensity as before, they have by implication scarcely purged themselves of their jealousy and intemperance, and a certain reading of the text will resist this view; such is the case with Qatādah (Rāzī, *Mafātīḥ*, p. 208). This latter view requires that those who chide Jacob are not the same as the brothers returning from Egypt who now *know* that Joseph lives. Concision and the economy of scene changes simply render the text ambiguous.
117. In the Qur'an Jacob has (imperfect) knowledge of the crime they have committed – the fact is repeated twice, vaguely: *bal sawwalat anfusu-kum amran* ('Your spirits have enticed you to devise some [evil]'). So too in the Torah, according to a message sent by Jacob to Joseph via his brothers posthumously (Genesis 50:15–17 'Thy father did command before he died saying, So shall ye say unto Joseph, Forgive now I pray thee the transgressions of thy brethren and their sin.' But in a text of recognition – constituted by definition of the divulgence of suppressed facts – it is significant to note what some interpreters require to remain hidden, thus obeying part of the broad morality of the tale: cf. Leibowitz, *Studies in Bereshit*, p. 564.
118. We should note that the epiphanic dimension of the Genesis version (and Qur'an following Genesis) is distinct from earlier material (Westermann, *Joseph*, p. 35): 'In the story of the patriarchs there are frequent reports which tell how God revealed himself to one of the patriarchs and gave him a word of instruction or promise. That is different in the story of Joseph, which contains no accounts of God's immediate self-revelation to human beings. This has to do with the Joseph story's origin in a later epoch with a more "enlightened spirituality".'
119. Rāzī relates a fascinating detail that salvages the respect due to parents in Islam (and the effective *ʿiṣmah* ('prophetic infallibility') of Joseph), i.e. it solves the problem of Jacob's prostration to Joseph: Jacob prostrated himself toward Joseph using Joseph simply as a *qiblah*, while he was in fact prostrating himself to God in thanksgiving for Joseph's deliverance (*Mafātīḥ*, p. 212): *jaʿalū-hu ka-l-qiblati thumma sajadū li-llāhi shukran li-niʿmati wujdāni-hi.*
120. When Rāzī (*Mafātīḥ*, p. 217) analyses the phrase *rabbi qad ātayta-nī mina*

l-mulki wa-min taʾwīli l-aḥādīth ('My Lord, You have bestowed some power on me and taught me something of the interpretation of tales'; Jones, *The Qurʾān*, p. 231) he provides an excellent example of how a theological nuance can emerge from piecemeal scrutiny of relatively minor points of grammar: the *min* is the partitive preposition 'some' (*li-l-tabʿīḍ*), thus establishing that both the knowledge and material stature accorded to Joseph by divine mediation was limited effectively to the needs of the narrative's providential design; *min taʾwīl al-aḥādīth* means effectively that Joseph could not interpret all dreams: indeed the first dream, his own, unfolds in subsequent events; it is never proleptically interpreted (by him at least); its very obscurity – paradoxically – becomes the symptom of a future gift (cf. also the partial observation of this point in Qushayrī, *Laṭāʾif*, p. 209, *min ḥarfu l-tabʿīḍi li-anna l-mulka bi-l-kamāli li-llāhi waḥda-hu* – '*min* is the partitive particle since complete and absolute sovereignty belongs to God alone'). A continuing paragraph in Rāzī interprets the phrase differently but adds nuance to our understanding: it provides a bridge between the material sphere of existence (*mulk* = *ʿālam al-ajsām*) and the spiritual sphere (*taʾwīl al-aḥādīth* = *ʿālam al-arwāḥ*); Joseph is a narrative medium contriving a conjunction between the two. Joseph's knowledge like his stature is relative, contingent and finite; the important thing is simply that he is invested with more of it than anyone else.

121. Hence Rāzī's theological view of the aesthetic point of the narrative.

122. It is *maʾāl* that differentiates between things and thus offers meaning (distinction); this is clear in Qushayrī's comments about the butler and the baker (*Laṭāʾif*, p. 186): *ishtarakā fī l-suʾāli wa-shtarakā fī l-ḥukmi wa-fī dukhūli l-sijni wa-lākin tabāyanā fī l-maʾāl: wāḥidun ṣuliba wa-wāḥidun qurriba wa-wuhiba wa-ka-dhā qaḍāyā l-tawḥīdi wa-ikhtiyāri l-ḥaqqi fa-min marfūʿin fawqa l-simāki maṭlaʿu-hu wa-min madfūnin taḥta l-turābi maḍjaʿu-hu*. And the same aesthetic view of the narrative encourages Qushayrī to give specificity of meaning to what ordinarily can remain generally didactic, such as his comment on *wa-lammā balagha ashudda-hu ātaynā-hu ʿilman wa-ḥukman*: *ʿalima anna mā yaʿqibu ttibāʿa l-ladhdhāti min hawājimi l-nadami ashaddu muqāsātan min kulfati l-ṣabri fī ḥāli l-imtināʿi ʿan dawāʿī l-shahwah*. Rāzī saw a temporal/chronological implication in the Qurʾanic phrase but was not so specific in ascribing meaning to it.

123. Cf. note 104 above.

2

Joseph in the Life of Muḥammad: Prophecy in *Tafsīr* (Exegesis), *Sīrah* (Biography) and Hadith (Tradition)

From the epistemology of a narrative paragon, Joseph in the the Qurʾan, we move on in this chapter to consider three case studies, one from each of the following genres: *tafsīr*, *sīrah* and hadith. These are all still emphatically religious textual corpora. The aim is to evince how echoes of the Joseph story inflect each of the three examples – the stories of Zayd ibn Ḥārithah, Salmān al-Fārisī and the slander against ʿĀʾishah, which are centred on prophecy, the early mission of Muḥammad, revelation and the ethics of communal conduct.

Tafsīr: The Seal of the Prophets and Accounts of Zayd ibn Ḥārithah

Early exegetical and biographical sources report that in Mecca the Prophet Muḥammad took one Zayd ibn Ḥārithah as his adopted son. This story is analysed in great detail by David Powers in two recent books.[1] One fascinating element in Powers' interpretation of this multi-part narrative, assembled mostly from the tradition of Qurʾanic exegesis, is the fact that he views it in significant ways as a rewriting of the story of Joseph. In Powers' reading, the story of Joseph is the underlying intertext of the way the story of Zayd is inflected, shaped and relayed in tradition.[2] Certainly, many elements of the two narratives bear comparison. In sum, they are both stories of family separation and recognition. But the family romance does not follow a standard course such as to end in a point of final resolution – of recognition and stable reunion. Indeed, in the story of Zayd ibn Ḥārithah, the main predicate of anagnorisis is not the establishment of kinship – rather a claim of kinship is repudiated – but the establishment of Muḥammad as the *Khātam al-Nabiyyīn* ('the Seal of the Prophets'),[3] a quite different kind of validated relationship. This crucial phrase in revelation follows up and qualifies – even intimates at an abrogation of – what Muḥammad had said before to Zayd years earlier, very humanly, when his father had come to reclaim him: 'I am the man you know full well.' With time, this claim of affection and adoptive kinship was abrogated by what came to be considered a critical issue of Islamic prophetic doctrine. One anagnorisis is effectively superseded by another.

In the story of Zayd there is progression from anagnorisis in the narrative background, or etiological exegesis of a Qurʾanic passage (quite standard hermeneutic elements according to generic norms), to anagnorisis in the Qurʾanic passage itself. That is to say, the postdating etiological narratives give a clearer sense of how the Qurʾanic passage can be read as an essential moment of culminating anagnorisis with what came to have huge doctrinal import.

The Qurʾanic passages should be read in the following sequence.

Part Ia

Qurʾan 33 al-Aḥzāb 37 and 40:

> 37 Consider when you said to the one whom God blessed you with and whom you yourself blessed, 'Go to your wife! Be pious towards God; and do not hide within yourself what God makes apparent. You fear people, yet God is more justly the one you should fear.' So when Zayd had fulfilled his desire of her, We then married her to you [scilicet, Muḥammad] so that Muslims would feel no shame about marrying the wives of their wards once the latter had fulfilled their desires of them. What God decrees is done . . .
> 40 Muḥammad is not the father of any of your men but the Messenger of God and the Seal of the Prophets; and God is omniscient.

Ad locum Q 33:37, al-Qurṭubī (d. 1273 AD) writes about the one blessed (*al-munᶜam ᶜalayhi*):

> The blessed one in this *āyah* is Zayd b. Ḥārithah . . . It was related that his paternal uncle found him one day when he came to Mecca for some business. He asked him, 'What is your name, young man?' He answered,

> 'Zayd.' So the uncle asked, 'Whose son are you?' He said, 'The son of Ḥārithah.' The uncle went on, 'And whose son is he?' Zayd answered, 'The son of Sharāḥīl al-Kalbī.' He went on, 'And what is your mother's name?' He answered, 'Suᶜdā, and I was among my maternal uncles of Ṭayy [when I was captured].' So the old man hugged him close to his chest. He sent word to his brother and his family and they arrived in Mecca. They wanted Zayd to stay with them. So they asked him, 'Whose son are you?' He answered, 'Muḥammad b. ᶜAbdullāh's.' So they went to Muḥammad and said, 'This is our son, so return him to us.' Muḥammad answered, 'I will give him the choice, and if he chooses you then take him by the hand.' Then the Prophet (Ṣ) asked him, 'What kind of companion have I been to you?' Zayd sobbed and asked, 'Why did you ask me this?' The Prophet said, 'I give you the choice: If you want to join their party then join them, but if you want to stay *then I am the man you know full well.*' He answered, 'I would choose no one over you.' His uncle dragged him towards him and said, 'Zayd, you have chosen captivity and servitude over your father and uncle!' He answered, 'Yes, by God – servitude with Muḥammad is more dear to me than to return among you.' [emphasis added]

Part Ib

There is a similar account *ad locum* Q 33:4 which adds emotion and poetry to the plight of Zayd's father.

> It was related about Zayd by Anas ibn Mālik and others that he was captured in Syria. Khayl b. Tihāmah took him captive and sold him to Ḥakīm b. Ḥizām b. Khuwaylid who gave him to his aunt Khadījah who in turn gave him to the Prophet (Ṣ). The latter freed him and adopted him (*tabannāhu*); and he stayed with him a while. Then his paternal uncle and father came wanting to ransom him, so the Prophet (Ṣ) said to them, and this was before his calling had begun: 'Give him the choice. If he chooses the two of you then he is yours without a ransom.' He chose to remain in servitude with the Messenger of God (Ṣ) preferring this over his freedom and returning to his people. So Muḥammad the Messenger of God (Ṣ) said at this point: 'O people of Quraysh, bear witness to the fact that I have a son who will inherit from me and from whom I will inherit.' He circled among

a group of Qurayshis making them testify to this fact. Both his uncle and father were pleased with this and departed.

When Zayd was first captured, his father roamed Syria, looking for him, reciting,

> 'I have cried for Zayd and know not what he has done
> Is he alive? is there hope? or has his term ended?
> By God, I do not know, though I ask,
> Did the plains or the mountains consume you?
> I wish I knew! Will you ever return?
> There would be glory in my world if you came back
> When it rises the sun recalls him to me
> And when it sets memory fades
> When the winds stir they rouse his image
> How long this sadness and fear has lasted!
> You are my life or else the cause of my death
> Every man dies, even if hope deceives him.'

He was then informed that Zayd was in Mecca; he went to him there and died. It is also related that the Prophet gave Zayd a choice [to stay or go] and when he made his choice his father left.

Part II

Q 33:37 also alludes to Zayd's divorce from Zaynab and the subsequent decree conveyed in revelation that a man may marry the divorced wife of his ward. The circumstances of the separation are recounted in detail in the exegesis. They go to lengths to avoid any censure attaching to the Prophet, as does the Qur'an itself, by depicting Muḥammad saying to Zayd, 'Take charge of your wife and be pious towards God!'

People have different interpretations of this verse. Qatādah, Ibn Zayd, and a group of exegetes, among them al-Ṭabarī and others, relate that:

> The Prophet came to find Zaynab attractive while she was still in Zayd's *ʿiṣmah*; he was keen that Zayd divorce her so that he could then marry her himself. Then when Zayd told him that he wanted a separation from her, complaining about her harsh and hurtful speech and her disobedience, the

Prophet said to him, 'Fear God. That is to say, regarding what you say about her. Take charge of your wife.' All the while, he hid his eagerness that Zayd divorce her. This is what he kept hidden within himself, as referred to in the Qur'anic verse. He adhered to a strict conduct of enjoining the proper behavior upon Zayd (*al-amr bi-l-maʿrūf*). Muqātil has said: 'The Prophet married Zaynab bint Jaḥsh to Zayd. She stayed with him for a while. Then one day the Prophet (peace be upon him) went to Zayd to ask for something, and he caught sight of Zaynab. She was fair-skinned, full-bodied and beautiful and among the most flawless women of Quraysh. He was attracted to her and said, "God Almighty – Disturber of hearts!" Zaynab heard these words addressed to God and mentioned them to Zayd. Zayd now understood the truth (*fa-faṭina Zayd*). He asked the Prophet, "O Messenger of God, allow me to divorce her, for she has an arrogant trait, lords it over me and insults me with her tongue." The Prophet replied (peace be upon him), "Take charge of your wife and fear God."'

It was also related that God *made a breeze blow and raised her veil*[4] while Zaynab was fully-dressed in her house. The Prophet glimpsed her and was affected by her. She herself was affected by the fact that the Prophet was affected by her, so she told Zayd, who was so affected that he divorced her.

Part III

Back to Q33:40:

> Muḥammad is not – and has not been – the father of any of your men but he is the Messenger of God and *the Seal of the Prophets. God knows all things.* [emphasis added]

Let us consider these three parts together, as a composite narrative. There are indeed elements similar to the Joseph story, as Powers suggests.[5] The captivity and sale of a young man of noble spirit; his move to another land, therein to become a figure of political significance; the young man's adoption within the household he serves (for a time); emotional reunion with his family (albeit fleetingly); the deep emotions of the father who has lost his son (like those of Jacob); and finally a revelation establishing his true identity vis-à-vis his earthly lord. To set out the facts this way – in order to see affinity with Joseph – is slightly tendentious but helps one understand certain generic elements of the composite narrative. The key recognition in the narrative is not about Zayd, nor his reunion with his father and other members of his biological family, but the establishment that Muḥammad is the Seal of the Prophets. In other narratives of the *Sīrah*, it is the *khātam al-nubuwwah* that enables and betokens the recognition of Muḥammad as Prophet. Such is the case most notably, as we shall see, in the complex, multi-part story of the conversion of Salmān al-Fārisī. It is inevitably tempting to read the two phrases *khātam al-nabiyyīn* and *khātam al-nubuwwah* as being semantically related to each other. It is impossible to establish which phrase was used first; the Qurʾanic phrase simply has greater textual authority, at least doctrinally. But it is possible to read the Qurʾanic phrase, in part, in the light of the way the other one functions in narratives of recognition in the *Sīrah*. On such a reading, Q 33:40 resolves the evolving narrative and anomalous romance of family found in the above passages of exegesis and culminating in Q 33:37: the epistemology of the story of Zayd is multi-layered and is resolved with revelation.[6] It is interesting, in this respect, that the ayah ends with reference to God's omniscience. These too are features the narrative shares with the story of Joseph.

Sīrah:[7] Community, Conversion and the Account of Salmān al-Fārisī

One of the most enchanting and well-crafted tales in the earliest corpus of Islamic literature is the account of Salmān al-Fārisī's conversion to Islam soon after the Prophet's migration to Medina, in or shortly after 622 AD. The chronology of the account is vague, in keeping with the character of this lengthy and elaborate narrative of transfiguration. The tale, with its marked folkloric features – its formulaic narrative blocks and the repetitive calibrating of its spatial and temporal dimensions – has an important part to play in Ibn Hishām's redaction and ordering of the discrete parts of the *Sīrah*.[8] The clue to this importance lies in the fact that an event that took place during the early Medinese period is placed as a bookend to the first part of the *Sīrah*, at the tail-end of a series of miraculous accounts of how the Prophet was fore-announced and recognised by a number of individuals before his birth or calling: to wit, by soothsayers in pre-Islamic Yemen, Christians of Najran,

Hanifs of the Hijaz, a famed Syrian monk, the Jews of Arabia and, finally, in this progressive array, a former Zoroastrian keeper of 'Magian' fires from Persia, Salmān al-Fārisī.[9]

It is a deftly hewn tale of recognition, certainly the most striking of its kind in Ibn Hishām. It deserves a detailed rendering here. We should stress that, key to its presentation within this chapter before the related materials that precede and follow it, is its bridging role: how it functions to underscore and effectively take stock of significant themes, then look ahead to Part II and especially to Part III of the *Sīrah*. One can argue that the narrative is an extended chronotope: it welds together space and time in a multi-part choreographed movement that leads into Medina at the time of the Prophet's arrival there, tracing, through the lands traversed until that moment, the future realms of Islam. This is vague, yet essentially true.

In a clearly determined sequence, the narrative reflects contact with Zoroastrians, then Christians, and then Jews, before the final conversion of Salmān to Islam following the recognition of Muḥammad in Medina. In this way, it brings together many of the elements of preceding shorter narratives, and looks forward, in one of its many semiotic inflections, to the troubled relationship with the Jews of Medina that supervenes in Part III. The negative role of the Jews (in addition to the Banū Kalb), who enslave Salmān and bring him to Medina in servitude, oblivious to the significance of his implacable quest for Muḥammad, appears to foreshadow later developments. It certainly keys in with the long commentary on Surah 2 – the only protracted exegesis of its kind in the *Sīrah* – that concentrates on the Jews of Medina's refusal to recognise in Muḥammad the Prophet foretold in their scriptures.

This contextual role notwithstanding, the conversion story is a tidy and self-contained narrative, with a few key elements that are redolent of the story of Joseph. Surah 12's account of the life of Joseph is far more complex,[10] but both narratives share a movement of disclosure towards recognition and, remotely, the story of Salmān provides support for the broad argument that the trials of Joseph were perceived to reflect, directly and indirectly, the life of Muḥammad.[11] A stronger sense of this can be gleaned from Chapter 3.

The Story

(My translation):[12]

ᶜAbdullāh b. ᶜAbbās related, Salmān al-Fārisī told me in person: I was a Persian from Isfahan, from a little village called Jayy where my father was the local *dihqān*.[13] I was the darling of his eye. Indeed, his love for me was so strong that he kept me confined to his house like a servant-girl. I was an adept of the Magian religion and became a keeper of the fire – the one who kindled it and kept it from going out.

My father had a large estate. One day he had to take care of some building work, so he told me, 'Son, this business will keep me away from the estate today. Go there yourself and look it over.' He gave me a few specific instructions. Then he said, 'Do not stay away for too long, for you are more important to me than my estate, and if you're gone for long you will distract me from all my affairs.'

So I set off for the estate. Along the way I passed by a Christian church. I heard voices inside in prayer, but I knew nothing about these people due to the fact that my father had kept me confined at home for so long. When I heard their voices, I went in to see what they were doing. I was struck with admiration for their liturgy and felt drawn towards them and their religion. I said to myself, 'This is better than our religion, by God!' And I did not move from that place until the sun had set. I forgot about my father's estate and never made it there. I asked them, 'Where are the origins of this religion?' They replied, 'In Syria.'

I returned to my father. He had sent people in search of me and had *been driven to distraction, neglecting all his affairs*. When I came to him, he asked, 'Where have you been? Didn't I make you swear not to stay away for long?' I answered him, 'Father, *I passed by some people who were praying in a church. I was struck with admiration for their religion, so I stayed there awhile listening until the sun set.*' He said, 'Son, *there is no good in that religion! Your religion – the religion of your forefathers – is better.' I answered, 'No, by God! It is truly better than our religion.*' He became fearful for me and placed shackles on my feet and *confined me in his house*.

I sent word to the Christians, saying, 'If one of your caravans arrives here from Syria tell me about it.' Soon a caravan of Christian merchants did come to them from Syria, so they sent word to me about their arrival. I said to them, 'Once they have finished their business and made preparations to return home, tell them about me.' So when they resolved to return home to their country, and I had managed to free myself of my shackles, I set off with them until I reached Syria.

Upon arrival there, I asked, 'Who here is the most knowledgeable about your religion?' They replied, 'The Bishop of the local church.' I went to him and said, 'I would like to convert to this religion. I want to abide with you and serve in your church, to learn from you and pray with you.' He said, 'Come in.' So I entered the church.

But he was a wicked man. He ordered and cajoled his people to give alms, but when they had amassed a significant amount he kept it all for himself. *He never gave it away as alms to the poor.* This went on until he had collected seven large jars of gold and silver. I despised him when I saw what he did.

He died and the Christians gathered to bury him. So I said to them, 'This was a wicked man. *He ordered and cajoled you to give alms* but when you brought it to him he kept it for himself. *He never gave a thing to the poor.*' They asked me, 'How do you know this?' I replied, 'I shall show you his treasure.' They said, 'Show us.' So I indicated the place to them *and brought out seven jars of gold and silver.* When they saw this, they said, 'By God, we shall certainly not bury him.' They crucified him and stoned him, and replaced him with another man.

I have never seen a man who doesn't pray five times a day (i.e. who is not a Muslim) more decent than him, more ascetic and desirous of the next world, more gallant both day and night, *so I loved him as I had never loved anyone before.* I remained with him for a long time. *When his death was near,* I asked him, '*O So-and-So,* I have stayed with you and *loved you as I have never loved anyone before, and your death is close, as God has ordained it, so to whom do you now confide me, and what instructions do you give me?*' He replied, 'My son, I know no one who behaves as I have, for men have changed and fallen into perilous ways; they have all abandoned most of their old ways, except for one man in Mawṣil. *His name is So-and-So. He is as good a man as I was, so go and abide with him.*'

When he died and was buried, I went and joined the man in Mawṣil. I said, '*O So-and-So, So-and-So confided me to you* when he died and advised me to join you; he told me that you comport yourself as he used to.' He answered, 'Abide with me.' So I stayed with him and found him to be the most decent of men, like his colleague, but *he was soon to die. When his death was close*, I asked him, '*O So-and–So, So-and-So confided me to you and ordered me to attach myself to you. You are close to death, so to whom do you now confide me? What do you instruct me to do?' He said, 'By God, I know of no man who is as we both were other than a man in* Naṣībīn. *His name is So-and-So, so attach yourself to him.'*

When he died and was buried I joined the man of Naṣībīn and *told him my story* and what my companion had instructed me to do. He said, '*Stay with me,' so I stayed with him, and found him to be like his two companions. He was the most decent of men, but, by God he was soon to be visited by death. I said to him, 'O So-and-So, So-and-So had confided me to So-and-So, then So-and-So confided me to you, so to whom do you now confide me? And what instructions do you have for me?'* He said, 'Son, by God, I know of no one left who behaves as we have – and whom I can instruct you to join – other than a man in Amorium in the land of the Byzantines. He is as we were; if you wish then join him for you will find him to be like us.'

When he died and was buried I joined the man in Amorium and *told him my story*. He said, '*Stay with me,' so I stayed with him, the best of men*, as guided to him and instructed by his companion. And I grew rich with him, acquiring cattle and flocks of sheep, then *when death was close, per God's decree, I said to him, 'O So-and-So, I was with So-and-So who confided me to So-and-So, and So-and-So confided me to So-and-So, then So-and-So confided me to you. To whom do you confide me, and what instructions do you have for me?'* He said, 'Son, I know of no one left today who is as we have been to whom I can instruct you to go, however the time of a prophet has drawn near and begun to cast its shadow upon us. He has been sent [to revive] the religion of Abraham, and will appear in Arabia. He will migrate to a town between two lava flows, a place among *palm groves*. He has the signs [of prophecy] upon him that cannot be hidden. He eats food that is gifted to him but not food intended as alms. Between his shoulders lies the seal of prophecy. *If you can get to that land, then do so.*'

Then he died and was buried. I stayed in Amorium as long as God willed it, until a party of merchants from the Banū Kalb passed through. I said to them, 'Take me with you to Arabia and I will give you both all my cattle and my flock of sheep.' They agreed. I gave them the livestock and they took me with them until they reached Wadī al-Qurā. There, they turned on me maliciously and sold me in servitude to a Jew. I was travelling with him when I saw *palm trees*, and hoped that this was the land that had been described to me by my last companion, but I was still uncertain (*lam yaḥiqqa fī nafsī*). While I languished with him, he was visited by a cousin of his from the Banū Qurayẓah of Medina. He sold me on to the latter who took me with him to Medina. When I saw the place, I recognised it immediately as the place that had been described to me by my companion. There I stayed. Meanwhile, the Prophet had begun his mission and was to remain in Mecca for a while yet. But I heard no mention of him, busy as I was with my work in bondage. Then he migrated to Medina. I was up in a *palm tree*, working for my master who sat beneath it, when a cousin of his came up to him and stood before him. He said, '*O So-and-So*, God smite the Banū Qaylah! for they are in Qubāʾ gathering around a man who came to them today from Mecca – and they claim he is a prophet!'

When I heard this, I trembled and thought I was about to fall upon my master. So I climbed down and asked his cousin, 'What is this you say? What is this you say?' My master got angry and struck me violently, saying, 'What business is this of yours? Get on with your work!' I answered, 'It is nothing, I wanted only to confirm what he was saying.'

I had with me some food which I had collected, so in the evening I took it to God's Apostle. I entered into his presence and said, 'I have heard that you are a righteous man (*rajulun ṣāliḥun*) and that there are immigrants with you in need of sustenance. Here is some food that I have kept as alms. I consider you more worthy of it than others.'

I brought the food close to him. God's Apostle said to his companions, 'Eat!' but he himself withheld his hand and ate nothing. So I said to myself, '*This is one sign!*' Then I left and gathered more food. In the meantime the Prophet had moved on to Medina. There I came to him and said, 'I noticed that you did not eat any of the food meant as alms, so here is a gift which I make to you.' The Prophet ate from this and he ordered his companions

> to eat with him. I said to myself, '*Now the signs are two*!' Then I came to the Apostle again when he was at the graveyard of Baqīᶜ Gharqad following the funeral procession of one of his companions. I was wearing two heavy robes. He sat later among his companions, so I greeted him then walked behind him to look at his back – to see if I could spot the seal which my companion had described to me.[14] When the Apostle of God saw that I had walked behind him he knew that I was trying to verify something that had been described to me, so he let his robe fall from upon his shoulders. I looked upon the seal and recognised it. I fell upon it, kissed it and sobbed. The Apostle said to me: 'Come round.' So I walked round and sat before him, *and told him my story* and *he was then keen for his companions to hear what I had recounted.*[15]

The rest of the story in this version tells of how the Prophet arranged to buy Salmān's freedom by semi-miraculous means.[16] The whole tale is woven with hagiographic qualities.

Several features and themes bear underscoring, in order to grasp the story's role and its placement in Ibn Hishām. The progression from one religious environment to another, from Magian to Christian to Jewish, culminating in the recognition of the Prophet and conversion to Islam in Medina, as foreseen by the religious man of Amorium, establishes a sequence marked by phases that repeat block motifs, their entire internal structure and key phrases reiterated verbatim. This is part of the oral quality of the anecdote, but also an aspect of its scheme of escalating an idea with accumulative strength and transmitting that force of value to the ultimate object of the story. There is a comprehensive move from pre-Islamic religion towards the beginnings of Islam, and this reflects the general arc of the *Sīrah* up to this point; more or less, the end of Part I and the beginning of the Prophet's mission.

Three names are key: the narrator Ibn ᶜAbbās, who lends the tale the authority that attaches to his person as one of the key transmitters of traditions; Salmān al-Fārisī, whose name is in fact absent, as he tells the story in the first person; and Muḥammad b. ᶜAbdullāh, the Prophet and Apostle of God, whose name too is absent, stressing his incipient mission. All other characters are nameless to a degree that is remarkable; this generates an aggregate effect of transition and erasure, signalled especially by the successive and patterned deaths of each of Salmān's Christian companions. The focus ends up being entirely upon the living Prophet and Salmān's conversion at his hands.

The geography, by contrast, is less anonymous: Salmān moves from Mesopotamia to Syria, to Mawṣil, to Niṣībīn, to Amorium, to Wadī al-Qurā and, finally, to Medina. In mechanical terms, the protracted geography serves to delay the ending; it builds up suspense and gathers evidence of Salmān's steadfast faith. It also clearly represents an expanse of land into most of which Islam would spread as teleological religious history traced its course. Islam was set to succeed Christianity within much of the story's geographical orbit. There is a sense that Christianity is a spent force historically and now stands on precarious footing; fewer and fewer pious men remain and the community is ready for a return to pristine monotheism.

There are villains in the story, too, and this coalesces with the precarious atmosphere that suffuses the vagaries and divagations of Salmān. He must flee his father, who shackles him and confines him to his family home; his first Christian mentor turns out to be a dishonest embezzler of religious funds; each of his mentors dies (it is as if a curse torments him); he is enslaved by the Banū Kalb; he is sold to a Jew at Wādī al-Qurā and then sold on again to a Jew of the Banū Qurayẓah headed for Medina. Chiming in with this precariousness is the fact that Salmān's last mentor, before dying, tells him to rally to the prophet who will soon appear, if he is able to. Nothing is a given. Obstacles lie in the way of a man seeking the new model religion. Precariousness is, as we shall see, a major theme in the accounts of Muḥammad's early life until he became established at Medina in the later years. The choreography of Salmān's sighting of the seal of prophecy (*khātam al-nubuwwah*) is almost gauche and surreptitious. But the Prophet grasps Salmān's unspoken intent and, in a silent gesture of reciprocal recognition, allows his cloak to drop from his back, exposing the seal.[17]

In addition to the *khātam al-nubuwwah*, Muḥammad's pious respect for alms is conceived as another token of prophetic identity. This detail of course contrasts with the actions of Salmān's first mentor, who was corrupt. The distinction is meant to establish the new religion as one that stamped out the corruption that had seeped into the old, even if a few good men still survived among the Christians. The proof: the last of them divined the coming of Muḥammad. The word for alms in Arabic is *ṣadaqah*, the semantic root of which conveys truth. As a token of religious veracity, it is quite felicitous, and we remark that Joseph reveals himself to his brothers in the Qurʾan on the heels of an ayah (Q Yusuf 12:88) in which they appeal to him for alms.[18] The revelation and the giving of alms are contrived so as to be linked, both being conceptually undergirded by honesty.

We should underline a few other details that are reminiscent of the story of Joseph. For one, Salmān's father dotes on his son. He is like Jacob in this respect, and also like one of those rich merchant fathers in the *Arabian Nights* who is blessed with a son in old age and hides him away protectively from public view, though a calamitous fate is never forestalled by such protective actions.[19] Here a sorry fate for the father turns out to be a blessing for the son. Such religious stories of hagiography are therefore a special variation on a theme of family romance. The story of Zayd b. al-Ḥārithah is similar in this respect: reunion with his father, after a long separation caused by capture and servitude, is subordinated unequivocally to the blessing of adoption by the Prophet. Like Joseph, too, Salmān is sold into servitude and taken to a foreign land. But it is an act of providence which holds great things in store for him. As in the Joseph story, the recognition makes apparent the hidden seams of providential agency.

The Beginning[20]

In what follows, I trace relevant materials and themes before and after Salmān al-Fārisī's conversion: the various religions on the eve of Islam; a world poised in transition; the precariousness of the situation as experienced by those gifted with foresight; the tension between matters kept temporarily hidden and their preordained exposure with Muḥammad's imminent mission; the dangers to the Prophet and the opposition of the majority of the Jews, who refuse to recognise as a community what several individuals foretold and what the nascent Islamic community was rallying to accept.

The arc we have alluded to begins with the dream of Rabīʿ b. Naṣr, king of Yemen. He called upon his community to interpret a vision *(ruʾyā)* that had terrified him. The legendary soothsayers, Saṭīḥ and Shiqq were summoned:[21]

> And Saṭīḥ arrived first . . . 'If you know the vision you will know what it means.' Saṭīḥ replied [in *sajʿ*]

> 'A fire you did see (*raʾayta ḥumamah)*
> Come from land and sea. (*kharajat min ẓulamah*)
> It fell on the low country (*fa-waqaʿat bi-arḍin tuhamah*)
> And devoured all that be.' (*fa-akalat kulla dhāti jumjumah*)

> The king exclaimed that this was distressing news and asked when these things would come to pass – in his time or after him? He replied: [again in rhyme] that more than sixty or seventy years must first pass. Would the newcomer's kingdom last? No, an end would be put to it after seventy years or more; then they would be slain or driven away as fugitives. Who would do this? Iram [aka Sayf] b. Dhī Yazan, who would come against them from Aden and not leave one of them in the Yemen. Further questions drew the information that their kingdom would not last, but a pure prophet to whom revelation came from on high would bring it to an end . . . His dominion would last to the end of time. 'Has time an end?' asked the king. 'Yes', replied Saṭīḥ, 'the day on which the first and the last shall be assembled, the righteous for happiness, the evildoers for misery.' 'Are you telling me the truth?' the king asked.

> 'Yes, by the dark and the twilight (*wa-l-shafaqi wa-l-ghasaq*)
> And the dawn that follows the night (*wa-l-falaqi idhā ttasaq*)
> Verily what I have told you is right.' (*in mā anbaʾtuka bihi la-ḥaqq*)

When Shiqq arrives, it is agreed that he has understood the dream to be the same, the difference residing merely in the choice of words. The style of his utterances is also typical of the Kāhins. His prophecy is essentially identical to that of Saṭīḥ, and what bears repeating is the apocalyptic associations of the era that the new prophet will usher in:

> His people will rule until the Day of Separation (*al-faṣl*), the day on which those close to God will be rewarded, on which demands will be made from heaven which the living and the dead will hear, men will be gathered at the appointed place, the God-fearing to receive salvation (*al-fawz*) and blessing (*al-khayrāt*) . . . By the Lord of heaven and earth, and what lies between them high and low I have told the truth in which no doubt (*amḍ*) lies.[22]

The eschatological tenor of Muḥammad's earliest teachings are perceptible in these mantic descriptions. Saṭīḥ and Shaqq are clearly meant to prefigure Muḥammad's early mission in both language and content.[23] In this final detail, the Dream of Naṣr b. Rabīᶜ is redolent of the story of Faymiyūn who is said to have brought Christianity to Najrān but whose greatest miracle is remarkably rooted in *tawḥīd*. Recognition lies internally within this lengthy account as a synecdoche reflecting the broader chronological account of Muḥammad's coming. Pre-Islamic Arabia is limned as a monotheistic, albeit religiously hybrid milieu steeped in a pregnant atmosphere of momentous transition. Here are the key elements of the story related on the authority of Wahb b. Munabbih:

> The one who brought Christianity to Najrān was a man named Faymiyūn who was a righteous and earnest ascete . . . He used to wander between towns, but as soon as he was recognized in one town he moved to another, eating only from what he earned; he was a builder by trade and used mud bricks . . . While he was practising his trade in a Syrian village, keeping himself withdrawn from other men, one of the inhabitants there called Ṣāliḥ perceived the kind of man he was and felt strong affection for him, so that unnoticed by Faymiyūn he would follow him from place to place, until one Sunday he went, as was his habit, out into the desert trailed by Ṣāliḥ. Ṣāliḥ found a hiding place and sat down where he could see him, not wanting him to know where he was. As Faymiyūn stood to pray a *tinnīn*, a seven-horned snake, came towards him and when Faymiyūn saw it he cursed it and it died. Seeing the snake but not knowing what had happened to it and fearing for Faymiyūn's safety, Ṣāliḥ could no longer contain himself and cried out: 'Faymiyūn, a *tinnīn* is upon you!' But he took no notice and carried on praying until he had completed them . . . *He knew that he had been recognized* and Ṣāliḥ knew that he had seen him. So he said to him: 'Faymiyūn, you know that I have never loved anything as I love you; I want to be with you always: go wherever you go.' He replied, 'As you wish. You know how I live and if you feel that you can bear such a life, well and good.' So Ṣāliḥ abided with him, and the people of the village were on the point of discovering his secret. For when an ailing man encountered him by chance he would pray for him and the man was cured; but if he was summoned

> to a sick man he would not go. [A man whose son was blind tricked him into attending his house whereupon the boy was cured.] *Knowing that he had been recognized* he left the village followed by Ṣāliḥ, and while they walked through Syria they passed by a great tree from which a man called out, saying: 'I've been expecting you, asking "When is he coming?" until I heard your voice and knew it was you. Don't go until you have prayed over my grave for I am about to die.' He did die and Faymiyūn prayed over him as they buried him.[24] Then he left followed by Ṣāliḥ until they reached the land of the Arabs who attacked them, and a caravan carried them off and sold them in Najrān. At this time the people of Najrān followed the religion of the Arabs and worshipped a great palm-tree there . . . Faymiyūn was sold to one nobleman and Ṣāliḥ to another. Now it happened that when Faymiyūn was praying earnestly at night in the house which his master had assigned to him the whole house was filled with light and shone radiantly . . . without a lamp. His master was amazed at the sight, and asked him about his religion. Faymiyūn told him and said that they were living in error; as for the palm-tree it could neither help nor hurt them; if he were to curse the tree in God's name, He would destroy it, for He was a single and peerless God. 'Then do so,' said his master, 'for if you do that we will embrace your religion and abandon our present faith.' After purifying himself and performing two *rak*ᶜ*ah*s, he invoked God against the tree and God sent a wind against it which tore it from its roots and hurled it to the ground. Then the people of Najrān adopted his religion and he instructed them in the law of ᶜĪsā b. Maryam.[25]

The reluctance of Faymiyūn to be recognised is striking and reflects both the dangers of living and worshipping in a pagan environment, as well as sensitivity, within the scheme of the teleological narrative, to the fact that true recognition will only come when Muḥammad's mission begins. His caution – which on some level betrays an ethos of self-effacement – shows that the discomforts of Muḥammad's early years as a prophet in Mecca had precedent. But what is more arresting even than this is the Islamic character of what Faymiyūn preaches and how he worships.[26] The account of 'ᶜAbdullah Ibn al-Tāhmir and Those who Perished in the Trench' develops some of the key foregoing elements. In the death, exhumation and reburial of ᶜAbdallah

b. al-Thāmir are elements of extraordinary symbolism in the context of the *Sīrah*.

In a village close to [Najrān] there was a sorcerer who used to instruct the young men [of the town] in his art. When Faymiyūn came there . . . he put up a tent between Najrān and the place where the sorcerer lived. Now the people of Najrān used to send their young men to that magus to be taught sorcery; al-Thāmir sent his son ᶜAbdullah along with them. When he passed by the man in the tent he was immensely struck by his prayers and devotion and began to sit with him and listen[27] until he became a Muslim and acknowledged the unity of God and worshipped Him. He asked questions about the laws of Islam and once he had been fully instructed therein he asked [Faymiyūn] what was the Great Name of God. Although he knew it he kept it from him, saying: 'My dear young man, you will not be able to bear it; I fear that you are not strong enough.' . . . ᶜAbdullah seeing that his master had kept the knowledge from him and was afraid of his weakness, collected a number of sticks and whenever he taught him a name of God he wrote the name on a stick. When he had got them all he lit a fire and began to throw them in one by one until when he reached the stick with the Great Name inscribed on it he threw it in, and it immediately sprang out untouched by the fire. Thereupon he took it and went and told his master that he knew the Great Name of God which he had concealed from him. The latter questioned him and when he heard how he had found out the secret he said, 'Young friend, you have got it, but *keep it to yourself*, though I do not think you will.'

Thereafter whenever ᶜAbdullah b. al-Thāmir entered Najrān and met a sick person he would say to him, 'Servant of God, will you acknowledge the unity of God and adopt my religion so that I may pray to God to heal you of your affliction?' The man would agree, acknowledge the unity of God, and become a Muslim, . . . in the end there was not a single sick person in Najrān but had adopted his religion . . . When news of this reached the king he sent for him and said: 'You have corrupted the people of my town: they have turned against me and begun to oppose my religion, the religion of my fathers.' . . . The king had him taken to a high mountain and thrown down headfirst, but when he reached the ground he was unhurt. Then he

> had him thrown into deep pool in Najrān from which no one had ever emerged alive, but he came out safely.
>
> Having thus got the better of him ᶜAbdullah told him that he would not be able to kill him until he acknowledged the unity of God and converted to his religion . . . The king then acknowledged God's unity and pronounced the creed of ᶜAbdullah; he hit him gently with a stick he had in his hand, killing him on the spot.
>
> . . . [I] was told that in the days of ᶜUmar b. al-Khaṭṭāb a man of Najrān dug up one of the ruins of Najrān intending to make use of the land, when they came upon ᶜAbdullah b. al-Thāmir under a grave; he was in a sitting posture with his hand covering the wound in his head and holding it firmly. When his hand was drawn away blood began to pour; but when they let go of his hand it returned to its former position and the flow of blood was staunched. On his ring was a gem inscribed 'Allah is my Lord.' A report was sent to ᶜUmar and he replied: 'Leave him alone and cover up the grave.' His orders were duly carried out.[28]

The power of *tawḥīd* is miraculous and engenders acknowledgement of the true religion – Christianity is cast in an Islamic mould, foreshadowing Muḥammad's calling, generations later, to set aright the degeneracy that had tainted monotheistic faith. The perception of historical and mythic transition portended by this marvellous tale of conversion is conveyed by the death of ᶜAbdallah as the morbid instantiation of *tawḥīd*. This augments the sense of precariousness in the practice of monotheism, alluded to above. However, there is a natural poetic justice in the uncovering of his body, and the recognition it entails, after the establishment of Islam. The wondrous unearthing touches on several issues:

- First, it reifies the connection between ᶜAbdallah b. al-Thāmir's Christianity and the Islam that superseded it chronologically (seeing a miracle from the past allows the past to weigh meaningfully upon the present).
- Secondly, it chimes, in the broadest sense, with the dynamic of concealment and exposure that runs substantially through the first two parts of the *Sīrah*. In this case, both exposure and concealment have double-edged

meaning. Exposure reveals the truth – it is a gesture of unearthing and a portent of the Prophet's future dispensation, but it reminds one of the dangers of exposure that hounded saints and men of like calling. Concealment connotes both the concept of hiding protectively from view and, more precisely here, entombing ritually in the past what belongs to the past as part of the numinous foundation of the present. The scene is highly paradoxical in its symbolism.

- Lastly, it is a recognition scene. Its tokens are religious (a ring inscribed with God's uniqueness) and miraculous (the unscarred stigmata of a providential death), and authenticate this, and by association, other Islamic hagiographic stories about the past.

Signs of the Prophet's Imminence

> The signs of our Lord are illuminating
>
> Abū al-Ṣalt b. Abī Rabīᶜah al-Thaqafī[29]

The father of the Prophet, ᶜAbdallah b. ᶜAbd al-Muṭṭalib, is known to have married Āminah bt. Wahb b. ᶜAbd al-Manāf, who was 'the most excellent woman among the Quraysh in birth and position at the time (*afḍalu mraʾatin fī l-quraysh nasaban wa-mawḍiᶜan*).'[30] On his way to the marriage, ᶜAbdallah was accosted by the sister of Waraqah b. Nawfal, who offered herself to him most forwardly: 'If you will take me you can have as many camels as were sacrificed in your stead (*la-ka mina l-ibili llatī nuḥirat ᶜanka*).' (She was referring to the camels sacrificed by ᶜAbd al-Muṭṭalib in order to release himself from the vow of sacrificing one of his ten sons to the God of the Kaᶜbah.)[31] He had no inclination to counter his father's wishes, so he consummated his marriage to Āminah the same day. She is said to have conceived the Prophet immediately with the consummation.

The following day, he met the woman who had proposed to him. 'He asked her why she did not make the proposal that she made to him the day before; to which she replied that the light that was with him the day before had left him, and she no longer had need of him. She had heard from her brother Waraqa b. Naufal, who had been a Christian and studied the scriptures, that a prophet would arise among the people (*anna-hu kāʾinun fī hādhihi l-ummah nabī*).'[32] She had recognised in the blaze that emanated from ᶜAbdallah's eyes the man who would sire the future prophet. But that light left him once his son was conceived. The light was effectively the vicarious light of Muḥammad – he was therefore, in a sense, physically recognised by a sign before his conception.

Muḥammad was suckled and fostered by Ḥalīmah bt. Abī Dhuʾayb after his father's death. She was approached by the Prophet's kin, but

> [t]his was a year of famine when [Ḥalīmah and her family] were destitute. I was was riding a dusky she-donkey of hers and we lead an old she-camel of ours which did not now yield a drop of milk. We were kept awake the whole night because of the weeping of our hungry child. I had no milk to give him, nor could our she-camel provide a morning draught, but we were hoping for rain and relief . . . When we reached Mecca, we looked for foster children. The apostle of God was offered to us; each woman refused him when she was told that he was an orphan, because we hoped to get payment from the child's father . . . and so we spurned him . . . Every woman we came with was given a child to suckle except me, but when we decided to depart I said to my husband, 'By God, I do not like the idea of returning with my friends without a suckling; I will go and take the orphan.' He replied, 'Do as you please; perhaps God will bless us on his account (*ᶜasā llāhu an yajᶜala la-nā fī-hī barakah*).'[33] So I went and took him for the sole reason that I could not find anyone else. I took him back to my baggage, and as soon as I put him in my bosom, my breasts overflowed with milk which he drank to his heart's content, as did his foster-brother also. Then they both slept, whereas before this we could not sleep with [our child]. My husband went to the old she-camel and found her udders full; he milked it and he and I drank of her milk until we were completely satiated, and we passed a happy night. In the morning my husband said: 'Do you know, Ḥalīma, you have taken a blessed creature?' I said, 'By God, I hope so.' . . . We continued to recognize this abundance as coming from God for a period of two years, when I weaned him.

Ḥalīmah was loath to return the Prophet to his family when the time came about five years later, but she was in the end forced to by the menacing recognition he received from Abyssinian Christians. This, at least, is how she experienced the attention he was attracting. We will encounter again this motif of a menacing ambience that infuses the first part of the *Sīrah*. In Ibn Hishām's account of this:

> A learned person told me that what urged his foster mother to return him to his mother . . . was that a number of Abyssinian Christians saw him with her when she brought him back after he had been weaned. They looked at him, asked questions about him, and studied him carefully, then they proposed to her, 'Let us take the boy, and bring him to our king and our country; for he will have a great future. We all know about him' (*naḥnu na*ᶜ*rifu amrahu*).[34]

Abū Ṭālib became the Prophet's guardian around the time of a similarly disquieting recognition:

> there was a man of Lihb who was a seer. Whenever he came to Mecca Quraysh used to bring their boys to him so that he could look at them and tell their fortunes. Abū Ṭālib brought [Muḥammad] along with the others when he was still a boy. The seer looked at him and then something else caught his attention. That disposed of he cried, 'Bring me that boy.' When Abū Ṭālib saw the man's eagerness he hid him and the seer began to say, 'Curse you, bring me that boy I saw just now, for by God he has a great future.' But Abū Ṭālib went away.[35]

The Recognition by Baḥīrā

The most celebrated recognition of the Prophet prior to his calling comes during his encounter with Baḥīrā as a young boy, when he accompanied his uncle Abū Ṭālib on a Meccan trading caravan to Syria. The account of it counters to some degree – in the attitude of its protagonist – the menace in the episodes we have just encountered, while confirming the existence of ambient enmity towards the Prophet from which he required protection. When Baḥīrā recognised Muḥammad by the descriptions foretold in the books that he had studied while secluded in his cell, he warned the boy's guardians of the need to watch carefully over him.

In addition to its obvious teleological importance, the encounter with Baḥīrā is detailed and engrossingly choreographed as narrative. There is a skilled delay woven into the first meeting. In other years, Baḥīrā had never taken notice of or spoken to the merchants who passed by his ascetic lodgings; this year, however:

> when they stopped near his cell he made a great feast for them. Some claim that this was because of something he saw while in his cell. They allege that . . . he saw the apostle of God in the caravan when they approached; alone among the people he had a cloud overshadowing him. They came and stopped in the shade of a tree near the monk. He looked at the cloud as it overshadowed the tree: its branches were bowed and drooped over the apostle of God until he was in the shade beneath it. When Baḥīrā saw this, he came out of his cell and sent word to them [inviting them to a meal; when the merchants arrived at Baḥīrā's lodging they had left the young Muḥammad behind guarding their baggage]. When Baḥīrā looked at the people he did not see the mark which he knew about having read about it in his books, so he said to them, 'Do not let any one of you remain behind and not attend my feast.' They told him that no one who ought to be there had remained behind except a boy, the youngest of them . . . thereupon he told them to invite him over . . . When Baḥīrā saw him he stared at him closely, scrutinizing at his body and finding traces of the description [he had read about in the Christian books. Baḥīrā began to ask Muḥammad questions, invoking the Meccan pagan goddesses, but he refused to answer until God alone was invoked] . . . So then he began to ask him about what happened in his sleep, about his habits and his affairs generally; what the apostle of God told him coincided with what Baḥīrā knew of his description. Then he looked at his back and saw the seal of prophethood between his shoulders in the very place described in his books. [Baḥīrā then addressed some questions to Abū Ṭālib] . . . when he asked what had become of the boy's father he answered that he had died before the child was born. 'You have told the truth,' said Baḥīrā. 'Take your nephew back to his country and guard him carefully against the Jews, for by God! If they find out about him what I know, they will do him harm; a great future lies before this nephew of yours, so take him home quickly.'[36]

Supplementary materials that follow this account tell how Zurayr, Tammām and Darīs,

> who were people of the scriptures, had noticed in the apostle of God what Baḥīrā had seen during that journey . . . They tried to harm him, but Baḥīrā kept them away and reminded them of God and mention of his description (*min dhikri-hi wa-ṣifatihi*) which they could find in the sacred books, and that if they conspired to harm him they would fail. And he kept on at them until they recognized the truth of what he said, left him and went away.[37]

This passage illustrates the ambivalence and precariousness of recognition. The Prophet's mission was a delicate affair in the way it was to come out into the open as a public calling to his fellow men. Recognition was at first equivocal; pristine understanding was hard to acquire, even by those attracted to his mystifying charisma. Sometimes divine protection was required: when he played once among fellow Meccan youngsters, carefree, an 'unseen figure slapped [him] most painfully saying, "Put your shirt on (*shidda ᶜalayka izārak*)."'[38] (i.e. Hide the mark of your prophethood – it is not time yet and dangers surround you.) The pain here is a minimal synecdoche of the pains and travails of prophetic emergence.

There is an incident later in the Prophet's early adult life that is overlaid with portentous poetry of a Homeric quality. This took place during the rebuilding of the Kaᶜbah before the Prophet's calling had begun. A quarrel ensued among the tribes as to who should reset the Black Stone in its corner. The Quraysh agreed that the next man to enter the Ḥaram would settle the matter. Sure enough, Muḥammad walked into the precinct and was asked to settle the dispute, which he did by having the Black Stone placed upon a sheet that was raised to its final position by four clans each holding onto a corner of the sheet, so that all were equally involved in the process. There was a snake that lived in the Kaᶜbah and terrorised those taking part in the refurbishment. Zubayr b. ᶜAbd al-Muṭṭalib said about the snake:

> I was amazed that the eagle went straight
> To the snake when it was excited.
> It used to rustle ominously
> And sometimes it would dart forth.
> When we planned to rebuild the Kaᶜba
> It terrified us for it was fearsome.
> When we feared its attack, down came an eagle,

Deadly straight in its swoop,
It bore it away, thus leaving us free
To work without further hindrance.[39]

The eagle is clearly a helper and an omen of transition. One is put in mind of the divine auspices witnessed by the suitors in the *Odyssey* when the terrifying displays of an eagle are to be read as portents, by the perspicacious, of Odysseus' return to Ithaca, indeed of his presence already on the Island in disguise. For those without faith in the king's rightful return, the results would be horrifying.

The Cosmic Paradox

In addition to Jewish rabbis and Christian monks, Arab soothsayers were cognisant of a prophet's advent, for they were inspired by their demon muses among the jinn. The circumstances that surround this mythic scenario create an interesting paradox, quite of a piece with many of the tensions that inhere in the entire narrative up to this point:

> As to the Arab soothsayers they had been visited by satans from the jinn with reports which they had secretly overheard before they were prevented from hearing by being pelted by stars. Male and female soothsayers continued to mention some of these matters to which Arabs paid no attention until God sent him and these things which they used to mention occurred and they recognized them.[40]

The actions of the jinn are explained further. They had begun to eavesdrop in the heavens, overhearing Qurʾanic verses before their communication to the Prophet. This was liable to bewilder mankind; therefore, they were blocked from listening further by being pelted from the heavens by meteors. But this visible cosmic spectacle itself became – and was associated with – a sign of prophetic imminence. Hence the paradox of the actions of the jinn who came to understand why they had been pelted:

> When the jinn heard the Qurʾān [once the Prophet had begun his calling] they realized that they had been prevented from eavesdropping previously so that revelation should not mingle with [snippets of] news from heaven thus perplexing mankind (*ahl al-arḍ*) . . . Then they returned to their jinn-

folk warning them, 'we have heard a scripture which was revealed after Moses confirming what preceded it; [it will guide believers] to the truth and to the straight path.' [Q al-Aḥqāf 46:28][41]

When the believers among the jinn recognised the Qurʾan, they did so very much in two senses: they *re*cognised mantic utterances that they had heard before, and this facilitated their acceptance of Muḥammad's apostolic mission.

'This is not the One'[42]

Unlike the jinn who recognised oddments of revelation that they had heard in heaven and thus became Muslims, the Jews, as characterised by the *Sīrah*, refused to recognise in Muḥammad the prophet described in their scriptures. The following two striking accounts lead into the story of the conversion of Salmān al-Fārisī. It is presented as a galling irony that Arab pagans who had heard the Jewish descriptions of the coming prophet recognised him in Muḥammad, while the Jews denied him despite what they had studied in their books.

> ᶜĀṣim b. ᶜUmar b. Qatāda told [Ibn Isḥāq] that some of his tribesmen said: 'What induced us to accept Islam . . . was what we used to hear the Jews say. We were polytheists worshipping idols, while they were people of the scriptures with knowledge which we did not possess. There was continual enmity between us and they would say, "The time of a prophet who is to be sent has now come. We will kill you with his aid as ᶜĀd and Iram perished." When God sent His apostle we accepted him when he called us to God and we realized what their threat meant[43] and joined before them. We believed in him but they denied him.[44] Concerning us and them, God revealed the verse in the chapter of the Cow: "And when a book from God came to them confirming what they already had . . ., when what they knew came to them, they disbelieved it."'[45]

Reference to the chapter of the Cow prefigures the lengthy commentary that supervenes in Part III of the *Sīrah*.[46]

Muḥammad's Call

The account of the first revelation is preceded (one may arguably say, 'prefaced') by reference to the Paraclete – 'the Comforter' – described in

John's Gospel. The passage quoted is John 15:23. It chimes well with the atmosphere of enmity that has obtained in the *Sīrah* up to this point, an environment that becomes especially charged and hostile after the beginning of the Prophet's call.

> Among the things that have reached me about what Jesus the Son of Mary stated in the Gospel which he received from God for the followers of the Gospel, in applying a term to describe the apostle of God, is the following. It is extracted from what John the Apostle set down for them when he wrote the Gospel for them from the Testament of Jesus Son of Mary: 'He that hates me has hated the Lord. And if I had not done in their presence works which none other before me did, they would not have sinned: but now they are puffed up with pride and think that they will overcome me and also the Lord. But the word that is in the law must be fulfilled, "They hated me without a cause" (i.e. without reason). But when the Comforter has come whom God will send to you from the Lord's presence, and the spirit of truth which will have gone forth from the Lord's presence he shall bear witness of me and you also, because you have been with me from the beginning. I have spoken to you about this lest you should be in doubt.'[47]

Doubt is one of the signal subjects broached in verse 1 of Surah 2 al-Baqarah: *Alif Lām Mīm: That is the book in which there is no doubt – a guidance for the pious and godly.* It is in essence the same kind of doubt referred to in John 15:23. Historically, however, the specific doubt against which al-Baqarah levels criticism, in sundry related but discrete passages, is the Medinese Jews' denial of Muḥammad's apostolic mission – the denial, chiefly, of those who were incapable of accepting the changing of the *qiblah* from Jerusalem to Mecca, the prescriptive heart of Surah 2, marking out the prayer of the Muslim community as distinct from what came now to be seen as the atavistic yet misguided practice of the Jews. (Paradoxically, the Medinese Jewish community's refusal to recognise the apostle may itself have provoked the redirecting of the *qiblah*.) Doubt, denial and recognition are tautly intertwined in the sūrah, as they are in the *Sīrah* where the resulting tension is related to the precariousness and instability we have identified intermittently throughout this chapter. Elsewhere, doubt troubles the Prophet himself before his recognition of Gabriel, although encouraged by the bracing reactions of Khadījah and Waraqah b. Nawfal. In a rare but telling oxymoron, doubt even troubles the arrogance of doubters: the pagan ʿUtbah b. Rabīʿah is clearly half way to recognising the Prophet after he hears the opening verses of Surah 41 Fuṣṣilat and is accused of being bewitched by his Meccan associates.

The First Revelation

The account of the earliest revelation is in two balanced parts; part two mirrors some elements of part one. First is the anxious encounter with Gabriel, then comes the reassuring dialogues with Khadījah and Waraqah b. Nawfal.

> [I]n the month of Ramaḍān in which God willed concerning him what He willed of His grace, the apostle set out to Ḥirāʾ as was his wont . . . On the night when God honoured him with his mission and thereby showed mercy to His servants, Gabriel brought him the command of God. 'He came to me,' said the apostle of God, 'while I was asleep, with a cover on which was brocaded some writing, and said, "Recite!" I said, "What shall I recite?" he pressed me with it so tightly that I thought it was death; then he let me go and said, "Recite!" I said, "What shall I recite?" He pressed me with it again so that I thought it was death; then he let me go and said, "Recite!" I said, "What shall I recite?" He pressed me with it a third time so that I thought it was death and said, "Recite!" I said, "What then shall I recite?" – and this I said only to deliver myself from him, lest he should do the same again. He said:
>
> > "[Recite] in the name of your Lord who created,
> > Who created man of blood coagulated.
> > Recite! Thy Lord is the most beneficent,
> > Who taught by the pen,
> > Taught that which they knew not unto men."
>
> So I recited it, and he departed from me. And I awoke from my sleep, and it felt as though these were words written on my heart. (Ṭ.[48] Now, none of God's creatures was more hateful to me than an (ecstatic) poet or a man possessed: I could not even look at them. I thought, Dear me! I am either poet or possessed – Never shall Quraysh say this of me! I will climb to the top of the mountain and throw myself down; I will kill myself and gain rest.

> So I set out to do so then,) when I was midway on the mountain, I heard a voice from heaven saying, "Muḥammad! You are the apostle of God and I am Gabriel." I raised my head towards heaven to see (who was speaking), and lo, Gabriel in the form of a man with feet astride the horizon saying, "Muḥammad! You are the apostle of God and I am Gabriel." I stood gazing at him, (Ṭ. And that distracted me from my purpose) moving neither forward nor backward; then I began to turn my face away from him, but towards whatever region of the sky I looked, I saw him as before. And I continued standing there, neither advancing nor turning back, until Khadīja sent her messengers in search of me and they gained the high ground above Mecca and returned to her while I was standing in the same place; then he parted from me and I from him, returning to my family.'[49]

The first five verses revealed to the Prophet in this celebrated and extraordinary Islamic beginning are about recitation, creation and knowledge. They are about process: recitation; and about content: creation and knowledge. The latter states very paradigmatically that God teaches mankind that of which he has no knowledge. This broadly stated paradigm of anagnorisis, of the movement from ignorance to knowledge, is itself emblematic of the entire encounter described, which is a synecdoche of the arc of Qurʾanic revelation now begun (scriptural revelation always, of necessity, has human ignorance as its backdrop and point of departure). Muḥammad's qualms and misgivings, which in one account of the vision led him even to consider suicide, reflect and translate a painful transition that is characteristic of the anxieties we find in many angelophanic encounters.[50]

Muḥammad recognises Gabriel in his dream vision, but he does not know that the angel is actually appearing to him – in real cosmic time, as it were. This is at first experienced as a disturbed reverie. The repetitions in the dialogue between the angel and the Prophet convey with great psychological force the anguish that Muḥammad felt. In the account as it survives in al-Ṭabarī, he is so distressed that he heads towards the summit of the mountain in order to throw himself into the abyss. This is hardly an act, or an attitude, of acceptance, however much he has recognised the figure of Gabriel in his dream.

Then a physical vision appears to him in his waking state, confirming both the identity of the angelic visitor and what Muḥammad has now become: the apostle of God. Like the iterative feature of the encounter in the dream vision, the second apparition happens twice, with words that are repeated verbatim. Such repetition works to break down resistance. Muḥammad turns his head away from Gabriel but sees Gabriel everywhere he turns. This powerful and extraordinary scene is the story of Jonah in miniature.

Now other messengers come to him. Difficulty suffuses this succession of charged moments. This time the messengers are from the real world: from Khadījah, and at first they cannot find the Prophet. The elusiveness of the whole situation subsists now on the most terrestrial level. Khadījah and Waraqah b. Nawfal, by turns, cajole Muḥammad into accepting the truth of the visions he has seen: To recognise and accept both Gabriel and his message. Khadījah encourages him first, but she also reports what she has heard to Waraqah. It is then Waraqah who, with compelling force, imparts to these encounters their significance and leaves Muḥammad on the threshold of acquiescence and transfiguration.

> Waraqa met [Muḥammad] and said, 'My nephew, tell me what you have seen and heard.' The apostle told him, and Waraqa said, 'Surely, by Him in whose hand is Waraqa's soul, you are the prophet of this people. There has come to you the greatest Nāmūs, who came unto Moses. You will be called a liar, and they will use you hatefully and cast you out and fight you . . . (al-Ṭabarī: Waraqa's words added to his confidence and lightened his anxiety.)[51]

With his words, Waraqah was warning the Prophet predominantly about the opposition he would face from the Meccan pagans. But once Muḥammad migrated to Medina in 622 AD, the main doctrinal opposition he faced came from the Jews whom the Qur'an then charged with wilfully misreading the scriptures regarding his calling. We have discussed Surah 2 (al-Baqarah) at some length elsewhere. The significance of the view set out above is corroborated in Part III of the *Sīrah* in an unusually extended and thematised commentary. It is clear, historically, that the surah was seeking an authenticated recognition of Muḥammad with the warning that, in religious terms, the truth, and whatsoever is malevolently concealed, inevitably comes to light. As we have had cause to say before, recognition and disclosure, together with their antonyms denial and concealment, are the fundamental leitmotifs of this surah.[52] The significance of this section also lies in that it comes before the bulk of the *maghāzī*, the accounts of Muḥammad's military raids, for the principal object of conquest, once the *qiblah* was changed, would have become Mecca. Recognition in the special sense it has in Surat al-Baqarah thus ties in with the ultimate motivation of the *Sīrah*, as a genre:[53] to give account of the Prophet's battle days and conquests.

Hadith: Personal Conduct and the Slander against ᶜĀ'ishah

> ... and moreover it is possible to discover whether a person has done something – or not
>
> Aristotle, *Poetics* 11 (ed. and trans. Halliwell, 1995), p. 67

The Affair of the Slander (*Ḥadīth al-Ifk*), in its fullest rendering, is the most expansive narrative in the corpus of authenticated traditions of the Prophet. It is a masterpiece of storytelling: of suspense and disclosure, moral cleansing and catharsis. It is a story of revelation and is, indeed, listed among the *asbāb al-nuzūl*[54] (those for example collected by al-Wāḥidī).[55] What draws our attention to it is the conjunction of two related things: the very deft way it cites Surah 12 (Yūsuf) and the fact that it is a narrative of anagnorisis in the broadest sense of the term.[56] Identity, the most common predicate of recognition in the Aristotelian scheme, is not overtly an issue in the story. However, the question of moral identity most certainly is: we come to know *what* a person is (her virtues) as much as *who*. The essence of identity is thus inextricably related to the moral quality of deed, action and general comportment; these are logically, of course, part of the ontology of identity – part of the semantics of its structure, in the terms of narratologist Tzvetan Todorov. And what a person has *not* done, as we shall see, is as important as the libelous verbal calumny that has been committed; this is especially important given that the alleged deed being coyly and yet perniciously alluded to throughout the narrative is the moral turpitude of the cuckolding of the Prophet of God.

The various links in *Ḥadīth al-Ifk* between anagnorisis and Surah 12 are explored below. That the two elements exist in the hadith may be fortuitous; but a purely chance conjunction seems unlikely, and the circumstantial as well as literary evidence suggests that the intertextual references in this narrative are as deftly woven into its fabric as one can hope to find in any well-wrought piece of literature: Surah 12 is evoked *overtly* to comment on a relatively subordinate theme of the narrative (ᶜĀᵓishah's summoning of fortitude); surrogately, however, it facilitates the consummation of one of the principal processes of the text, the anagnorisis which it both foretokens and of which it may itself be considered a part. This is all the more surprising and striking given the fact that the tale is told retrospectively by ᶜĀᵓishah who paints a picture of herself at the time of these events as the very icon of innocence and naivety. This superb narrative is far from naive in its execution. It is hardly plausible that ᶜĀᵓishah can scarcely recall Jacob's name and yet be sensitive to the full aesthetic and ethical implications of summoning Surah 12 in the way that she does. The hand of a skilled redactor seems to operate here. Either she herself crafted her narrative with the benefit of years of hindsight – she may have become a canny raconteuse – or someone else, or both.[57]

A Telegraphic Synopsis[58]

> Before setting off on any expedition the Prophet Muḥammad would draw lots in order to select which of his wives would accompany him. On the expedition against the Banū Muṣṭaliq (of *c*.6 AH) the kismet fell to ᶜĀᵓishah. Returning from the raid, the army encamped by night near Medina. ᶜĀᵓishah strayed off on foot in order to answer nature's call and lost a necklace. She was delayed returning to search for it; in the meantime the army struck camp and her minders loaded her howdah upon her camel failing to notice that she was not inside. In a gloss, ᶜĀᵓishah attributes the lightness of women in those days to their meagre diet. (Scilicet: if she hadn't weighed so little her bearers would have noticed her absence.) A straggler from the fighting force, a young man called Ṣafwān b. al-Muᶜaṭṭal, discovered her, placed her upon his camel and led her off towards Medina. ᶜĀᵓishah was immediately slandered and the chief slanderer is named, ᶜAbdullāh b. Ubayy. She fell ill upon her return to Medina; confined to her home, she learnt nothing of what had been said about her. Only Muḥammad's unusual behaviour towards her left her suspecting that something was amiss. One night, on a visit outside to answer nature's call (which is a corporal leitmotif of the narrative), she learnt of the calumny from Umm Misṭaḥ, whose own son, Misṭaḥ, was among the faction of

> slanderers. The Prophet allowed his young wife to move temporarily to her parents' house. She spoke with her mother, Umm Rūmān, who was apprized of the scandal; ʿĀʾishah spent that night and following day weeping. Meanwhile, Muḥammad consulted with ʿAlī b. Abī Ṭālib and Usāmah b. Zayd about what he should do. He asked ʿĀʾishah's servant Barīrah to testify to the character of his young wife. She had only good things to say of her mistress. The Prophet then spoke publicly about the scandal, defending his family. A public wrangle ensued between the (leaders of) the Aws and Khazraj tribes of Medina. Muḥammad visited his wife – who was still in tears – asking her to confess her sin if she was guilty. She maintained her innocence, unfalteringly. The Revelation of Qurʾan 24:11ff. follows, in which ʿĀʾishah was unequivocally vindicated. Abū Bakr, ʿĀʾishah's father, withdrew support from his ward, Misṭaḥ, for his part in the slander. Qurʾan 24:22 was then revealed, castigating actions such as those of Abū Bakr – this is part of the process of communal reconciliation, thus Abū Bakr rescinds his decision. ʿĀʾishah expressed her gratitude to her co-spouse Zaynab, sister of Ḥamnah (one of the chief slanderers). In contrast to her sister, Zaynab spoke only well of ʿĀʾishah during the affair, even though she stood to gain in the Prophet's marital favour.

A complex tension runs through the piece, which consists of a series of interwoven dichotomies: the alternating and interpenetrating manifestations of knowledge and ignorance, often suffused with dramatic irony; the shifting perspectives of public and private spheres of daily life; the silencing of facts (or of the sordid details of events, if only as a retrospective textual protocol) when gossip is apparently rife in its own sibilant way; screening and disclosure, veiling and unveiling; the pronounced separation between human and divine levels of existence (the humanity of the Prophet is markedly etched in this narrative – he is cast as the decidedly human medium of divine revelation); and finally, as a factor of the latter antonymy, we can posit the distinction between the transcendent eloquence of divine discourse (the Qurʾanic revelation that is adduced in the denouement) and the unseemly words of human calumny. Revelation, once it has been received after a disconcerting hiatus, is accented and determinative in its influence on the lives of the community. It is not hard to contrast this with the drawing of lots – the loose, somewhat happy-go-lucky, way in which the episode begins. (Is there a tension here, too? Is God's will behind the whole affair? Or does He simply clear up the human mess?) Anagnorisis, in all events, resolves the tension that inheres in each of the constitutive doublets listed above.

The community of Muslims was in effect divided into active perpetrators and passive victims of ignorance in this affair. Those that were active were the scandalmongers whose names have been relayed to posterity; they were eventually punished and made examples of, most notably Ḥassān b. Thābit, the Prophet's own 'court poet'.[59] Passive ignorance is harder to define precisely; it is the inability to resist the insidious effect of the slander; once heard the affair was not readily forgotten and suppressed; suspicion lingered, a fact copiously illustrated in the helpless reaction of ᶜĀᵓishah's parents. Although mother comforted daughter, showing astute understanding of the uxorial jealousies that fanned the flames of the affair, Umm Rūmān could not find words to speak when ᶜĀᵓishah pleaded with each of her parents in turn to exonerate her in the presence of her husband who, in a transparent and telling inconsistency of the narrative sequence in some versions, had already proclaimed publicly that he 'knew' only good of his family; they each replied, 'I do not know what to say to the Prophet.' Their ignorance and impotence to say or do anything is stressed in the verbatim repetition of their words (*wa-llāhi mā adrī mā aqūlu li-rasūli llāhi*).[60] ᶜĀᵓishah was passive too, but as a victim of the conspiratorial ignorance of others: she was talked about, ignored – and then absolved; she was indeed given the epithet al-Mubarraᵓah ('the vindicated') as a result of this episode. But in Arabic 'being ignorant' can be construed – it is certainly parsed – as an active process; someone who is ignorant is *jāhil* (an active participle). It is also, in a sense, a transitive process. A paradox thus can be seen to emerge in that the predication of ignorance is itself an anagnorisis of sorts; the fact that 'they' did not know that 'she' was innocent is – especially from the reader's perspective – tantamount to saying more straighforwardly in the end: 'She was innocent.' (This is certainly an important element of the teleological syntax of this narrative, whose literary success is in part due to its quality of delaying this predication and anagnorisis for rhetorical effect.)[61]

The Qurᵓanic verses which were revealed as a result of this incident are typically terse and allusive (Q al-Nūr 24:11ff.); the affair in all its details is silenced in some sense with an ordinance that such calumny is a punishable sin. The words of the gossip may be evoked in the minds of those who originally heard them; posterity, however, will never know how exactly the slanderers made their accusation: what words they used, what motives they gave, what epithets were ascribed to the victims of their insidious conjecture. This simultaneous muting of the affair even while it is the subject of the narrative is itself one of the recurring features of the text. For example, in the slightly elaborated recension of Ibn Isḥāq (which we have received in the *Sīrah* of Ibn Hishām) the phrase *qāla ahlu l-ifki mā qālū* passes over – and silences – the words they actually spoke.[62] In the same recension we learn that ᶜĀᵓishah never spoke to Ṣafwān b. al-Muᶜaṭṭal (*fa-mā kallamat-hu*), just as she refused to address the Prophet with gratitude after the Qurᵓanic disclosure of her innocence. This curtness, in the latter instance, is ᶜĀᵓishah's own delayed retaliation to the Prophet's laconic and hurtful, 'How is that woman?' (*kayfa tīkum*), when inquiring after his sickly young wife earlier in the affair.

In addition to the citation of Qurᵓan 12:18, the only other Qurᵓanic verse included in the narrative is 24:11. Taken in its proper context it is at once a disclosure of truth (both particular and prescriptive) and identity, albeit the identity of the scandalmongers remains typically anonymous within the text of the scripture. But the effect of the words (Q 24:11) *alladhīna jāᵓū bi-l-ifki ᶜuṣbatun min-kum* ('those who spread the slander are only a group among you') is significant in its anonymity and reference to a small group in confining the damage that has been done to a community that had risked sliding back towards erstwhile internecine dispute. There is a marked scaling down here of the perpetrators of a moral improbity that had seemed at one point to touch the whole community; when, in the early stages of her ignorance, ᶜĀᵓishah is the sole individual unaware of the gossip it is the whole community that seems tainted by the perjury. The toning down of indecorous details of the intrigue in terse reports of it, years after the fact, is most striking in the Kufan hadith related from Ḥuṣayn[63] (from Abū Wāᵓil); its source is not ᶜĀᵓishah but her mother, Umm Rūmān:[64]

> When a woman of the Anṣār came in to us she exclaimed, 'May God afflict so-and-so with such-and-such!' ᶜĀᵓishah's mother asked, 'Why so?' She

> replied that her son was among those who had spread the 'saying'/the 'talk' (*al-ḥadīth*); she asked, 'And what is that?' She replied, 'Such-and-such.' At which ᶜĀᵓishah asked, 'Does the Prophet know?' 'Yes.' 'And does Abū Bakr (her father) know?' 'Yes.' At which she – ᶜĀᵓishah – fell to the ground in a swoon.

But could ᶜĀᵓishah really imagine the Prophet to have been ignorant of such common knowledge? The paralogism is explained in some measure by this fact: the community, and ᶜĀᵓishah with it, is utterly discountenanced by this affair. That the Prophet should have known, together with her father, simply intensified her feelings of ignorance and exclusion – *everybody* knew, even those who, out of fear or respect, might have been spared exposure to the calumny. That the Prophet should have known of this tawdry matter was abhorrent to ᶜĀᵓishah; for him not to know, of course, would have been equally unsettling.

Slouching Back to Jāhiliyyah

We might now consider another way that ignorance is inscribed into this tale. We turn our gaze thus from the deeply private to the public and societal sphere of events. The scandal opens up wounds in the conflict between the tribes of the Anṣār: during the Prophet's public *khuṭbah* in which, with measured obliqueness and tact, he addresses the matter of the slander, Saᶜd b. ᶜUbādah (of Khazraj) accuses Saᶜd b. Muᶜādh (of Aws) of lying; the latter becomes much exercised and the exchange between the two men threatens the fragile peace that exists between the two tribal groups. The Arabic locution that paints his change of humour is significant: *wa-kāna qabla dhālika rajulan ṣāliḥan wa-kāna ḥtamalat-hu l-ḥamiyyah* ('Before this he was an upright man but he was taken by the zeal of ignorance'). Represented by these men, the community as a whole is sliding backwards toward a pre-Islamic state of existence, a time of ignorance. To explain the point we need simply consider the use of the phrase '*ḥamiyyat al-jāhiliyyah*' in Q 48:26 which describes a time: 'When those who disbelieved set fierceness in their hearts, the fierceness of the age of ignorance (*ḥamiyyat al-jāhiliyyah*), *and God sent down his reassurance to his messenger and to the believers*, and fastened on them the word "piety", to which they have the best right and are worthy of it. *God is aware of everything.*' It is divine omniscience that will drag the blundering community back into a state of enlightenment through revelation.

Elements of Surah 12

When the Prophet defends his young wife in the public *khuṭbah* during the course of the scandal he repeats verbatim the words that have been voiced to him reassuringly – but in private – by Usāmah b. Zayd: *lā naʿlamu illā khayran* ('we only know good things') → *wa-llāhi mā ʿalimtu ʿalā ahlī illā khayran* ('by God!, I have only learnt good things about my family'). These words are evocative of Surah 12:51 (*lā ʿalimnā ʿalay-hi min sūʾ*; 'we know nothing of evil about him') in which the women of Egypt (Zulaykha's cohort of admiring guests) declare and confess their knowledge of Joseph's innocence. Surah 12 in fact furnishes more than this detail to the narrative of the scandal; by evoking the Qurʾan, the hadith in fact borrows and modulates the epistemological strength of anagnorisis from the sacred narrative. When ʿĀʾishah claims astonishingly she had no knowledge of the gossip while it raged, she uses the words: *lā ashʿuru bi-shayʾin min dhālika* ('I sensed nothing of this'); that is, she associates herself unwittingly through her choice of words with a kind of incognisance or *agnoia* ascribed to the scheming brothers at Surah 12:15. The connection may be tenuous at this point (observable only with hindsight as matters unfold) but worth highlighting, for in her later, markedly more tangible invocation of the Joseph story, she associates herself even more with the brothers. The quotation of Surah 12 is indeed fascinating, for we can confidently reconstruct the pattern of associations in ʿĀʾishah's mind: sensing that her parents do not believe her even though she tells the truth, she raises the spectre in her inchoate thoughts of the plaintive words of Joseph's brothers (12:17): *wa-mā anta bi-muʾminin la-nā wa-law kunnā ṣādiqīn* ('You wouldn't believe us even if we were telling the truth'); the evocation is fragile, because unspoken, yet unmistakable and it puts her more consciously in mind of Jacob's forbearance in the following ayah (12:18), 'Sweet forbearance! God's help is to be sought against what you describe' (*fa-ṣabrun jamīlun wa-llāhu l-mustaʿānu ʿalā mā taṣifūn*), thus rescuing her from any compromising association with the perjury of Joseph's brethren. In this way, perjury, as a theme, is evoked and sustained, but so too are introduced the themes of forbearance (which she now needs and calls upon) and the pending disclosure of truth foretokened (at least contextually) by these verses in the Qurʾan.[65] Seen in this light, *The Slander* is, indeed, a stylised narrative; the deft manner in which ʿĀʾishah is led to adduce pertinent details of Surah 12 makes us sensitive even to the way the quotation is couched: *mā ajidu lī la-kum mathalan illā abā yūsufa idh qāla* ('I can find nothing exemplary to say to you all except [the words of] the father of Joseph when he said (sic)'), which elliptical locution seems be to patterned on *idh qāla yūsufu li-abī-hi* ('when Joseph said to his father'). It is not farfetched to suggest some retrospective enhancement of the style of the narrative in this instance, as in others.[66]

Of some significance in sustaining the relationship between this hadith and Surah 12, is the vocabulary ʿĀʾishah uses to express her hope of absolution; her self-effacing reverie is that a prophetic *ruʾyā* (vision) will exonerate her. This is a key word in Surah 12 used to describe Joseph's dream, the event that sets the whole story in motion. However, an interesting secondary issue emerges: in the words and sentiments of ʿĀʾishah, this type of mantic vision is categorically subordinated to revelation such that Joseph's 'historical' vision can be understood to have been ultimately subsumed in Qurʾanic revelation. The Qurʾan thus promotes and enhances the mantic constitution of evolving prophetic history.

In Ibn Hishām's version, from Ibn Isḥāq, the scene in which ʿĀʾishah asks her parents to utter words in her defence before the Prophet contains a phrase that is absent from the text of other redactors: *fa-lammā ani staʿjamā ʿalayya staʿbartu fa-bakaytu* ('When my parents were unable to speak I wept'). They have already at this point said, '*wa-llāhi mā nadrī bi-mādhā nujību-hu*' ('By God, I do not know what to answer'). Their words set a tone of verbal inadequacy that will be offset effectively when ʿĀʾishah responds by quoting from the Qurʾan. A further detail should be noted in this respect: Surah 12 is one of a number of chapters that begin by vaunting the eloquent – Arabic/*ʿarabī* – qualities of Qurʾanic diction (12:2 *innā anzalnā-hu qurʾānan ʿarabiyyan laʿalla-kum taʿqilūn*; 'we have sent it down as an Arabic Qurʾān so that you may understand'). Eloquence – that is, Arabic – is the medium of enlightenment; by contrast, the root *ʿajama* ('gabbling like a foreigner', the root of *istaʿjamā*) can be, as it is here, a metonym for a state of moral torpor.

The Prophet seeks reassurance, exposes his own doubts in private, yet tries to impose himself staunchly in public in defence of his wife: publicly he proclaims – apparently without equivocation – that he knows no wickedness about his wife. Ostensibly this is a declaration of what he knows, yet *we* know it to be inflected with doubt for he simply repeats in this *khuṭbah* the very words he has heard from Usāmah b. Zayd (except in the altered sequence of Ibn Hishām). There are no short cuts in this narrative; *agnoia* must work itself through a whole series of stages and events. The upshot is of course *deus ex machina*, in a rather enhanced scriptural sense, but the body of the narrative would nevertheless please some of the European renaissance commentators on Aristotle's *Poetics*.[67] In some measure, there is contrived deferment in the narrative, in the form of '*istilbāth al-waḥy*': the Prophet is deprived for nigh on a month from divine revelation about the affair; the retardation of the revelation gives rise to doubt, and somehow we suspect the doubt in turn delays futher revelation.[68] It is a psychological vicious circle as well as a teasing providential irony.

Ṣafwān b. al-Muᶜaṭṭal's Eclipse

Towards the end of the material contained in the account of *The Slander* in Ibn Hishām's *Sīrah* survives a terse revelation related, again, on the authority of ᶜĀᵓishah: 'They asked about Ibn al-Muᶜaṭṭal, and they found him to be impotent, he never approached women, then he died a martyr.' This provides further absolution of ᶜĀᵓishah. But the psychology of this detail is intriguing, and has been canvassed astutely by Denise Spellberg.[69] One is allowed to conjecture that the wounds of the accusation were never properly healed and the matter may never have been forgotten in the fullest sense. Years after the event, it is still ᶜĀᵓishah who tells us that the man was sexually inadequate. But what is the psychology of this revelation? In some sense, the terms of the disclosure are inherently paradoxical – who would or even could testify to such a matter? It is surely, at most, circumstantial conjecture. But when the thought floats about, with ᶜĀᵓishah's figure furtive in mind, one wonders whether the wounds and scars of the scandal had ever truly healed. And one questions why she did not have the presence of mind to avert her gaze and suppress a report about which people could so easily and damningly rejoin, How could you be so certain? Here we should turn our attention to the other victim of this intrigue. The shadow cast upon Ṣafwān by the affair must have been painful to bear: he was falsely accused and, even more intolerably, subjected to the scrutiny that would reveal, publicly, in the end a humiliating flaw in his manhood – in some sense, this is a negation of the integrity of his identity; anagnorisis reveals a half-figure. He is silenced by the text and muted physically as a man. Apart from his *istirjā*ᶜ, which is a form of impersonal, ritualised speech, no words of his are ever transmitted; he is spoken *of*, rendered passive, and never allowed to put his own case to posterity. He is finally then gagged by his death as a martyr – his only recompense will be other-worldly. This detail of Ṣafwān's damaged virility, in the ambiguous chord it strikes, has some affinity with the epilogue to this affair relayed in al-Wāqidī's *Maghāzī*.

Al-Wāqidī's Ambiguous Codicil

Al-Wāqidī's account is substantially the same as that of al-Bukhārī and Ibn Hishām, but there are also some significant departures from the earlier redactions, especially in the wider contextualisation of narrative material. There are some differences, on the one hand, and some enhancements of the original themes, on the other. As a prologue, al-Wāqidī adds to the narrative we are familiar with from al-Zuhrī a short account of how ᶜĀᵓishah lost her necklace on a different occasion. This other episode is preserved in the sources, and seems to have occurred some time after *The Slander*. Coincidentally, it too gave rise to a verse of revelation, in this case the *āyat al-tayammum* (the verse licensing Muslims to perform their ablutions with sand when deprived of water, on a journey, or in analogous situations).[70] Gregor Schoeler has remarked about this episode:

> A chief feature of Waqidi's recension is the bringing together of two separate occasions on each of which ᶜĀᵓishah lost her necklace and thereby leading to a revelation. The loss of her necklace during one Razzia is attributed by Ibn Isḥāq to discrete occasions. Moreover, Ibn Isḥāq has it that the first loss occurred during the raid that led to the scandal and the second led to the revelation of the *tayammum* verse (allowing travelers to do their ablutions with sand). Al-Wāqidī reverses the chronology of events.[71]

(The author adds in a footnote (*loc. cit.*) that Ibn Saᶜd, al-Wāqidī's pupil, followed his teacher in this collocation and ordering of the events – in a terse version of a mere five lines.)[72]

It may be that al-Wāqidī was simply careless in juxtaposing the two similar events. He may not have intended them to be read as constituting events on a single raid, rather he presented the incident placed first in his edition as a sort of thematic foreshadowing of the larger unfolding affair. He introduces the players, and paints the character of their private lives. The material also suggests that a carefee and insouciant spirit was the measure of ᶜĀᵓishah's youthful character in general; such was her disposition and temperament before the intrigue broke out. This appears to be the point of the prologue in al-Wāqidī's editorial scheme: ᶜĀᵓishah had a careless knack of losing necklaces; she was therefore certainly far from scheming to be alone with the wandering straggler, Ṣafwān b. al-Muᶜaṭṭal.

The most intriguing detail in this descriptive prologue is the frolicsome spirit that subsists in the interaction between the Prophet and ᶜĀᵓishah. They race each other playfully once the tension of the occasion has passed, and we are reminded that they had raced in this way before. Their relationship is depicted as having been close and strong, in general. (The importance of contiguous, or near-contiguous materials, as a technique in composition, will be addressed again in consideration of the way al-Wāqidī bookends the episode with an intriguing narrative envoi that is relayed perhaps uniquely in his redaction of the *The Scandal.*)

In general, conjecture and doubt is heightened in al-Wāqidī in the salient use of the verb *ẓanna*. In the advent to the start of the rumour, the verb is employed three times: 'I had *thought* – mistakenly – that even if I stayed absent for a whole month they would not leave until I was in my Howdah'; 'I returned to look for [the necklace] and found it in the place I *thought* I had left it'; 'they loaded up my camels with my canopy *thinking* that I was in it.' These instances stress a subjective category of cognition. It is conjectural thought that is implied in *ẓanna*; one can be correct in one's assumptions but things are really hit-or-miss. The community will think – be forced to countenance the unbearable suspicion – that ᶜĀᵓishah has cuckolded her husband, but it is mistaken, prompted by the malice and perfidy of a few. There is, of course, a difference between *ẓanna* and *ᶜalima* (between thinking and knowing). However, an intriguing detail in the psychology of *The Slander* is that even *ᶜilm* is inflected with doubt in the course of the narrative: the repeated phrases of the kind, 'I only know good of her', are tacitly equivocal in that they delineate the circumscribed (empirical) parameters of an individual's knowledge. When the Prophet repeats this phrase publicly, having heard it privately from the mouth of Usāmah b. Zayd, it suggests desire and scruple rather than certainty; at least, this is the case for the reader of the text of the hadith who can place these two scenes side by side. The Prophet's knowledge is prompted and vicarious, and therefore is not knowledge at all in this instance, but rather a personal desire and a tentative machination of political expediency. One is tempted to label this 'ergative' knowledge: the effort to be sure of what one wants to know.

A theme of blindness informs al-Wāqidī's narrative which renders intriguing the physical atmosphere of the initial encounter between Ṣafwān and ᶜĀᵓishah; it occurred during *ᶜamāyat al-ṣubḥ* (literally, 'the blindness of dawn'). That is, the encounter occurred at the cusp of darkness and light, an atmospheric and cognitive limbo which is sustained until the final revelation of Qurᵓan 24:11ff. It would be needlessly glib to expatiate on this point. But one detail that needs still to be made is that the sole human recognition of identity in this narrative takes place in a dusky crepuscular light. Ṣafwān sees a distant silhouette, approaches it and then recognises ᶜĀᵓishah despite the half-light. He is forced, one imagines, to come right up to her, by which time it is too late to retreat, though it might have been better – and the thought may well have occurred to him – had he never seen her at all! The community at large encountered the rumour in an analogous way.

In the cognitive lexicon of the narrative, al-Wāqidī's version contains a detail which does not quite crystallise in the earlier redactions; it pertains to the description of ᶜĀᵓishah's illness in the days after the inception of the rumour and her anxiety at receiving from the Prophet none of the kindness and concern she was accustomed to. Here is the way ᶜĀᵓishah describes her response to the Prophet's aloofness: *qad ankartu min rasūli llāhi luṭfa-hu bī wa-raḥmata-hu fa-lā aᶜrifu min-hu l-luṭfa lladhī kuntu aᶜrifu ḥīna shtakaytu inna-mā yadkhulu fa-yusallimu fa-yaqūlu kayfa tīkum* ('I did not recognize in the Prophet the usual kindness and concern he showed me whenever I fell ill; [on that occasion] he simply entered the household and asked curtly "How is she?"').[73] We notice in this charged description the verbal doublet *ᶜarafa*/ *ankara*. It is difficult to translate *ankartu* such as to convey its full semantic sweep; one is forced to paraphrase diffusely: 'I failed to recognise, frowned upon, disapproved, considered *munkar*.' To be influenced in one's demeanor by an unfounded rumour is *munkar*.[74] There is an ethical undercurrent to Muḥammad's unusual comportment that feeds on the common ethical antonymy, *maʿrūf* and *munkar* ('the right and the wrong'). It is problematic, to say the least, to ascribe *munkar* to the actions of the Prophet (and it would be easier to do so if the verb used here by ʿĀʾishah were *istankartu*), but we can be confident in positing that there is an ethical dimension to the epistemology of this detail in the narrative as there is throughout. Ignorance is both a literal deficit of knowledge as well as an injurious, deleterious comportment. Knowledge is at the heart of the ironies of the text: when ʿĀʾishah fails to recognise Muḥammad, it is because she does not understand his motives, which in turn is simply a function of her ignorance of the scandal that has seeped through the community like some insidious poison.

In the excerpt of ʿĀʾishah's description of the Prophet above, we included his terse words in asking after his wife ('*kayfa tīkum*'). We have noted already that this is part of the muting of the scandal in the use of a curt telegraphic language. Regarding ʿĀʾishah, there is more to the matter: her name, her very identity (her enhanced status, certainly), has been dismissively diminished with this abrupt and impersonal question; this is a form of *inkār* ('rejection') in a sense. One might conjecture that her name is not given back to her until the vindication afforded by the revelation of Q 24:11ff. Although the scripture mentions no specific name, her name is always attached to this ayah (except in the Shiʿi tradition which prefers a distinct etiology, identifying the Prophet's Coptic concubine, Maryam, as the implied referent of the verse). When the Prophet addresses the crowd in his *khuṭbah* he of course omits any mention of names, referring to those aggrieved by the calumny as members of his *ahl*. This is also to muzzle the affair in some measure, while also reflecting the general decorum of discretion that obtains throughout the *récit*; it is the same propriety that has led to the seclusion of the Prophet's womenfolk. The diminished identity of ʿĀʾishah is engraved further into the narrative when, having defended herself robustly (adducing Surah 12, as discussed), she recoils from arrogating to herself the distinction of being absolved in the Qurʾan itself; she dared only hope that the Prophet might receive some other mantic inspiration – a *ruyʾā*, a vision. There is prescience in this facet of *méconnaissance*.

The final anecdote relayed by al-Wāqidī in a section entitled *Dhikr ᶜĀᵓishah (raḍiya llāhu ᶜan-hā) wa-aṣḥāb al-ifk* ('An account of ᶜĀᵓishah and the perpetrators of the slander'), can be read as a functionally and hermeneutically inserted epilogue. Its links with the main part of *The Slander* beg consideration; it is a short anecdote with its own recognition and revelatory significance. In some sense, it sustains the human ambivalence of the scandal; it gestures at the fact that truth is a divine privilege which a person cannot aspire to, but sometimes she/he should simply avoid situations that cannot be resolved in finite human understanding. (Similar sentiments are conveyed in the Qurᵓan: 'Do not ask, for you may receive an answer you are not ready to cope with.')[75] While it is tacked on at the end as an epilogue, in its chronology it fits squarely within the storyline of the scandal, which is not insignificant given the way ancillary recognitions, across genres and across cultures, often chime in with the main revelation of a text.[76] In most literature, this is achieved proleptically, here the effect is analeptic: it is a choice and tantalisingly ambivalent envoi with something of a sting in the tail. The epilogue contains its own anagnorisis, therefore we can harbour the conjecture, so essential to this study as a whole, that recognition and revelation – even when separated in the sequence of a narrative – are symptoms of each other.

The episode relates events that occurred during the return to Medina in the early stages of the slander. ᶜAbdallāh b. Rawāḥah wished to press on home to Medina from the final encampment ahead of the army while the Prophet still slept. Abū Muḥammad Jābir b. ᶜAbdallāh, ᶜAbdallāh's interlocutor, refused to accompany him, but the latter insisted that he would set off, remarking that this practice had not been proscribed by the nascent religion. So, he returned home to find his house lit up by a lamp and espies a tall figure next to his wife. He presumed (*ẓanna*) this to be a man, fell upon the ground and regretted his rash and hasty homecoming. He was then about to strike them both with his sword, when he thought better to nudge his wife with his foot. She awoke screaming, though half asleep. He said, 'It's me, ᶜAbdallāh – who is this?' She replied that it was Rujaylah:[77] 'We heard that you were coming so I summoned her to dress my hair and she ended up staying over.' He slept and in the morning, still troubled – and no doubt shamed – by the incident, he set out again to meet the Prophet, finding him at Biᵓr Maᵓūnah. The Prophet was riding between Abū Bakr and Bashīr b. Saᶜd; he turned to

Bashīr and said: 'Abū Nu^{c}mān, ^{c}Abdallāh's face would suggest that he regrets (*kariha*) having returned home last night [or: has met with something he disliked upon his return].' ^{c}Abdallāh explained what had happened, upon which the Prophet indited, 'Do not return home to your wives at night!' It is this proscription and prophetic teaching that furnishes the point of the episode.

The episode has its own epilogue, describing in skeletal detail the return from another campaign on which occasion two men ignored the prophetic injunction and returned home at night to see 'what they were loath to see'. This brief codicil exists in two short versions in al-Dārimī's *Muqaddimah*. The second of the two is less equivocal in its ending: on the authority of Sa^{c}īd b. al-Musayyab, who was one of al-Zuhrī's main informants:

> *kāna rasūlu llāhi idhā qadima min safarin nazala l-mu^{c}arrasah thumma qāla lā taṭruqū l-nisā'a laylan fa-kharaja rajulāni mimman sami^{c}a maqālata-hu fa-ṭaraqā ahlay-himā fa-wajada kullu wāḥidin min-humā ma^{c}a mraʾati-hi rajulan*
> (When the Prophet returned from a certain raid he camped at night [before entering Medina] and announced, Do not return home to disturb your women during the night.' But two men among those listening returned home and each one found his wife with another man.)

Is it really plausible that the ambiguous and insinuating effect of ending the episode of *The Slander* with such material escaped the attention of al-Wāqidī? Did he intend there to be a loaded semantic connection with the main narrative? Was this collocation and arrangement a tacit suggestion of the open-endedness of the entire *Slander* narrative on a purely human level? Or was it simply an afterthought, added for the sake of comprehensiveness in recording the events of the fateful night in question? The answer cannot be unequivocal and definitive, but one can conjecture that it might in each case be 'Yes', thereby muddying the waters left so apparently limpid after the revelation of Q 24:11ff.; Al-Wāqidī leaves to posterity interconnected material that is more humanly uncertain than divinely omniscient.

Envoi

We might end simply with a postscript of our own. The two men found with the wives of the returning raiders exhibit behaviour anathema to the chaste and faithful Joseph. Now, ᶜĀʾishah was no Zulaykha (for she never in fact betrayed her husband); but this statement may even be slandering Zulaykha who was, of course, redeemed in *qiṣaṣ* material. According to the apocrypha, when Joseph was eventually married to her, he found her to be a virgin; her honour was figuratively and physically intact and Potiphar, like Ṣafwān b. al-Muᶜaṭṭal, was discovered to have been impotent. These are all then ambivalent themes. On the granular level, the lives of people, prophets and otherwise, hold many discoveries to be made.

Notes

1. David Powers, *Muḥammad is not the Father of any of your Men: The Making of the Last Prophet* (Philadelphia: University of Pennsylvania Press, 2009), esp. ch. 7 *passim*, pp. 132ff.; Powers, *Zayd* (Philadelphia: University of Pennsylvania Press, 2014).
2. Powers, *Muḥammad*, pp. 132ff.
3. This phrase is a Qurʾanic *hapax*. The dominant understanding of the phrase is that it signifies that Muḥammad was the last of God's prophets; it also may originally have carried the sense of authenticity (this can be determined in part by comparison with the use of its Hebrew cognate; the existence of the non-Qurʾanic cognate Arabic phrase *khatam al-nubuwwah* to describe the mark of authentic prophecy between Muḥammad's shoulder blades supports this semantic nuance). These two meanings can (and do) clearly overlap. For a full discussion of this phrase warranting the status of Muḥammad as Seal of the Prophets in every sense, see Uri Rubin's excellent and comprehensive study 'The Seal of the Prophets and the Finality of Prophecy: On the Interpretation of Sūrat al-Aḥzāb (33)', *Zeitschrift der Deutschen Morgenländischen Gesellschaft* 164:1 (2014), pp. 65–96.
4. This charming motif is found in one of the inserted tales of Nizami's *Haft Paykar.*
5. See Powers, *Muḥammad*, pp. 132–3.
6. The idea of authentic prophecy is contained in the phrase *khātam al-nubuwwah* – even if it also came to be (or was always) understood to mean 'the seal of the prophets'.
7. Most readers have access to this in Alfred Guillaume's *The Life of Muhammad: A Translation of Ibn Ishaq's* Sirat Rasul Allah (I have used the Karachi: Oxford University Press, 2010, 23rd reprint). Guillaume's translation and study is based

on the Arabic copy 'which must have reached Ibn Hishām . . . whose text, abbreviated, annotated, and sometimes altered, is the main source of the original work' (*The Life*, p. xvii). For other sources from whom other original material of Ibn Isḥāq can be recovered, see Guilluame, *The Life*, p. xxxi.

8. For a study of the anomalous character of this story in the context of the *Sīrah*, see 'Salmān al-Fārisī' by J. Horovitz in *Der Islam* 12 (1922), pp. 178–80.
9. For further readings relevant as background to the interpretive approach adopted in this chapter, see Adrien Leites, '*Sīra* and the Question of Tradition', in Harald Motzki (ed.), *The Biography of Muḥammad: The Issue of Sources* (Leiden: Brill, 2000); Wim Raven, 'The biography of the Prophet and its scriptural basis', in Stefan Leder (ed.), *Storytelling in the Framework of non-fictional Arabic Literature* (Wiesbaden: Harrassowitz, 1998); invaluable is Jonathan E. Brockopp's collection *The Cambridge Companion to Muḥammad* (Cambridge: Cambridge University Press, 2010), especially the editor's Introduction and 'The Arabian Context of Muḥammad's Life' by Walid A. Saleh.
10. We refer to the Joseph story in the Islamic tradition writ large together with its apocryphal accretions.
11. The strongest case for this is made by A. L. de Prémare in *Joseph et Muhammad. Le Chapitre 12 du Coran* (Aix-en-Provence: Publications de l'Université de Provence, 1989).
12. The following translation is mine. Rendered in italics are elements that can be deemed formulaic within the narrative by dint of verbatim or near-verbatim repetition, in many cases of extended blocks of text. For the Arabic original, see Ibn Hishām, *Al-Sīrah al-nabawiyyah*, ed. Muḥammad Fahmy al-Sirjānī, 4 vols (Cairo: al-Maktabah al-Tawfīqiyyah, 1978), I, pp. 222–38.
13. *Dihqān* or *dehqān*: 'A class of land-owing magnate during the Sassanid and early Islamic period.' See https://www.google.ae/?gfe_rd=cr&ei=lOghVsbYGsLL8gfbiZ34CA&gws_rd=ssl#q=dihqan. See further '*dehqān*' in *Encyclopaedia Iranica*. The title was used well into the Abbasid period, as evinced in the *fārisiyyāt*, the Arabic poems with Persian lexical elements, of Abū Nuwās (d. *c.*813 AD).
14. See Saleh, 'The Arabian Context', p. 30: 'the physical seal of prophecy, a birthmark that Muḥammad is supposed to have had on his body . . . is connected to the Qur'ānic concept of the seal of prophets, a title given to Muḥammad in Q 33:40 [see Chapter 3]. The *Sīra* is thus emphatic about the role of mythology in presenting the significance of Muḥammad.' See also Boaz Soshan's *Popular Culture in Medieval Cairo* (Cambridge: Cambridge University Press, 2002), p. 29: The much maligned popular hagiographer Abū al-Hasan al-Bakrī relates

that 'Ridwān, the Keeper of Paradise, stamps upon the baby [Muḥammad]'s shoulder the special seal of Prophecy (*khatam*).'

15. It is clear that a story such as this serves to authenticate the mission of the prophet. It is not merely for the aesthetics of the account that the prophet wished his companions to hear it. Such is the function of the *Sīrah* in general for posterity.
16. Essentially it involves the planting of a palm grove with the prophet's help, and thus follows through a motif contained earlier in the story – one of the descriptive tokens of recognition being that the prophet foretold by Salmān's last Christian companion would live in a town full of palm groves.
17. There was a time in his early life when it was necessary for the young Muḥammad to conceal the physical sign of his future calling, as we shall read in other anecdotes.
18. 12:88 . . . *wa-taṣaddaq ᶜalaynā inna llāha yajzī l-mutaṣaddiqīn*; 89 *qālū aᵓinnaka la-anta yūsufu* . . .
19. See, for example, the father of the eponymous ᶜAlāᵓ al-Dīn Abū al-Shāmāt.
20. Note Gordon Newby's *The Making of the Last Prophet: A Reconstruction of the Earliest Biography of Muhammad* (Columbia: University of South Carolina Press, 1989) argument about the *Sīrah* in the earliest redaction of Ibn Isḥāq, non-extant as a single *oeuvre* or in a single source, beginning with the biblical prophets.
21. Ibn Hishām, *Sīrah*, I, p. 16ff.
22. Rendering adapted from *The Life of Muhammad*, trans. Guillaume, p. 5. Ibn Hishām, *Sīrah*, I, p. 19.
23. One of the most captivating and richly told stories prophesying Muḥammad's coming features Sayf b. Dhī Yazan himself; it is conveyed in other sources. Sayf foretells Muḥammad's mission to a delegation from Mecca that is headed by the prophet's grandfather, ᶜAbd al-Muṭṭalib. See Julia Bray's 'ᶜAbbasid Myth and the Human Act: Ibn ᶜAbd Rabbih and Others' in Philip F. Kennedy (ed.), *On Fiction and* Adab *in Medieval Arabic Literature* (Wiesbaden: Harrassowitz Verlag, 2006).
24. This brief encounter remains a mysterious recognition – it is a blind motif, but it seems to have a part in setting an ambience of mystical expectation.
25. Translated and adapted from Guillaume, *The Life*, pp. 14–16. For the Arabic, see Ibn Hishām, *Sīrah*, I, pp. 31–3.
26. The story of Faymiyūn is clearly not of Islamic origin but is judged to fit the scheme of Part I of the *Sīrah*. See Gordon D. Newby, 'An Example of Coptic Literary

Influence on Ibn Isḥāq's *Sīrah*', *Journal of Near Eastern Studies* 31 (1972), pp. 22–8. Raven ('The biography', p. 422) observes how Newby 'establishes a parallel between the story about the Nadjrānī Christian ascet (sic) Faymiyūn . . . and a Coptic hagiology about Pachomius. In this story the Prophet does not occur; yet saints' legends may well have contributed to other parts of the *sīra*.' For a broader discussion of the subject, see Garth Fowden, *Empire to Commonwealth: Cosequences of Monotheism in Late Antiquity* (Princeton: Princeton University Press, 1993). Fowden is discussed in Saleh ('The Arabian Context', pp. 24–5): he had 'various cultural overlays in mind when he assessed the significance of the rise of Islam: "The Islamic Empire was implicit in late antiquity, but nothing quite like it had ever been seen before." The same could be said about the life of Muḥammad as it came to be told by Muslims in the *Sīra* . . . His life mirrored the expectations one would find in the biographies of holy men from late antiquity and fashioned them in a uniquely Arabian fashion.'

27. This motif puts one in mind of a similar element in the story of Salmān al-Fārisī and foreshadows accounts of conversion to Islam through captivation by early Meccan ayahs.
28. Rendering adapted from Guillaume's translation (*The Life of Muhammad*). For the Arabic, see Ibn Hishām, *Sīrah*, I, pp. 34–6. This episode has some kinship with the unearthing of Abū Righāl at Madāʾin Ṣāliḥ during the expedition to Tabūk. See Jaroslav Stetkevych, *Muhammad and the Golden Bough* (Bloomington: Indiana University Press, 1996).
29. Ibn Hishām, *Sīrah*, I, p. 60: *inna āyāti rabbinā thāqibāt.*
30. See Guillaume, *The Life of Muhammad*, p. 67; Ibn Hishām, *Sīrah*, I, p. 163.
31. See Guillaume, *The Life of Muhammad*, pp. 67–8; Ibn Hishām, *Sīrah*, I, p. 162.
32. Guillaume, *The Life of Muhammad*, p. 69; Ibn Hishām, *Sīrah*, I, p. 163.
33. This phrase is reminiscent of Q Yusuf 12:21.
34. Adapted from Guillaume, *The Life of Muhammad*, p. 73; Ibn Hishām, *Sīrah*, I, p. 174.
35. Adapted from Guillaume, *The Life of Muhammad*, p. 79; Ibn Hishām, *Sīrah*, I, p. 185.
36. Adapted from Guillaume, *The Life of Muhammad*, pp. 80–1; Ibn Hishām, *Sīrah*, I, pp.187–8.
37. Adapted from Guillaume, *The Life of Muhammad*, p. 81; Ibn Hishām, *Sīrah*, I, p. 188.
38. Ibn Hishām, *Sīrah*, I, p. 189.
39. Guillaume, *The Life of Muhammad*, pp. 86–7; Ibn Hishām, *Sīrah*, I, p. 205.

40. Adapted from Guillaume, *The Life of Muhammad*, p. 90; Ibn Hishām, *Sīrah*, I, p. 211.
41. Adapted from Guillaume, *The Life of Muhammad*, p. 90; Ibn Hishām, *Sīrah*, I, pp. 212–13.
42. Adapted from Guillaume, *The Life of Muhammad*, p. 93; Ibn Hishām, *Sīrah*, I, p. 219.
43. *Wa-ᶜarafnā mā kānū yatawaᶜᶜadūnanā.*
44. *Kafarū bi-hi.*
45. Ibn Hishām, *Sīrah*, I, p. 218.
46. We are not often told the very words that convey the denial of Muḥammad's teaching in this context. The second account is therefore a notable naturalistic rarity. Adapted from Guillaume, *The Life of Muhammad*, p. 93; Ibn Hishām, *Sīrah*, I, p. 219: 'Salama b. Salāma b. Waqsh ([who] was present at Badr) said: We had a Jewish neighbour among B. ᶜAbduᵓl-Ashhal, who came to us one day from his house . . . He spoke of the resurrection, the reckoning, the scales, paradise, and hell. When he spoke of these things to the polytheists who thought that there could be no rising after death, they said to him, "Good gracious man! Do you think that such things could be that men can be raised from the dead to a place where there is a garden and a fire in which they will be recompensed for their deeds?" . . . When they asked for a sign that this would be, he said, pointing with his hand to Mecca and the Yaman, "A prophet will be sent from the direction of this land." . . . and by God, a night and a day did not pass before God sent Muḥammad his apostle and he was living among us. We believed in him, but he denied him in his wickedness and envy, when we asked, "Aren't you the man who said these things?" he said, "Certainly, but this is not the one."'
47. Adapted from Guillaume, *The Life of Muhammad*, pp. 103–4; Ibn Hishām, *Sīrah*, I, p. 239.
48. The following detail within brackets is relayed in al-Ṭabarī but does not survive in Ibn Hishām who likely edited out materials which he was too uncomfortable with.
49. Guillaume, *The Life of Muhammad*, pp. 105–6; Ibn Hishām, *Sīrah*, I, pp. 242–6.
50. See James L. Kugel's excellent discussion of this psychology and epistemology during the encounter between prophets and angels in *The God of Old*, ch. 2, 'The Moments of Confusion', pp. 5–36.
51. Adapted from Guillaume, *The Life of Muhammad*, p. 107; Ibn Hishām, *Sīrah*, I, p. 247.
52. This relates to the prescriptive heart of the surah: the changing of the *Qiblah* and

its implications for *ṣalāt* and the greater onus now on the conquest of Mecca. For an Arabic commentary on much of the narrative background and content of Q 2 (al-Baqarah), see especially Ibn Hishām, *Sīrah*, II, pp. 123–31 (i.e. on the reponse of the Jews to Muḥammad's teaching in the early Medinese period, and in particular the changing of the *Qiblah* – p. 131).

53. On the significance of the *maghāzī* ('raids or expeditions') as the original focus and framework of the biographies of Muḥammad, see Saleh ('The Arabian Context', p. 27): 'The work of Ibn Isḥāq grew out of an already active literary tradition that was attempting to record the life of Muḥammad. The heroic Muḥammad was the first to be celebrated, and all evidence points to the fact that early Muslims kept the memory of his deeds as a military leader and as the head of his community in Medina. His exploits were recorded in what we call *maghāzī* literature.' (See also J. M. B. Jones, 'The Chronology of the Maghāzī – A Textual Survey', *Bulletin of the School of Oriental and African Studies* 19:2 (1957), pp. 240–80; quoted in Saleh, 'The Arabian Context'.)
54. The literature describing, largely anecdotally, the causes of revelation, i.e. the background and etiology of verses and clusters of verses in the Qurʾan.
55. Abū al-Ḥasan ʿAlī ibn Aḥmad al-Wāḥidī, *Asbāb al-nuzūl* (Beirut: ʿĀlam al-Kutub, n.d.).
56. We should be reminded that the expanded predicates and applicability of Aristotelian 'discovery' were explored especially by the Italian renaissance commentators; see, for example, Terence Cave, *Recognitions: A Study in Poetics* (Oxford: Clarendon Press, 1988), p. 64, on Ludovico Castelvetro: 'If anagnorisis may be extended to include the discovery of an occulted fact without revelation of identity, then clearly the range of plots that can lay claim to the prestige of a recognition scene is immeasurably widened. Anagnorisis would seem, indeed, to become virtually coterminous with peripeteia, since peripeteia always implies the epiphany of some form of knowledge previously withheld from characters or spectators.'
57. The aesthetics of the narrative – its qualities in conveying the important subject it treats – is broached by the hadith collector and classifier Ibn Shihāb al-Zuhrī (d. 741 or 742 AD) in a brief initial gloss on his method in assembling the narrative from four sources: 'Al-Zuhrī said, "Each of them told me a part of what she [ʿĀʾishah] had narrated; some of this material is more complete than others and sounder as a story (*athbatu la-hu qtiṣāṣan*); I have included in [my] account what I have received from each [authority] as told to him by ʿĀʾishah; their anecdotes support each other mutually"' (Guillaume, *The Life of Muhammad*, p. 494; Ibn

Hishām, *Sīrah*, III, p. 211). Al-Zuhrī has put together a core narrative that is the best of all possible versions – among hadith this is indeed *aḥsan al-qaṣaṣ*.

58. The synopsis which follows is essentially a translation of Gregor Schoeler's excellent, clear and judicious analytical breakdown of the main narrative (collated by al-Zuhrī) into sixteen main themes or motifs (see Schoeler, *Charakter und Authentie der muslimischen Überlieferung über das Leben Mohammeds* (Berlin: W. de Gruyter, 1996)); they form the core of the fullest versions of the Hadith in the *sunan* as well as those of both Ibn Isḥāq/Ibn Hishām and al-Wāqidī, though the latter two change the order of certain elements and add details and passages that are missing from al-Zuhrī's consolidated account. Some of these addenda will be discussed where relevant below in consideration of both Ibn Isḥāq and al-Wāqidī, according to our own programme of analysis. An excellent modern rendering into English of *The Slander* can be had in *The Expeditions: An Early Biography of Muhammad* (Library of Arabic Literature) by Maᶜmar ibn Rāshid, trans. and ed. Sean Anthony (New York: New York University Press, 2014) [paperback, English only edition published in 2015].
59. A reading of Natalie Zemon Davis' *The Return of Martin Guerre* (Cambridge, MA: Harvard University Press, 1983) offers some insight into the way a community reacts psychologically after the revelation of truth about a scandalous affair that has divided it. Anagnorisis, when it is final and conclusive (as it is in the tragic demise of Bernard de Tilh), immediately tinctures (even stains) the text – or the lives of players in a narrative – analeptically: all the players realise that they have been living a lie, both actively and passively sustaining a deceit. The *Ḥadīth al-Ifk* does not ponder these matters in its epilogue but the effects on the collective psychology of the community must nevertheless be considered to be there.
60. There are a number of rhetorically significant repetitions in this text, none more noticeable than the Prophet's repetition publicly of words of assurance made to him in private. The repeated references to ᶜĀᵓishah's toiletry – the most exclusively physical of bodily functions – is ironically at the heart of an affair that will issue in revelation.
61. Not every version of the affair achieves this effect; the version in al-Bukhārī's *Ṣaḥīḥ*, related on the authority of Hishām b. ᶜUrwah, to give but one example; this is quite significantly truncated, omitting the very dramatic initial scene of how the necklace was lost and the rescue by Ṣafwān b. al-Muᶜaṭṭal (it either assumes knowledge of the story, or omits it for the sake of decorum).
62. It is also, one perceives, the hint of a deterministic view of the events of the *récit*.

63. Abū l-Hudhayl Ḥuṣayn b. ᶜAbd al-Raḥmān al-Sulamī, one of the *ṣughrā min al-tābiᶜīn*, lived in Kufa and died 136 AH.
64. In al-Bukhārī, *Ṣaḥīḥ*: *al-Maghāzī*, no. 4143, p. 841.
65. For a complementary view of the function of intertextuality in this narrative, see Ashley Manjarrez Walker and Michael Sells, 'The Wiles of Women and Performative Intertextuality: ᶜĀᵓisha, the Hadith of the Slander, and the Sura of Yusuf', *Journal of Arabic Literature* 31 (1999). It is the issue of *kayd*, and its full implications for *The Slander*, that is thoroughly and persuasively explored in this article. The greatest coalescence of perspectives between this article and the present study lies in the identification of *ᶜuṣbah* as an 'intertextual link' between Surah 12 and Qurᵓan 24:11 (pp. 61–2).
66. For example, in the story of the conversion of Salmān al-Fārisī, which has an important role in the *Sīrah* – see above. The use of Surah 12 in this hadith puts one in mind of the way it is evoked on another occasion in the life of Muḥammad (cf. de Prémare, *Joseph*, p. 5): 'Al-Wâqidî, l'auteur du *Livre des expéditions militaires* du prophète de l'islam nous raconte que Muhammad, après avoir été en butte à l'opposition de ses compatriotes mekkois, entra finalement en vainqueur à la Mekke. Il effectua alors une longue station au Sanctuaire de la Kaaba et en acceptant les rites traditionels; puis il ressortit et, s'adressait à ses frères vaincus, il proclama: "Je dis comme a dit mon frère Joseph: Pas de reproche à vous faire aujourd'hui: Allâh vous pardonne, car il est, par excellence, le miséricordieux."'
67. The character of the narrative in *Ḥadīth al-Ifk* in fact illustrates the observations of a sixteenth-century Italian commentator on *The Poetics*, Robortello (Cave, *Recognitions*, p. 77): 'anagnorisis implies . . . a drawing-out of the movement from *agnoia* [or ignorance] to full knowledge, and hence of course a mediation between the two states.' This is qualified in further comments: 'The reversal, when it occurs, . . . does not rest on a crude binary principle. *Recognition pervades as it were the whole structure of the plot; it is the paradigm of poetic epistemology*.' This may work in two directions, for recognition – as we have had occasion to observe – normally sheds retrospective light on a text.
68. The phrase *istalbatha l-waḥy* ('revelation was delayed') is reworked effectively later in the narrative in the words *wa-qad makatha shahran lā yūḥā ilay-hi fī shaᵓnī shayᵓun* ('he spent a whole month without anything being revealed to him about me').
69. See 'The Accusation of Adultery and Communal Debate', in Denise Spellberg, *Politics, Gender and the Islamic Past* (New York: Columbia University Press,

1996). For a further discussion of this episode, see also Barbara Stowasser, *Women in the Qurʾān, Traditions, and Interpretation* (New York: Oxford University Press, 1994), pp. 94–5.

70. Qurʾan 4:43; 5:6.

71. Schoeler, *Charakter*, p. 137: 'Es gilt vor allem aber auch für ein Hauptcharakteristikum der –Wāqidī-rezension: die Verknüpfung zweier verscheidener Ereignisse miteinander, bei welchen ᶜĀʾisha ihre Halskette verlor (und damit Anlass zu einer Offenbarung gab) . . . er . . . legt das zweimalige Verlieren der Haskette auf ein und dieselbe Razzia, während in der Tradition nach Ibn Isḥāq ausdrücklich von zwei verschiedenen Razzien die rede ist. Ausserdem hätte nach Ibn Isḥāq zuerst der Skandal und dann das die *tayammum*-Offenbarung hervorrufende Ereignis stattgefunden, während bei al-Wāqidī die Reihenfolge der Episoden umgekehrt ist.'

72. Ibid, p. 137: 'Ibn Saᶜd, al-Wāqidī's Schüler, der in seiner sehr kurzen Behandlung der Razzia gegen die Banū l-Muṣṭaliq eine ganz knappe Zusammenfassung (5 Zeilen!) des Wāqidī'sschen Berichtes gibt (*Ṭabaqāt* 2/1/46f.), ist seinem Lehrer hierin gefolgt, und weitere haben sich ihm angeschlossen; s. *Fatḥ* 2/250ff. Dass ein zweimaligeṣ Verlieren der Halskette bei einer Razzia historisch – milde ausgedrückt – unwarscheinlich ist, haben schon kritische Köpfe unter den einheimischen Ḥadīt-Gelehrten bemerkt; vgl Ibn Ḥagar in *Fatḥ* 2/250.'

73. The version in Ibn Isḥāq describes her reaction to the Prophet's uncharacteristic lack of tenderness towards her during her illness, thus: *ankartu dhālika* ('I found that strange, unusual and unbecoming'; the verb is used twice in three lines); compare this with the words in al-Bukhārī: *lā arā mina l-nabī l-luṭfa lladhī kuntu arā* ('I did not see from the Prophet the kindness I was used to'). Al-Wāqidī is perhaps the most interesting due to a combination of roots that allow us to discuss the ethical doublet, *maᶜrūf* and *munkar*.

74. *Lā aᶜrifu*, we should notice, imparts the same meaning as *ankartu*, viz. 'I [did] not recognise'.

75. Cf. Qurʾan 5 al-Māʾidah 101: *yā ayyu-hā lladhīna āmanū lā tasʾalū ᶜan ashyāʾa in tubda la-kum tasuʾ-kum* ('O Believers! Do not ask about things which will harm you when they are disclosed to you').

76. This is part of the effect of synecdoche and metonymy relevant to much of the material in this volume.

77. This may be her name – in any case it casts an ironic shadow on ᶜAbdallah's impetuous assumption that this was a man, a *rajul*.

3

Joseph and his Avatars

Given the importance of Surah 12 as the paragon of all storytelling in the Qurʾan, it should not surprise us to find refractions and transfigurations of the story in postdating religious and literary narratives. The texts examined in this chapter all borrow themes, rework structures and seek the cognitive reassurance of anagnorisis from the scriptural epitome and its apocryphal accretions. Each of the works – which range, in distinctive styles, from the mystical epic *Conference of the Birds*[1] to the popular Arabian Nights' *Romance of Ghānim b. Ayyūb*[2] – features recognition and discovery either as a central theme or as an element more essentially contingent upon defining features of the generic cast in which the given story is fashioned.[3]

These kinds of rewritings have been studied widely in the Christian and Jewish traditions. Such poignant samples as we find, in Friedrich Klopstock's (d. 1803 AD) *Der Messias*, to name but one example,[4] exist also in the Arabic, and more broadly the Islamic, corpus. (Turkish and Persian romances are included below showing how Islamic materials work across a cultural palette of highly cognate texts.) Evocations of the Joseph story in narratives of recognition that we will examine below are of two kinds: (1) direct citation or reference (clear outcrops of textual influence, which can simultaneously operate as hidden seams); and (2) the more delicate, recondite and even sublimated allusions which can be woven into the entire structure of a text in a variety of ways.[5] In the latter case we are reminded of remarks about the influence of the *Arabian Nights* on Coleridge: '[T]o attempt to trace the prints of the *Arabian Nights* . . . in "The Rime of the Ancient Mariner," and "Christabel," and "Kubla Khan," were like seeking the sun and the rain of vanished yesterdays in the limbs and foliage of the oak. But the rain and sun are there.'[6]

Comparison at a glance between the two versions of the full Joseph story in Genesis and the Qurʾan evinces a glaring omission in the latter. No account of the imbroglio between Judah and Tamar (Genesis 38) exists in the Qurʾan nor, apparently, in the Islamic tradition at large. This type of quasi-romance, tainted by the spectre of sexual indelicacy, is not unheard of in that tradition (indeed *The Slander* has certain elements in common with it). However, Judah is absent by name from Surah 12, hence part of the ethical function of Genesis 38 – to show Judah's incipient moral transfiguration: remorse for his sin realised by means of the tokens of identity Tamar shows him – is superfluous; and for obvious reasons, concerning distinct religious genealogies, the Qurʾan does not need to show the cleansing of sins and restoration of the moral qualities of the patriarchal ancestor of King David, Judah's lineal descendant. Nonetheless, in so far as Genesis 38 establishes the dynamic of anagnorisis and shores up the importance of the theme in the fuller narrative of Genesis 37–50, it is germane to observe how the Joseph story, in another cultural context – to wit, in its full Islamic apocryphal amplifications – serves to enunciate certain nuances of the same, or a similar, dynamic in other Islamic narratives of discovery.[7] A wide-ranging survey of elements of Joseph in Islamic – not exclusively Arabic – materials, provides insight into one of the most notable intertextual clusters in Arabic and related literature.

The following close readings of the selected texts explore some reincarnations of Joseph in a diverse body of writings, which are utterly oblivious to generic boundaries. The stories vary immensely in style and sophistication and appear in practically all genres of writing. I have chosen not to arrange them in any obvious order, for the proliferation of anagnorisis in narrative has made it impossible to give a full survey of or exhaust its manifestations even in the Arabic narrative tradition let alone the far more capacious body of Islamic literatures, in all languages. Equally, it is next to impossible to sum up in a nutshell the ways in which anagnorisis functions in the production of meaning. We have seen in the preceding chapters three examples of the workings of anagnorisis in crystallising what knowledge means and how it informs the Islamic faith and worldview in the Qurʾan, in articulating prophecy in Islamic terms and how Muḥammad embodies this prophecy in his person and conduct in the Prophetic Tradition. I now move to Arabic stories, particularly narratives of disclosure, which grapple with faith-based ethics of living, and demonstrate the abiding presence of the Qurʾan and Prophetic Tradition in Arabic writings. These examples, I hope, will through the avatars of Joseph give a glimpse of the moral universe of Arabic stories. The fragments in the examples, like stones in a mosaic, come to a sharper focus in the last example, a story from the *Arabian Nights*, to yield a fuller view of the moral canvas of Arabic storytelling.

Jacob's Punishment and a Mother's Joy

Nāṣir al-Dīn al-Rabzūghī's (*fl.* thirteenth–fourteenth centuries) Turkish redaction of the *Qiṣaṣ al-Anbiyāʾ* ('Tales of the Prophets'), like all materials of this ilk, fills in much of the background to the elliptical Qurʾanic narrative of the Joseph story.[8] The collection is largely naive in its register but remarkably canny in its collocation of themes. As a whole the work is methodical and fashions a much more detailed narrative than the succinct epitome that subsists in Surah 12. Withal, many recognition scenes drawn from the Islamic apocryphal tradition, writ large, complement those that are in the original text of the Qurʾan; we have already encountered some of these in Chapter 1. For instance, concerning Q 12:79, 'for then we would be unjust', al-Rabzūghī recounts the reactions of Judah when Joseph refuses to release Benjamin (p. 248):

> When they had lost hope of convincing Joseph, Judah said: 'Oh brothers, together with the caravan, are you not a match for this army? I am a match for the king. Or if you prefer, you attack the king and seize him, and I will be a match for the rest of the army.' Joseph knew how strong and fierce his brothers were. When they became angry, their hair stood on end and came forth through their clothes. They would not grow calm until they had destroyed a country. Otherwise their anger would only subside if a person who was like themselves a descendant from the prophet Jacob rubbed their backs with his hand. Judah told his brothers: 'Stand aside from me; just let me attack them.' When Joseph saw that Judah was angry, he told his young son: 'Go and rub the back of that man with your hand.' As soon as the boy went and did this, Judah's anger subsided. Judah remarked to his brothers: 'There is a descendant of the prophet Jacob in the land of Egypt.'

Judah's intuition begins to foreshadow the recognition scenes that resolve the Qurʾanic narrative. Other, similar, moments of epiphany work a comparable function of adumbration. But the most striking in this redaction is the apocryphal story told just prior to the moment when Jacob recognises the scent of Joseph (Q 12:94), when it dawns on him that his son is alive in Egypt. The positioning of this apocryphal story is purposeful and quite emblematic within the scheme of reading we are concerned with in this chapter. The story is a rare curio in *qiṣaṣ* collections. The episode begins with a question and answer:

> Question: Jacob and Joseph were both prophets. What was the reason for this separation of eighty [*sic*] years? Answer: When Joseph was small, the prophet Jacob had a female slave named Mubashshira. That slave had a son named Bashīr. One day, while he was playing with Joseph, he slapped Joseph in the face. Joseph went crying to his father. Jacob swore to sell Bashīr. In the end he did take him from his mother and sell him. His mother Mubashshira stayed behind, weeping. The Lord, He is exalted, ordained: 'Oh Jacob, since you separated Bashīr from his mother and sold him, I, for my part, will separate Joseph from you and sell him. The whole world must learn that one must not separate the nail from the flesh.'
>
> It has been related: Mubashshira had lost her sight crying over her son Bashīr; Jacob lost his sight too. Mubashshira went before the prophet Jacob, weeping. Jacob prayed: 'My God, will Mubashshira be reunited with her son? Will I be reunited with my son?' God addressed him: 'Oh Jacob, until I have reunited Mubashshira with her son, My providence will not reunite you with Joseph.' The prophet Jacob told Mubashshira this good news. Mubashshira became hopeful. She made a shelter on the road to Canaan and sat down there.
>
> Her son Bashīr was a slave in Egypt. When he heard the news about Joseph, he mounted a she-camel and set out in order to tell Jacob the happy news. Bashīr went in front and Reuben after him. When Bashīr arrived in Canaan, he saw the shelter where his mother was sitting and asked her for water. His mother gave him water. She asked: 'Where have you come from and where are you going?' Bashīr said: 'I've come from Egypt and I'm going to Canaan. I'm going to tell the prophet Jacob the happy news about his son Joseph.' His mother said: 'You are lying.' Bashīr said: 'Old woman, what do you know about me that you call me a liar?' His mother said: 'My son has

> been separate from me. In reply to the prophet Jacob's prayer the Lord, *He is exalted*, has informed us: "Until I have reunited Mubashshira's son with his mother, I shall not reunite Joseph with you." I have received no good news about my son; how can Jacob receive good news about Joseph?' Bashīr replied: 'What is your name?' His mother said: 'Mubashshira.' 'What is your son's name?' She said: 'Bashīr.' When he heard this, he threw himself from the camel and fell at his mother's feet, saying: 'Behold, I am your son!' Mubashshira embraced her son and she recovered her sight.[9]

This highly typological anecdote supports the argument about the role of synecdoche in the kind of literature we are reading. Just as elements of the Joseph story may be evoked and cited to enrich and give depth of scriptural meaning to an overarching narrative of disclosure, so the anagnorisis of Mubashshirah and Bashīr works to similar effect in this *qiṣaṣ* redaction of the Joseph narrative itself. It signals to us also that recognition of this kind is part of the ethical dynamic of the story. It is remarkable that God states, 'My providence . . .', thus underscoring the point that these are fundamentally providential stories: recognition scenes often throw attendant moral and broadly religious issues into sharp relief.[10]

The Scent of Joseph

An ethical epistemology, developed and distended across a relatively long anecdote, by the standards of *adab*, exists in the story of the troubled conversion to Islam of the Ghassanid Phylarch, Jabalah ibn al-Ayham (*fl.* early seventh century AD). The account discussed here is taken from Ibn ᶜAbd Rabbih's *Al-ᶜIqd al-Farīd*. During the caliphate of ᶜUmar ibn al-Khaṭṭāb, he made known his intention to convert to Islam, but upon arrival in Medina he was disappointed that the new religion only diminished the worldly status that he had enjoyed in the *Jāhiliyyah*, the 'Age of Ignorance'. He, therefore, quit Medina as an apostate and ensconced himself in Constantinople at the court of Heraclius (d. 641 AD). There he was visited by an envoy from the caliph ᶜUmar who found him decked out in ostentatious splendour, with gold dust sprinkled on his greying beard. For the austere and sanctimonious Muslim envoy, this vision was too ungodly for comfort, hence his reaction upon seeing Jabalah: 'I looked at him but could not recognize him/I disapproved of him' (in Arabic, *fa-naẓartu ilay-hi fa-ankartu-hu*). The envoy returned to Medina and conveyed to ᶜUmar Jabalah's terms for reacceptance of Islam. He also conveyed gifts from Jabalah to the poet Ḥassān ibn Thābit who had been his court poet in the *Jāhiliyyah*. Ḥassān was now a blind old man, but he recognised the scent of Jabalah upon the envoy's person. 'I smell the scent of the people of Jafnah upon you.' These words in Arabic are highly charged and significant, borrowed as they are from the Qurᵓanic phrase which the blind Jacob utters when he detects that his son Joseph still lives – words that precede the restoration of his sight when the shirt of his lost son is cast upon his face in Surah 12:96. In the Qurᵓan, the episode is part of the movement of recognition in the final unfolding stages of the narrative (as discussed in Chapter 1). Ḥassān's eloquently charged locution, by carrying the force of the intertextual link, is a significant gesture of recognition. The old poet's sight is not restored, to be sure, but the statement itself is an act of numinous vision, and it is rendered in contrast to the ignorance of Jabalah who has been figuratively blinded – until it is too late – by his overweening sense of worldly status. It is in this light that we interpret the envoy's earlier words of denial – his inability to recognise, that is, accept Jabalah (*naẓartu ilay-hi fa-ankartu-hu*). Jabalah's final change of attitude comes too late, for he dies before the envoy can reach him again to bring him back into the Islamic fold.[11] The epistemology of the story, with its various recognitions and equivocations, is brimful of ethical significance. It is both about recognition and recognition-that-comes-too-late. There is, indeed, a sorry humanistic contrast between this story and Jacob's happy epiphany in Surah 12.

The Writing on the Wall

The most unique quasi-narrative to shed light on our subject is inscribed on the inner courtyard frieze of *Madrasat al-Firdaws* in Aleppo. The *Firdaws* is an Ayyubid building[12] described in detail by Yasser Tabbaa in *Constructions of Power and Piety in Medieval Aleppo*.[13]

> In sheer length, these inscriptions stand out in Ayyubid architecture, whose inscriptions rarely exceed a purely functional plaque above the entrance. They are, furthermore, written in legible and very elegant script: a large, slightly attenuated *thuluth* that represents the zenith of monumental

> cursive calligraphy. Their legibility is further enhanced by their relatively low placement – a little more than four meters above ground level in the courtyard and about 2.5 meters above ground level around the elevated iwan. *These inscriptions were meant to be read.* [p. 171; emphasis added]

Here is a full account of the frieze:

> [p. 173] The religious inscription [in the inner courtyard] is one of the most outstanding in all Islamic architecture . . . [p. 174] The inscription is important and uncommon enough to require a full translation:
>
> Praised be those people who when night falls you hear from them a groan of fear and when morning comes you witness a change of mood:
>
> When night falls they resist [sleep]
> It leaves them while still prostrate
> Longing has dispelled their sleepiness, so they rose
> Whilst the righteous people of the world are asleep
>
> Their bodies withstand worship and their feet support them in their night vigil. Their voices and pleas are not in vain as they pass the night kneeling and prostrating. They are called by the caller and entertained by the cantor:
>
> O men of the night exert yourselves
> For so many voices are not answered
> Only the serious and persevering
> Will stay up the whole night
>
> Even if they wanted to sleep for one hour, they are disturbed by longing for Him [God]; so they arise attracted by love and ardor for Him, and they roam. The aspirant of the Divine Presence (*murīd al-ḥaḍrah*) chants for them and sends them off; he impels them to pray lovingly and insists:
>
> Encourage your mounts and strive
> If you have any passion in your heart
> Time has come to bring out the hidden
> And expose the texts: be prepared!
>
> Their beds beckon them and their pillows regret their absence. Sleep is distant from their eyes and rest has departed from their sides. Night for

> them is the most precious time, and their companion during their night vigil herds the stars:
>
> I was visited by Your Apparition,
> And when it wanted to depart I held on
> How I wish my night were eternal.
> And I never saw the morning star
>
> They shunned sleep during the dark; and were graced by long stay. They spoke to their Lord with the sweetest words; and forgot their suffering by the proximity of the Knowing King. If they stayed away from Him one hour during the night, they would dissolve; and if they departed from Him one instant, they would not be well. They continue their vigil till dawn and anticipate the reward of their alertness and wakefulness. We have heard that God, the Blessed and the Supreme, manifests Himself for those who love Him. He says: 'Who am I?' they answer 'You are God (*anta Allāh*); You are our Sustainer *(māliku rizqinā)*.' And He tells them, 'You are my beloved ones; you are the people of my care and solicitude (*antum ahlu wilāyatī wa*ᶜ*ināyatī*). This is my face; contemplate it. This is My speech; hear it. This is My cup; drink it. {And their Lord offered them a pure drink}' (Qur᾿an LXXVI, 21). When they drink it they feel healthy and ecstatic; when filled with ecstasy, they stand up; having stood up, they roam about [perhaps whirl]; having roamed, they are frenzied. This frenzy brings them to life. When the Ṣabā wind carried the scent of Yūsuf's shirt, only Yaᶜqūb could decipher its secret. It was not known by the Canaanites and whoever came with them nor by Yehuda, and he was the carrier.

In astonishing detail, the mural inscription of the *Firdaws Madrasah* describes the mystical process – and the personal epiphanies – of its devotees. Ḍayf Khātūn, the patroness of the institution, may have been influenced by, and instrumental in reviving, an *ishrāqī* approach to mystical rites four decades after the execution of the eponymous founder of the illuminationist school, Suhrawardī Maqtūl (d. 1191). Tabbaa suggests that the text

> refers to the night vigils of Ramaḍān. It is well known that the month of Ramaḍān was a time of heightened piety and awareness of proximity to God, for both lay Muslims and the mystic. Many of the faithful would

> gather in the mosque after *Ifṭār* – as they still do today – to perform the special prayer of *Tarawīḥ*, whose length and rhythms may in fact have influenced Sufi practice. [p. 176]

Whatever the case may be, it is clear that in the account of the Sufi progress charged elements of the Joseph story – Jacob sensing the scent of Joseph, regaining his sight having been blinded by sorrow, and seeing the face of God in the providential act – resolve in moments of measured textual beauty the highly personal movement towards privileged mystical knowledge and recognition[14] which the Sufis of this *madrasah* both practiced and celebrated.[15]

The Fugitive: Ibrāhīm b. al-Mahdī's Deliverance

In his anthology *Majānī al-adab* ('A Harvest of *Adab*') (4:236) the Jesuit scholar Luwīs Cheikho (d. 1927) relays a story of which we find traces in a number of medieval sources.[16] Al-Maʾmūn entered Rayy in pursuit of his uncle Ibrāhīm b. al-Mahdī who had set himself up as alternative caliph in 818 AD. Ibrāhīm fled into the backstreets in disguise and ended up taking refuge in the house of a cupper (*ḥajjām*). The latter was a humble man who supposed that Ibrāhīm must have found his profession distasteful. Once Ibrāhīm had eaten his dinner, the cupper invited his guest to share a draught of wine; he then requested Ibrāhīm, who was a glorious musician, to sing:

> 'Sir, I do not have the status to ask you to sing, but your sense of decency will urge you to oblige me; if you see fit to honor a slave it would be most appreciated!'
> Ibrāhīm asked, 'But how do you know that I can sing well?'
> He explained, 'Dear Lord! You're too famous to ask such a question – you are Ibrāhīm b. al-Mahdī, our former caliph, for whose capture al-Maʾmūn is offering a thousand dirhams.'
> Ibrāhīm then continued his story: When he said this I began to hold him in high esteem and was certain that he would behave with integrity towards me; so I took the lute, tuned it and sang – with thoughts of my family and son passing through my mind, feeling the bite of separation from them:
>
> > Perhaps the One who provided Joseph's family with sustenance
> > And gave him strength while he languished in prison

> May answer our prayer and bring our kinfolk together – God is the Lord of the Worlds and All Powerful![17]

It appears, initially, that the recognition of Ibrāhīm by his host, the cupper, evokes the Joseph story and the series of recognitions by which it is characterised. At this level, the evocation may be subliminal. The cupper then asks modestly to sing in his turn. He takes the lute and recites a song of the long toils of night for those separated from their loved ones. The third line is noteworthy for use of the verb *yastabshirūn*: 'When the harmful night approaches those suffering passion despair; yet others announce *good fortune* when it comes.' The root *b-sh-r* ('good news') is associated with Joseph in the Qur'an, as we have seen, in the form *Yā Bushrā!* – the call of the Midianite forager which is essentially a proleptic cry announcing the blessings that Joseph will bring to all associated with him.

Ibrāhīm, sensitive to the burden of hospitality he imposes on his host, determines to leave and tries to pay the cupper for his efforts. But the cupper refuses all payment and insists that Ibrāhīm stay on for a while, 'Until God provides you with deliverance!' But Ibrāhīm eventually leaves in disguise and, while crossing a bridge, is recognised by one of al-Ma'mūn's soldiers who had served him previously. Ibrāhīm pushes the man into the river, makes his escape, and takes refuge in a nearby house. There he is given cover by the woman of the premises. The soldier shows up and explains what he is looking for. She takes care of the soldier's wounds but keeps silent about Ibrāhīm's presence in her house. She simply says to Ibrāhīm, once the soldier has left, 'I think you are the man in his story!'

Ibrāhīm takes his leave again and this time comes upon one of his former servant women (*mawlāt*). She takes him in and disappears to the market place (to buy provisions, or so he thinks) but she returns with a retinue of al-Ma'mūn's soldiers. She has betrayed her former master.

Brought before al-Ma'mūn, Ibrāhīm admits his guilt and states that the caliph has every right to punish him for his treachery, though forgiveness, he stresses, is also in the sovereign's gift. When al-Ma'mūn consults his advisors, they all reply that Ibrāhīm should be punished. All but one. For Aḥmad b. Abī Khālid advises, 'If you kill him, you will be like all others who exert that right. If you spare him, you will be unique.' The words persuade al-Ma'mūn, who speaks to Ibrāhīm – his uncle – these loaded words, '*lā tathrība ᶜalayka l-yawm*' ('No blame attaches to you today').[18] These are the very words, though here addressed grammatically to a single person, that Joseph addresses to his brothers in Egypt after he has revealed his identity to them. They are the words that enable the family's reconciliation. Thus the truth of the blessing contained in the root *b-sh-r* has come to pass, and one can recognise these words as resolving the earlier mention in the story by the cupper of the plight of Joseph's family. It is interesting, relatedly, to note that al-Maᵓmūn rewards the generous and selfless acts of both the cupper and the woman who protected Ibrāhīm from the soldier who trailed him. The recognition built into this story, borrowing the evocations of the Joseph narrative, shows the concept shading into the deep ethical and cognitive semantics of *maᶜrūf*.

Borrowing the Qurᵓanic Language of Recognition

In *Quṭb al-Surūr fī Awṣāf al-Khumūr* ('The Pinnacle of Delights in the Description of Wines') Al-Raqīq al-Nadīm tells a version of a story also contained in al-Iṣfahānī's *Kitāb al-Aghānī* about the famous musician Maᶜbad, whom we will encounter further in Chapter 4.

> Abū al-Faraj al-Isfahānī said:[19] Yūnus al-Kātib related that Maᶜbad had taught a servant girl called Ẓabyah who belonged to a family of Medina. He made great efforts to educate her until she became a skilled songstress. An Iraqi man bought her from her family, took her to Basra and became passionately fond of her. She instructed several of his singing girls in song then died in his household. Due to his great fondness for her and the intense sorrow he suffered he became obsessed with Maᶜbad and inquired after him constantly until word of this search reached Maᶜbad himself. The latter was told that the man was a gentleman of some means and so he traveled to find him in the hope of serving his own interests. When he arrived in Basra he discovered that the man had just left for Ahwaz. Maᶜbad hastened to follow him, soon catching up with the boat on which the man was traveling. The man asked him, 'Where are you headed?' Maᶜbad replied, 'Ahwaz.' He asked, 'What do you do?' he replied, 'I sing and was hoping to fall into the company of singing girls and their owners.' When the man heard this he invited him on board and received him generously, preparing a special rug

for him; neither man knew who the other was. They ate and drank. The man had brought with him the servant women whom Ẓabyah had trained. He ordered them to sing. One of them sang the poem by al-Nābighah al-Dhubyānī beginning

Suᶜād has gone, the ropes that bound us together severed . . .

to a tune by Maᶜbad himself, but she did not perform it well. So he said to her, 'There are some flaws in your singing.' The man responded to him, 'Are you so well trained in music that you can perceive faults in such singing?! Mind your place!' So he kept quiet. She carried on singing several songs until she made a complete hash of one; when Maᶜbad pointed this out the man said to him, 'Easy now, you impertinent man!' So he kept his peace again until she had stopped singing. Then Maᶜbad himself was moved to sing the first tune. When he finished the servant women all shouted, 'Beautifully done, by God! Sing it for us again!' He declined then sang the second tune at which the women said to their master, 'This must be the finest singer alive; ask him to repeat this for us all just once more so that we can learn it from him. We'll never come across anyone equal to him.' He replied, 'We were rude to him just now and you heard his reply. I dare not ask him for anything now.' No sooner had he finished singing than the earth shook and the man sprang to kiss Maᶜbad's head and apologized. When he had calmed down Maᶜbad asked, 'Where did these servant women learn these songs?' He replied, 'They learnt them from a songstress I use to own called Ẓabyah whom I bought in the Hijaz and who studied under Maᶜbad. She was my very body and soul but God decided to take her for Himself, and ever since she died I have been seeking Maᶜbad and his music.' Maᶜbad said, 'It is really you! I am Maᶜbad, by God! And I have been looking for you.' The man was thrilled and kissed his head, and the servant women all came out to kiss his hands and feet. Maᶜbad then said, 'By God! I will stay with you until I have made each of your servant women like Ẓabyah and more.' He spent a whole year with him and received generous treatment and compensation.

This is an uncomplicated version of a kind of anecdote that exists in more intricate forms, as we shall see in Chapter 4. Yet it has a charming linear simplicity, represented in its tidy geography and displacements: from Medina to Basra to Ahwaz, leading towards an easy and predictable climax. Most noteworthy about the inevitable recognition scene are the words Ma^cbad utters when he realises he has found the man he has been looking for. The English translation ('It is really you!') evokes nothing in particular and seems empty of underlying significance. However, in the Arabic original the words '*wa-inna-ka la-anta huwa*' are a pointed evocation of the words Joseph's brothers utter in Surah 12 (verse 90) when Joseph reveals himself to them (*a-inna-ka la-anta yūsuf*). The phrase is an enhanced flourish in an otherwise relatively unadorned anecdote, highlighting this story's plain but appealing affinity with the unfolding of plot in Surah 12.

A False Note: Exposing a Base Miser

The *Maqāmah Khamriyyah* ('*Maqāmah* of Wine') of Ibn Nāqiyā (d. 1092 AD)[20] quotes Surah 12 in an enchantingly duplicitous way. It describes a saturnalian scene attended by men of taste and dominated by a gifted 'singing-girl' or *qaynah* (whose name is not given, though she is referred to as *Dumyat al-miḥrāb*, 'the Idol of the Prayer Niche'). She enchants her audience with a gifted performance of singing. At a certain point in proceedings al-Yashkurī, the rogue hero of Ibn Nāqiyā's series, shows up and the rest of the episode consists of the long exchange between himself and the *qaynah*. She has been set up by the other carousers to try and wrest al-Yashkurī's signet ring from him in order to prove his miserliness and meanness of spirit – for the carousers know it is an attempt that is doomed to failure.

By and by, he asks the songstress to perform a *nawbah* (song cycle) from among the repertoire of ᶜUbayd ibn Surayj.[21] Al-Yashkurī says: 'This is the missing gem (*al-ḍāllah*) – now found – which no one but you is capable of performing.' His words of praise introduce the note of discovery that will take a warped turn as events transpire. She performs a number of other requests, including a song of Nuṣayb b. Rabāḥ which he claims most performers are incapable of singing correctly. When she recites it beautifully, he makes a start and cries in admiration, 'Now the truth has come to light!' (*al-āna ḥaṣḥaṣa l-ḥaqqu*; Q 12:51). As we know, these are the words uttered at Pharaoh's court when Joseph's innocence is established. They are a favourite phrase in medieval and modern Arabic literature, often borrowed to express any significant situation in which truth comes to the fore. This is now the turning point of the *maqāmah*, after its picaresque fashion. Al-Yashkurī has already claimed that a lost jewel has been found in the consummate skills of the *qaynah*, but the truth that will come to light is that he will not part with his ring (*khātam*), which she now makes repeated attempts to extort from him. His ring indeed will be the token of the miser that he is. She asks for the ring to remember him by. He prevaricates and objects and their struggle continues till dawn when he utters words that evoke teachings of the Prophet to the effect that he will have nothing to do with dalliance; disingenuously, he denies a significant part of himself. The locution of his phrase toys with the language of lineage: I am not of dalliance nor is dalliance of me! (*ʾilayka ʿannī! Lastu min dadin walā dadun minnī!*) The light of dawn now broke forth and his ignoble character came through. This, and no other, is the sorry truth that comes to light!

The Conference of the Birds

The introduction to Davis and Darbdandi's translation of Attar's celebrated Persian romance provides a summary notion of Sufi thought while illustrating the natural gravity exerted by the vocabulary of recognition in its expression, in primary and secondary texts alike (pp. 11–12): '[T]he soul is trapped within the cage of the body but can, by looking inward, recognize its essential affinity with God.' This theme is developed in a kaleidoscopic way throughout *The Conference*; but there is also a looming climax, and the passage which steers us to the point in the narrative when the birds discover the Simorgh is entitled 'Joseph's brothers read of their treachery':

> When Malek Dar bought Joseph as a slave, / The price agreed (and which he gladly gave)
> Seemed far too low – to be quite sure he made / The brothers sign a note for what he'd paid;
> And when the wicked purchase was complete / He left with Joseph and sealed the receipt.
> At last when Joseph ruled in Egypt's court / His brothers came to beg and little thought
> To whom it was each bowed his humbled head / And as a suppliant appealed for bread.

> Then Joseph held a scroll up in is hand / And said: 'No courtier here can understand / These Hebrew characters – if you can read / This note I'll give you all the bread you need.'
> The brothers could read Hebrew easily / And cried: 'Give us the note, your majesty!'
> (If any of my readers cannot find / Himself in this account, the fool is blind.)
> When Joseph gave them that short document / They looked – and trembled with astonishment.
> They did not read a line but in dismay / Debated inwardly what they should say.
> Their past sins silenced them; they were too weak / To offer an excuse or even speak.
> Then Joseph said: 'Why don't you read? You seem / Distracted, haunted by some dreadful dream.'
> And they replied: 'Better to hold your breath / Than read and in so doing merit death.' [pp. 217–18]

In this brief passage the brothers have a knowledge of Hebrew, but it lulls them momentarily into a false sense of security and they plunge with rash alacrity into the dark trap that has been set for them – the textual snare that will force their conscience to revisit them (for they are not innately wicked). The passage is ingenious in showing how apprehension is generated internally, thus establishing the fundamentally personal implications of their transfiguration from a state of moral torpor to one of moral awakening; this process amplifies a tacit detail in the Qurʾanic anagnorisis. In the Qurʾan, as here, Joseph does not tell them candidly, 'I am Joseph', rather he allows the fact to dawn on each of them from within his own stirring conscience. So, in a passage that speaks volumes of the inner horror concomitant with their sudden insight, we find a pregnant, uneasy, guilt-ridden silence.

Revelation emerges more clearly in the ensuing passage of the poem, the final epiphany, which is fashioned precisely as a recognition of the birds' own individual images in a mirror set up for them at the very goal of their quest.[22] In what follows we notice that it is still Joseph – as a borrowed figure – who both shores up and embellishes recognition and spiritual epiphany (pp. 218–9):

The thirty birds read through the fateful page / And there discovered, stage by detailed stage,
Their lives, their actions, set out one by one – / All that their souls had ever been or done:
And this was bad enough, but as they read / They understood that it was they who'd led
The lovely Joseph into slavery – / Who had deprived him of his liberty
Deep in a well, then ignorantly sold / Their captive to a passing chief for gold.
(Can you not see that at each breath you sell / The Joseph you imprisoned in that well,
That he will be the king to whom you must / Naked and hungry bow down in the dust?)
The chastened spirits of these birds became / Like crumbled powder, and they shrank with shame.
Then, as by shame their spirits were refined / Of all the world's weight, they began to find
A new life flow towards them from the bright / Celestial and ever-living Light –
Their souls rose free of all they'd been before; / The past and all its actions were no more.
Their life came from that close, insistent sun / And in its vivid rays they shone as one.
There in the Simorgh's radiant face they saw / Themselves, the Simorgh of the world – with awe
They gazed, and dared at last to comprehend / They were the Simorgh and the journey's end.
They were the Simorgh – at themselves they stare, / And see a second Simorgh standing there;
They look at both and see the two are one, / That this is that, that this, the goal is won.
They ask (but inwardly they make no sound) / The meaning of these mysteries that confound
Their puzzled ignorance – how is it true / That 'we' is not distinguished here from 'you'?

> And silently their shining Lord replies: / 'I am a mirror set before your eyes,
> And all who come before my splendour see / Themselves, their own unique reality.'

The Conference is a protracted poem of nigh epic length; in the Davis-Darbandi translation it extends to 4455 verses. In its expansive descanting there is space for multiple references to the Joseph story; the final reference cited above – the one most organically woven into the text – is, according to a certain view of the work, pre-figured by earlier references, which collectively illustrate the paradoxes that run through the tale as leitmotifs, and which are clearly part of its diverting and didactic mystical discourse. But despite the epic's apparent ambiguous hedging, Joseph helps to articulate the message of *The Conference* almost to a greater degree than any other borrowed theme. One could argue that the recurring motif of a king and his servant, the core players in a number of exemplary anecdotes, is as important, if not more so; but occurrences of the latter type are in the main topically explained, whereas Joseph is drawn from recognisable Islamic *qiṣaṣ* material, and this aggregated apocryphal cycle certainly provides the work's dominant religious and prophetic motif.

The Romance of Ghānim b. Ayyūb[23]

> The Joseph of the Koran, very different from him of Genesis. We shall meet him often in the Nights . . .
>
> Burton, *The Book of the Thousand Nights and a Night*, X, p. 13

A shrewd anagnostic stencil for reading the Joseph story as a latent, sublimated and sustained archetype behind a given romance can be gleaned from Andras Hamori's study of the story of Qamar al-Zaman in *The Arabian Nights*:[24]

> Let us begin at the beginning. Not at the beginning of the tale of Qamar al-Zaman, but with what is the master-text behind it: the story of Joseph in the legends of the Prophets. That legend, familiar to all, was used by Qur'an commentators and pondered by mystics. It is an example of what I shall call perfect romance: its conclusion resolves both familial and erotic dissonances. In the legend man and woman too have their *cognitio* and

> blossoming harmony. The temptress, after a share of suffering, experiences moral rebirth, and is married to Joseph. She has been we find a virgin all along: a felicitous defect in her first husband makes for a nice parallel to her moral renewal. This legend echoes in our tale [Qamar al-Zaman]. There are reminders of the evidence of the bloody clothes brought to Jacob, and Jacob's building of a *bayt al-aḥzān*. The Zulaykha figure is split: the temptress who slanders the chaste hero reappears in Qamar al-Zaman's wives, while the woman who for love of the hero forsakes her idols and is reborn in the law reappears – somewhat as in the Haggadah – in the next generation, in the Magian's daughter. Perhaps we have in distributive form what was sequential in the story of Joseph, when we find al-As^{c}ad in the Magian's dungeon while his brother al-Amjad is named the king's vizier.

An analogous case of sustained textual influence can be made for the Tale of the Two Viziers in which, as in Surah 12, the details of dreamy imaginings cause resentment. There are other elements, however, which evoke Surah 12 more pointedly. At intervals the son of Nūr al-Dīn, the hero Badr al-Dīn Ḥasan, is convinced that he has been entrapped in a dream, and in the final scene he repeatedly exclaims in bewilderment, *anā fī aḍghāthi aḥlām* ('I am in tangled nightmares').[25] This phrase exists in a number of other *Arabian Nights* stories; it can merely be loosely oneiric. Whether or not it is meant to be read as a sharp outcrop of the Joseph story's influence must depend on the weight of other evidence. I would like to highlight just two other elements. First, we should bear in mind the importance of the itinerary in this tale, which is finally resolved with a journey into Egypt. This vague evocation of the Joseph story is shored up and made palpable in other details. Shams al-Dīn tells his brother's wife before escorting her to Egypt from Baṣra: *mā hādhā waqt bukāʾ hādhā waqt tajhīzika li-l-safar ma*^{c}*a-nā ilā diyār miṣr* ^{c}*asā allāh yajma*^{c} *shamla-nā wa-shamlaki bi-waladi bni akhī* ('this is no time to cry; this is time to prepare for a trip down into Egypt in the hope that God will reunite us with my brother's son'). This evokes in both word and meaning Surah 12:83 in which after the loss of Benjamin, Jacob cries out, *fa-ṣabrun jamīlun* ^{c}*asā llāhu an yaʾtiya-nī bi-him jamī*^{c}*an*. These details occur in a noticeably random order; more persuasive is the following excerpt in which the cook in Damascus offers protection to Badr al-Dīn and adopts him as his son: *yā* *sayyidī badr al-dīn i*^{c}*lam anna hādhā amrun* ^{c}*ajībun wa-ḥadīthun gharībun wa-lākin yā waladī iktam mā ma*^{c}*ak ḥattā yufarrij allāh mā bi-ka wa-q*^{c}*ud* ^{c}*indī fī hādhā l-makān wa-anā mā lī waladun fa-attakhidhu-ka waladī* ('Badr al-Dīn, good sir, you should realize that these are very strange circumstances but keep them to yourself until God grants you deliverance; stay with me, meanwhile, for I have no offspring and can adopt you as my son'). Two ayahs from Surah 12 are broken into this passage: (12:5) *yā bunayya la taqṣuṣ ruʾyā-ka ilā ikhwati-ka* ('my son, do not relate this dream to your brothers') and (12:21) *akrimī mathwā-hu* ^{c}*asā an yanfa*^{c}*a-nā aw nattakhidha-hu waladan* ('receive him generously in our house in the hope that he will benefit us or we can adopt him as a son').[26]

But for an example of how Surah 12 can affect the ethos of a story in the *Thousand and One Nights* we must turn to The Romance of Ghānim b. Ayyūb contained in the very readable anonymous English translation entitled *Arabian Nights' Entertainments*.[27] It exists in this early eighteenth-century 'Grub Street' edition chiefly because of its previous inclusion in Antoine Galland's own French rendering (and selection) of *Nights*' tales. Since it does not survive in the so-called Syrian recension, Galland must have found the story in some extraneous *Nights* material to which he had access in manuscript form. Subsequently, perhaps even as a result of Galland's original popularisation of the story, it became part of the Egyptian recension.[28] The chronological implications set out here are tentative not trenchant. However, they are tenable and allow me to present this tale the way I'm inclined, though the gambit will be anathema to those for whom there must be such a thing as an authentic and privileged Arabic original. My leaning is to give some credit to the English translation, from the French translation, which depending on the view one adopts, either enhances the elements of the Joseph romance of the Būlāq Arabic version, or at the very least provides a complementary reading along lines established in the Arabic. There is an obvious irony here – one of involved cultural exchange and interference – but we should by now have come to accept that the literary history of the *Nights* includes and embraces some of its manifold textual progeny.[29] In this particular case, a tale's reworking of significant elements of the Joseph romance has been detected by the translator and has then been very finely embellished, independently of the Arabic version.

Here is the synopsis, adapted from the précis provided in the Second Appendix of the Oxford 1995 Mack edition based on Henry Weber's 1812 edition; italicised is a section which is essentially added to the Arabic original:

> Ghānim, son of the merchant Abū Ayyūb of Damascus, travels to Baghdad following his father's death in order to sell what remains of his father's goods. One evening he stumbles upon a group of slaves secretly and hurriedly burying a large chest under cover of darkness just outside the city walls. When the slaves depart Ghānim retrieves the chest and, opening it, discovers Qūt al-Qulūb, the favourite of the caliph Hārūn al-Rashīd, drugged and nearly dead inside. Ghānim rescues her and takes her to recover at his own home in Baghdad. It soon becomes clear that Zubayda, the caliph's jealous wife, has had Qūt al-Qulūb poisoned with sleeping potion and was the one responsible for attempting to have her buried alive. Qūt al-Qulūb realizes that she must for her own safety maintain a low profile while living with the merchant Ghānim. Ghānim, for his own part, has fallen hopelessly in love with the beautiful young favourite.
>
> Zubayda has meanwhile told Hārūn al-Rashīd that Qūt al-Qulūb has died. Even when Qūt al-Qulūb finally manages to communicate news of her whereabouts to the caliph, he believes her to have been perversely unfaithful to him. Rather than welcoming her back to court and rewarding her rescuer, Hārūn orders his servants to kill Ghānim and forcibly return his favourite to his palace. Disguised as a slave, Ghānim manages to escape, but his house is levelled in the attack. *Not content with this misplaced retribution the caliph then orders that Ghānim's relatives be located in Damascus. He instructs the sultan there – Mohammad Zinebi – to prosecute Ghānim's mother and sister, Fitna. The two innocents are paraded through the streets, but a sympathetic populace refuses to jeer at or ridicule them. They are nevertheless disgraced in their home-town, and decide eventually to head for Baghdad.*
>
> Qūt al-Qulūb meanwhile has been imprisoned in a dark tower; only after a long incarceration does she have a chance to tell her story to Hārūn and to plead Ghānim's case. The caliph relents and wishes to forgive Ghānim, but he cannot be found. Qūt al-Qulūb has in the meantime asked the syndic of some merchants to distribute money amongst the poor. The syndic tells her that two women – obviously noble but distraught – have recently arrived in

> Baghdad who seem to be particularly worthy of her charity. Qūt al-Qulūb rescues the two, who are revealed to be Ghānim's mother and sister. The caliph, who has by now been fully convinced of the extent of Zubayda's treachery, rejects his wife and marries Ghānim's sister Fitna. He then offers Ghānim's mother to Ja^{c}far, his grand visier. Ghānim finally reappears in Baghdad, and he and Qūt al-Qulūb are happily reunited.[30]

In what follows, analysis of this happy and comic romance is informed by a two-part agenda: (1) to show that aspects of the structural model of romance set out in Northrop Frye's *Secular Scripture* are particularly felicitous in identifying features of this narrative with details of the genre to which it so transparently belongs. This is another way – in addition to its textual history – that the tale strides with generic confidence outside the margins of Arabo-Islamic culture. Romance, of which a recognition scene is such an important constituent element, is the genre of narrative art which Arabic literature appears most conspicuously to share with other cultural traditions;[31] and (2) to discuss the evocations of the Joseph romance which are threaded through the story and embellish its tissue of disclosures.

First, one should call attention to an omission in the English synopsis. In the Arabic of the Būlāq edition, the three black slaves who bury the chest containing Qūt al-Qulūb exchange tales to explain how and why they had each become eunuchs. The first slave's anecdote is prurient in the extreme: he took the virginity of his foster sister while she was still dressed in robes; this lewdness, we should further observe, was mildly progressive, for he had been at first content simply to fondle her genitalia with his own. The second anecdote can be passed over and the third slave has no time to tell his tale in full. However, the gist of it is essential, indeed its sparseness renders its message all the more crystalline: *anā aḥkī la-kum sababa qaṭ^{c}i khuṣāya wa-qad kuntu astaḥiqqu akthara min dhālika li-annī kuntu niktu sayyidatī wa-bna sayyidī wa-l-ḥikāyatu ma^{c}ī ṭawīlatun wa-mā hādhihi waqtu ḥikāyati-hā li-anna l-ṣabāḥa yā awlādu ^{c}ammā qarīb*. This, the Būlāq version, does not then avert its gaze from unseemly details of moral and sexual transgression – this is not the tenor of the text according to a strict narrative or literary protocol imposed by or upon a prudish author or redactor; hence the chastity which marks the main part of the story, rather than being a dictate of narrative decorum has – or must be seen to have – a purpose.[32] We can be even more precise on this, for the transgression which the third slave performed was that of *sleeping with his master's wife*, an especially odious infidelity and one that sets off by contrast the deportment of Ghānim.[33]

The synopsis cited above nowhere indicates the refrain uttered by Ghānim at intervals throughout the story, yet it is crucial to the following interpretation. When Ghānim learns the identity of Qūt al-Qulūb, he announces his own death – rather like Ṣafwān b. al-Muᶜaṭṭal's *istirjāᶜ*: 'Alas! madam . . . I have just saved your life, and this embroidery is my death!' It is not simply that she is the caliph's favourite concubine that threatens his existence but the added and complicating fact that he has already ceded his heart to her. That this love is now stymied is expressed as a fatality, and he will have cause to reiterate the point: that he both loves her and yet that his love for her must be restrained. That it should kill him ('dying entirely yours') connotes figuratively that his love will consume him; it also contains the sublimated threat that were his love to be consummated he would risk death at the hands of the jealous caliph. Indeed this threat exists even while he remains loyal to his sovereign, for it is what the caliph *perceives* that dictates the lot of those in his domain.

The following declaration contains the important refrain that runs through the tale: Ghānim addresses Qūt al-Qulūb having learnt that she belongs to Hārūn al-Rashīd:

> But how great soever he [the caliph] is, give me leave madam, to declare, that nothing will be able to make me recall the present I have made you of my heart. I know, and shall never forget, that *what belongs to the master is forbidden to the slave*; but I loved you before you told me that you were engaged to the caliph . . .[34]

The refrain occurs on five subsequent occasions, corresponding in fact to what we can identify as four supervening stages in the development of events. In this first instance, we should note, Ghānim makes a vow of abstinence while declaring his love; he speaks of his own affections only and we have no indication here that Qūt al-Qulūb returns his sentiments (it would in any case be irrelevant and add to the affective impasse). But the situation develops and, having learned that Qūt al-Qulūb does not 'look upon all [his] care with indifference' ('while she knew what she owed to the caliph'), the refrain recurs: 'He was not ignorant, "*That what belongs to the master, is forbid to the servant.*"' Further, the double-bind of lovers is glossed intermittently: 'As fond as they were of each other, their respect for the caliph kept them within those bounds that were due to him, which still heightened their passion.'[35] This knowledge has come to constrain them, while, with the passage of time, their imminent separation casts its shadow upon them.

The third instance of the refrain occurs after a significant psychological detail: Ghānim has discovered and reported to Qūt al-Qulūb (confined as she is in his house) that among the people of Baghdad she is believed to be dead, the obvious tell-tale sign being that Zubayda, the caliph's malificent wife who had arranged to have her buried alive, has built a mausoleum in her memory; he is thus tempted:

> Would to God, that, taking advantage of this false report, you will share my fortune, and go far from hence to reign in my heart! But whither does this pleasing notion carry me? . . . Supposing you could resolve to give [the caliph] up for me, and that you would follow me, ought I to consent to it? No, it is my part always to remember, that, *what belongs to the master, is forbidden to the slave.*[36]

This passage lends itself to an easy interpretation: the situation at large has allowed him to fall prey to temptation and in this respect his relationship with Qūt al-Qulūb has progressed to another stage; however, he responds to his own self-questioning with unequivocal rejection – the refrain – and in the end the show of a moment's weakness simply betrays the measure of his love while reaffirming his fidelity to the caliph. The humanity of the lovers is etched into the story, and we are reminded – pointedly, one is bound to claim – of the Qurʾanic phrase (of 12:24): *wa-hammat bi-hi wa-hamma bi-hā law-lā raʾā burhāna rabbi-hi* ('she desired him and he would have desired her had he not seen the proof of his Lord').

Between this and the next three instances of the refrain, a turning point in the narrative supervenes. Hārūn al-Rashīd, like Potiphar, will punish a man though he is innocent; but the man escapes and Qūt al-Qulūb is incarcerated in a dark tower to suffer alone. She has been falsely condemned. But the truth emerges when the caliph, walking alone within the enclosure of the palace, overhears her complaining (to herself but in audible words) of the lovers' innocence. As Frye has written in *Fables of Identity*, 'A humor is restored to normal outlook by being confronted . . . with a reflection of its own illusion.'[37] Qūt al-Qulūb relates to the caliph the whole story of her encounter with Ghānim and comes to the crucial point of fidelity; she tells Hārūn al-Rashīd: 'as soon as he [Ghānim] heard that I had the honour to belong to you, "Alas, madam," said he, "*That which belongs to the master is forbidden to the slave.*" From that moment . . . his behaviour was always suitable to his words.' Two important substantive notions issue from this revelation: (1) the caliph's pleasure, which will eventually afford the lovers' their ease, and (2) the confession, made with striking delicacy, that Qūt al-Qulūb has 'felt some tender inclination growing in [her] breast'. Love has been reciprocal and has been growing in this respect; there is a marked vector of increase in the dynamic of this version of the story. Honesty or candour – ancillaries of truth – are betokened here and are further enhanced with the reiterated theme of fidelity, for

> He [Ghānim] perceived it [i.e. Qūt al-Qulūb's sentiments], but was still far from taking an advantage of my frailty: and notwithstanding the flame which consumed him, he still remained steady in his duty, and all his passion could force from him, was those words I have already told your majesty, '*That which belongs to the master is forbidden to the slave.*'[38]

This is not a religious text, nor, principally, a romance of patrimony but a tale of lovers, and so at this crucial point in the narrative the caliph facilitates the erotic romance: he will give Ghānim to Qūt al-Qulūb for a husband. But the youth has gone absent, and multiple recognitions and reunions will supervene before the final occurrence of the refrain; the latter has come to work a paradoxical effect, for having once stood as barrier to affection (by virtue of prescribing a restrictive morality) it has now ratified the betrothal of lovers in return for that very morality betokened. With anagnorisis – the crucial point of discovery in a text – comes peripety, a reversal of fortune. The caliph's realisation of the truth is the chief anagnorisis in the text, for it brings about the reversal of fortune that is only subsequently realised materially in those other ancillary recognitions and reunions that mark the final third of the comedy as a sustained movement from ignorance of family to knowledge and discovery. At the beginning of the story Ghānim is an obscure young merchant living in Damascus who has lost his father. His sphere of existence is circumscribed; he has his genealogy and family identity but in the wider world that lies beyond his home he cuts an anonymous figure, and having travelled to Baghdad his identity is further taken from him when he is forced to abandon all and flee for his life; his mother comes to believe he is dead. But, all along, he shows himself to be a good Muslim; this emerges as a metonym of his fidelity as a subject of the caliph, the very righteous sovereign he has angered, and it is an affecting marker of restituted identity that the tale should end with this principled citizen and the caliph exchanging compliments and moral pledges *face-à-face*. Ghānim warrants his fidelity to his sovereign in person ('a slave has no will but his master's own, on whom his life and fortune depend') and in the process he effectively asks for the caliph's concubine's hand in marriage. His identity is restored to him in this supreme act of worldly acknowledgement, and the tale's denouement is marked as a sort of mundane resurrection. The refrain has previously resolved Ghānim's attitude to Qūt al-Qulūb, but in the end it is more clearly rendered what it has always *also* been, a general statement of *religious* duty. The Arabic of the Būlāq edition has *sayyidī* three times for 'my master' and *mawlāya* once;[39] but another version (perhaps even a putative original Arabic) could easily have had *rabbī*, thus hewing closer to Qurʾan 12:23 (*inna-hu rabbī aḥsana mathwāya*) and highlighting also the semantic ambiguity that attends this instance of the word in the scripture, where it is redolent of Joseph's attitude to his Lord, God, as well as his earthly master.

The assertion that the story of Joseph is a romance in literary terms has been made before and is practically unassailable. The generic label romance is indeed accentuated by the Islamic tradition in the way Joseph's relationship with Zulaykha is perceived, imagined and developed. Even in the scant Qurʾanic narrative there is an aspect of moral reformation in her comportment, for it is she who declares publicly the truth of Joseph's innocence before Pharaoh's court: to wit, that it was *she* who tried to seduce Joseph and not vice versa. This moral restitution is rewarded in the later *qiṣaṣ* tradition where her feelings for Joseph are understood not as concupiscence but true love; furthermore, her sentiments are requited in marriage. And he too has loved her all along (or so it can appear in apocrypha), thus his earlier abstinence and restraint need some explanatory gloss. Qurʾan 12:24, like 12:23, is ambiguous; the discussions in *tafsīr* show this to be the case: *hamma bi-hā* seems according to the sequence of events to describe the passion of the moment and is always described more in physical rather than spiritual terms of attraction; the spirit is never so impulsive (a sense of the weakness of a single moment, after weeks or months of moral steadfastness, is most clearly conveyed in the Haggadah). The point relevant here is that while the Qurʾanic Zulaykha may be remembered for her lustful villainy and she became Joseph's lover (though in apocrypha), it was the latter who was rewarded for his fidelity to his earthly master, this being a metonym for his religious scruple (his constant eye to the pleasure of his Lord). To read Ghānim as Joseph is not difficult (both were tempted and resisted temptation); and with certain adjustments (that is, with an awareness of the *full* sequence of events pertaining to Zulaykha in the *fullness* of the Islamic accounts of the prophets) we can glimpse Zulaykha as a model for Qūt al-Qulūb.

The evidence for such a reading, which depends substantially on the nature of the refrain, is offered below (culled from three complementary sources):

- Genesis 39:7 And it came to pass after these things, that his master's wife cast her eyes upon Joseph; and she said, Lie with me. 8 But he refused, and said unto his master's wife, Behold, my master wotteth not what is with me in the house, and he hath committed all that he hath to my hand; 9 There is none greater in this house than I; neither hath he kept back any thing from me but thee, because thou *art* his wife: how then can I do this great wickedness, and sin against God?
- Qurʾan Surah 12:23 The woman in whose house he lived tried to seduce him. She shut the doors and said, 'Come on.' He replied, 'God be my refuge. *[Your husband] is my master.* He has given me good lodging. Those who do wrong do not prosper.'
- And here, finally, is the pertinent detail in al-Kisāʾīʿs *Qiṣaṣ*[40], though it adds little to the Qurʾanic original: 'O Joseph,' [Zulaykha] said, 'I am yours!' 'But where is your husband Potiphar?' asked Joseph. 'I have nothing to do with him,' she answered. 'You are the only one for me. I am yours!' 'O Zulaykha, I fear this house will be a house of sorrow and

a spot of hell.' 'O Joseph, I love you with all my heart. Lift up your head and look at me in the fullness of my beauty!' '*Your master has more right to you than I do.*'

A cardinal insight into the thematic function of the refrain can be gleaned from the comments of Claus Westermann on Joseph's 'innocent downfall'[41]

> [On Genesis 39:8] 'But he [Joseph] refused . . .' On this Gunkel remarks: 'The narrator contrasts the lasciviousness of the Egyptian woman with the chastity of the Israelite youth.' And Procksch entitles it, 'the motif of the pure man confronting the impure woman,' and then remarks, 'Through the projection (of the Egyptian's intentions) onto Joseph, the contrast between the modest Semite and the wicked Hamite is artfully brought into play.' Both of these commentators have totally missed the meaning of the story. According to them, the contrast which governs the narrative is that of the two characteristics (chastity and licentiousness; purity and impurity) personified by the principal characters. But such a juxtaposition of attributes misunderstands the story, and at its decisive points. This failure to understand can be explained in terms of the profound involvement in abstract and moralistic thinking in which we live, a kind of thought which is totally alien to this narrative. If this kind of contrast were really the point, what could we make of the remark that Joseph's acquiescence would have meant a breach of trust? If the purpose had really been to highlight the contrast between chastity and lasciviousness, that could have been done much more effectively if no other motives had contributed toward the decision.
>
> In another of his comments, Gunkel refers to the real scope (*skopos*) of the narrative: 'Joseph rejects her demand because it would be a serious breach of confidence, and this is a feature which recurs in every version of the story.' [Including the Qurʾanic version]. Thus Joseph refuses to betray the trust which his master has deposited in him. All of the talk about the 'chaste Joseph', then, misses the real meaning of the story, as do all of the numerous graphic portrayals of this scene which are predicated on this error. What Joseph says to his master's wife in reply to her proposition is based on this argument: 'nor has he kept back anything from me except yourself, because you are his wife.'

On this view, the theme of chastity is ancillary to fidelity to a master. Hence the decorum of the translated adaptations of the text can be explained as due simply to the coy filter of the European milieu – the literary salons for which these Oriental tales were drafted in their original French rendering. The carnal aspect of the Arabic original does not hinder this reading, but rather in fact enhances it. To explain this, we can take a comment by the French scholar Edgard Weber as a point of departure; he notes a curious reversal that takes place when Ghānim discovers Qūt al-Qulūb's identity:[42]

> Aussitôt il change d'attitude envers sa bien aimée, bien que celle-ci devienne alors plus entreprennante qu'auparavant. Il dresse même deux lits pour que chacun puisse dormir seul . . . Il s'opère dans le conte un curieux renversement. A partir du moment où Ghânim décide de demeurer chaste, la jeune fille manifeste la liberté qu'elle s'est refusé jusqu'alors.

When Ghānim shows his loyalty to the sovereign by making, and then sustaining, his vow of chastity, it becomes necessary simultaneously for Qūt al-Qulūb to test his resolve with her own increasing cupidity. But to view her behaviour as a kind of deliberate male-chauvinist characterisation of feminine desire is to ignore the mechansim according to which the narrative is obliged to function: desire must needs exist for fealty to be tested, hence the baton of chastity is relayed from one player to the next at the crucial point of Ghānim's discovery of her identity. Chastity is thus subordinated to fidelity very much in accordance with the comments of Claus Westermann.

Is a happy ending inevitable? The point of greatest suspense is the question: can it turn out to be a lovers' romance? Given the theme that marks the narrative as a refrain (we label this the Joseph refrain), we can be confident that it will at least be a romance of kinfolk: the family will be reunited (the sister, Fitna, has been identified by name so she must surely reappear after Ghānim's first departure from Damsacus). Of course, there are some variables: the mother may perish with age, but in this case the sister will doubtless be reunited with her brother (though for the canny reader who picks up echoes of Jacob's situation waiting for a lost child patiently, even the mother should not die). But on the other hand the refrain strengthens the, at first, inchoate image of Zulaykha and hence may increasingly evoke the lovers' union in the Joseph romance. The refrain indeed calibrates the progress of love – it is a constant and fixed phrase that punctuates and undergirds the text, while their love is growing, at first stymied and then sanctified. And this in turn both exacerbates and intensifies the tension, the divide between what the reader may allow herself to wish for the lovers, and the duty that binds them (the protagonists) ever more cruelly as their love waxes stronger. In the Grub Street version more noticeably than in the Arabic there is a growing reciprocity in their affections at the same time that their situation becomes increasingly forlorn, and we can measure this increase each time the refrain is uttered, for the refrain is never spoken without the situation of the lovers having changed or developed. But there is a turning point in the sequence of events, and after this is reached the refrain will no longer bind the lovers but contribute to releasing them. The refrain thus represents both the barrier that separates them and the quality that will eventually facilitate their betrothal.

All hinges on the caliph. Hārūn al-Rashīd cannot be deceived and he instills both fear and fidelity, sentiments that are intertwoven.[43] The caliph is in some sense the incarnation of anagnorisis in the *Nights*, as the numerous tales in which he disguises himself and descends incognito among his citizens show: they are all characterised by the suppression and eventual disclosure of truth. He hides behind his modest camouflage and the hidden secrets of quotidian Baghdad are revealed to him (this narrative motif exists here in a slightly adapted placement[44] and form, for the caliph is not masquerading when he overhears the truth but strolling within the palace precincts). And it is not so much that the caliph cannot but *should* not be lied to, for he is the defender of Islam and, for later generations that heard this tale, he was the champion of its golden age. In some sense the audience of this fiction cannot hope for the caliph to be cheated in order for the lovers to be united; a conflict of sentiment and interests therefore subsists. How then can the romance be sustained? (There are enough cases of death in love to caution the reader away from the unwarranted and complacent expectation of a happy ending.)

The caliph holds the solution even while embodying its hindrance. According to normal protocol only death could force the separation of the caliph from any of his concubines. No one dies in this tale, yet the notion of death fills the narrative as a sort of leitmotif which modulates as reality, figure (or metaphor) and illusion: at the very outset Ghānim's father dies (allowing for the standard motif of the son's pecuniary inheritance); in Baghdad Ghānim, after attending the funeral of a 'prime merchant', witnesses the burial of a chest – the murder of Qūt al-Qulūb, and for a while she *is* indeed considered deceased (she is *deemed* to have died by the caliph and is *known erroneously* to have been murdered by Zubayda who has disposed of her body); for a moment even Qūt al-Qulūb herself is under the illusion that she is in 'the undiscovered country', witness the words she utters as she regains consciousness in the company of Ghānim: 'At length looking about, and perceiving she was in a burial-place, she was in a mighty fright. How now, cried she, much louder than before, is this the resurrection of the dead? Is the day of judgment come?'[45] When the predicament of the lovers dawns upon them they feel the dark and murderous threat of the caliph's wrath; and to accentuate the theme Zubayda builds a marble memorial for the concubine of whom she deems herself to be rid; Hārūn al-Rashīd accepts the significance of this entombment when he digs up the body: he suspects his wife (or the circumstances of Qūt al-Qulūb's reported death) but accedes – piously in fact – to the evidence of the shroud that covers a wooden effigy of her; he therefore literally then mourns for his *maḥẓiyyah* (favourite courtesan)[46]: 'The caliph sent for ministers of his religion, the officers of the palace, and the readers of the Alcoran; and, whilst they were calling together, he remained in the mausoleum, moistening the earth, that covered the phantom of his love, with his tears.'[47]

There are two interpretative functional aspects to this theme of death; the first may not be wholly convincing, the second, however, is essential to the psychology and evolution of events. The belief that a loved one is dead and gone is not far from the mind as one reads through the Joseph romance. However, it is hard to secure this allusion, and it must also be stated that in the Islamic tradition neither Jacob nor the scheming brothers expressly state their belief that the missing Joseph is actually dead. With this proviso, therefore, we should simply accept that there is an element – there is certainly the attitude – of mourning for lost ones; and, furthermore, the biblical Joseph is *literally* mourned by a grieving Jacob, which testifies at least to the emotionally laden psychology of what one might call the primordial background narrative. The connection between the caliph in this tale and any figure in the Islamic narrative of Joseph cannot be sharply made, especially when we add to what we have already set out that Ghānim's mother also comes to give credence to the fact that her son is dead (and not merely missing).[48] The figure or role of Jacob is thus vague and distributed among more than one character,[49] and one may wonder therefore whether the point is worth making at all except as some easily creditable generic observation: that both are romances and that these themes are the natural corollaries of a painful severance.

But if we tend to dismiss the parallels between this romance and the story of Joseph, some details nevertheless provide some striking parallels; thus Qūt al-Qulūb: she is left to her death in a grave then rescued, and subsequently rewarded for her show of faith (her innocence) by being imprisoned in a dark tower. The succession of events that befall Joseph are not dissimilar: the pit, the temptation of Zulaykha and his resistance to this, and his subsequent imprisonment. No single person is cast according to the model of Joseph, but details of both narratives have to some extent randomly distributed affinities with each other.

The clever modulations and sustained treatment of the theme draw us towards a functionalist reading of the text. There does in fact appear to be a very important transference enabled by the treatment of death, and this extracts the narrative sequence from the deadlock already broached above (to wit, how can the caliph be made to give up his favourite concubine?) It is a problem of the plausibility of narrative contrivance within certain cultural and generic constraints. The release in the end comes not from the material external world but from within, for the fact that he has mourned her encourages a mental process by which he can eventually be separated from her; it performs a sort of cathartic severance. These psychological propositions are not explored explicitly by the narrative but they seem nevertheless to lie behind the obvious symbolism of this very conspicuous theme.

The Symbolism of the Veil

There is a fascinating detail in the scene in which Qūt al-Qulūb's identity is revealed to Ghānim. She has been brought from the burial ground to his house:

> When they had eaten some small matter, Ghānim observing that the lady's veil, which she had laid down by her on the sofa, was embroidered along the

> edge with golden letters, begged leave to her to look upon that embroidery. The lady immediately took up the veil, and delivered it to him, asking whether he could read? . . . Ghānim took the veil, and read these words, 'I am yours, and you are mine, thou descendant from the prophet's uncle.' That descendant from the prophet's uncle was Haroun Alraschid, who then reigned, and was descended from Abbas, Mahomet's uncle. When Ghānim perceived these words, 'Alas! Madam,' said he, in a melancholy tone, 'I have just saved your life, and this embroidery is my death!'[50]

It is a striking contrivance of symbolism that the item of clothing which is to announce her identity should be a veil and a gift from the caliph. For a veil is that which more normally conceals and protects; that which creates a barrier between the one who wears it (or owns it) and the outside world; it imposes an unbreachable divide between the private and the public spheres, between the women of the harem and strange unrelated men. The veil here is no empty parchment or cipher that carries a neutral message (the gilt words embroidered upon it); it is rather a message in its own right; it simultaneously reveals, conceals and enforces a separation. Here then, in this translucent silk raiment, is one of the symbolic cusps of the story,[51] the material point of conjunction between what is suppressed and hidden, on the one hand, and what is confessed and revealed, on the other. Wraps and veils often and typically feature in narratives of suppression and disclosure; the most pertinent example in the Islamic sphere among the narratives we have already encountered exists in the account of *The Scandal* (see earlier this chapter). But, the veil need not be culturally specific in its literary manifestations: an excellent instance of the potent symbolism of the veil in a recognition scene is found in Joseph Conrad's *Under Western Eyes*. Cave gives a perceptive account of this, referring to the scene in which Natalia is given to know that it was Razumov who had betrayed her brother Haldin – the shock of which news caused her to drop the veil from her hand:

> In a rather special sense, Natalia's veil operates in this scene in the manner of a recognition token. The play that Conrad makes with it is certainly not motivated by demands of realist fiction: it may be plausible that she should wear a veil and remove it on coming indoors, but when she drops it, when Razumov picks it up and carries it off . . . and when he subsequently sends

> her his diary [his confessions] wrapped up in it, we know, and the text knows we know, *that it is placed as a significant detail for us to interpret.* [52]

We now reach a turning-point in our own analysis. Having suggested the importance of this symbolic inscription, we may have to abandon it as an untenable variant of the story, for the Arabic (of Būlāq) is quite distinct in respect of this detail: it is a trouserband not a veil that in a moment of dalliance discloses Qūt al-Qulūb's relationship to the caliph. A barrier is thus set up between the lovers when Qūt al-Qulūb's chastity is finally *and only immanently* at risk – it is not identity that a trouserband veils but concupiscence itself. Indeed, this version of the story is far less chaste all round, a point best exemplified in the fact that Qūt al-Qulūb reciprocates the sentiments of Ghānim from the outset of their installation in his house. The well-drawn vectors of intensifying pain followed by requital are not so clearly traced in the Arabic of the Būlāq edition. However, there is a strong ulterior reminiscence of the chaste Joseph in the circumstances in which the embroidery on the trouserband is read. In the mainstream *tafsīr* tradition the temptation Joseph felt before wresting himself from Zulaykha is surprisingly graphic:[53]

> Joseph unfastened the belt of his trousers and sat before her 'as the circumciser sits'; she lay down for him and he sat between her legs; she lay down on her back and he sat between her legs and loosened his garment (or her garment); he dropped his pants to his buttocks; he sat with her as a man sits with his wife . . . What these scenarios have in common is that the action stops short of actual intercourse.

It is in fact just such a situation that is symbolised by Qūt al-Qulūb's trouserband, which can thus be viewed as a final but effective barrier between desire and an infidelity.

Here then is the critical question. Has Galland, and the Grub Street English translator following the Frenchman, amplified and enhanced the atavistic allusions to the Joseph romance which we have set out in detail above? Which is to say, has Galland interpreted expansively, in narrative form, the allusions and intertextual relationships which he detected in the original Arabic? Or has he fashioned a substantively new story which only by happenstance, perhaps due to the prominence of Joseph in the Judeo-Christian tradition, happens to echo and even develop aspects of the Islamic prophetic romance? The evidence of available Arabic versions of the story persuades us of the greater truth in the first suggestion.[54] Galland produced a coherent design for the story in which there was a natural dovetailing between Islamic sensibility (chastity as evidence of fidelity) and the strait-laced tastes of his principal readership.[55]

Epilogue: Two Definitions of Romance

> Most romances end happily, with a return to the state of identity, and begin with a departure from it. Even in the most realistic stories there is usually some trace of a plunge downward at the beginning and a bounce upward at the end. This means that most romances exhibit a cyclical movement of descent into a night world and a return to the idyllic world, or to some symbol of it like a marriage . . .[56]

And even more aptly:

> The symbolic spread of a romance tends . . . to go into its literary context, to other romances that are most like it in the conventions adopted. The sense that more is meant than meets the ear in romance comes largely from the reverberations that its familiar conventions set up within our literary experience, like a shell that contains the sound of the sea.[57]

The next two chapters return to reading 'works' – whole anecdotes that reflect on the larger work and genre within which they lie. There is now an attempt to detect strategies of reading. The motivation is literary, earnest as well as playful engagement with the structures of knowledge – and relatedly, of narrative – within what comes across cumulatively as a generic network of intertextuality.

In Chapter 4, I take the idea of *al-faraj ba*ᶜ*d al-shiddah* as both episteme and narrative pattern that permeate a body of writing in Arabic, particularly *adab* and storytelling, which in turn reflect and refract the Qur᾽anic paradigm. I look at intertextuality diachronically (chronologically from the Qur᾽an to the fourth century, modulating registers from the 'sacred' to the 'profane') and synchronically (the proliferation of 'recognition' as literary 'chronotope' across a variety of genres within the Arabic tradition, dialogically, as well as in its intersections with other structures of knowledge and narrative – e.g. *al-amr bi l-ma^c^ruf wa l-nahy ^c^an al-munkar*). All this contributes to the elaboration and nuancing of the ethics of living.

Chapter 5 takes on the more 'scandalously playful' engagement with the faith-based ethics of living, and looks at the various manifestations of a conceptual (perhaps even an existential) interrogation of 'epistemes' inherent in sacred texts and *adab*.

Notes

1. The Persian mystical romance, *Manṭiq al-ṭayr* of Farid ud-Din Attar.
2. *Qiṣṣat Ghānim ibn Ayyūb.*
3. This latter feature is particularly true of romance.
4. See Piero Boitani's 'A spark of love: Medieval recognitions', in *The Tragic and the Sublime in Medieval Literature* (Cambridge: Cambridge University Press, 1989), p. 121. Among the treasures of anagnorisis unearthed by Boitani from the pre-modern Christian canon, Friedrich Klopstock's eighteenth-century masterpiece *Der Messias* is particularly compelling in the way it draws on Joseph for the topical, thematic and cognitive sustenance that evocations of the biblical narrative can deliver. In the following excerpt the subject is Doubting Thomas' demurred recognition of Jesus: 'After the eleven [apostles] tell him of Jesus' appearance [after the crucifixion], [Thomas] spends a horrible night in the graveyard debating with himself and in total solitude the problems of death, resurrection, and faith. In his praying and in his delirium, Thomas cannot reach any conclusion by reasoning (or, as Aristotle would have called it, *syllogismos*), but . . . he is prompted to accept the mystery by a voice which speaks to him from the darkness. And the voice is that of Joseph, Jacob's son, the protagonist of one of the most spectacular recognition scenes ever invented: a scene which Klopstock's Jesus recounts to the two disciples walking towards Emmaus and which they quote to the apostles when they reach Jerusalem. [In these scenes the author is] implicitly resorting to the ancient exegetical method of typology. Joseph, a traditional *figura* of Jesus, manifested himself to, and was recognized by his brothers, who believed him dead – after resurrection, Jesus appears, is recognized, and "believed in" by the apostles. In fact, Klopstock has the post-resurrectional recognition scenes culminate in a series of triumphal epiphanies and theophanies . . . which involves all the patriarchs and in one of which Joseph, talking to Benjamin, recalls "the sweetest of (his) earthly hours", that of anagnorisis.'

5. Cf. the kind of textual sublimation discussed persuasively by Daniel Beaumont in '"Peut-on . . .": Intertextual Relations in *The Arabian Nights* and Genesis', *Comparative Literature* 50:2 (1998), pp. 120–35.
6. Robert Irwin, *The Arabian Nights. A Companion* (London: Penguin, 1995).
7. Here Joseph – a kind of narrative incarnation of epiphanic disclosure – functions much as a fictionalised Homer does in foreshadowing the denouement in Heliodorus' *Aethiopica* (Terence Cave, *Recognitions* (Oxford: Clarendon Press, 1988), p. 21): 'The allusive character of the work as a whole, its literary inbreeding, is perhaps best epitomized by an extended reference to Homer . . . There is a quotation from Homer (the *Iliad*) about recognizing gods when they visit humans in disguise, and this is followed by a long quasi-biographical digression in which Homer is said to have been an Egyptian, illegitimately fathered by the God Hermes . . . This anecdote not only reveals considerable interest in Homer on Heliodorus' part, but actually creates the elements of an unresolved recognition story, so that the epic narrator *par excellence* becomes a character in a fiction that bears some resemblance to his own . . . It is as if Heliodorus were trying to frame intertextually not only his own narrative and the *Odyssey* but even Homer himself, thus *closing off all legendary narratives in a domain of their own.*' [my emphasis]
8. See *Al-Rabghūzī, The Stories of the Prophets: Qiṣaṣ al-Anbiyāʾ: An Eastern Turkish Version*, vol. 2, trans. H. E. Boeschoten, J. O'Kane and M. Vandamme (Leiden: Brill, 1995).
9. Al-Rabghūzī, *Qiṣaṣ*, pp. 264–5.
10. One wonders if the Qurʾanic phrase '*Yā Bushrā*' (Q 12:19) is not ultimately the source of inspiration for Mubashshirah's story.
11. For a detailed discussion of this anecdote (in Ibn ʿAbd Rabbih's version) and its significance, see Julia Bray's 'ʿAbbasid Myth and the Human Act: Ibn ʿAbd Rabbih and Others', in Philip F. Kennedy (ed.), *On Fiction and* Adab *in Medieval Arabic Literature* (Wiesbaden: Harrassowitz Verlag, 2006), esp. pp. 34–9. Other versions of the story are discussed in Julia Bray's 'Christian King, Muslim Apostate: Depictions of Jabala ibn al-Ayham in Early Arabic Sources', in Arietta Papaconstantinou (ed.), *Writing 'True Stories'* (Turnhout: Brepols, 2010), pp. 175–203.
12. We do not yet know if it has survived the depradations Aleppo has suffered in the current civil war.
13. Yasser Tabbaa, *Constructions of Power and Piety in Medieval Aleppo* (University Park: The State University of Pennsylvania Press, 1997), p. 171.

14. An exquisite short story of mystical recognition with allusions to Joseph, told as an allegory of shame and redemption, exists in Ibn Sīna's *Salamān and Absāl*. An abridged account can be read in Henry Corbin's *Avicenna and the Visionary Recital* (Princeton: Princeton University Press, 1988), pp. 224–5. It features one of the most astonishing bed tricks in Islamic literature.
15. Tabbaa, *Constructions of Power*, p. 180.
16. A version is told in Abū ^{c}Alī al-Muḥassin al-Tanūkhī's *Al-Faraj ba^{c}d al-Shiddah* (F 349), but the latter is quite distinct; the story here is, in fact, closer to the *Faraj* story told about al-Faḍl b. Rabī^{c} in flight from al-Maʾmūn (F 465). The abbreviation 'F 349' refers to *Faraj* story number 349 in the five-volume edition of ^{c}Abbūd al-Shāljī (Beirut: Dār Ṣādir, 1978), III, pp. 334–8.
17. *Qiṣaṣ al-^{c}arab*, ed. Muḥammad Abū al-Faḍl Ibrāhīm *et al.* (Beirut: al-Maktabah al-^{c}Aṣriyyah), 1, pp. 215–17.
18. Qurʾan 12 Yūsuf 92.
19. Abū Isḥāq Ibrāhīm ibn al-Qāsim Al-Raqīq al-Qayrawānī 'al-Nadīm' (b. in the fourth century Hijrī/tenth century AD) probably found this story in Abū al-Faraj al-Iṣfahānī's *Kitāb al-Aghānī* (Cairo, 1927), vol. I, p. 48.
20. For detailed discussion of Ibn Nāqiyā's opus of ten *maqāmāt*, see Stefan Wild, 'Die zehnte Maqāma des Ibn Nāqiyā: eine Burleske aus Baghdad', in W. Heinrichs and G. Schoeler (eds), *Festschrift Ewald Wagner zum 65. Geburtstag. Band 2: Studien zur Arabischen Dichtung*, (Beirut: Franz Steiner, 1994), pp. 427–38; Geert Jan van Gelder, 'Fools and Rogues in Discourse and Disguise: Two Studies', in Robin Ostle (ed.), *Sensibilities of the Islamic Mediterranean: Self-Expression in Muslim Culture from Classical Times to the Present Day* (London: I. B. Tauris, 2008), pp. 27–58; Philip F. Kennedy, 'Reason and Revelation or A Philosopher's Squib (The Sixth Maqāma of Ibn Nāqiyā)', *Journal of Arabic and Islamic Studies* 3 (2000), pp. 84–113.
21. 'One of the great singers of the early Ḥid̲j̲āzī school of Arabic music, was born in Mecca in 40/660 . . . He used to improvise his songs and to accompany himself on the Persian flute. He set to music poems of ^{c}Umar b. Abī Rabī^{c}a and other poets. He moved his audience to tears, for his song came from the heart, not from the head. Some of his melodies go under the name of his son-inlaw Sa^{c}īd b. Mas^{c}ūd al-Hud̲h̲alī. He died of elephantiasis in Mecca in 96/714, but other dates (even as late as 126/744) are also given. His death was lamented by Kat̲h̲īr b. Kat̲h̲īr (al-Sahmī).' Quoted from *Encyclopaedia of Islam* (2nd edn) article by J. W. Fück.
22. Cf. in Ibn Ṭufayl's *Ḥayy b. Yaqẓān* (trans. Lenn Evan Goodman – Chicago:

University of Chicago Press, 2009) the recognition of the eponymous hero's own differentiated self in the sphere of the Active Intellect.

23. For the Arabic versions of this tale, see *Alf laylah wa-laylah*, Būlāq, I, pp. 125–38; Calcutta II, I, pp. 320–50; Breslau, IV, p. 365 – V, p. 34; for Antoine Galland's original French translation, see his volume VIII, pp. 1ff. (republished lately in *Les Mille et une nuits* (Paris: GF-Flammarion, 1965), vol. 2, pp. 377–421); for the anonymous English 'Grub Street' rendering of Galland's French in Henry Weber's 1812 orthographic adaptation, see R. L. Mack (ed.), *Arabian Nights' Entertainments* (Oxford, 1996), pp. 535–71; see also, Edward William Lane, *A New Translation of the Tales of the Thousands and One Nights* (London: Charles Knight & Co., 1838–40), I, pp. 487ff.; Richard Burton, *The Book of the Thousand Nights and a Night* (London, 1885–8), II, pp. 1–76. The tale is not part of the extant Syrian recension and is not therefore in Haddawy's recent translation – Husain Haddawy, *The Arabian Nights* (New York: Norton, 1988). All Paris (Bibliotheque Nationale) manuscript versions of this story correspond closely to the Arabic of Būlāq and Calcutta II, except for the spurious Arabic of BN 3616 folia 141–80 which is Dom Denis Chavis' late eighteenth century translation into stilted Arabic of Galland's already freely adapted French translation.
24. See Andras Hamori, 'The Magian and the Whore: Readings of Qamar al-Zaman' in Kay Hardy Campbell *et al.* (eds), *The 1001 Nights: Critical Essays and Annotated Bibliography* (Cambridge, MA: Dar Mahjar, 1985), pp. 25–40. Given that the majority of material examined in this section is culled from *The Arabian Nights,* we should also bear in mind the subtle processes of textual influence and transformation discussed in Dan Beaumont's 'Peut-on'; the author suggests intriguingly that, and shows in detail how, essential elements of the story of Abraham and Isaac have been distilled and condensed in the *Arabian Nights*' story of the Merchant and the Genie.
25. The phrase appears in the Egyptian recension of the *Nights* only; it is absent from the so-called Syrian recension edited by Muhsin Mahdi.
26. In one of al-Tanūkhī's *Faraj* anecdotes (F 208; see Chapter 4 below) the events are set in motion by the prospect of a family reunion; this is to take place in Egypt and, strikingly, some of the names involved include Yūsuf, Yaᶜqūb and Isḥāq – a transparently evocative conjunction. (This is manipulating the evidence somewhat, since the full names are: Abū Muḥammad al-Ḥasan b. Yūsuf, the brother of the narrator Abū l-Ḥasan Aḥmad b. Yūsuf al-Azraq b. Yaᶜqūb b. Isḥāq, who is to escort the wife and sister of a third brother, Abū Yaᶜqūb Isḥāq b. Yūsuf, to Egypt to be reunited with husband and father. But in some sense,

by virtue of marked repetition, the full names lay even greater stress on the patriarchs; see Julia Bray, 'Place and Self-image: the Buhlūlids and Tanūḫids and their family traditions', in Antonella Ghersetti (ed.), *Quaderni di Studi Arabi* 3: *Luoghi e immaginario nella letteratura araba* (Rome, 2008), p. 53). Predictably, recognition is an important feature of this tale of deliverance. Other stories of reunion in Egypt carry the same nomenclatural significance. See the popular story, *Geschichte Jussufs und des Indischen Kaufmanns*, Christian Maximilian Habicht, *Tausend und eine Nacht: Arabische erzählungen* (Leipzig: F. W. Hendel, 1926), pp. 179–97 [540th–542nd nights].

27. Mack, *Arabian Nights' Entertainments*, pp. 535–71.
28. For a detailed discussion of the way Galland worked with and transformed the Arabic materials at his disposal, see Muhsin Mahdi, *The Thousand and One Nights*, vol. 2, ch. 1; Irwin, *The Arabian Nights*, pp. 54–62; and more recently, Eva Sallis, *Sheherazade through the Looking Glass: The Metamorphosis of the Thousand and One Nights* (London: Curzon Press, 1999), pp. 47–50.
29. Eva Sallis has discussed this extensively in *Sheherazade through the Looking Glass*. See also Philip F. Kennedy and Marina Warner (eds), *Scheherazade's Children: Global Encounters with the* Arabian Nights (New York: New York University Press, 2013).
30. When we compare Arabic and translated versions of this tale, the nomenclature can appear problematic and deserves a clarifying note: Galland called the hero of the story Ghānim but changed the name of his father from Abū Ayyūb to 'Abou Aibou'; Chavis then turned the father's name back into an impossible Arabic name of Abū l-Hibū (BN 3616 f. 141); Galland gave Qūt al-Qulūb (Ghānim's beloved) the name Fitna (Ghānim's sister), and to Fitna he gave the name 'Force de coeurs', which Chavis turned back into Arabic as Quwwat al-Qalb. The Grub Street English translation sustains Galland's inversion of names, giving the name Alcolomb to the sister and Fetnah to the hero's beloved. However, although the inversion is sustained these names themselves are closer to the original Arabic than Galland's and suggest some access to the original Arabic independent of the Frenchman's published translations.
31. My study is also informed by the work of the late and lamented Peter Heath ('Romance as Genre in the Arabian Nights', parts I and II in *Journal of Arabic Literature* 18 and 19 (1989)) and to a lesser extent that of Edgard Weber (*L'Imaginaire arabe et contes erotiques* (Paris: L'Harmatton, 1991)). See below.
32. The omission of these elements from Lane's Victorian translation provides us

with an obvious gauge to their lascivious content. Galland of course had omitted these elements long before Lane. Burton, true to form, includes these elements fully in his translation.

33. Peter Heath has already made the point in 'Romance as Genre', part II, p. 2. It will be important in the end to stress fidelity to one's master over the general quality of chastity – see below.
34. Mack, *Arabian Nights' Entertainments*, p. 543.
35. Ibid., p. 546.
36. Ibid., p. 548.
37. Northrop Frye, *Fables of Identity: Studies in Poetic Mythology* (New York: Harcourt Brace and World, 1963), p. 116.
38. Mack, *Arabian Nights' Entertainments*, pp. 561–2.
39. The Arabic is *alladhī li-mawlāya yuḥarram ᶜalayya; wa-kull shayᵓ li-l-sayyid ḥarām; kullu-mā huwa makhṣūṣ li-l-sayyid ḥarām ᶜalā l-ᶜabd.*
40. Al-Kisāᵓī, *The Tales of the Prophets of al-Kisaᵓi*, trans. with notes by W. M. Thackston (Boston: Twayne Publishers, 1978), p. 174.
41. Claus Westermann, *Joseph: Studies of the Joseph Stories in Genesis* (London: Bloomsbury, 1996), pp. 24–5.
42. Weber, *L'Imaginaire arabe*, p. 205.
43. See the tragic *Thousand and One Nights'* romance of ᶜAlī b. Bakkār and Shams al-Nahār for the best example of the stifling unease that fear and respect for the caliph can engender (in Haddawy, *The Arabian Nights*, pp. 354ff.).
44. It normally occurs at the beginning of a narrative.
45. Mack, *Arabian Nights' Entertainments*, p. 540.
46. See Shawkat M. Toorawa (ed. and trans.), *Consorts of the Caliphs: Women and the Court of Baghdad* by Ibn al-Sāᶜī (New York: New York University Press, 2015) for a discussion of women and their roles in the intimate entourage of the caliphs.
47. Mack, *Arabian Nights' Entertainments*, p. 549.
48. See her words of warning when her son first sets out from Damascus.
49. For the reactions of the mother, see especially (Mack, *Arabian Nights' Entertainments*, p. 557) how she is exhorted to patience (*ṣabr*), claims certain knowledge of her son even while she is distressed by his absence, and then makes a comment on the nature of her complaint, all individual features redolent of Jacob's privileged yet imperfect knowledge: 'I know my son . . . I have educated him very carefully, and in the respect which is due to the commander of believers. He has not committed the crime he is accused of; I dare answer for his

innocency. But I will give over muttering and complaining, since it is for him that I suffer, and he is not dead.'

50. Mack, *Arabian Nights' Entertainments*, p. 541.
51. Just as death, Janus-like, with the march of events can represent both death *and* rebirth together.
52. Cave, *Recognitions*, p. 482
53. See Barbara Stowasser, *Women in the Qur'ān, Traditions, and Interpretation* (New York: Oxford University Press, 1994), p. 52.
54. The only Arabic version of the tale which corresponds closely to Galland's translation is the mansucript (Bibliothèque Nationale 3616) of Dom Denis Chavis' phony Arabic version, itself clearly and at times ludicrously based on Galland's French. See note 22 above.
55. Two other fairytale romances which merit analysis to the same degree as the story of Ghānim in framing the Joseph story across many aspects of the narrative are *Codadad and His Brothers* (see Mack, *Arabian Nights' Entertainments*, pp. 583–604) and *The Story of the Forty Maidens* contained in *Kitāb al-ḥikāyāt al-ʿAjībah wal-akhbār al-gharībah*, ed. Hans Wehr (Wiesbaden: Franz Steiner, 1956), pp. 105–21. The latter was recently translated by Geert Jan van Gelder in *Classical Arabic Literature: A Library of Arabic Literature Anthology* (New York: New York University Press, 2012), pp. 318–32.
56. Northrop Frye, *The Secular Scripture: A Study of the Structure of Romance* (Cambridge, MA: Harvard University Press, 1976), p. 54.
57. Ibid., p. 58.

4

Intertextuality and Reading: The Myth of Deliverance in *al-Faraj ba^{c}d al-Shiddah*

Medieval Arabic anecdote collections regularly contain pious stories of deliverance (*faraj*) after distress (*shiddah*) in which recognition inflects the relief with which such narratives tend to end. These stories cater to and display popular sentiment on the whole, though they are preserved in highbrow belles-lettristic (*adab*) collections of prose.[1] Deliverance[2] from evil, as a Christian might be more linguistically primed to say, is occasionally highlighted at the end of a story as a didactic message that accrues from events; however, the cognitive mechanism that unfolds and unveils *faraj* is rarely perceived in any kind of informal gloss or in a statement of poetics, which may take the form of a verse epilogue appended to the end of a tale. We may consider briefly, from the *Arabian Nights*, 'The Island King and the Pious Israelite'[3] which ends with just such a feature. It is a tale of a family's vanished prosperity, flight and separation wrought devastatingly by shipwreck (that old chestnut). The father is separated from his wife and two young sons during their voyage to a land where no one knows them in order to escape the ruthless exploitation at home by evil creditors. By and by, and rather more quickly than seems credible, the father becomes the king of a prosperous island to which visitors are attracted from far and wide. Among them, after discrete and staggered arrivals, are his two sons, whom he fails to recognise, and his wife, who does recognise their two sons from the *retrouvailles* that takes place between them, for they have been recounting their past lives audibly while keeping a wary eye over the imposing figure of their as yet unknown mother. Their stories are those that mark and signal their identities – the story of their shared diaspora – and in this sense they are classic '*hommes récits*', though accounts of their tribulations are relatively bare given the brevity of the tale. Their childhood severance becomes the very foretoken of their reunion, which is in the end a happy paradox.

This tale is fashioned from the barest ingredients of family romance, with two of the genre's most archetypical motifs: shipwreck, and the telling and overhearing of tales.[4] It is structured in crystalline fashion: one recognition leading to another, and the latter, within the short compass available to the redactor, being delayed as far as possible so as to end with the optimum discharge of pent up emotion. Nothing rescues the text from its cloying register: it is too terse and schematic (barely two pages in Būlāq) to escape this pitfall, for there is little room for nuance or refinement. The significance of the short tale lies in the lines of poetry – and statement of poetics – with which it ends, as referred to above, encapsulating its themes in the form of a moral lesson. It is a tale about *faraj* (deliverance) after *shiddah* (distress) expressed through the analogous Qurʾanic *yusr* after ᶜ*usr* (the latter doublet having the greater authority because it is scriptural). Recognition is not explicitly considered a theme per se; it is at most only a silent corollary. It is not even clear how the theme would be expressed and conceptualised in medieval Arabic.[5] Recognition remains simply part of the tacit technique of a tale of family reunion and providential design. There is no parody here, just a bland lesson in a certain kind of conventional emplotment.

Yet so unassuming – indeed so transparent – is the tale that it has its charm. The way the father loses his money is no more credible than the contrivance of *deus ex machina* by which he is rewarded with another fortune: a mysterious and disembodied voice instructs the lucky castaway, 'Dig in such-and-such a place and uncover great wealth.' One unlikelihood (implausible treasures to be unearthed, pinpointed as if on a map by an unknown voice) is the recompense for another (the depletion of his inherited wealth by sharpsters who, taking advantage of an oath he had made to his dying father that he would never swear a solemn oath, prevent him from swearing that the debts they claimed against him were entirely fraudulent!).

There are far more sophisticated anecdotes than this in the *Faraj ba*ᶜ*d al-Shiddah* as well as other *adab* collections, including al-Tanūkhī's other collection of anecdotes, the *Nishwār al-Muḥāḍarah*.[6] Broadly speaking, the anecdotes set out below, across the remainder of the chapter, display a number of features. By and large they have been arranged to exhibit increasing complexity. The sophistication of the stories lies either in their relatively deft structure (e.g. the final two romances of the series) or in the ambiguity of their content: in the series of brigand stories moral and emotional ambiguity emerges from the recognition scene; characters display picaresque traits yet the recognitions between the main players tend to underline their laudable and face-saving human virtues. Another feature which comes through from the chapter as a whole is that of the connection between reading and recognition; this subsists between the players within a story but also reaches out towards the story's readership which sees, just as the players do, the connections that make recognition a process of gleaning the qualities that bind people together in an evolving and unspoken social contract of providential goodness.

Far more sophisticated in Arabic than our short *Arabian Nights* exemplar of the 'Pious Israelite' are those tales that al-Tanūkhī (d. 994 AD) brought together in his multi-volumed collection. *Faraj* 158[7] is a good example, and one that is appropriate to a subject that brings different generic corpora of literature together, for it is precisely about the crossing of sectarian boundaries along the Muslim-Byzantine marches during the ninth century AD. Its attribution to an anonymous source suggests from the outset that it is in fact a substantially tall tale, artfully devised.

> *The Story.* A man from Kufa related: We were with Maslamah ibn ᶜAbdallah [an Umayyad general] on the Byzantine marches where he took numerous prisoners. Many were put to the sword, and when a weak old man appeared before him still he ordered his execution.
>
> 'What need do you have to kill an old man like me?' he asked. 'If you let me live, I will bring you two young Muslim prisoners [from among the Byzantines].'
>
> 'Who will guarantee me this?' asked Maslamah.
>
> 'I keep the pledges I make,' replied the old man.
>
> 'I do not trust you,' said Maslamah. So the old man asked leave to search the camp for someone who might warrant his pledge until he returned with two prisoners of war. Maslamah delegated someone to accompany him around, ordering him to keep a watchful eye. The Shaykh wandered around

awhile, inspecting the faces of those he came across until he passed by a young man from the Banū Kilāb who was grooming his horse (*farasahu*).

He said to the young man, 'Act as my guarantor with the Emir.' Then he explained the whole situation. 'I will do it,' said the young man who then went to Maslamah, and pledged his guarantee, whereupon the old man was released. When he had left, Maslamah asked his guarantor:

'Do you know the old man?'

'No, by God!'

'Why then did you act as his guarantor?'

'I saw him inspecting people's faces, and he chose me from among them, so I was loath to disappoint his impression of me.'

On the following day, the old man returned accompanied by two Muslim prisoners of war whom he delivered into the hands of Maslamah. He then asked,

'Would the Emir allow me to take this young man, my guarantor, away with me to my camp so that I can reward him for what he has done for me?'

Maslamah replied to the young man, 'If you are willing to go, then go with him.'

When the two arrived at the old man's camp, the latter said, 'Young man, did you know that you are my son?'

'How can I be your son when I am a Muslim from among the Arabs and you are a Byzantine Christian?'

The old man then said, 'Tell me about your mother. What is her ethnicity?'

'Byzantine,' replied the young man.

'I will describe her to you,' said the old man. 'If I am right about her will you then believe me?'

'Please, go ahead.'

In unerring detail the Byzantine described the mother of the young man, who then said,

'She is indeed as you say, but how did you know I was her son?'

'From resemblance, by the way souls recognise each other, and by the grace of astute physiognomy (*firāsah*).'

He then brought a woman out to him, and when the young man saw her, he was sure it was his mother, due to their great resemblance. Then an old woman came out, also his mother's spitting image. They approached the man and kissed his head and hands.

The Shaykh said, 'This is your grandmother, and this is your aunt.'

Then he rode out from his camp and summoned some young men from the desert. They came and he spoke to them in Greek. They kissed the youth's head and hands, upon which the old man said, 'These are your maternal uncles and cousins, and your mother's paternal cousins.'

He then brought out many jewels and sumptuous clothes for the young man, saying, 'These are your mother's and have been safeguarded by us since she was taken prisoner. Take them with you and give them to her. She will recognise them.' He then gave the young man much money for himself, prepared pack animals, escorted him to Maslamah's camp and left him. The young man returned to his house and took out all the things he had been given and which the Shaykh had said belonged to his mother. She saw them and cried . . . As he kept pulling things out, she asked, 'My son, where did you get all these clothes from? Would you describe the people of the place from which all of this came?'

He then described the fortress and the locale, as well as her mother and aunt, and the other men whom he had seen. She cried and was upset.

'Why do you cry?' he asked.

'The old man is my father, by God, and the old woman my mother; and the other one, my aunt.'

So he told her the story, and took out the rest of what her father had given him, handing it all over to her. *Finis.*

Recognition, together with the virtual and momentary reunion it facilitates between the members of a family separated by war, clearly overrides the theme of deliverance for which it is the principal narrative vehicle of enunciation. Marvellous recognition is explained rationally and attributed to physical resemblance, but also irrationally according to spiritual affinities (the classic 'call of blood' motif). The most interesting theme developed in this respect is that of physiognomy (*firāsah*),[8] for this 'science' (and its role in many narratives like this one)[9] pretends to be entirely rational, yet so many of the stories in which it features undermine its apparently rational premises.[10] Here it is the old man who observes physically the features in a person's face that tell him he is in the presence of his grandson. The son, for his part, is introduced to us grooming his horse – that is, his *faras*, a noun that shares the root of *firāsah*, surely a deliberate element of textual paronomasia, suggesting by simple semantic association the reciprocal process of recognition. The young man innately recognises the merit of his grandfather's perceptions before he has any idea as to who he is, and is eventually rewarded for his trust and hospitality (both are often ancillary themes of recognition, especially in Arabic texts where semantic roots are shared). Here we refer to the loaded semantics and etymology of the word *maᶜrūf*. It means 'known' or 'recognised', literally, but it has the important ethical sense of 'charity' specifically, and the 'good' and the 'right' more generally.[11] Withal, however, there is much providential manipulation in the story – a limpid transcendent scheme emerges that is scarcely rational and more convincingly immaculate. Indeed, physiognomy in general is rarely more than a rationalising charade for luck and destiny's tricks – here the very comforting tricks of familial deliverance managed with deliberate and measured timing.[12] The point is obvious but merits mention: the tokens used in the story are purely physical but the message is human, ecumenical and quite spiritual.

Symmetry, Form and Meaning

Reunion as a theme has shape: it is in a sense the closing of a circle and can be experienced as such in reading. Sometimes this kind of resolution, or closure, is enhanced by other patterns of composition, tending towards the physical symmetry of form. Use of such highly determined epitomes aids the rhetorical expression of meaning. Al-Tanūkhī's F 157 displays in an uncomplicated and quite short anecdote the relationship between recognition and narrative equilibrium-cum-symmetry. It is the story of a certain Muḥammad b. al-Faḍl al-Jarjarāʾī who used to run the estate of al-Muᶜtaṣim's general, ᶜAjīf b. ᶜAnbasah, at Kaskar until accused of mismanagement and leading the place to ruin. He was arrested and brought in chains before his employer at Samarra. When threatened with being stripped and flogged, he was terrified and urinated upon himself. He was then saved by the intercession of ᶜAjīf's secretary, who advised that the matters be investigated before any punishment be meted out. ᶜAjīf was then summoned by al-Muᶜtaṣim to accompany him on the campaign against Amorium in Anatolia (in 838 AD) and was subsequently one of the officers put to death for conspiracy upon the caliph's return. Thus Muḥammad al-Jarjarāʾī was released and found employment thereafter running several estates between Mosul and Raʾs ʿAyn.

One of these estates was known as Karāthā. On arrival there one day, he found the privy of the house in which he was staying to be cramped and unclean and so he relieved himself by urinating outside upon a mound of earth at the edge of the desert. Witnessing this, the owner of the house came out after him and asked, 'Do you know what you have urinated upon!?' He replied, 'A mound of earth.' The man laughed and said, 'This is the grave of a man known as ʿAjīf, one of the caliph's generals who was brought here in chains and executed.' In the closing words the protagonist adds, recognising a tidy biographical symmetry: 'I marvelled at having urinated upon myself when he terrified me then urinating on his grave.'

Recognition can restore identity. In a similar way, it restores or establishes the equilibrium of justice, as it does here where, with the identification of ʿAjīf's grave the protagonist, together with al-Tanūkhī's reader, sees the wheel of justice turn full circle to put right an iniquity. It is poetic justice we witness as much as the equitable execution of social affairs: the protagonist urinates twice in a state of ignorance, of fear and innocence, and then gleans the machinations of fortune in a quintessentially private, and normally quite trivial, corporal experience. Small events are linked to a greater scheme and acquire significance. The final recognition is clearly not coterminous or synchronous with deliverance in this case, but a reminder of it that adds fortune's ironic signature to the happy turn of events.

Recognition and Ethical Expression

The ethical and moral gloss that recognition imparts to a text is seen in the Indian story that al-Tanūkhī (F 466)[13] relays from a famous traveller who heard it from 'one of the Indian *Maisur* (a word which means one who is born in India as a Moslem)'. It is more apparently folkloric[14] than most stories in al-Tanūkhī's collection, but it is a valuable tale to adduce by virtue of its quite archetypal structure, and because it provides a paragon of a kind of recognition that issues in a clear moral lesson about hospitality – about the ability to recognise someone unknown and to receive that person with, and in effect as, *maʿrūf*.

The setting is vague and ahistorical: 'a certain Indian state where the King was of good character'. At the outset, an important feature (or oddity) of regal practice is described, which is that the kings of India would give and receive gifts and other physical objects with their hands held out behind their backs, as if to gesture at the reversals that matters can or must suffer in life. This is a well-judged detail in a story that is built upon two fully antithetical cycles of changing fortune. Power in this kingdom is usurped by a villain, the king dies and his rightful heir flees, but

> it is a practice of the Indian kings that if one of them leave his seat for any purpose, he must have a vest, with a pocket containing all sorts of precious gems, such as rubies, folded in satin. The value of these gems is sufficient for the establishment of a great kingdom should a disaster compel him to take flight.[15]

That they are gems also marks them out potentially as tokens of identity, flagged glaringly for the reader to note at the start of the young heir's adventures. He takes the vest and flees.

Destitute, tired and hungry along the open road, he encounters a well-to-do itinerant man 'with a wallet on his shoulder'. They travel together for seven days; the prince hopes to be offered food and sustenance by this traveller but is offered nothing during the whole week. When they come upon a village, the heir decides to stay and seek 'employ for a wage'. He is taken on by the foreman of a building site, and displays the odd habit of taking and giving mortar 'in accordance with the royal custom':

> I kept turning my hand behind my back to hand them the mortar: only whenever I recollected that this was a mistake and might forfeit me my life, I hastened to correct it and turn my hand in the right direction before I attracted attention.[16]

A woman does, however, notice this behaviour and infers that he must be of royal stock. She treats him kindly and they marry. Four years later, strangers appear seeking the rightful heir to their kingdom in order to instate him upon its throne. But they have no trace of him. At this prompting, the young prince identifies himself to their spokesman:

> Do you know me? He said, No. – I told him that I was the person he was seeking, and produced the tokens: he admitted the truth of what I said, and made obeisance. I bade him conceal our business till we had reached the country, and he agreed. I then went to my wife and told her the facts – the whole story![17]

He is returned to his kingdom and established on his rightful throne, his tokens eventually warranting his birthright.

Though the story could end there, it has a significant surplus. 'He ordered a vast mansion to be erected, to which everyone who passed through his territory should be brought to be entertained there for three days, and furnished with provisions for three more.'[18] He took to inspecting his guests, for he sought the appearance of the man who had refused him succour. Then one day,

> he saw [him] among the people. When his eye fell on him, he gave him a betel leaf, which is the highest honour that a sovereign can bestow on a subject. When the king did this the man made obeisance and kissed the ground. The King bade him rise and looking at him perceived that he did not recognize the King. He ordered the man to be well looked after, and entertained, and when this was done summoned him and said: Do you know me? The man said: How could he fail to know the King, who is so mighty and exalted! The King said: I was not referring to that: Do you know who I was before this state? The man said, No. The King then reminded him of the story and how he had withheld food from the prince for seven days when they were on the road. The man was abashed, and the King ordered him to be taken back to the mansion, and entertained. Presently he was found dead. The Indian liver is abnormally large, and chagrin had been too much for this man, whose liver it affected, so he died.[19]

Structurally, these events are tidy and balanced: what is lost is recouped in clean sequential stages, and exile is followed naturally by return (in a mini, and decidedly unepic, *nostos*). Tokens of identity and status are flagged conspicuously and then play a part in recognition scenes that are thus transparently foreshadowed. They hold little surprise and are largely determined by convention. More significant is the fact that the themes of the tale are explored on two levels: there is a broad political plot of sovereignty lost then regained, and the personal plot of the dealings between the prince and his miserly companion. The first is larger, more general, broadly providential and less interesting, though it pretends to proffer ethnographic insights. This rather smacks of pseudo-ethnography. It is the personal plot of the king's dealing with the unknown individual that carries the ethical force of the story. And it is privileged by its structural placement, giving the subplot an enhanced quality. Recognition is built into the story at several moments and on two levels: the final anagnorisis, which resolves the subplot, carries the strongest moral dividend, and the other moments of recognition can be read as leading into it according to an inexorable epistemological momentum. In such a scheme, the recognitions of the heir-in-hiding first as a nobleman and then as rightful king, by his wife and his subjects, respectively, are moments of synecdoche, parts-for-the-whole of this recognition story, before the final message about the ethical and moral duty of hospitality. The second anagnorisis is dwelt on in relative detail, and thus underlines the terrible shock to the abashed visitor. His recognition is blatantly moral as well as cognitive – an agonising, and literally unbearable, object lesson about right (ethical) and good (moral) principles of hospitable conduct.[20]

Recognition, Kindness and Moral Imperatives

There is always at least a minimal measure of dramatic quality in a recognition scene, however high or low the register. The few examples we give below are of far greater nuance and realism, thus more moving and more memorable. Still, the ethical aspect of recognition is quite patent; recognition is indeed palpably part of the resolving syntax of ethical expression. In F 447 the obligation to receive a stranger kindly is spun as a beautiful narrative of symmetry and coincidence with, as in other stories, the bitter historical animosity between the Umayyads and the Alids as its backdrop.[21] The intensity of that hostility drives home the point of kindness and hospitality all the more. Al-Tanūkhī's illustrious literary colleague Abū al-Faraj al-Iṣfahānī is claimed as its source.

The Story. At the start of each fiscal year, Muḥammad b. Zayd al-ᶜAlawī, a scion of ᶜAlī ibn Abī Ṭālib, used to review the government coffers of Tabaristan and disburse the surplus from the previous year among the

Qurayshīs, the Anṣār, the *fuqahāʾ*, *et al.* One year when he had finished distributing money to the Hashemites and summoned the Banū ᶜAbd Manāf, a man stood up. But he kept his silence when asked to which clan of ᶜAbd Manāf he belonged. Muḥammad b. Zayd questioned him further and confirmed his growing suspicion that the stranger belonged to the line of Yazīd b. Muᶜāwiyah (d. 683 AD), the most loathsome to the Alids on account of their role in the killing of al-Ḥusayn b. ᶜAlī. So he railed against the stranger thus: 'If you have come in ignorance of the circumstances [that you find yourself in], then this is the most abject ignorance! If you have come with evil design, then you are truly risking your life!' But, though, with these words, Muḥammad expressed deeply ingrained animosity, when the entire audience in attendance leered at the stranger threateningly, Muḥammad warned them against their evil intentions explaining that killing this man would be illegitimate vengeance for the murder of al-Ḥusayn at Karbala. And he told a story about an act of noble clemency that transcends the ingrained sectarian hatred between the Alids for the Umayyads.

The story was told by his grandfather, also named Muḥammad b. Zayd (and great grandson of al-Ḥusayn b. ᶜAlī). While performing the pilgrimage in Mecca one year the caliph al-Manṣūr was shown a gemstone that had been found in the Ḥaram; he recognised it as having once belonged to Hishām b. ᶜAbd al-Malik, and knew also that it was now in the possession of Hishām's son, Muḥammad. Assuming Hishām's son to be present in Mecca, a trap is sprung. The following day, al-Manṣūr instructs his men to lock the gates of the holy precinct during prayer, allowing people to exit only by one designated gate, the easier to stake out his quarry. When the gates are closed, Muḥammad b. Hishām realises what is afoot and becomes visibly distressed. Muḥammad b. Zayd, the great grandson of al-Ḥusayn, is present and notices the man's distress, realising that he is the individual being sought, though he still does not know who he is. He pledges to protect him unconditionally, and only then finds out his identity. Apologising in advance for the mistreatment he will receive during a scheme to enable his escape, he dresses the man in rags, and in full view of the men guarding the gate gives him a heavy beating, claiming him to be a truant camel driver. He is thus given an escort to lead the man back to his caravan. Now safe, Muḥammad b. Hishām kisses his saviour's head and offers him (another) gem as a gift. But the gift is refused with these words: 'We do not accept recompense for goodness that is a moral duty (*maʿrūf*).' The gem as a classic token is here transcended by the moral gift of hospitality.[22] When he finishes his story Muḥammad b. Zayd gives his unlikely Umayyad protégé his share of the fiscal surplus.

While ostensibly sectarian (an Alid meets an Umayyad in a relationship of potential enmity), both the frame story and the embedded story are more particularly about the moral responsibility of helping a stranger, in one case disbursing money and in another saving a life. In each case, the *mise en scène* turns on the discovery of identity and, of the two, the embedded tale even manages with some originality to work in a mysteriously misplaced gem as a token of identity. The question to ponder over residually is whether or not personal recognition works to help the articulation of the moral message. It is certainly not as clear in this story on the whole as it is in many other *adab* anecdotes. In each of the two mini dramas of recognition, an identity emerges that challenges the generous to rise above sectarian prejudice. The rather uncomplicated message itself remains for the audience to discern for, while the processes of disclosure and didacticism complement each other, their lines of articulation are not clearly superimposed upon each other. Thus the didacticism of recognition remains essentially a readerly exercise, as is often the case in narrative.

Two Ethical Stories: A Diptych of Lost Purses

Al-Jāḥiẓ's short anecdote about the miser from Merv, with its dispiriting disclosure for the narrator who is forced to face up to the fact that he has dealings with a man of utter meanness, is in ethical temperament effectively the antithesis of a pair of stories in al-Tanūkhī's *Faraj baʿd al-Shiddah*,[23] a compelling diptych about lost purses turning up adventitiously, being recognised according to their conspicuous *ṣifah*s, and delivering their owners from years of misery.

Here, first, is the anecdote from al-Jāḥiẓ's *Kitāb al-Bukhalāʾ* (*Book of Misers*):[24]

> A man of Merv folk used regularly to go on pilgrimage and trade, staying (always) with a man of the Iraqi people, and the latter would entertain him and provide him with his victuals. Many a time he would say to this Iraqi:

> 'I do wish I might see you in Merv so that I could make you some return for your long-standing kindness and the fresh solicitude you show me each time I come, but here Allah has put me in need of you.' . . . Now, after a lengthy interval, business in the province (Merv) came the way of this Iraqi, and one of the things that made bearable enduring the journey and the loneliness of going to a strange place, was the man from Merv's being there. So when he arrived he went straight on to him in his traveling clothes – his turban, under-cap and (woollen) mantel – to unload his baggage at his house – as a man does with a trusted friend and place familiar to him. So when he came upon him sitting among his companions he bent down over him and embraced him, but he did not recognize him nor did he ask him the sort of questions any person who had ever seen him would ask. The Iraqi said to himself: 'Perhaps he does not recognize me because of the cloth covering my head.' So he threw his cloth aside and started to ask him things, but he showed even less recognition of him. So he said: 'Perhaps it may be the turban that has got him.' So he snatched it off. Then he told him his name and patronymic and started afresh to ask him things, but he found him utterly failing to recognize him. He said (to himself): 'Perhaps it is just the (under)-cap that has got him.' The man from Merv (now) realized that there was nothing left onto which a person making pretence at being unaware and not recognizing could fasten, so he said: 'If you were to take off your skin I still would not recognize you.'

Finally the man who resists being recognised recognises and confesses to the grotesque ingratitude in his true nature. Quite the contrary to this is al-Tanūkhī's engaging diptych, the first part of which, F 245, is told by a merchant from al-Karkh, on the western outskirts of Baghdad, who used to do business with a Khurasanian trader every year and made his livelihood from their transactions. One year the Khurasanian ceased to appear and, gradually, over four years, his continued absence left the Karkhī destitute and burdened with debt. Then one day, while out walking along the banks of the Tigris, his foot unearthed an object from the wet sand and, as he pulled on it, he found a leather purse full of dinars. His spirits restored by the lucky find, he decided to use the money to set his affairs in order and place the full sum aside in the purse, so as to return it to its rightful owner should he ever make himself known. Three years later, he was again a wealthy man. After seven years had passed since the Khurasanian's last appearance, a dishevelled pilgrim showed up at his shop door. He assumed that he was a beggar, but when offered some loose change, the man turned aside to leave. Puzzled by this behaviour, he stood up to look at him closely, and lo! he recognised him as his old partner from Khurasan.

Now the latter tells his story: about losing a purse that had been entrusted to him by the Emir of his home region; of a priceless gem he had been carrying in it together with a thousand dinars; and of his charge to sell the gemstone and return with a list of goods that were to have been bought with the proceeds of the sale. However, while swimming in the Tigris he carelessly left the purse on the riverbank and lost it. Upon his return home, he was financially ruined and spent seven years in the Emir's prison. Hearing of these misfortunes, and recognising the description of the purse, the Karkhī tells his friend: 'Some of your lost fortune has returned to you!' He produces the item; the Khurasanian emits a groan of delight and asks for a knife to cut open a secret pouch in which the gemstone had been safely concealed. He returns home to Khurasan, restores his affairs and delivers the gem back to the Emir, who in turn begs forgiveness for having mistreated him.

In F 246, the second episode of the diptych, the lost purse is made of silk and contains three thousand dinars. It is the possession of a pilgrim – the narrator – who loses it when he sets it aside to urinate along the way to Mecca. He then forgets to retrieve it. A man following behind chances upon it and uses the money to pay off some debts but, as in F 245, resolves to restore the full sum to its owner one day – but only upon detailed description of the purse as a warrant of rightful possession. In this case, the man who lost the purse barely notices the loss at first, for he is wealthy, but he squanders his fortune and comes to regret it. One day, years later, his wife is about to give birth and sends him out to buy some food for sustenance. He spends his last few pennies doing so but, on the way home, breaks the container he has bought, spilling and losing the groceries. At this he breaks down in the street bewailing his sundry misfortunes. When a passerby hears his distress, he comes to his assistance and asks to hear his story.

'I used to be so wealthy,' he begins, 'that even the loss of a purse with three thousand dinars went unnoticed. Now I cry over the breakage of a pot worth nothing more than one sixth of a dinar!' When the man asks to hear the description of the lost purse, the narrator moans that he is being made a mockery of, but he calms down when invited to take refuge at the man's house. Over a period of months, the man loans the narrator significant sums of money with which to do business and reconstitute his wealth. Eventually, one day, the benefactor pulls out a purse – *the* purse – and asks: 'Do you recognise this?' Of course, the narrator gets the purse back having already recouped much of its contents in the form of the loans he has received over several months, being thus restored in the process to healthy business practices.

These two stories seem deliberately to have been set side by side by al-Tanūkhī as a diptych. Both are charmingly told, with endearing human details about: on the one hand, forgetfulness and negligence, the quintessential insouciance of urinating in the sand without a care in the world; on the other, constancy and fidelity to an upright decision. The simple point to retain is that in each case recognition is part of the mechanism of deliverance, and is so marked as to feed (and indeed be fed by) the epistemology contained in the fraught concept of *ma*ᶜ*rūf*. For these are essentially stories about that broadly recognisable quality of goodness inhering in *ma*ᶜ*rūf* as much as they are about *faraj*. The terms are indeed two sides of a blessed coin: recognition of a person and a purse is recognition of pious action, for the reader, and provides two examples of providence's varied schemes of deliverance for the living.

Ethics, Equivocation and Prophetic Apparitions

There is a short paragraph in the first chapter of al-Tanūkhī's *Faraj* titled 'Accounts of the prophets' that provides an epitome of the Joseph story. It illustrates the didactic theme of *faraj ba*ᶜ*d al-shiddah* effectively and with great economy. There is scarcely any engagement with the narrative: no stress is laid on any particular element, except in giving equal status to Jacob and Joseph as protagonists of the story and as paragons of the virtue of patience (*ṣabr*). No attempt is made to link the surah with the material in chapter 6 of the *Faraj* with which it has such a clear affinity, that element in which dreams foretoken felicity after distress. This fact is even stranger given that the very title of chapter 6 echoes Surah 12 in two ways: (1) by differentiating between 'false dreams' and those that enunciate the truth ('*bushrā manāmin*' – 'good news announced in a dream' – and '*kidhb aḥlām*' – 'lying dreams' – correspond respectively to the roles played by '*ruʾyā/aḥādīth*' – 'vision/events related in dreams' – and '*aḍghāth aḥlām*' – 'tangled nightmares' – in the Qurʾanic narrative); and (2) the very word '*bushrā*' evokes the forager of the Midyanite caravan who calls back to his people upon finding Joseph in the pit: *yā bushrā*! ('Happy news!').[25]

The Joseph story is perhaps too obviously paradigmatic for al-Tanūkhī to have made a meal out of in gleaning an interpretive moral payoff. Yet this is precisely why we are justified in looking for echoes of it in other material that is less familiar. In this respect, chapter 6 of *Faraj* is the most propitious, consistently showing up varying details of affinity with the Joseph narrative. But the most interesting feature is how the theme of hesitation and equivocation is used.[26]

A Preamble: Recognising ᶜAlī ibn Abī Ṭālib

Faraj 199 is titled by al-Shāljī 'Why [the Caliph] al-Muᶜtaḍid never harmed or killed the ᶜAlawīs during his [reign]'.

> Muḥammad b. Yaḥyā b. Abī ᶜAbbād al-Ḥusnī related: When al-Muᶜtaḍid (d. 892) was in his father's [prison he had a dream in which] he saw what seemed to be an old man sitting by the banks of the Tigris stretching his hand into the water scooping it all up in his palm, at which the Tigris dried up. He then released [the water] back [into the river] . . . and the Tigris resumed its normal state . . . I asked him about [the identity] of this man, and he answered that it was ᶜAlī b. Abī Ṭālib (the Prophet Muḥammad's cousin).[27]

Recognition of ᶜAlī is the corollary of the more important fact of recognising his authority, such that al-Muᶜtaḍid relents in the oppression of Shiᶜites (ᶜAlawīs/followers of ᶜAlī) during his reign (in contrast to the severe policies of Hārūn al-Rashīd (d. 809 AD) and other predecessors). No attempt is made to account for how al-Muᶜtaḍid validates the identity of his interlocutor; it is as if ᶜAlī is associated with the belief in veridical dreams normally attaching to the person of the Prophet Muḥammad, viz. that if he visits you in a dream and you understand him to be the Prophet then he must indeed be the Prophet, for the Devil cannot take on his form in human reverie.[28]

The second and more detailed version of this story adds greater drama to the issue of identity. It is the miracle of diverting the waters of the Tigris that establishes the veracity of the man's claim to being ᶜAlī b. Abī Ṭālib, though the latter is not in fact recognised by his facial or corporal aspect. The anecdote may, reductively, be pursuing a simple logic: al-Muᶜtaḍid had never actually seen the Prophet's cousin, thus it would not be by his aspect that he could know him. We might also note that the fact of being in prison is a reflection of Joseph's biography: al-Muᶜtaḍid acquires a confidence while still physically detained, reflecting Joseph's story and his emerging strength of character as a prophet. The difference is that al-Muᶜtaḍid's confidence is expressed far more in material than religious or doctrinal terms. When al-Muᶜtaḍid is released from prison, he soon becomes caliph and his successful function as an administrator is described in some detail. Are there echoes here of Joseph's 'being made powerful in the land' (*tamkīn fī l-arḍ*) after release from prison? Whatever the case may be, this is not the only story of a man achieving high office after a period of incarceration, following some numinous preordainment.

A Doublet of Prophetic Apparitions

In two further anecdotes, it is not ᶜAlī but the Prophet Muḥammad who appears to a man in his dream. These materials, placed together below according to our own contrastive scheme of selection, give nuance to the varied semantics and the metonymy of recognition. In one instance, the Prophet has to identify himself while, in the other, the dreamer appears more immediately to intuit his identity – to recognise him more literally in the first place, thus allowing other implications to accrue to the fact. Across these two stories, if we are justified in holding them up interpretively as a diptych, there is a distribution and relaying of the varied rhetorical and structural roles of recognition and misrecognition.

Faraj 206, titled by al-Shāljī 'Al-Muᶜtamid releases two innocent men from his prison on the basis of a dream *(li-manāmin raʾā-hu)*' is told in two variant versions, the second of which is itself in twin parts and contains a complication – a twist – that insinuates a stunning ambiguity into the moral reflections of the denouement. The first account is told on the authority of Aḥmad b. Yazīd al-Muhallabī:

> We stood before al-Mu^c^tamid one night when wine was brought to him and his head began to droop from sleepiness. He said: 'Let nobody leave!' Then he slept for half an hour, waking as if he had drunk a bit and saying: 'Summon to me from the prison a man known as Manṣūr the camel-driver.' The latter was brought in and the caliph asked him: 'How long have you been detained?' He answered: 'It has been three years, now,' at which the caliph requested him to tell his story, but truthfully. He began [his tale]: 'I am a man from Mawṣil. I used to own a camel that provided my livelihood, and I raised my family with what I earned from renting it out. But as my income grew steadily slim in Mawṣil, I decided to set out for Samarra where work is less hard to come by. Upon approaching the city, I came across a group of soldiers escorting brigands whom they had arrested. Their number had been recorded by the post-master (*ṣāḥib al-barīd*). They were ten, one of whom bribed the soldiers to release him, which they did, arresting me in his stead to make up the numbers. They seized my camel, though I pleaded with them invoking God's exalted name, and explained to them my plight. But they refused [to listen] and imprisoned me. Some of those taken have since died and I remained alone.'
>
> Al-Mu^c^tamid said at this point: 'Bring five hundred dinars.' They were brought and he continued: 'Pay them to this man, and pay him a further stipend of thirty dinars per month, and put him in charge of our camels.' He – the caliph – then approached us, saying: 'Just now I saw the Prophet in a dream; he said: "Aḥmad, send someone to the prison and have Manṣūr the camel-driver released, for he has been falsely accused; and give him generous recompense." So I did what you have just seen me do.'

This first version of the story is the more straightforward of the two. The second one develops it in a number of significant ways. Al-Tanūkhī himself tells us that the second is the fuller rendering (*bi-atammi min hādhihi l-riwāyah*). It has, as we would expect, a different oral source, though in this case the writer's informant is yet another boon companion (*nadīm*) of the caliph – a companionship which, in evoking some measure of decadence, itself becomes relevant as the meaning of the events unfold. One element of distinction lies in the prefatory description of the caliph (al-Mu^c^tamid, d. 870 AD) as being of a quarrelsome nature when drunk, though in normal circumstances he was both tolerant and generous. Few gatherings were spared his querulous deportment when he became inebriated. On one occasion, once the caliph had already given his companions (*julasāʾ*) leave to exit, he gave orders for the narrator to be brought back to him in the middle of the night. The latter feared he was to be made the object of the caliph's caprice. Once in the presence of the caliph, the latter ordered the chief of police to be summoned, a command that intensified the narrator's anxiety. However, when the police chief arrives he is ordered to have so-and-so the camel-driver summoned from prison. The latter's story is similar to the one told in the first version, though this time the treachery to which he is exposed in being robbed of his camels is even more wicked and calculating: he is truly set up and set upon, being blamed for the act of brigandage of a group of Kurdish highwaymen. Having told his story, the man is released from prison and compensated.

At this point, we encounter a significant addition to the *récit*: the caliph orders the release of a second imprisoned individual – so-and-so the blacksmith – according to a similar sequence of events. Again the man has been wrongly accused: this time of killing the apprentice of the man he was working for. He too is set free by the caliph and generously recompensed; are we here, incidentally, brought back to the detail with which the *récit* begins according to which the caliph, in his normal comportment, is described as generous and tolerant? The narrator too is in a sense released from the anxious state in which he attended the caliph: he says of himself, 'The caliph dismissed me/dispelled my cares' (*farraja ʿannī*), transparently using the root *faraj* – underlining the full generic force of the anecdote. We can at the very least posit that there is a semantic (indeed, organic) relationship between the elements and details of the anecdote. This will emerge yet further.

Once these two astonishing acts of justice are completed, the caliph explains himself: he had seen a vision of the Prophet in his dream; it is here that the most significant detail in this particular version occurs, for the identity of the apparition is not immediately seized:

> I saw in my dream a man (*rajulan*) who said: 'There are two men in your prison who have been wrongly condemned; one of them is called Manṣūr the camel-driver, the other is so-and-so the blacksmith. Have them set free

> immediately and recompense them justly.' I woke up terrorized – then fell back to sleep. But no sooner had my limbs grown heavy again than the very same figure appeared to me, saying: 'Curse you! I ordered you to set free two injured men from your prison who have languished there . . . and you just fall back to sleep! I will hurt you for this!' And he was about to lay his hands upon me when I asked: 'Who are you?' He replied: 'I am the Prophet Muḥammad.' Whereupon I kissed his hand, explaining: 'O Prophet of God, I did not recognize you! If I had, I would not have dared to delay in discharging your orders.'[29]

This act of equivocation – of *méconnaissance*[30] – seems significant in two ways. First, it is a symptom of the unfolding themes of the text: of the fact, for instance, that the narrator himself has failed to recognise why he has been summoned to see the caliph in the middle of the night. The atmosphere that pervades the text – indeed its very subject – is that of misapprehension in both a literal and physical sense (the sense of wrongful arrest) and its more standard cognitive one. In this anecdote, the truth is resisted in a variety of ways, and grotesque miscarriages of justice provide the backdrop of this general theme.

For the second detail, we must look to the astonishing epilogue of the narrative:

> On the following evening I went to see the caliph at court; he was sitting drinking and I deemed it a good idea to let his company know what had happened the previous night so that he might be pleased, for I knew that he took great pleasure in being praised and eulogized; whenever he committed an act of kindness he mentioned it often in subsequent conversations, exalting in it, even if the deed was in fact quite paltry. I asked: 'What would the Commander of the Faithful say to my informing his servants about the miracle of last night and of the Prophet's attention to the affairs of his caliphate? His response to this was: 'And what is that?' I replied: 'Your summoning of myself and the chief of police, together with the camel-driver and the blacksmith, and [your] dream of the Prophet and how he ordered you to act in their regard.' He said that he didn't remember any of this, [insisting]: 'I was drunk and slept all night; I never woke up.' 'Indeed you did!' I replied. But again he denied this, saying: 'Will you play tricks with

> me and deceive me with lies?' Then he called upon his intimate servants who nevertheless confirmed what I had said; at this his astonishment was apparent and quite palpable, yet he swore that he had no recollection of anything. Now, I know of no more curious and novel event than the conjunction of [his] marvelous dream and his subsequent obliviousness to it.'

If we allow ourselves to restructure the text, to transpose the order of events in time (or juxtapose them synchronously, in effect), we come to a certain appreciation of the significance of al-Muᶜtamid's failure to recognise the Prophet upon his first appearance. That he should have fallen asleep after such a striking vision is, on the one hand, a simple inflection of realism – the caliph was blind-drunk. On the other hand, it also stresses the theme of *méconnaissance*: a failure both to recognise and act upon the instructions of the Prophet of Islam; this is appropriate given that he is, in the first place, inebriated and habitually given to such indulgence. The plain fact seems to be that the forgetting of the dream works in tandem with the failure to recognise and has some ethical significance linked with the caliph's general comportment. Epiphany, together with the implicit reward of grace it offers,[31] is spoiled, or essentially attenuated, by drunkenness. In sum, failure to recognise is rendered as a symptom of a moral failing, but the oneiric Prophet has justice on his mind – the release of the wrongfully imprisoned man – more than the goal of gifting the caliph with the blessing of his own apparition, which would surely be commensurate with cherished remembrance.

In F 208, the nature of prophetic recognition is quite distinct: it is ostensibly less problematic, yet misrecognition is inscribed significantly into the narrative in another way. The events are set in motion by the prospect of a family reunion: this is to take place in Egypt and the names of the family members include Yūsuf (Joseph), Yaᶜqūb (Jacob) and Isḥāq (Isaac) – a conspicuous onomastic conjunction.

Placing interpretive emphasis on these patriarchal names may be slightly underhand and unwarranted, since the full names of the characters are: Abū Muḥammad al-Ḥasan b. Yūsuf, the brother of the narrator Abū l-Ḥasan Aḥmad b. Yūsuf al-Azraq b. Yaᶜqūb b. Isḥāq, who is to escort the wife and sister of a third brother, Abū Yaᶜqūb Isḥāq b. Yūsuf, to Egypt to be reunited with husband and father. But in some sense, of course, the full names lay even greater stress on the biblical Patriarchs. That the order of the patriarchal lineage is scrambled tells us that if some version of (or generic allusion to) the Joseph narrative ensues it is likely to be both sublimated and kaleidoscopic. The fact that these individuals were real members of a prominent family of al-Tanūkh ('the Buhlūlids of al-Anbār and Baghdad'), with whom the author of *Faraj* had intimate contact, renders this interpretation of the names problematic, since at face value real people are telling what purport to be real events.[32] But does this fact necessarily disqualify a semantic reading of the narrative's poetics? Perhaps the author was aware of the aggregate significance of the names, a fact which may have affected the exact form the story acquired and the meaning thus conveyed when it was finally set down in writing – if only on some subliminal level.

The Story. Abū Muḥammad sets off for Egypt with his two female wards as part of a large caravan; in the heart of the desert of Samāwa they are betrayed by their guards and are set upon by Bedouins. The caravan is despoiled and Abū Muḥammad is left destitute together with all his travelling companions who are left bereft of mounts, provisions and a guide. Their choice was to meet their certain death either by passively staying put, in supine submission, or to make a forlorn effort to seek their salvation (*ṭalab al-khalāṣ*). The understanding at this juncture, that only God can actually save them, should He will, shares the simple theology of Surah 12.[33]

Eventually they come upon some Bedouin dwellings. The inhabitants are at first inhospitable (*ankarū-nā*) but they are soon prevailed upon to offer shelter and sustenance. Abū Muḥammad fares especially well with his host, for he has an aura of gravity and is well versed in the Qurʾan. After some time, Abū Muḥammad asks his host to escort him and his wards to Damascus, where he surmises that word will have spread of the caravan's fate and where – he also assumes – his brother will have made arrangements with friends to provide succour should Abū Muḥammad chance to show up. There, the Bedouin is told, he will be recompensed with whatever he desires. These are the actual words of Abū Muḥammad's assumption: *qaddartu annī idhā dakhaltu dimashqa wajadtu bi-hā min aṣdiqāʾi akhī man ākhudhu min-hu mā urīdu* ('I considered that if I were to go to Damascus I would find a friend of my brother to provide me with whatever I needed').[34]

We will encounter them again. In the hermeneutic code of this text, this is what Roland Barthes would call a snare (*une leurre*).[35]

Upon arriving in Damascus, survivors of the caravan seek out their friends and acquaintances. Abū Muḥammad, for his part, is recognised and met by a man who is apprised of both his *kunyah* (cognomen) and *nasab* (genealogy). Though he does not know this man from Adam, the familiarity he shows and articulates does not surprise him, for he assumes this to be a friend of his brother. In *Great Expectations* (Charles Dickens), when Pip assumes his benefactor to be Miss Havisham, he neither doubts this fact nor is he able to divulge his suspicions for he is sworn to silence, living thereby according to his misapprehension, which is reinforced with time. Albeit to a much smaller extent, a similar element exists in this narrative: 'I spent two days with this man living a life of ease; I asked him nothing, nor did he ask me . . .' At this point, the culmination of equivocation supervenes, for to recompense the Bedouin who had brought Abū Muḥammad to town, the Damascene host offers his guest whatever he desires to pay him off: 'Take all the money you wish' (*khudh mā turīd mina l-māl*). These words echo Abū Muḥammad's own previous thoughts, and never is he more certain that he is in the company of his brother's putative friend. Hence the force of surprise that ensues immediately afterwards:

> The Damascene asked me: 'Which country were you headed for? And how much money do you need/what expenses will you incur?' When he uttered these words I began to doubt him and said to myself: 'If this were one of my brother's friends . . . he would know my goal.' I asked: 'How much did my brother instruct you to pay me?' He answered: 'Who is your brother?' I told him: 'Abū Ya^c^qūb al-Azraq al-Anbārī, the administrator in Egypt'. He said he had never heard this name and did not know my brother. I was astonished and said, 'I thought (*ẓanantu*) that you were a friend of my brother and that your munificence towards me was on his account. This is why I was so forthright with you; if I hadn't been under this impression I would have been more restrained. Why have you [then] treated me thus?'[36]

Here we reach the third and last part of a composite anagnorisis: the Damascene explains that the Prophet had appeared to him in a dream instructing him to find Abū Muḥammad al-Azraqī and to give him what he needed. Hearing this Abū Muḥammad, profoundly moved, cries effusively and asks his helper what his name is. We are told in this version of the story, Fulān b. Fulān al-Ṣābūnī (So–and-So the Soapseller). A particularly subtle detail in the text is that Abū Muḥammad had indeed mentioned the name of this man more fully but Abū l-Ḥasan, the narrator, then admits to having forgotten it. It is a clever inflection of misrecognition suggesting the two sides of a coin: on the one hand, that the man most obliged to acknowledge charity does not forget the name of his helper, and, on the other, that the narrator who owes nothing to the charitable man allows it to slip his mind. The epilogue reveals providential design: Abū Yaᶜqūb indeed becomes a friend of the Ṣābūnī – Abū Muḥammad's assumption that they were friends had been significantly proleptic. Further, this friendship is in the end to the Ṣābūnī's advantage for, in subsequent years, he is himself succoured in time of hardship by his friend. This is an 'anecdote of destiny'.

In order to evaluate the two sides of recognition in this story, we should be reminded of the verb used when the Bedouin first balk from offering charity to the victims of the despoiled caravan: *ankarū-nā* ('They denied us'). To deny charity is simultaneously 'not to know' and/or 'to be in a state of ignorance'. In this anecdote, the ethical knowledge from which charity issues is at first inchoate and emerges in a three-part movement of anagnorisis. But in the first story of our diptych about al-Muᶜtamid (F 206), misrecognition occurs around the person of the Prophet Muḥammad. Can there exist a parallel narrative agenda? For, in contrast to F 206, the vision of the Prophet here is succinct and unequivocal: 'I saw the Prophet in a dream' (*raᵓaytu l-nabī fī l-nawm*). Why, we should ask, is there no obstacle to recognition here, as before? The answer may lie in the fact that the issue of recognition, with its facets of equivocation that can render it more real than hollow, has already been explored and developed elsewhere in the story. The vision of the Prophet, or its function in the development of the narrative, now simply resolves the relatively complex movement of anagnorisis. In both anecdotes, one can trace a movement from ignorance to knowledge, but anagnorisis does not simply inhere in the recognition of the Prophet, however moving and special such a vision may be in the life of the dreamer. Rather the whole concatenation of incidents – equivocations and disclosures – leads up to this point and is part of the hermeneutic apparatus of recognition's broad metonymic significance.

Recognition and Reading

In stories, and stories within stories, where recognition and reading as anagnostic processes are closely interlaced, there is often a moral epistemology to be read from connections between descriptive details and events. F 389 is about the destitute but haughty Muznah, wife of the Umayyad Marwān II (744–50/127–32) who is given refuge long after her husband's demise by Khayzurān, wife of the caliph al-Mahdī, and the Abbasid princess, Zaynab bt. Sulaymān. The story of Muznah is told by Zaynab as an exemplum to illustrate the fact that iniquities come back to haunt those who commit them.[37]

The framing and enframed stories are set up as follows: The narrator of the outer frame, a client of al-ᶜAbbās b. ᶜAbd al-Muṭṭalib, wanted to marry 'Kitāb', one of Zaynab's servant women. His diffidence in asking for permission to do so – for fear of rejection – provokes Zaynab to tell a story illustrating why she would never obstruct such a match and thus abuse her status. She claims that her story is more exquisite than any 'book', punning wilfully on the word 'Kitāb', the servant woman's name. The bookish tale, more worthy even than 'Kitāb', becomes Zaynab's endorsement of the betrothal. There is a clear show of poetics in this play on words: a sense of the function of narrative and how it can work to deliver meaning according to formal and thematic constructions.

Here are the crucial details of the story which Zaynab tells about Muznah:

> [I was with Khayzurān at her *majlis*] one day when one of her servant women came in and said: 'My lady, there is a woman at the door; I have never seen such a combination of exquisite features and terrible physical condition. She is wearing a ragged garment which in covering one part of her body simply uncovers another. She is asking for permission to see you.'
>
> [Khayzurān] turned towards me and asked: 'What do you think?'
>
> I answered, 'Ask her what her name is, and what the matter is, then let her enter . . .' The servant woman said: 'I have tried my utmost already, but she will not tell me; she insisted on leaving but I prevented her from doing so.'
>
> So I said to Khayzurān: 'There's no harm then in your giving her leave to enter. You can receive her honorably and gain recompense in God's eyes.'

> So she gave her leave to enter.
>
> The woman who entered was even more striking than the maid's description of her, though she tried to hide herself . . .
>
> She greeted us and we replied. Then she said to Khayzurān: 'I am Muznah the wife of Marwān al-Ja^c^dī.'
>
> . . . when her name fell upon my ears I sat up straight, then asked: 'Muznah?'
>
> She said: 'Yes.'
>
> I said: 'May God take your life and keep you away from us! God be praised for stripping you of your life of ease, upending your status and afflicting you with such exemplary punishment! Do you remember, you enemy of God, how you behaved when the womenfolk of my family asked you to petition your husband to take Ibrahim b. Muḥammad[38] down from the wooden blocks on which he was languishing? And how you then dismissed them?! God be praised for taking away your prosperity.' At these words [Muznah] laughed, almost cackling, and revealed her beautiful teeth.
>
> She said: 'My cousin, how marvelous indeed that God has done this to me. . . I did this to your womenfolk so he delivered me to you hungry, humbled and naked. Yet this is how you thank Him for subjugating me to you!' She turned to leave in a demeanor quite distinct from that of her entrance. I said to Khayzurān: 'She must be a secret gift from God revealed to us . . .' So I ran after her.[39]

In the ensuing story, Muznah is received into the household of Khayzurān according to her lofty status, of which she is only too aware, chiding the servants who attend to her and refusing shows of affection or embrace before being restored to her physical dignity. As in so many stories of *Faraj*, there is mutual recognition here, in this case, of social status. Told as an exemplum, the story of Muznah is didactic; in this and other senses revelatory. It is also, to reiterate, a 'bookish' story worthy of guaranteeing 'Kitāb's' marriage to the narrator, which is rendered in a clever semantic gesture of the anagnostic value of narrative. Recognition here is a token – a synecdochic element – of the exemplum's power. What is delightful, too, within this scheme are the details that support the subject, such as the phrase with which Muznah is described when she first appears in the *majlis*: '[She] was even more striking than the maid's description of her, though she tried to hide herself'; so too the detail of the ragged garment that when covering up one part of Muznah's body only uncovers another. Beauty can only be revealed, for all that it will try to hide; by the same token, a beautiful story cannot but reveal itself as part of God's blessing. This is the point of Zaynab's description of Muznah as 'some hidden treasure of God revealed to us' (*Makhbaʾat Allāh*). It is the revelation of the message that is important, and this is how the recognition – gratitude to God and hospitality to one's fellow – works to deliver its message to the frame story, guaranteeing the marriage of the narrator to 'Kitāb', the woman whose name in effect carries the blessing of a providential exemplum.

The anagnostic features of this story are redolent of F 242, which is about the marriage of the legendary Mālik b. Ṭawq and a certain al-Muhannāt bt. al-Haytham al-Shaybānī. The relevant detail lies in the way that recognition of the meaning of a story, and the verses that lie at the heart of it, make it possible for a marriage to take place. The tale begins when the narrator, Muḥammad b. ᶜAbd al-Ḥamīd al-Jushamī, returns from Mecca one year after the pilgrimage. Alighting at some unnamed spot, he noticed a woman of extraordinary beauty begging for alms. She was like the full moon and the radiant sun. He averted his gaze, seeking God's protection from the lure of temptation. She kept doing her rounds among the visitors, then returned to his mount and stood still. The narrator's curiosity now gets the better of him, so he asks her:

> 'Are you not embarrassed to show your face in such a place, in front of all these people?'
>
> She simply slapped her face, as a woman does in grief, and recited this poem:
>
> I was not used to showing it until my resourcefulness was exhausted // . . .
> It troubles me to do so, but fate is cruel and full of injustice;
> I used to guard my face and kept it veiled // . . .
> But circumstances have forced me to reveal it; God is my witness and knows this.
> Time unveiled its cruel self to me in a place where I have few friends and it is hard to earn a Dirham . . .

> I was amazed by the combination of her beauty, manners and eloquence, so I excused her and asked her what her name was.[40]

On his way home, the narrator stayed with Mālik b. Ṭawq at al-Raḥbah and, when asked what wonders he had seen, he told the story of the woman. Some time later, having returned to Syria, the narrator was visited by messengers bearing gifts of money and clothing from Mālik. He was puzzled by their charge, but they explained that Mālik had been so taken by the narrator's account of al-Muhannāt that he sent his men into the desert to seek her out. Eventually finding her, they brought her back and he married her, for he had perceived her exquisite qualities in the tale told about her and, more significantly, in the poem she had composed about herself.

The imagery of the poem and the mechanism of the narrative work together, somewhat hand in hand, for they are both about unveiling. She is literally unveiled, that is, forced to keep her face uncovered in order to beg, and acts to reveal her qualities in a poem that, as if to underline the theme, is itself about time 'unveiling' its effects upon the destitute. This tidy harmony of disclosure works its effect upon the astute and sensitive Mālik b. Ṭawq.

In F 484, a man faints when a fragment of his lyric poetry is set to music and sung by Maᶜbad, the renowned musician. Maᶜbad then asks him to explain his story. It is about his passionate love for a girl and her father's machination to impede their marriage because his daughter has been mentioned publicly in verse by her suitor. Much later Maᶜbad attends Jaᶜfar b. Yaḥyā al-Barmakī's court and sings the same two verses. Jaᶜfar is struck by the song and asks: 'Whose is this?!' When the story of the lyric verses is told to him he summons the boy and tells him that the young woman he has been forced to forsake is under his protection. The following day they tell the story to Harūn al-Rashīd; equally struck by the verses and the circumstances of the affair, he summons the father of the girl together with his daughter and the two lovers are united in matrimony. It is the symbolism of the poetry's role more than the actual (rather bland) poetry itself that is important. It represents a purity of spirit, enhanced by song, and these virtues are recognised by the sensitive people that hear it. That Jaᶜfar should have recognised the young lady in question as being in his jurisdiction is the kind of enchanted coincidence we are used to in tales of deliverance; it simply resolves providential design. Recognition thus works on two levels.

The function of poetry in F 492, the final anecdote in al-Tanūkhī's collection, works in a manner akin to this. It is about a wife who, having preserved a steely silence against her husband for a lengthy period of time, finally realises the error of her ways. She admits:

> The reason I began to shun him was silly and slight but I was possessed by spite in the way that lovers can be, and then I became obstinate, and the Devil showed me that I had right on my side. And so I remained until a while ago when I leafed through a book I had at hand and my eyes fell upon the words of a poet:
>
> Life is too short to waste by calling others to account
> Make the most of moments as they come, for they are fleet – like the clouds
>
> I realized this was a lesson to me, and that I should not anger God by angering my husband.[41]

This is not momentous poetry but perhaps the Qurᵓanic allusion in the phrase *fa-murūru-hā marra l-saḥābi* ('moments passing fleet *like the clouds*')[42] enhances the effect of the lesson for the wife. The higher registers of Arabic can work their magic on characters in *Faraj*.[43]

A Story about Music

Faraj 254 about the musician Ibn Jāmiᶜ is a relatively complex story in the significant sub-genre of stories about music. He suffered severe financial hardship while in Mecca, awaking one morning with a meagre three dirhams to his name. That same day, he noticed a servant woman walking to a watering hole with a jar on her head, singing a plaintive song. Enchanted by this, more by the music than the poetry, he asked her to sing it again so that he could learn the tune. She does so, but insists on being paid for her trouble. He gives her his last three dirhams, but she predicts, as if to console him, that he will one day earn three times a thousand dirhams from the song she recites to him. He then makes his way to Baghdad where upon arrival he finds himself praying at the mosque of al-Faḍl b. Rabīᶜ. When the prayer ends all the people leave, except for one man and his entourage. He turns to Ibn Jāmi^c and observes that he must be a stranger. Ibn Jāmi^c tells him he is a singer and the man departs. He is informed by one of his servants that this is Salām al-Abrash, the eunuch Ḥājib who served three caliphs from al-Manṣūr to al-Rashīd. He is then escorted to the caliph's compound. There, in one of the residences, he is cleaned, refreshed, and introduced into a *majlis*. A servant appears from behind a screen and is ordered to sing; he sings verses to a tune of Ibn Jāmi^c but not well, rendering it in mixed keys. Another servant comes and sings, also to a tune of Ibn Jāmi^c. And this relay carries on, three female singers and a man by turns singing a series of songs by Ibn Jāmi^c and other musicians, including extracts from the poetry of ^{c}Umar b. Abī Rabi^{c}ah[44] (twice) and the celebrated *ṣu^{c}lūk* poem by ^{c}Urwah b. al-Ward.[45] At this point, Ibn Jāmi^c himself is invited to sing. He performs three songs and is asked at the end of each: 'Whose song is this?' He replies each time: 'It is mine.' And each time is accused of lying, with the words: 'This is by Ibn Jāmi^c!' After the third exchange, Ibn Jāmi^c sees the caliph, Hārūn al-Rashīd, and Ja^{c}far ibn Yaḥyā al-Barmakī emerge from behind the screen. When they ask him to sing again, he recalls the song he had been taught by the servant woman in Mecca. Upon request he sings this three times in a row and is rewarded on each occasion with a purse containing a thousand dinars. On being handed the third sum he remembers the prophecy that the Meccan girl had made: that for an investment of three dirhams he would see a return of three thousand dinars. The caliph now notices a smile on his face and he is prompted to explain the whole story. It is as if in symbolic terms the caliph represents the incarnation of this revealed blessing, a ritualistic role that operates in a particularly involved way at the end of the cycle of 'The Porter and the Three Ladies of Baghdad' from the *Arabian Nights*.

Recognition is woven into this story in layers. First, Ibn Jāmi^c hears his own tunes being sung while he attends a scene incognito. He then reveals himself to his audience, and finally he understands, in the events that have followed sequentially up to this point, that a human prophecy has been realised: the three stages are clearly part of a sustained momentum of disclosure. That the anecdote was constructed according to an enhanced literary self-consciousness – a sense of applied poetics – may be suggested by examining the second and last three line excerpt of ^{c}Umar b. Abī Rabī^{c}ah sung by the third woman. It has intertextual relevance since these three verses are the climax of a longer narrative poem in which an adventurous ᶜUmar in disguise is recognised by his female playmates; the whole episode is relayed vividly by al-Iṣfahānī in the *Aghānī* together with an etiological backstory.[46]

The story is told by ᶜUmar b. Abī Rabīᶜah in the first person:

> Years ago Khālid al-Khirrīt ('The Guide') came up to me and said, 'O Abū l-Khaṭṭāb, four women just passed by me before the evening prayer making for such-and-such a place. I've never seen women like these among either the Bedouin or town-dwellers. Hind bt. Al-Ḥārith the Murrite was among them. Would you like to go to them in disguise and eavesdrop on their conversation and enjoy the vision you'll have of them while they do not know who you are?' I answered: 'Curse you! How am I supposed to hide my identity?' He said: 'You dress in Bedouin clothes and ride on a young camel; then you go to them, greet them, and they will think nothing more than that you have chanced upon them.' So I did what he said. I mounted on a young camel, went up to them, greeted them then stood nearby. They asked me to recite poetry to them and to converse with them, so I recited the poetry of Jamīl and al-Aḥwaṣ and Nuṣayb and others. They said: 'Curse you, Bedouin man! How sweet and charming you are! Will you not dismount and converse with us today? Come evening you can be on your way in God's keeping.' So I made my camel kneel and conversed with them and recited poetry. They were delighted with my company and admired my conversation. Then they started to wink at one another and to say to each other, 'It would seem that we know this man! How he looks like the very image of ᶜUmar b. Abī Rabīᶜah!' Then one of them said, 'By God, it is ᶜUmar!' Hind then stretched her hand towards me, took my turban and threw it from my head saying: 'O ᶜUmar! Do you think you have been deceiving us all day? Well it is us who have been deceiving you with the cunning help of Khālid, for we set him up to send you to us in the worst aspect possible yet we are as you see us!' Then we began to converse and Hind told me: 'My dear ᶜUmar, listen to me: If only you had seen me the other day when I was with my family: I put my head in my robe and looked at my vagina and it was swollen – the very object of a man's desire. I called out: ᶜUmar! ᶜUmar.' So I called out, 'I'm here, I'm here!' – three times

and lengthened the vowel on the third occasion. So she laughed. We spoke together awhile, then I said farewell and left. These are the verses composed on the occasion:

> When we halted and uttered a greeting, bright faces shone to meet me whose beauty made it impossible for them to hide themselves behind a veil.
>
> When they saw me and recognized me their behavior became playfully foolish. They said, 'A searching man has arrived all weary, having traveled apace!'
>
> They drew in the ropes of love for a heart-broken man who drew in an arms length of rope for every inch of theirs.

In a textual gloss following the poem, al-Iṣfahānī notes that these verses were set to music by several musicians, among them Ibn Jāmiᶜ. He also notes that there are several versions of this poem; therefore the exact context of the three verses varies. However, whichever version one opts to read, their role in an amorous narrative is clear. Undoubtedly, the theme of recognition, of a disguise shuffled off in a playful setting, keys in well with the dynamic of al-Tanūkhī's story about Ibn Jāmiᶜ. Spotting the connection seems to be part of the underlying literary intent of the anecdote.

Intertexuality in Brigand Stories

The image of effaced desert traces, one of the very cornerstones of the Arab poetic experience (and of Arabic literary culture in general), lies at the heart of F 448[47] an anecdote about the Shiᶜi partisan poet, Diᶜbil ibn ᶜAlī al-Khuzāᶜī (d. 869 AD), and his encounter with a Kurdish brigand. This is one of a number of brigand tales that paint the figure of the outlaw as an astute man of eloquence, a type who, though a criminal, displays his own innate nobility. The tale, told on the authority of the poet's son, which both signals and explains its unadulterated sectarian leanings, develops the contrary themes and impulses of suppression and recognition, impulses that cut intertextually across registers, informing both verse and prose. Or, put another way, the line of poetry cited at intervals in the narrative can be read as being an integral part of the thematics that the anecdote unfolds in a tidy symmetry.

The Story. When Diᶜbil visited Alī al-Riḍā in Khurasan and recited his poem in praise of the Alids, he was told to keep the composition to himself and firmly under wraps: 'Do not recite this to anyone until I tell you!' The prescription is somewhat of a piece with the opening image of the poem itself, the hemistich that is quoted: 'Effaced traces of the signs [of habitation] are no longer legible' (*Madārisu āyātin khalat min talāwatin*). Di^c^bil keeps faith with the Imam's instruction and when asked by al-Ma^ʾ^mūn to recite this poem, he claims: 'I do not know it, Commander of the Faithful.' Suppression, erasure, denial – in effect, the placement of a poem and its imagery beyond clear exposure and recognition – are details that key in with each other. The remainder of the anecdote can be read as mitigating, and then reversing, the severity of the constraint. First, in the presence of the caliph, who reports Di^c^bil's denial of authorship to the Alid Imam, ^c^Alī al-Riḍā gives the poet license to recite his poem. It receives much admiration for which he is rewarded with a precious silk robe and other refined garments, including a shirt. This is one form of recognition: acknowledgement and recompense. Then, travelling out of town, Di^c^bil's company is attacked by Kurdish brigands, known as Mārīkhān. He is robbed – divested in every sense – of his recent gains. Contemplating the devastation of the scene, he notices that one brigand holds his precious clothes and begins to recite his poem 'Effaced traces . . .' But unable to complete the verses he merely then weeps. It is the idea that the scene has been devastated – erased in a very particular and of course quite violent sense – that seems to evoke and provoke the line of poetry:

> (p. 229) When I witnessed this I marveled at a Kurdish highwayman expressing Shī^c^ī sympathies, and found myself desiring to repossess my shirt and raincoat.
>
> So I said: 'Sir, whose Qaṣīdah is this?'
>
> He replied, 'What has that to do with you? Curse you!'
>
> I said: 'There is a reason [for my question] about which I will inform you presently.'[48]
>
> He said: 'It is too famous [a poem] for its author to be unknown.'
>
> I asked: 'Who is he?'
>
> He said: 'Di^c^bil ibn ^c^Alī al-Khuzā^c^ī, the poet of Āl (the family of) Muḥammad, may God reward him.'
>
> I said to him: 'By God, sir, I am Di^c^bil and this is my poem.'

Though it takes a moment for the brigand to be persuaded, he soon acknowledges Di^{c}bil as the poet he claims to be, and inevitably returns the goods he has robbed; indeed, the entire company receives back its property. The short postscript to this anecdote is also significant, containing in miniature a recognition of its own that can be read as a gesture of authentication: 'The narrator of this anecdote [Di^{c}bil's son] said, 'I told this story to ^{c}Alī b. Behzād al-Kurdī, and he said, "By God! it was my father who did this".' The pattern of the two fathers' situation is carried over in miniature into the meeting between their two sons years later. So it is that the poem of erasure leaves a trace that is in the end quite legible in the morality and providential spirit it conveys. Read as a whole, the tale has a hagiographic quality, in condensed fashion authenticating the Alid beliefs that it celebrates and upon which it is built.

F 449 is another tale about a noble brigand told as an autobiographical episode by al-Tanukhī's father, though it too, like so much else in the *Faraj*, smacks of the often tidy and reassuring patterns of fiction. He tells of how he had a *bawwāb* (gatekeeper) when living in al-Karkh who was treated like one of the family, free to come and go without leave and at leisure. The *bawwāb* had a son of about ten years old at the time whom al-Tanūkhī senior treated indulgently, as the young offspring of a faithful servant. Upon quitting al-Karkh, al-Tanūkhī senior lost track of the man and his family. Then one day travelling downriver on his way to Wasit his flotilla was set upon by heavily armed river pirates. The attack surprised al-Tanūkhī at this particular time, as the stellar augury for the trip had been auspicious:

> [As I considered this matter of the stars] the boat with the pirates' leader came up alongside mine so that he could inspect what was there for the taking. When he saw me, he forbade his men from taking anything from my boat, and boarded it on his own. He contemplated me for a long while, then bowed to kiss my hand. He was masked and I could not recognize him.
>
> I was alarmed, and said: 'What's wrong with you, my man!?'
>
> He removed his mask and asked: 'My lord, do you not recognize me?'
>
> I took a good look at him, in despair, and didn't know him.
>
> 'No, by God!' I said.
>
> He said: 'Yes [you do], I'm your servant, the son of so-and-so from al-

> Karkh, your former gatekeeper. I'm the boy you raised in your own house; you fed me with your own hand.'
>
> So I looked hard at him again, and lo! his face was that very face, except that his beard had changed him in my eyes. I was put at ease. And asked: 'How is it that you have come to this, my man?'[49]

The brigand goes on to defend himself eloquently, with a measure of social comment about the straits of a felonious livelihood into which some men are forced. He was brought up to wield a weapon but, when old enough to work, no government office would retain him, so he was driven inexorably to brigandage. The argument is short but forceful, as far as it goes, etching the image of a man whom society has unjustly sidelined and disenfranchised. The recognitions are mutual, without quite condoning piracy and clearly, for al-Tanūkhī senior, the moment of recognition is commensurate with both deliverance and reassurance, in the end, that the stars had not lied. This is providential anagnorisis scored into the visible firmament.

In F 448 a brigand disguised as an emir argues, citing al-Jāḥiẓ's *Kitāb al-Luṣūṣ*, that stealing from merchants who do not know the meaning of *zakāt* – that is, who horde their wealth without paying charitable taxes – is permissible. This brigand is astute, educated, recites poetry and knows grammar and philology. The narrator, Abū Aḥmad al-Ḥārithī, is so impressed by him that he composes verses in praise of him, and, at the end of the anecdote, he addresses him as 'Emir' in spontaneous recognition of his qualities. In F 398[50] a brigand is forced to realise which of his actions in his past he is being rewarded for when, cast from a high rock face, he twice survives the attempts to murder him along with other, less fortunate, captives. The moral epistemology of brigand stories – the coming-to-see of the goodness of people or actions despite their criminality – appears varied but quite consistent in al-Tanūkhī. These are close in nature to the *maqāmāt* in the cast of players they contain but their recognition scenes, albeit set in ambiguous anecdotes, are edifying rather than dispiriting.

Redolence of the *Maqāmah*

In Arabic literary history, 'The Weaver of Words' story (F 291) was the first to be held up in the West as a possible generic model for the *maqāmāt*[51] – as the kind of text al-Hamadhānī may have been inspired by, both formally, according to cognitive structure, and thematically: a man pretending to be one thing turns out to be quite another, and in the meantime has shown himself to be educated and eloquent, though morally flawed. Al-Ḥarīrī (d. 1122 AD, author of the most celebrated collection of fifty *maqāmāt*) was in fact quite aware of the model and crafted one of his own narratives upon it (*maqāmah* 22), as observed in al-Sharīshī's (1222 AD) commentary to that text which even signals the 'Weaver of Words' – al-Tanūkhī's story – as its ultimate source. F 454 features a blind man who is not in fact blind. This too is a common motif in tales of trickery, and both al-Hamadhānī and al-Ḥarīrī's collections have their fair share of blind conmen.[52] It is the way the theme is configured into a tidy plot that is particularly redolent of the *maqāmah* in this case.

The story is told by one burlesquely named 'Dosh and Dates the Man from Wasit' (*al-Danānīrī al-Tammār al-Wāsiṭī*) who worked as a businessman's agent at al-Ubillah on the banks of the Tigris, north of Basra. He was charged one day with conveying 500 dinars from Basra to al-Ubillah. He placed the money in a cloth purse and hired a boatman to take him. On the outskirts of Basra, they encountered a blind man on the banks of the river reciting the Qurʾan exquisitely. The boatman tried to shoo him away with curses, but this only increased the merchant's indulgence. So they took him along. When the blind man had alighted at al-Ubillah and the merchant was about to make his own way home, he found that his purse was missing. He exchanged heated words with the boatman; the latter accused the blind man of the theft and, after a thorough search of the boat, nothing showed up. So he wandered off in despair. Disconsolate and roaming the streets, he was approached by a man who asked him what was troubling him. When he explained, he was told to visit an old man in the gaol of the Banū Namīr. He did exaxtly as instructed and fed the old man, receiving further mysterious instructions about what to do next:

> (p. 253) Go immediately to the quarter of the Banū Hilāl, and make for a certain lane; proceed to the end. There you'll see a ramshackle door; open it and make your way in without asking for permission. You'll find a long hallway leading to two doors. Go in through the right hand one. That will

> take you into some living quarters in which there is a room with pegs; on each peg is a sash and robe. Take off your clothes and hang them on [a] peg and put on the robe that's hanging on it. Sit down and some people will arrive, doing as you do exactly. When they are served wine, drink a few cups with them, then take a big cup, fill it, then get up and say:
>
> 'This is to the health of my uncle Abū Bakr al-Naqqāsh!'
>
> They will laugh and be happy and say:
>
> 'Is he your uncle?' Say: 'Yes' . . . when they have all drunk to my health and have settled down, say to them: 'My uncle greets you and instructs you: "My boys, give back to my nephew the cloth purse which you stole from him yesterday by the river at al-Ubillah." They will return it to you.'

Inevitably, with instructions flagged so precisely, things turn out in accordance with every detail described. Having thus recouped his money he asked them to tell him how they stole it and, at this, one of them says:

> 'Do you recognize me?' I looked at him closely and lo! It was the Qurʾan reciter who had been pretending to be blind. He gestured towards another man, and asked, 'Do you recognize this man?' I looked hard and lo! It was the boatman.

He explains their ruse, the nature of which is now patent to the reader. This quite detailed anecdote has several noticeable qualities: the relatively unexpected surprise about the boatman, for we expect the blind man to be recognised but not quite so much that the boatman should be his accomplice. In the closing scene of the story, it is the narrator himself who acts the impostor, as if in a mechanical way a minimal measure of lying is needed to bring out the truth. Structurally, the long description of the thieves' hideout and the ritual behaviour the narrator can expect to witness authenticates the influence that the old man, Abū Bakr al-Naqqāsh, exerts upon this underworld, although he himself languishes in gaol. It conjures mystery and delays the recognition with unusual elements and a skilful measure of suspense. There is a surplus to this mysterious story that might easily engender a sequel.

Like Magwitch in Dickens' *Great Expectations*, the figure of a mysterious benefactor comes to light in F 301, yet another of several stories about noble brigands in al-Tanūkhī's collection. The transmission chain is vague, almost non-existent – 'it reached me' – but the story is an exquisite tale of changing fortunes, told vividly in a first person narrative. The narrator was a charming, educated, gregarious man whose fortunes waned, then diminished completely, leaving a once popular man destitute – a shunned social pariah and an impoverished prisoner in his own house. Then, one evening, he heard the sound of hooves outside his house and then a man banging on the door, announcing: 'Someone whose anonymity I must keep greets you and says, "I am a private person, and can stand the company of few people. But would you be kind enough to visit me so we can converse into the night?"'

In an endearing detail, the narrator notes, as if signalling the private nature of the relationship he is headed for:

> I could not find anything to wear so I put on my wife's robe and went out. I was handed a skitty horse to ride and led to the home of an august and handsome man. He embraced me, ordered food and drink, and we fell into conversation. Towards dawn he requested that we meet regularly but on condition that I make no inquiries about him.[53]

Before departing the narrator was offered money but refused to accept it, finding it awkward and undignified to do so. These visits were repeated on several occasions and, each time, the narrator refused monetary recompense for his attendance until his wife berated him for returning penniless. Eventually he promised her, on pain of divorce, to accept whatever he was offered in the future. His material well-being was thus restored and he found favour again in society among fickle fair-weather friends. Then, all of a sudden, contact with the anonymous patron ceased and his messenger stopped coming.

One day, some time later, walking near his house he heard a commotion and saw a crowd gathered around an individual. The people claimed they were struggling to apprehend 'So-and-So, the highwayman' who had been wanted by the Sultan and finally traced to the quarter. The narrator approached the crowd, looked closely at the man, and lo! it was his mysterious host, fighting back the crowd with a drawn sword. The people heaved backwards and forwards with his successive lunges. The narrator got off his horse, led it to the man at a moment when the people stood back and told him, 'Take the horse and save yourself.' The man mounted and fled, escaping his pursuers.

At this the narrator was arrested for aiding and abetting a criminal, but privately he explained the full background and circumstances of what he had done to the investigating Emir. The latter replied in a whisper, out of earshot of those standing around: 'You did the right and proper thing! (*aḥsant!*).' He then explained away the narrator's actions as a misadventure of which the brigand had simply taken advantage. The narrator never saw his brigand host again.

In the abstract, this story is about *iḥsān* – doing the right thing. *Iḥsān* is sometimes translated as 'generosity' and has a meaning similar, in certain contexts, to *ma^{c}rūf*; it is in part its verbal form. The point about the narrator's *iḥsān*, which is appreciated and condoned privately by the investigating Emir at the end, is that it is a reciprocation of *iḥsān* previously received from his unknown benefactor, and is thus entirely morally justifiable. Recognition in this story can in some measure be deemed reciprocal. Although the narrator is the one who sees and recognises his benefactor, he has been recognised by the latter in a more profound sense from the outset, establishing the *bonhomie* between the two men that remains forever shrouded in mystery. The two men only come to know each other fully at the moment when they are forced to part company forever. Recognition is evidently the catalyst of a crucial and dynamic moment in the plot. But it also enhances for the reader the effect of seeing the truth and, beyond that, the moral message. It is a synecdochic signature of the story, a view supported by the fact that, while recognition happens in full view of the crowd, it remains a very private affair. This is a story that takes a consistently grim view of the people, of hypocrites who are nothing but fair-weather friends. It is the secluded private experience of friendship that the tale celebrates, which is why the Emir – a nobleman – condones the narrator's actions in a private whisper, out of earshot of the audience that surrounds him, as if the public should not know what it cannot grasp for itself. The Emir's reaction makes him in effect partake in the meaningful particular knowledge that binds together the narrator and his benefactor, spiritually if not forever physically. Generally, it is true that the more private the experience that recognition celebrates the more powerful the emotive discharge it delivers in narrative.

Layered Romances, Complex Stories

Part 1 – 'Servant-Girls Lost and Regained'

Al-Tanūkhī's F 469 is a long and intricate romance rendered beautiful in its incidents by its musical elements, though these details are incidental to the generic form that it takes, for it belongs much more clearly to the separate sub-category of stories about lovers whose self-absorption and financial insouciance cause their demise and separation. They are reunited in the end after their misadventures, in a way that bears a somewhat ponderous message. Geert Jan van Gelder has produced a short study of this story type entitled 'Slave-girl lost and regained';[54] he gives examples of some twenty such tales from various sources including al-Iṣfahānī's *Aghānī*, Ibn Ḥabib's *Muḥabbar*, Ibn ᶜAbd Rabbih's *ᶜIqd al-Farīd*, al-Marzubānīs *Nūr al-Qabas*, several from al-Tanūkhī's *Faraj* and several also from the *Arabian Nights*.[55] He suggests a nugatory summary of events as follows: union/possession; separation/loss; reunion/repossession. This is difficult to argue against; however, the cognitive aspect that inheres in these stories – their recognition scenes – is not conveyed, and we might consider this an oversight.

The Story. Two lovers in Baghdad become destitute when all their money is spent; they attempt to stave off disaster by earning their keep as musicians but, by and by, the woman, a slave-girl, is sold off, upon her own suggestion, to a Hashemite trader who takes her to Basra by boat. The man meanwhile falls asleep in a mosque and is fleeced of the money earned from the sale. Having now lost everything, he tries to commit suicide by throwing himself into the Tigris but is rescued by bystanders. He befriends a man who advises him to leave Baghdad; at the market of the Kutubiyyīn, he buys secret passage upon a merchant's boat downriver to Wasit by bribing the boatmen and disguising himself as one of them. The boat, he learns, belongs to a Hashemite trader of Basra from whom he must keep his true identity hidden. Some time after embarking, he recognises his beloved upon the boat attended by two servants, but he keeps his knowledge of her to himself. On route she is prevailed upon to sing, though she resists. Hearing her he sighs and faints in anguish and the boatmen begin to wonder why they ever agreed to accept this apparently deranged man into their company. They decide to get rid of him at the first opportunity. During a halt along the banks of the river, the lover sneaks behind the screen from which his beloved had been singing and retunes the lute she had been playing. When she picks up the instrument, she immediately recognises that only her lover could have tampered with it – for this was his favourite tuning. The Hashemite reveals himself for his part simply as an amateur of music, and promises to manumit the woman when they arrive in Basra and to marry her off to her lover.

However, a second cycle of separation and reunion supervenes. During another halt, the lover falls asleep inebriated on the river bank having stepped off the boat to urinate, and is forgotten by his companions when they depart. Thus the theme of insouciance crops up again – although this is to be the last time he is stung by delinquent foibles. Abandoned and alone, he has no way to find his beloved or her master in Basra, for he had thought it too presumptuous to ask the noble Hashemite his name. He decides to settle alone in the same city working for a greengrocer and is rewarded by and by for his application by being married off to the grocer's daughter. He tends carefully to the grocer's financial affairs and even discovers the embezzlements perpetrated by the other employees. After two years, still pining after his old flame, he decides to seek word of her or her company at al-Ubillah one Palm Sunday when people thronged to the quarter. There he recognises the Hashemite's boat and his former companions upon it. He tells them his story while they relate to him how they thought he had drowned two years earlier by falling into the river. His beloved had mourned him all this time: she had smashed her lute, given up singing, taken to wearing black, and built a mausoleum for her dearly departed lover. When reunited with him again, she gasps so violently he thought she would die. He marries her, after divorcing the grocer's daughter (and paying her contractual dues), and settles down to a happy life with his beloved in circumstances of material ease similar to those they had known at the very outset of the story.

In addition to recognition, which uses the medium of music according to a familiar trope simply to convey the deep aesthetic affinity between the two lovers, other themes stressed by this story are those of money and death.[56] The financial aspect of deliverance is common in *Faraj*: although wealth is by turns granted, taken away and returned according to providential schemes of bad and good fortune, just as often inscribed in theses tales is the fact that good housekeeping and financial management can be learned and that pious gratitude goes hand in hand with monetary good sense. In the first part of this story the lovers fritter away their wealth carelessly and, when the beloved is sold off, the gains from the sale are immediately stolen as if to underline the crass folly of the transaction. By contrast, in the latter half of the tale, in Basra, the lover becomes a wise and honest financial steward and rectifies his patron's affairs. It is only once he has effectively done penance in this way over time that he is rewarded providentially by reunion with his beloved. (The small matter of divorcing his first wife, discarding her once reunited with his beloved, seems callous to contemporary taste, but the detail intends no negative judgement upon him so long as he pays her legal monetary dues in being separated from her.)[57]

As we have intimated, death is also written in various ways as a metaphor into the story. Financial ruin is perceived as a mortal torpor. The lover attempts suicide once unsuccessfully, and he contemplates it a second time when things go awry all over again. Then, when left behind by his boating companions, he is thought actually to have died and the woman mourns him intensely. In the grocer's house, he excuses his chronic melancholy spuriously (but indicatively) as a bereavement for acquaintances and family members who have passed away. Cumulatively, recognition and deliverance are thus invested with the force of resurrection. Romantic recognition – and the related heightened aesthetics of musical empathy – is supplemented by a moral lesson about money. In many respects – and to modern taste – this is anti-romance in the second cycle.[58]

Part 2 – 'I am your Father!'

The late A. F. L. Beeston suggested in 'Genesis of the *Maqāmāt* Genre'[59] one of the many kinds of anecdote that may have influenced al-Hamadhānī in honing his picaresque narratives; he proposed a particular text from the *Faraj* (F 341 – the 'Weaver of Words') of al-Tanūkhī in which ᶜAmr ibn Masᶜadah, despatched by the caliph and descending the Tigris by boat, encounters on the riverbank a tatterdemalion seeking food and shelter. Once aboard, the stranger behaves impertinently but speaks with astonishing eloquence, and he boasts detailed knowledge of the functions of a *kātib* (secretary) – far more knowledge, it transpires, than that of his bureaucratic host. It is disclosed, at the end, that his fortunes have reversed themselves and that he is (or had been) a government functionary. He is now down on his luck. Beeston observed in the stranger's eloquence and the consequent recognition of true identity the anecdote's essential affinity with al-Hamadhānī's corpus of *maqāmāt*. More significant for our purposes is the fact that al-Tanūkhī may have taken a similar view of the material, since he too implicitly privileged recognition as the key defining rhetorical device of the anecdote.[60]

This emerges from the fact that the anecdote appears to be part of a diptych. The episode that follows it in F 342 relates another version of ᶜAmr ibn Masᶜadah's encounter on his boat (*wa-qāla muʾallifu hādhā l-kitābi wa-qad balagha-nī ḥadīthun li-ᶜAmr b. Masᶜadah fī zullāli-hi bi-khilāfi hādhā*), this time, according conceivably to a deliberate symmetry of contrast, travelling upstream rather than down. In this version, the man rescued from the riverbank tells his own, much longer story. It is a relatively complicated romance rendered in miniature[61] with the staple ingredients of love, severance, travel and reunion. This man, after an absence of twenty-eight years, returns home to a son he has never known and is brought together with the wife he had long presumed to be dead. Withal, the vagaries of the plot – the loss of equilibrium followed eventually by its return – provide the structure for some telling symbolism, especially regarding the organic intersections of love, narrative, procreation and material wellbeing (*rizq*). What makes this pertinent to the discussion of the *maqāmah* – which brings us back to Beeston's original point and then develops it – is that al-Ḥarīrī, al-Hamadhānī's illustrious successor, wrote what may be considered to be a highly self-conscious and parodic counter-text to the kind of literature that this romance of deliverance represents.

The Full Translation[62]

> I have heard a different [version of the][63] story about ᶜAmr b. Masᶜadah on his boat: ᶜUbaydullāh b. Muḥammad b. al-Ḥasan b. al-Ḥafā al-ᶜAbqasī, whose family were relatives of the Banū Māriyah, the inhabitants of al-Ṣarāt, related: My father told me: I heard the old folk of al-Ṣarāt relate:
>
> > That ᶜAmr b. Masᶜadah was travelling up river from Wasit to Baghdad in terrible heat. As he sat on his river boat, a man called out to him: 'Sir! Whoever owns this riverboat, for God's sake will you not take a look at me!?'

So ^{c}Amr drew back the drapes [that protected him from the heat] and saw a bare headed, decrepit old man.

'You can see the state I am in,' the latter said. 'Yet I can find no one to take me aboard with them; earn yourself God's blessing by doing me the favour; tell your crew to take me among the oarsmen until we arrive at some habitation where I can alight.'

^{c}Amr b. Mas^{c}adah continued: I took pity on him, so I said, 'Take him aboard.' So they took him at which point he fainted; he almost died from the torment of having walked in the sun. When he awoke I said to him, 'Old man, how did you get to your state? – What is your story?' He started: 'It's a long one.' So I reassured him, tossed him a tunic and handkerchief, and ordered some dirhams to be given to him. He thanked me. I said: 'You must now tell me your story.' He began:

'I used to be a wealthy man by God's grace and majesty. I was a money changer. I bought a servant woman at a cost of five hundred dinars. I fell intensely in love with her and I could not bear to be separated from her for even an hour. Whenever I went to the shop I was overcome by deranged longing so I would return and sit with her the entire day. This went on until my shop went bankrupt and my earnings dried up. I then began to spend my capital until virtually nothing was left of it – even so I could not bear to be separated from her. She then became pregnant. So I began to sell the remnants of my household until nothing remained and I had no means left to me. When she went into labour she said to me: "Listen! I am dying here, so find a way to get me some honey, flour, sesame oil, and meat, or I really will die!"

'I cried and despaired, and wandered off aimlessly. I went to the Tigris to drown myself but remembered the delights promised in the Hereafter to the good soul and the fear of chastisement so I stopped myself. Then I wandered off all the way to Nahrawan, and continued from village to village until I reached distant Khurasan. There I chanced upon a man who knew me. I worked on his estate, earned a large sum of money and became well off. I stayed there many years, without news of my household back in Baghdad but certain somehow that my maid servant had died. The years went by languorously until I accumulated a wealth of twenty thousand dirhams. I said to myself: "Now that I am so well off, why not return home?"

'So, with all my wealth, I bought chattels from Khurasan and set off for

Iraq by way of Fāris and al-Ahwaz in lower Iraq. Midway between the two, my caravan was set upon by brigands. They took all I had. I escaped with nothing but my clothes and returned thus poor to my homeland. I entered Ahwaz at a loss as to what to do until I told my story to a local I knew there; he gave me enough to get to Wasit. There I ran out of money so I walked to this spot. I was about to die when I appealed to you for help. It has been twenty-eight years since I left Baghdad.'

I was amazed at all this and said to him: 'Go, and find out your family's news then come to me for I will take upon myself to grant you what you need to set your affairs in order, as I would for anyone like you.' He thanked me and said a prayer [for me]. Then we entered Baghdad. Quite a while passed during which time I forgot about him. One day as I mounted my horse to go to the palace of al-Maʾmūn, lo! there the old man stood at my door riding a well appointed donkey, dressed in fine clothes and with two black slaves in attendance. When I saw him, I welcomed him and asked him what his news was. He said: 'It's a long story; I'll come to you tomorrow and tell you all.' On the following day he came to me. I told him: 'Tell me your story, for I am delighted at the fact that things have turned out well for you and how well you obviously seem.' He said: 'I left your riverboat [that day] and made for my house; there I found the wall that adjoins the road just as I had left it. However, the front door was clean and well appointed, with a doorman and shops on either side of it, and there was also a donkey attended to by a hireling. I said to myself [mournfully]: "We belong to God and to Him do we return! My slave woman has died and another man has taken possession of the house; it has obviously been bought by one of the Sultan's men." Then I went up to a grocer whom I used to know in the district and found a young man in his shop. I asked him:

"How are you related to the grocer?"

He said: "I am his son."

"When did he die?"

"Twenty years ago."

"Whose house is this?"

"It belongs to the son of the caliph's wet nurse who is now in charge of the treasury."

"What is his name?"

"He is the son of So-and-So the money changer." – And he named me.

"Who sold him this house?"

"It was his father's house."

"Is his father alive?"

"No."

"Do you know anything about them?"

He said: "My father told me that this boy's father was a prominent money changer who lost his wealth and that when the boy's mother went into labour the father went out to fetch something but he got lost and perished. My father said: 'The mother's messenger came to me asking me for something to sustain her so I provided her with what she needed for the birth. I gave her ten dirhams.' She hadn't even spent them when news came that a son had just been born to Hārūn al-Rashīd. The child had rejected all the wet nurses who had been brought to him . . . The caliph was now anxious to find a wet nurse. The woman charged with finding one came to this boy's mother and took her to the palace of al-Rashīd. When the infant's mouth was brought to the woman's breast he accepted it. So she nursed him. The infant was al-Maᵓmūn. She thus came to have a prominent place among the caliphal family and received rich compensation.

"Then al-Maᵓmūn moved to Khurasan and the woman accompanied him there, taking her son along. We heard no more about her until recently when al-Maᵓmūn returned along with his retinue. We saw that the young child had become a man. I had never seen him before. My father had already died.

"Everyone says: 'He is the son of So-and-So the moneylender and the son of al-Maᵓmūn's wet nurse; he rebuilt this house and spruced it up.'"

I asked: "Do you know anything about his mother: is she dead or alive?"

"She's alive. She spends a few days at the palace of the caliph and spends the other days with her son."

I thanked God for this state of affairs, went up to the house and entered among a crowd of people. I saw a courtyard at the far end of the house. There was a *majlis* arrayed in splendid carpets. At the centre was a man surrounded by secretaries and financial agents. He was checking their accounts. Scattered around the *majlis* were agents with piles of money and balances set before them.

I looked at the young man and saw my likeness in him and so I knew he was my son. I sat hidden among the people until I was the only person left behind. He then came up to me and asked:

"Old man, do you have a request for me?"

I replied: "Yes, but it is a matter only you must hear."

He thus signalled to his servants standing around him to leave. He then said, "God give you strength – [please begin]!"

"I am your father."

When he heard, this his face changed and he leapt up in a hurry leaving me where I was. Presently, a servant came up to me and asked me to accompany him. He led me up to a screen in a pleasant room before which a chair had been placed. The young man was sitting on another chair next to this. He said: "Sit, old man!"

I sat on the chair, the servant came in and then there was movement behind the screen. I said: "I suppose you wish to test the truth of what I said with so-and-so [your mother]." I then mentioned the name of my servant woman, his mother.

Then the screen opened and the servant woman came out to me. She fell upon me with tears and kisses, calling out: "My lord!"

I saw that the young man looked amazed, uncomfortable and confused.

I asked the servant woman: "What is your news?"

She replied, "Never mind my news; it is enough that I see you before me, by God's grace! Tell me first what happened to you."

So I told her my story from the day I left her behind to that very same day. And she told her story just as the grocer had told me, yet more amazingly and in greater detail, and all this took place within sight and earshot of the young man. When we had finished talking he exited the room and left me where I was. Then a servant came up to me and asked me to go out and meet my son. I exited as asked and when he saw me from a distance he stood up and said: "I ask God's forgiveness and yours, father, for having treated you unfairly; you surprised me when you first came to me with a story I could not imagine possible, and now – well, all this is God's blessing granted to you, and I am your son. The caliph has courted me for a while now: he would like me to give up brokering and to work in his palace. But I have not done so out of desire to stick to this profession. But now I will ask him to return your job to you so that I can serve him in other ways. Come quickly! Set your affairs aright!"

I was escorted to the bath and washed; they brought me robes and dressed me, and was taken to his mother's quarters where I sat and waited. Then I was taken in to the see the caliph. I told him my story. He granted me robes of honour and appointed me to the job that my father had occupied before. He awarded me a stipend of such and such a month and appointed my son to the most noble positions, increasing his salary many times over, employing him to take care of his most intimate affairs.

I come now to thank you for the kindness you did me and to inform you of the fact that my wealth has been restored.'

ᶜAmr b. Masᶜadah said: 'When he named the young man, I knew that it was the son of the caliph's wet nurse, just as he had said.'

This richly layered family romance of sundered lovers is relatively complex, both in its two-part structure and in its varied, often quite original content conceived according to an overall cohesion of themes and certain generic norms. One notices inevitably the contrast between the concrete historical specificity of some characters (the narrator ᶜAmr b. Masᶜadah, Harūn al-Rashīd and al-Maʾmūn) and the sustained anonymity of others, chiefly the protagonist and his family: the *ṣayrafī* (money changer), his *jāriyah* (slave-girl) and their son. Their names are never mentioned, though there is ample opportunity for such naming given that it is largely a text of retrieved identity; indeed, as the story comes to a close the profusion of phrases of the kind *fulān al-fulānī* (so-and-so) becomes conspicuous and seems almost to be deliberately contrived. We suggest that ᶜAmr b. Masᶜadah's role anchors the story concretely in history, setting and even disguising the fiction behind a façade of reality, while the anonymity of characters within the story he tells draws in the reader to experience their vagaries. It thus becomes a representation of universal human experience where that experience is, if not the very letter and detail of the story itself, at least the desire for a story and the sense of personal fulfilment a narrative can provide. It is paradoxical that a recognition narrative should be so anonymous in leaving its protagonists unnamed, yet the experience thus related acquires a measure of the archetypal.[64]

The structure of F 342 is relatively sophisticated when compared to most tales in al-Tanūkhī's collection. It is reminiscent, indeed, of Heliodorus's *Aethiopica*, which is the most complex of the Hellenistic romances of sundered families and lovers brought together in a final recognition scene. Both romances begin with an enigmatic scene then tell a retrospective story that leads at the approximate midpoint of the narrative into the opening scene, thus explaining it and providing its context; the rest of the narrative carries on from that point to the end in linear time. Like the *Aethiopica*, this story is thus made up of two major cycles. Here we should simply observe that the end of the first cycle is familiar to the reader and recognised as a return to the opening moment, and the cognitive aspect of this feeds the movement of the whole story as a coming-to-know. The end of the first part is poised loadedly at the moment of return in a physical, geographic and narrative sense.

One of the key themes of the story is common to many in *Faraj*, to wit: the loss and recovery of wealth. The theme is common too in romance generally, but the *Faraj* canon adds a didactic gloss to the subject as we have already seen, prompting one to gather that responsible thrift – the healthy management of wealth – is the optimal way of receiving and showing gratitude for God's material blessing: of deserving deliverance, before, during, and even after the fact.[65] Fate's role in giving and taking away at random is simply the other side of livelihood's coin, nurturing the piety of patience and acceptance. In this story, there is somehow equivalence between material prosperity, narrative fortune and the begetting of progeny. The loss of wealth happens initially at the point when the narrator presumes to have lost his family. He then, much later, tells his story and recovers his family in addition to wealth; so much is clear. But, as if to underline the theme of the father-son relationship and its connection with the regenerative power of the story, when the money changer returns to Baghdad, his initial encounter is with the son of the local grocer, who is now dead; it is this filial figure who gives preliminary account of the money changer's own son. Sustaining the family theme is the fact that, when she begets her son, and having lost her husband, the *jāriyah* becomes the wet nurse to the child of Harūn al-Rashīd, al-Ma᾿mūn. As a result, she is virtually adopted into the caliphal family. Her account of rearing not just one child but two will be part of the full story that warrants the reunion with the lost father. Narrative, paternity and material capital develop as themes, feeding off and into each other reciprocally. This fact is driven home on the level of language when the money changer returns home to find his former house 'exactly as he had left it' twenty eight years earlier. In Arabic he says: 'as I had left it' (*ka-mā khallaftu-hu*) which also means also 'as I had begotten it', evoking the fact that his son was born at the moment he had abandoned his home. Thus, just as he recognises his old house at first, so he comes to recognise his son. This semantic overlapping is part of the well fashioned cohesion of the text.

One of the great ironies of F 342 lies in the fact that, when the narrator is furthest from home in Khurasan, displaced from his roots and former identity, he imagines his beloved slave-girl and the child she had borne to have perished long ago. Yet all this time they are there, living among the retinue of al-Maʾmūn as the foster mother and milk brother of the caliph, respectively. The dramatic irony of this situation works on several levels: to show that the sense of impedimentary distance in separation exists chiefly as a trauma of the mind, showing up the essentially psychological character of alienation, and to emphasise the temporary disjunction of family bonds and relations while simultaneously underlining the very theme of kinship. If, for heuristic purposes, we envisage the theme of family as a pictorial icon, that icon exists out of focus in Khurasan: two family images exist independently and disjointedly, the one is a foster family, the other is real and biological. The lines of the familial icon come mentally into focus in a single cohesive form only when the grocer's son enlightens the narrator about the survival of his child and slave woman. Emotionally, the image is filled out, or coloured in, as it were, in the two ensuing recognition scenes, first between father and son and then between father and concubine.

That all three family members are to be found in far-flung Khurasan yet unaware of each other's presence is related also to another detail. Romances, however comic and happy they may turn out to be, tend to feature characters tossed around by fate; the players can seem like passive pieces on the chess board of life moved hither and yon according to the will of a transcendent narrative force, which is trying and destructive at first, then restorative. For this reason, we notice the conspicuously recurrent use by the money changer and the narrator of the Arabic verb *ṭaraḥa*, meaning 'to fling' or 'cast away'. The money changer asks initially 'to be cast' among the oarsmen of the river boat when appealing to the crew to take him aboard; he wishes then to be conveyed to and 'cast upon' some other location; finally, the narrator speaks of 'casting' a shirt upon him when he receives him into his company for the first time. These locutions contribute, on a deep semantic level, to the picture of a person haphazardly 'thrown about', of his own diminished responsibility until that point when the narrative visibly acquires its full shape and he is reunited with his family. This casting about is a subtheme of the narrative.

Another subtheme that keys in both with the mechanism and semantics of the move towards recognition is that of exposure. The whole tale shapes a disclosure, with felicitous results, of what has been hidden from view – the circular fact that the slave woman's pregnancy, experienced initially as a hardship, will allow her to become wet nurse to the caliphal household, thus reconstituting her own family. Physical exposure abets this theme in various ways: the money changer as an old man in the opening scene appears with his head 'exposed' to the elements (*ḥāsir al-raʾs*); this detail is followed closely by the 'drawing back of the screen on the river boat' before he is taken aboard, a dramatic gesture that foreshadows his reunion with his wife later in Baghdad when, having recognised him, she appears from behind a screen to embrace him. His initial destitution is described as the 'stripping bare of his shop or enterprise' (*taᶜaṭṭala dukkānī*); furthermore, it comes as a result of the spending and exhaustion of his capital, '*raʾs al-māl*' (lit. 'the head of money') which somehow conjures and leads to the baring of his head. Metaphorically, the telling of his story is expressed as the 'exposure of his story' (in Arabic, in the first person, *kashaftu khabarī*).

At some level, as we have already suggested, this story is about giving birth and adoption: the creation of life and the establishment of family relations. Yet on another, the consequences of this are experienced variously as death. When the money changer is first brought onto ᶜAmr b. Masᶜadah's riverboat, he is close to death and passes out; when his servant woman goes into labour, she instructs him to buy some honey 'lest she die'. He fails to purchase anything and, for twenty-eight years, he assumes she is indeed deceased. When he gets to the end of his story, to that point when he arrives on ᶜAmr b. Masᶜadah's riverboat for succour, he reiterates the fact that, at that moment, he was on the very point of expiring. Death is a theme of 'descent' in Frye's structural terminology of romance, after which the 'ascent' of a happy denouement can be experienced as a rebirth. Such are the recognition scenes in F 342.

There are three moments of recognition: (1) the money changer's realisation that his family has survived and flourished in their old home, information garnered from the grocer's son; (2) the meeting with his son in which he announces himself; and (3) the final reunion with the mother who emerges from behind her protective screen. These are the broad lines of the story. This dominant theme of the narrative is supported in a minor key by incidental recognitions that occur during the money changer's peregrinations: when he first arrives in Khurasan, he 'chanced upon a man who knew him' and who provides him with the opportunity of salvaging his livelihood (*ṣādaftu bi-hā man ʿarafa-nī*); when he arrives in Ahwaz, having been robbed on the way of his Khurasanian fortune, he 'reveals his story to a man there whom he happened to know and who gave him [enough assistance] to get to Wasit.' The root ʿ*arafa* in both instances evokes from the context the semantics of *maʿrūf*: 'good, generosity, succour, assistance'. Both instances thus foreshadow the positive, nigh life-giving, effect of recognition as it develops through the story. They are subsidiary instances of the succour afforded by ʿAmr b. Masʿadah whose own good turn in helping the money changer is repaid in the very telling of the story in two parts: first on the riverboat and then much later in Baghdad, once all matters of family reunion and recovered status have been resolved.

The second encounter between ʿAmr b. Masʿadah and the money changer, before the latter tells the second half of his story, is introduced by a significant and tell-tale detail: ʿAmr had just mounted his horse in order to visit al-Maʾmūn when he saw the man standing before him. Thus the figure of the caliph gives the story a sort of blessed teleology: on the one hand, ʿAmr b. Masʿadah was doing the caliph's work when he met the money changer travelling up the Tigris and, on the other, the latter's family fortune is restored through their one intimate and quite different sort of association with the caliph. The divinely invested figure of the sovereign occupying the background is part of the story's providential character.

On a purely formal level, recognition feeds often off of suspense and offers the sense of an ending: anagnorisis is primed to release the greatest charge of effect upon the reader when it is delayed. The very fact of this story's structure in two parts contributes deftly to this fact; on a minor level of detail, the second part contains its own dramatic deferral when the money changer, appearing before ^{c}Amr b. Mas^{c}adah, tells him he will return to recount the final complement of his story the following day. It is as if every possible structural aspect of the story is deliberately measured and weighted to enhance its shape, that shape that is seen normally most clearly in a recognition scene or, even prior to that by the reader, in the steadily crystallising knowledge that a recognition scene is, according to narrative expectations, inevitable.

In F 342 ^{c}Amr b. Mas^{c}adah gives succour and has authority, while the money changer is a master of his own complex narrative of identity. In part I, he narrates to ^{c}Amr; in part II, he narrates also to ^{c}Amr, but in four stages, namely, what the grocer's son relates to him, what he relates to his own son, what he relates to his wife, and finally what his wife relates to him. In the closing gesture of the anecdote, ^{c}Amr stamps his considerable authority upon the whole affair, authenticating the recognition that has preceded, by verifying with personal knowledge the identity of the money changer's son. These are the closing words: 'When he named the young man, I knew that he was indeed the son of the caliph's wet nurse.' ^{c}Amr hereby places an official seal, so to speak, on the restoration of identity – he is a bureaucrat after all. These are structural aspects of the unfolding issue of identity and, as such, are more transparent than certain more latent thematic features. The way various details of the whole, many of those outlined in the foregoing paragraph, shape up together in the recognition scene can be gleaned finally if we consider the actions of the son when told: 'I am your father'. In Arabic his immediate response, as reported by the money changer, is *taraka-nī makānī*: 'he left/abandoned me in my place'. This seems to be an act of denial and rejection: the son rejecting his father's claim. When the son shortly thereafter witnesses the *retrouvailles* between his parents confirming this claim he again 'exits and left me where I was' (in Arabic, *kharaja wa-taraka-nī makānī*). In the latter instance, he leaves to prepare a scene of acknowledgement of his father: to cement the final recognition. It is as if the two sudden exits re-enact the father's abandonment that set the whole chain of narrative events in motion. The recognition between father and son thus viewed acquires in miniature the stamp of the entire narrative. In this respect, the filial anagnorisis can be seen to be privileged above the one between the parents: this is anagnorisis given weight after the manner of *Pericles,* we might say, rather than *The Winter's Tale*. What is clear is that this is uplifting romance according to an archetypal pattern and temperament of narrative. Recognition can seem to define the very genre exhibited here. Ironically, recognition can undermine the process too in another very significant mood of storytelling. And this can sometimes seem to be what the parodistic, flippant and facetiously eloquent *maqāmah* is all about.

Notes

1. For a helpful working definition of *adab*, see Tarif Khalidi's review of Robert Irwin's anthology of medieval Arabic literature, *Night and Horses and the Desert*, in *Times Literary Supplement* 5061 (31 March 2000), p. 8. See also Geert Jan van Gelder, *Classical Arabic Literature* (New York: New York University Press, 2012), p. xiv: 'The term *adab* is often applied to literary output that is entertaining and edifying at the same time, based on the notion that ethics and aesthetics should go together – though not all classical literature is edifying by any means.'
2. Arabic *faraj*, together with its Qurʾanic conceptual sibling *yusr* (see Q al-Sharḥ 94:5–6: *fa-inna maᶜa l-ᶜusri yusra / inna maᶜa l-ᶜusri yusra*; 'for with hardship comes ease / with hardship comes ease').
3. Burton, *The Book of the Thousand Nights and a Night*, V, pp. 290–4; *Alf laylah wa-laylah*, Būlāq edition, I, pp. 653–5.
4. The most celebrated example of this is Odysseus among the Phaeacians in Book VIII of the *Odyssey*. Hasan El-Shamy indexes this as one of the categories of recognition in his *Folk Traditions of the Arab World. A Guide to Motif Classifications* (Bloomington: Indiana University Press, 1995), vol. I, p. 151.
5. See Appendix.
6. Partially translated into English by D. S. Margoliouth as *The Table-Talk of a Mesopotamian Judge*.
7. Al-Tanūkhī's tales are normally referenced according to their sequential numbering in the five-volume edition of ᶜAbbūd al-Shāljī (Beirut: Dār Ṣādir, 1978); *Faraj* 158 (F 158) is in vol. II, pp. 29–31.
8. The following of physical traces and tracks.
9. On physiognomy in Arabic-Islamic literature see the recent essay by Robert G. Hoyland, 'The Islamic Background to Polemon's Treatise', in Simon Swain (ed.), *Seeing the Face, Seeing the Soul: Polemon's Physiognomy from Classical Antiquity to Medieval Islam* (Oxford: Oxford University Press, 2007), pp.

227–80. Relevant anecdotes of the kind referred to above are the apocryphal story about the pre-Islamic poet Imruᵓ al-Qays (how he was tested and identified by his canny betrothed; see Abū al-Faraj al-Iṣfahānī's *Kitāb al-Aghānī* (Cairo: Wizārat al-Thaqāfah wa-l-Irshād al-Qawmī, 1927–74), vol. IX, pp. 101–3) and especially the story of the four sons of Nizar, an important story in pre-Islamic Arabian tribal lore, related in Masᶜudi's *Muruj al-Dhahab* (*Meadows of Gold*), his multi-volumed history. (A recognisable version of the four sons of Nizar crops up notably in Voltaire's 'conte orientale' *Zadig* – an enlightenment tale that tries to, but cannot, square the circle between rational thought and providential, transcendental serendipity. It was written long before *Candide* and still has faith in providence as a guiding principle in life.)

10. See our discussion of *Firāsah* and the irrational in a forthcoming essay entitled '*Firāsah*, Recognition and the Irrational in Narratives of Detection'.
11. See further discussion in Chapters 1 and 5.
12. See the lengthy tale of ᶜUmar ibn al-Nuᶜmān; Burton, *The Book of the Thousand Nights and a Night*, II, pp. 77–283; for the Arabic, see *Alf laylah wa-laylah*, Būlāq edition, I, pp. 139–228. Similar tales of conflict and contact across these borderlands make up a large part of the popular epic *Sīrat al-Amīra Dhāt al-Himmah*. These comments may suggest that the story, and others like it, read like surreal fiction. There is, however, a certain naturalism in its details and in its relatively sober literary temperament, which sets it apart from analogous, and far more popular, tales in the *Arabian Nights* that develop similar themes of family reunion on the Byzantine-Muslim borderlands. For relevant discussion of these kinds of materials, see Remke Kruk's *The Warrior Women of Islam: Female Empowerment in Islamic Popular Literature* (London: I. B. Tauris, 2014).
13. *Faraj* 466, IV, pp. 300–5; for the English translation of D. S. Margoliouth used here, see Robert Irwin, *Night and Horses and the Desert* (London: Penguin, 1999), pp. 155–8. The original appeared in D. S. Margoliouth, *Lectures on Arabic Historians* (Calcutta: University of Calcutta, 1930), pp. 142–6.
14. It is characterised by the fanciful ethnography of seafarers' tales, of which this is no doubt one.
15. Irwin, *Night and Horses and the Desert*, p. 156.
16. Ibid., p. 157.
17. Ibid., p. 157.
18. According to Islamic custom, one is obliged to receive a stranger for three days only.
19. Irwin, *Night and Horses and the Desert*, p. 158.

20. One can showcase similarly the story of ᶜUqbā al-Ḥusnā from the *Jalīs al-Ṣāliḥ* of al-Nahrawānī as a tidy story delivering a clear moral message, though not about hospitality in this case but deliverance from a series of evil malefactors. See Abū al-Faraj al-Muᶜāfā b. Zakariyyā al-Nahrawānī al-Jarīrī (d. 1000 AD), *al-Jalīs al-Ṣāliḥ Wa-l-Īnās al-Shāfiᶜī*, ed. Muḥammad Mursī al-Khūlī (Beirut: ᶜĀlam al-Kutub, 1981), vol. I, pp. 189–92. This is popular hagiography, and it begins with the archetypal motif of the wife calumniated by the husband's sibling, a variant of 'the-son-calumniated-by-the-lascivious-stepmother' – the so-called 'Phaedra motif'. The story of Judah and Tamar in Genesis 38 is also closely akin.
21. For other Alid stories cf. the tale of Diᶜbil b. ᶜAlī below in the sections on 'Intertextuality' and 'Recognition and reading'.
22. This part of the story is told without its frame in other sources. See Salma Jayyusi (ed.), *Classical Arabic Stories* (New York: Columbia University Press).
23. Though the epistemological mechanism is exactly the same.
24. See al-Jāḥiẓ, *The Book of Misers (Al-Bukhalaᵓ)*, trans. R. B. Serjeant (Reading: Garnet Press, 1997), pp. 18–19.
25. Albeit some Qurᵓanic commentaries suggest, less compellingly, that Bushrā may have simply been the name of a companion whom the forager was calling back to.
26. See James Kugel, *The God of Old: Inside the Lost World of the Bible* (New York: Free Press, 2003), pp. 5–36.
27. *Faraj*, II, p. 209.
28. See John C. Lamoreaux, *The Early Muslim Tradition of Dream Interpretation* (Albany: State University of New York Press, 2002), p. 32. How the Prophet is recognised in the first place is another matter of interest. Briefly, it may be a consequence of intuition, of unthinking assumption, or some physical attribute may be observed, e.g. a glimpse of the tooth the Prophet broke at the battle of Uḥud and which became visible when he laughed (see for example Ibn ᶜAsākir, *Tārīkh Dimashq*, ed. ᶜAbd al-Qādir Badran (Damascus: 1911), vol. 3, p. 132, who tells how the *muḥaddith* Ibn ᶜUkāsha (d. *c.*840 AD) sees the Prophet in a dream, recognising him by his broken tooth: *rubāᶜiyyah maksūrah*).
29. *Faraj*, II, p. 247.
30. In the usage of Vladimir Jankélévitch; see *Le Je-ne-sais-quoi et le Presque-rien* (Paris: Seuil, 1981).
31. Prophetic apparitions are surely metonymic tokens of *thawāb* – other wordly recompense.
32. See Julia Bray, 'Place and self-image: the Buhlūlids and Tanūḫids and their

family traditions', in Antonella Ghersetti (ed.), *Quaderni di Studi Arabi* 3: *Luoghi e immaginario nella letteratura araba* (Rome, 2008), pp. 39–66. The linear genealogy of this family lays as much stress on the relevant patriarchal names as that of the brothers in the attribution of al-Tanūkhī's story: Abū Yaᶜqūb Isḥāq ibn al-Buhlūl (d. 867 AD) was father of Yaᶜqūb (d. 865 AD) who was father of Abū Bakr al-Azraq Yūsuf (d. 941 AD) who was father of Abu Yaᶜqūb Isḥāq (no dates) – the latter was of the generation of this narrative.

33. We are put in mind especially of verses such as 12:67.
34. *Faraj*, II, pp. 255–6.
35. See Roland Barthes, *S/Z* (Paris: Le Seuil, 1970).
36. *Faraj*, II, p. 257.
37. The version of the story contained in al-Masᶜūdī's *Muruj al-Dhahab* is discussed in Julie Scott Meisami's, 'Writing Medieval Women: representations and misrepresentations', in Julia Bray (ed.), *Muslim Horizons* (London: Routledge, 2006), p. 69.
38. 'The Imām Ibrāhīm ibn Muḥammad ibn ᶜAlī had been the head of the Abbasid family, Muzna's second cousin – and Zaynab's husband's father. He had given the order that would eventually overthrow Marwān, who imprisoned him in Ḥarrān, where he died in 132/749. Marwān, more generous than Muzna, returned Ibrāhīm's body to Zaynab.' See Meisami, 'Writing Medieval Women', p. 69.
39. *Faraj*, IV, pp. 75–82.
40. *Faraj*, II, p. 360.
41. *Faraj*, IV, p. 428.
42. See Q 27:88.
43. The long and relatively complex F 197 has been studied in an article by Andras Hamori. See 'The House of Brotherly Love: A Story in *al-Tanūḫī's Niŝwār al-muḥādara* and in *The Thousand and One Nights*', in Miklós Maróth (ed.), *Problems in Arabic Literature* (Piliscsaba: The Avicenna Institute of Middle Eastern Studies, 2004), pp. 15–26.
44. The celebrated Meccan love poet of the Banū Makhzūm (b. 644 AD). He was known for his highly erotic, often dramatised, verse and modelled himself in two or three instances on the pre-Islamic poet, Imruᵓ al-Qays of the Banū Kindah (*fl.* early sixth century AD).
45. A late pre-Islamic brigand poet or *ṣuᶜlūk* (pl. *ṣaᶜālīk*).
46. For the full poem, see ᶜUmar b. Abī Rabīᶜah, *Dīwān ᶜUmar b. Abī Rabīᶜah* (Beirut: Dār Ṣādir, 1971), pp. 227–9.

47. Ibid., pp. 227–30.
48. Al-Tanūkhī, *Faraj*, IV, pp. 234–7.
49. *Faraj*, IV, p. 236.
50. *Faraj*, IV, pp. 97–101.
51. See note 59 below.
52. See in al-Hamadhānī the *maqāmah* known as '*al-Makfūfiyyah*' and al-Ḥarīrī the *maqāmah* of Barqaᶜīd (discussed below and in Daniel Beaumont's 'Trickster and Rhetoric in the *Maqāmāt*', in *Edebiyât* 5 (1994), pp. 1–14).
53. *Faraj*, III, p. 178.
54. Geert Jan van Gelder, 'Slave-girl lost and regained: transformations of a story', in Ulrich Marzolph (ed.), *The Arabian Nights in Transnational Perspective* (Detroit: Wayne State University Press, 2007), pp. 65–82. This version of the 'sold slave-girl' motif and its relation to the 'Weaver of Words' and variants, are discussed at length as families of tales and motifs in Julia Ashtiany Bray, '*Isnād*s and Models of Heroes', *Arabic and Middle Eastern Literatures* 1:1 (1998).
55. Van Gelder identifies the following staple narrative blocks: (1) *A man owns a slave-girl.* (2) *The man and the slave-girl love each other.* (3) *They become destitute.* (4) *The man sells the girl.* (5) *The slave-girl's new owner becomes aware of their attachment.* (6) *He generously returns the slave-girl to her lover.*
56. Cf. F 342.
57. Cf. the analogous treatment of the wife Zubaydah in the tale of Aladdin of the Moles from the *Arabian Nights*.
58. The two most complex stories of the kind in van Gelder's study are perhaps the tale of Zumurrud and Ali Shar in the *Arabian Nights* (discussed in vol. II) and the tale of Ṭalḥah and Tuḥfah relayed in the anonymous *al-Ḥikāyāt al-ᶜajībah wa-l-akhbār al-gharībah*. [Ed. Hans Wehr (Wiesbaden: Franz Steiner, 1956), with the German title *Das Buch der wunderbaren Erzaehlungen und seltsamen Geschichten*.] The structure is relatively complicated and the epistemology is intensely moralistic, sustaining throughout the language of truth, fidelity, generosity and nobility; both these features come through in the story's various recognition scenes.
59. 'The Genesis of the *Maqāmāt* Genre', *Journal of Arabic Literature* 2 (1971).
60. Al-Sharīsī made a similar, and indeed more tangible, connection between a *maqāmah* of al-Ḥarīrī (not al-Hamadhānī) and the 'Weaver of Words' in his commentary to the latter's *Maqāmāt*.
61. Compared with the length of such tales in the corpus of Hellenistic novels.
62. *Faraj*, III, pp. 314–20.

63. Whether it is another story or simply another quite distinct version of F 341 is left ambiguous by the phrase *bi-khilāfi hādhā* in Arabic.
64. Al-Ḥarīrī may have been aware of this a century later in writing a generic counter-text in the form of his *Maqāmah* 5, of Kufa, and one or two other texts from his collection.
65. We have seen that in the discussion of F 469.

5

Imposture and Allusion in the Picaresque *Maqāmah*[1]

> [He] experienced the freedom that lies behind the mask, within dissimulation, the freedom to juggle with being, and, indeed, with the language which is so vital to our being.
>
> Angela Carter, *Nights at the Circus*, p. 103

The Poetics of Family Stories

Recognition stories lend themselves to easy parody. A few examples exist in the *Arabian Nights*, depending on how one leans in interpretation.[2] There is a case to be made that the *maqāmāt* (sing. *maqāmah*, often rendered 'séances' or 'assemblies') are in large measure parodies of the art of storytelling or of the values with which stories can be burdened by a culture. Intrigues of disguise and imposture all make for good stories in which manifold deceit is veiled at first, and then exposed. Sometimes the story itself may be exposed, for a good story about forgery will stir suspicions that the story too has been fabricated. Allusive narratives exacerbate the point since they are texts in which much detail and significance lie under the surface in the play on language. The rhetorical figures of al-Ḥarīrī's *maqāmāt* emphasise the sensation that one thing – a word, or even just a phoneme – can have two very different, and sometimes even contrary, meanings.[3] Indeed, they mirror Cave's remarks about Western literature:

> in the Aristotelian tradition of antiquity, anagnorisis is . . . a focus for reflections on the way fictions as such are constituted, the way in which they play with and on the reader, their distinctive markers as fiction – untruth, disguise, trickery, 'suspense' or deferments; the creative effects of shock and amazement, and so on.[4]

These comments were originally made about both Odysseus and the *Odyssey*. With Homer's Greek, we are culturally a far cry from the Arabic *maqāmah*. But to insist on the distinction is on some level spurious, for the poetics of disguise and disclosure – of the art of telling stories in a long cycle of itinerant impostures so fundamental to the divagations and return of Odysseus[5] – justify the stretched comparison. What are the *maqāmāt* if not a long cycle of wandering impostures? Within the distended literary reception of Homer's epic, Kilito, in his analysis of al-Harīrī's fifth *maqāmah, al-Ghāʾib* ('The Absentee'), already some years ago, made the comparison between the rogue hero Abū Zayd's utterly fictional wife Barrah and the resourceful Penelope who spun a yarn to stave off her suitors while waiting for Odysseus's return.[6] What is curious about the figure of Barrah is that she does not exist, but bodies forth only as a fiction within a fiction – Abū Zayd admits that she is the product of his cunning fancy. She works her effect on Abū Zayd's audience, though – which is the object of his ruse. More curious even is the icon painted of her in al-Wāsiṭī's illustration of the *maqāmāt* where she dominates the image in which she appears, eclipsing Abū Zayd himself who appears diminished and to one side, as if the power of the story is bound to bring her back to life. Fiction, fancy, imposture, or the mere threat of imposture, all survive the disclosure of truth, like Barrah in al-Wāsiṭī's iconic imagination.[7] A fake story survives if it is memorable, because fancy can attach itself mnemonically and by attraction to its easy contours, rather than by merit of its veracity. That point comes across in 'The Absentee'[8] in the actions of Abū Zayd's obtuse audience who, as we will see, unwittingly preserve a fictional story in writing for posterity's edification, but thereby only in fact record in perpetuity their idiocy in being duped by it; they expose and preserve themselves as the dull object lesson of the perils of fiction.

There is a close affinity between fakery, fiction and storytelling – of the relating of real events in fanciful ways. Fancy is part of the self-conscious way in which we like stories to take shape. Fiction can tell us more about storytelling poetics or give us the same insights more acutely and intensely than stories dulled by reality and mundane fact. In an unpublished essay Robyn Creswell describes eloquently the self-conscious poetics that often appear to inhere in anagnorisis, which has a 'double function':

> It serves both as a decisive moment in the structure of a plot, as well as a means for representing an epistemological drama – the drama of hesitation and denial, assertion and revelation. In other words, recognition scenes are bits of narrative that contain, perhaps more explicitly than other bits, their own poetics. A successful reading of such scenes should, ideally, produce not only an interpretation of the text, but also an account of how it knows itself – or . . . its own theory of fiction.

Creswell quotes Cave aptly: 'The recognition scene is the mark or signature of a fiction, so that even if something like it occurs in fact, it still sounds like a fiction and will probably be retold as such.'[9] This is critical to a reading of the *maqāmah* in view of its status as the first highbrow fictional genre in Arabic literature that is also more or less avowedly fictional – displaying the avowal, in part, by putting so much stress on the recognition scene. On the one hand, fact acquires the flavour of fiction with anagnorisis; on the other, fiction itself likes to pretend that it imitates fact but is exposed as fanciful by the tug and lure of anagnorisis.

The picaresque *maqāmāt* which flourished from the tenth century AD onwards reveal 'the capacity of language to articulate at once the most persuasive visions of harmony and truth and the most insidious simulacra of that truth.'[10] While exploring and toying with the idea that eloquence need not be commensurate with veracity, these anecdotes engage also in a number of intertextual diversions,[11] parodying Hadith, pious sermons, stories of wise fools, romance form, aspects of theological discourse, Isma^{c}ili stories of initiation and, in certain instances, the mythic tales of Shi^{c}i Imamic hagiography – that is, those anecdotes of sightings, encounters with, and recognitions of, the occulted Twelfth Imam,[12] who was believed while in occultation to attend incognito the pilgrimage in Mecca every year.

The Return of the Missing Husband, Part 1: al-Ḥarīrī's Fifth Maqāmah

The fictional narrator, al-Ḥārith b. Hammām, was in attendance one night in Kufa amid a gathering of intellectual and literary soulmates when a man knocked at the door seeking alms. The latter's silver tongue in describing his forlorn condition prompts them to allow him in. With the aid of a lamp that is brought into the room, the narrator recognises him as Abū Zayd, al-Ḥarīrī's ubiquitous rogue hero. Since the recognition of Abū Zayd and his game of deception normally take place at the closure of the anecdote, this *maqāmah* is a conscious variation upon a theme. Al-Ḥārith now proceeds to request the telling of one of Abū Zayd's *gharāʾib*, or marvellous stories. The following is the unlikely tale, which in the original Arabic is linguistically ornate and exquisitely told.

Earlier that very night in Kufa itself he had sought alms at another stranger's house.[13] A young boy came to the door, apologising in precocious language for the impoverished state of the household. In the young boy's bleak description of the plight of his mother, who had been abandoned by her husband while pregnant years before, Abū Zayd realises that he is in the presence of his son, Zayd. But, unable to offer any material assistance, he turns away in shame. There, Abū Zayd ends his dismal tale. His audience is so taken by it that they have it recorded in writing. They all promise him money for the restitution of his family, and he receives their pledges the following morning. (All the other events have taken place at night under the auspices of a rising and setting moon with whose mutable aspect Abū Zayd is clearly linked. To some extent, the moon, once it has disappeared below the horizon, is transfigured in the person of Abū Zayd.) When he is about to depart, al-Ḥārith asks to accompany him in order to meet his offspring, and only then does it dawn on him that Abū Zayd has invented the whole story.

Vaguely, this *maqāmah* parodies romance;[14] more pointedly it undercuts some of the complacencies of the very cult of storytelling, as evidenced wryly in the way the protagonist's own name is deconstructed: Abū Zayd means 'the Father of Zayd', which is on this occasion a fiction. The third and final recognition in this *maqāmah* sheds retrospective light, as most recognitions tend to, on the nature of the first – on who and what exactly Abū Zayd is and is not. He is indeed Abū Zayd the wandering, deceitful and shape-shifting trickster; he is not the biological father of Zayd. The very name Abū Zayd becomes ontologically contradictory, just as the *maqāmāt* are in general.[15] If it is not a son Abū Zayd fails to deliver it is something else: some metonymy of the truth that disappoints.

The Return of the Missing Husband, Part 2: Non-fiction

Is this kind of imposture really the preserve of fiction? Or does imposture simply become more heightened in fiction? Striking recognition stories do survive in one of the most mundane textual genres of all: legal court histories. Because of their concern with the status of the individual, they can shed light on issues of identity, social and religious stature, testimony and truth in legal theory. An engrossing example is an episode described by Bernard Haykel.[16] One of two variants is taken from *al-Badr al-Ṭāliᶜ* or *Rising Moon* by the eighteenth-century Yemeni Sunni revivalist theologian and lawyer, Muḥammad ibn ᶜAlī al-Shawkānī (d. 1734). The work is a biographical dictionary and relates the lives of prominent legal scholars and jurists, detailing the issues and events that marked their vocations. Under the entry about al-Sayyid al-Ḥusayn ibn Yaḥyā ibn Ibrāhīm al-Daylamī al-Dhamārī, we find the following episode:

> Soon after the turn of the 18th century CE, a man known as Muḥammad ibn Ḥusayn, one of the sons of al-Mahdī Ṣāḥib al-Mawāhib (a Yemeni patrician, d. 1727), disappeared from his home town for about twenty years. During this time his family received no trace of news from, or even about, him. Then a man arrived in town claiming to be the missing individual. The family of the absent man – his wife together with his mother and brothers and sisters – believed him and word spread around town that he was now again sleeping with his spouse. Things continued in this vein for some days until a man from Bayt al-Najm, an inhabitant of Zabīd (a distant coastal region), appeared on the scene; he informed the people of Dhamār and its governor that this man was not in fact the missing person, but rather a member of the family of Ṣaᶜṣaᶜa, who were commoners from Shaᶜsān: [he was] an outcast, a sharpster and a wandering thief. He had – so the informant claimed – upon his arrival in town simply assumed the lofty sartorial aspect of the family he had infiltrated. The governor (Al-Sayyid Al-Dhamārī) summoned [the claimant] but determined that he was indeed the person he professed to being – Muḥammad ibn Ḥusayn, a member of the noble family. He based his judgement on the fact that his claim was corroborated by the mother, the wife and the siblings of the missing man . . . It was only afterwards that other witnesses testified to the fact that he was indeed a commoner from Ṣaᶜṣaᶜa. He was thus convicted of fraud by the Imam, physically castigated, expelled, and he died soon afterwards. Al-Dhamārī – the subject of this biographical entry – had ruled in the

> impostor's favour on the basis of external evidence (*istinādan ilā l-ẓāhir*), viz. the original deposition of the family. He was investigated [for his lack of judgement] by the [religious] authorities and later exonerated, and he continues to practice to this day. He is exemplary in his comportment: he strives to enforce what is good and forbids all manner of reprehensible behaviour (*qāʾimun bi-l-amr bi-l-maʿrūf wa-l-nahy ʿan al-munkar*).[17]

For al-Shawkānī, the point of recording this story in his book was to illustrate how a normally fine and gifted judge – one exemplary in his conduct and the practice of law – was taken in by superficial evidence such as to issue a flawed judgement. But few texts could be more tantalising. It is all too short, the mere synopsis of a splendid tale of imposture, and the more we pore over it the more we yearn for a fuller, more expansive version that develops the ambiguities of the situation, accentuating the nuances and tensions that surely inhered in the lead-up to the final epiphany: the unmasking of the interloper and, along with him, the muted and perhaps tacit connivance of whole sectors of the community. We have in our reading of this skeletal anecdote been spoiled by the detailed surviving archive of a closely analogous historical event – the very epitome of al-Shawkānī's self-same story which took place two centuries earlier in the French Pyrenees: the notorious *Return of Martin Guerre*.[18]

Even the most cursory comparison of the Martin Guerre and Ṣaʿṣaʿah stories reveals one crucial element that is missing from the Yemeni text: the final appearance of the absentee husband, the dramatic '*retour*' (return) of the real Martin Guerre, recognised by his wife in court, enabling, indeed forcing the disclosure of a truth that has threatened to surface for so long. Up to that critical point there had been much collusion with the impostor, whose real name was Arnaud du Tilh. Whilst the community of Artigat was in the end divided over the affair, identity had for a long time been established not by a well-grounded epistemology of character, but rather by desire and delusion – most notably by the desire of a wife to have the husband whom she wanted or whom she allowed herself to think she desired for three years until the dramatic *peripeteia* involved in the true spouse's return. It is curious in al-Shawkānī's version of this archetypal narrative that even the mother is duped; perhaps she was simply dithering in old age and suffered dementia.

Although this is a striking added feature, it does not diminish the problem of the wife's acquiescence in the impostor's claim. If the wife is implicitly exonerated by al-Shawkānī's text, one is struck nevertheless by how muted this particular aspect is. What else has been quieted? Quite possibly, the spectre of material opportunism or, worse, uxorial betrayal.

In all events, tales of imposture are typically shot through with ambiguity. Of Martin Guerre's wife, Bertrande de Rols, Cave muses:

> [S]he is the unknown quantity, the one who knows what men don't know, the faithful wife who may also have abetted the impostor. Any reading of Martin Guerre's story is bound to make Bertrande central to the uncertainty of the recognition (whom did she recognize behind the scenes, in bed?) . . . Central, yet always, in a male dominated society peripheral: which is exactly why she is a blind-spot.[19]

Although details may come to light that allow us to flesh out the parallels between these two women, we should set aside the imaginary promise of putative, at best undiscovered archives to address another issue. One of the most interesting aspects of Martin Guerre's 'return' is the intertextual dimension in the accounts that have come down to us. As Cave continues:

> The cultured sixteenth-century narrators of the story (and *a fortiori* later ones) regarded it as a drama, part comedy, part tragedy, remembering no doubt Plautus' *Amphitryon*, where Jupiter seduces a woman by disguising himself as her husband and where, in the Prologue, the term 'tragicomedy' was first used. In this way, Martin Guerre immediately enters the inter-textual labyrinth composed by the literary memory of Western civilization. His story cannot be recovered as a unique event, experienced by living individuals: it is shaped *ab initio* by existing narrative structures and interpretation . . . Shakespeare's plays, the first of which were written during Martin's lifetime, flourish on materials of which his story is made, and make it difficult to read that story as anything but an implausible yet disturbing tale.[20]

One wonders if this kind of 'anxiety of influence', or intertextual gravity, exists correspondingly in the Yemeni narrative. Some signature of literary enhancement might subsist in the finely alliterative and sibilant description of the rogue (the *rajul min bayt ṣaᶜṣaᶜah l-mazāyinah ahl shaᶜsān ṣuᶜlūk mutaḥayyil mutalaṣṣiṣ kathīr al-siyāḥah*: 'the man from the house of Ṣaᶜṣaᶜah, the barber of the people of Shaᶜsān, a wandering rogue and thieving trickster'); this is certainly verbal enhancement and lends the entire account a kind of literary inflection. On such a reading, a distant textual antecedent for the literary type would be al-Ḥarīrī's fifth *maqāmah*.

Excursus: The Perils of Aspect and the Virtues of Disparity

Stories of imposture, brought together by Jorge Luis Borges in a virtual cross-cultural conspectus in his exquisite tales 'Tom Castro, the Implausible Impostor' and 'The Masked Dyer, Hakim of Merv',[21] thrive on the dramatic tensions between appearance and latency. Such tension holds morality in suspension until the truth emerges into light. The messy ambivalence that normally inheres in stories of imposture, casting morality into doubt, is conveyed dazzlingly in Borges's creative meditation on the problematic nature of human appearance in acts of personal deception. It is worth quoting at length from 'Tom Castro' since it is such a carefully fashioned story – conscious of its own poetics – about a returning family member, in this case a son. It is a 'true' story that takes on a classically fictional form; indeed, Borges's version of this notorious nineteenth-century affair is superbly sculpted, infused with a dark and sinister fatalism:

> Tichborne was a gentleman, slight in build, with a trim, buttoned-up look, sharp features, darkish skin, straight black hair, lively eyes, and a finicky, precise way of speaking. Orton was an enormously fat, out-and-out boor, whose features could hardly be made out; he had somewhat freckled skin, wavy brown hair, heavy-lidded eyes, and his speech was dim or non-existent. Bogle got into his head that Orton's duty was to board the next Europe-bound steamer and to satisfy Lady Tichborne's hopes by claiming to be her son. The plan was outrageously ingenious . . . He knew that an exact likeness of the long-lost Roger Charles Tichborne was an outright impossibility. He also knew that any resemblance, however successfully contrived, would only point up certain unavoidable disparities. Bogle therefore steered clear of all likeness. Intuition told him that the vast ineptitude of the venture would serve as ample proof that no fraud was afoot . . . A further assurance

> of success lay in Lady Tichborne's unrelenting, harebrained advertisements, which showed how unshakably she believed that Roger Tichborne was not dead and willing she was to recognize him.[22]

Imposture may be superficial, heaping emphasis on appearance, yet showing simultaneously that appearance is meaningless because what one desires to see can be stronger than what one sees in reality. Imposture thus preys on psychology: the will to believe may be stronger than the clear ability to discern. The psychological tension in these materials at times may be one way of explaining away and mitigating a sense of moral contamination. Michael Cooperson probes two aspects of this issue compellingly in his discussion of the mystic Bishr al-Ḥāfī (b. 767 AD); Cooperson's observations are important, principally, for hinting through his juxtapositions that distinct narrative moods and different textual genres can and do meet on some central ground of ambiguity:

> As if fascinated by the carefully cultivated inscrutability of their fellow citizens, classical writers played obsessive variations on the theme of discovery. The most common of these variations consisted in narratives that reveal a character to be other than he appears. In [the Sufi saint] Ma^c^ruf [al-Karkhī's (815 AD)] biographical anecdote, for example, the Sufi surprises his disciples by revealing his solicitude for the sinners. Fictional compositions, notably the *maqāma*, played even more complex variations on this theme. Al-Hamadhani, the inventor of the genre, made the saint and the sinner into a single character and derived the plot of his stories from the narrator's obsessive curiosity about this character's true identity. The narrator, ^c^Isa b. Hisham, frequently comes upon the protagonist Abu al-Fath in a public space such as a mosque or the market-place, where the latter delivers a sermon that reduces the audience to tears of penitence – except, that is, for the narrator, who instead feels only curiosity that compels him to pursue the preacher and uncover him for a beggar, a rascal, or a drunkard. This pattern recurs in the *Maqāmāt* of al-Ḥarīrī, where the hero Abu Zayd evinces both a private and a public personality . . .
>
> When the mysterious Bishr al-Hafi tried to conceal his identity from his visitor, the man continued to press him until Bishr finally divulged his *kunya*, Abu Nasr. But this attempt to skirt the issue (Abu Nasr was

> a common name) failed when the man revealed that he too was Abu Nasr and, encouraged by this coincidence, divulged to Bishr that he was searching Baghdad in hopes of meeting the great mystic Bishr al-Hafi. The *Maqāmāt* play a more elaborate version of this game by making the narrator and the protagonist practically identical, and then engaging them in a recurrent game of deferred recognition. Both ᶜIsa b. Hisham and Abu al-Fath travel the mashriq in a variety of guises, alternatively rich, poor, old, and young; both prize and practice eloquence, and both earn their living in illicit ways. ᶜIsa seeks to repress any awareness that he resembles Abu al-Fath, and vice versa: most implausible, he again and again fails to recognize his Doppelgänger. For his part, Abu al-Fath is never surprised to see ᶜIsa, which makes sense only if he is not really a separate personality but rather a repressed portion of ᶜIsa's.[23]

Veiled identity is significant in purposefully and functionally religious material, as well as in the picaresque. There is much imposture even in religious lore.[24] The marked antitheses in imposture stories between what is latent and apparent and what is true and untrue – complicated by the fact that truth may lie hidden while untruth is apparent – alert us on some level to the strained and tense relations between genres, a reflection that turns us back to consider further the parodic ridiculing which tales of imposture can inflict upon tales of edifying or religious content. Tales of husbands who return after a prolonged disappearance do not always force the pious to avert their gaze; such earnest stories may be the textual objects of parody that a *maqāmah* like the fifth of al-Ḥarīrī (the *Maqāmah* of Kufa) has in its sights. There are, for example, two stories of returning claimants to note here before discussing the *Maqāmah* of Kufa in greater detail. The first is the *Arabian Nights* story of 'al-Mutalammis and his Wife Umaymah', adapted below from the translation by Burton:[25]

> It is related that [the pre-Islamic poet] al-Mutalammis once fled from al-Nuᶜman ibn Mundhir and was absent so long that folk deemed him dead. Now he had a beautiful wife, Umaymah by name, and her family urged her to marry again; but she refused, for she loved her husband al-Mutalammis very dearly. However, they were urgent with her, because of the multitude of her suitors, and importuned her till she at last condoned,

> albeit reluctantly; and they espoused her to a man of her own tribe. Now on the night of the wedding, al-Mutalammis came back and, hearing in the camp a noise of pipes and tabrets and seeing signs of a wedding festival, asked some of the children what was the merry-making, to which they replied, 'They have married Umaymah wife of al-Mutalammis, to such a one, and he goes in to her this night.' When he heard this, he planned to enter the house amongst the mob of women and saw the two of them seated on the bridal couch. By and by, the bridegroom came up to her, whereupon she sighed heavily and weeping, recited this couplet,
>
> > 'Would heaven I knew (but many are the shifts of joy and woe) / In what far distant land you are, my Mutalammis, oh!'
>
> Now al-Mutalammis was a renowned poet; so he answered her saying:
>
> > 'Right near at hand, Umaymah mine! Whenever the caravan / Halted I never ceased to pine for you, I would have you know!'
>
> When the bridegroom heard this, he guessed how the case stood and went forth from among them in haste improvising,
>
> > 'I was in bestest luck, but now my luck goes contrary: / A hospitable house and room contains your love, you two!'
>
> And he returned not but left the two to their privacy. So al-Mutalammis and his wife abode together in all comfort and solace of life and in all its joys and jollities, till death parted them. And glory be to Him whose command the earth and the heavens shall arise!

This is simple and unproblematic romance. There can scarcely be a moral agenda to speak of. Al-Mutalammis's prolonged disappearance is not questioned, and the story seems simply to be the excuse for a citation of one of the poet's verses. It is this poetry that provides the authentication of the returning man's identity; the etiology of verse is often fanciful. This is emphatically demotic literature that celebrates a renowned poet. The basic point to glean from it is that the recognition scene is not coy of being taken at face value: it is straightforward, and both simplistically and emotionally uplifting.

A more interesting – and marvellous – return is told about the legendary figure Tamīm al-Dārī:[26]

> The Lakhmid Tamīm al-Dārī Abū ᵓl-Fawāris ('the Father of Knights') . . . was converted to Islam from Christianity. Tamīm was supposed to have been the first to light lamps in mosques, and is supposed to have been the man who taught the Prophet the signs and wonders which would herald the appearance of the Antichrist. In the Tamīm legend, the Prophet, when about to die, prophesies that Tamīm will experience unheard-of adventures. Some are fantastic, others allegorical [categories that are not mutually exclusive, as below]:
>
> One day a hideous afreet kidnapped Tamīm from his home at the hour of prayer. He vanished for seven years. So long was his absence that his wife assumed that he had died; she asked permission of the caliph ᶜUmar b. al-Khaṭṭāb to remarry. The caliph hesitated, but in the end agreed, and she accepted the suit of a man of the tribe of ᶜUdhrah. On the day she was to be wed, Tamīm unexpectedly descended from the sky. No one recognised him. A dispute arose between him and the ᶜUdhrī over possession of the wife, and the caliph was obliged to arbitrate. Tamīm then told his tale: the afreet had transported him to an island; their flight had lasted half a night, although the distance they had traversed was equal to seventy years.

Hideous creatures thrived on that island in frightful variety. The dimensions of the continuing story are immense, in time and space: decades spent adrift, travelling distances beyond the ken of man. Marvellous elements include: encounters with jinn and a symphony of angels whose wise instructions go unheeded; wanderings amid towering mountains, fortresses of snow, and deserted cities of myriad palaces suspended in the air, among mysterious men, good and evil, followed by eventual arrival at the legendary Iram of the Columns. The appearance of Elias marks the spiritual centre of the story, more or less. He will guide the hero home should he be dutiful. A ship conveys him and among the crew is a sailor who owns the oldest book of Moses that prophesies the coming of the Prophet Muḥammad; after time adrift two colossal black mountains appear and, there, Tamīm al-Dārī finds a youth clad in green who feeds him dates; cast about again he meets with: a stunning maiden, a black dog guarding a cave's entrance and, within, a one-eyed grey-bearded old man lying fettered and manacled to a stone bed. Mystery has piled upon mystery but he learns that the maiden was the world, the one-eyed creature the Antichrist. Eventually two billowing dark clouds loom, one filled with furious angels, the other with angels of mercy; the green youth then reappears declaring himself to be Khiḍr – and so some mystical point of resolution has been reached. By and by, after all this agonistic journeying, the hero is transported home, transfigured . . .

> The tale concluded, the caliph ᶜUmar now had to judge who was the lawful spouse. He consulted ᶜAlī b. Abī Ṭālib, the Prophet's son-in-law, who vouched for Tamīm's honesty, and the wife was given the final choice. She asked to be reunited with her husband, the ideal Companion.[27]

Tamīm al-Dārī was said to have instructed the Prophet about the eschatology of the Antichrist; it is these elements of the story, therefore, that authenticate the identity of the returning claimant. Paradoxically, the entire narrative, which is about lost identity, identifies the man; Tamīm al-Dārī is the perfect paradigm of an *homme récit*, known ontologically, as it were, for this kind of story which by turns effaces and contrives his identity. The edifying aspect of the story lies in the fact that it is an allegory of loss and gain in a journey through the symbolic realms of belief, unbelief and pious conversion. Of further interest is that the overarching epistemological scheme of marital rights and recognition is reflected in miniature in the disclosure of al-Khiḍr. The role this Gnostic knower plays is a common trait in popular allegorical stories: his late and functional appearance establishes a traveller's tale as one of spiritual discovery; often in such stories the enunciation of al-Khiḍr's identity signals the attainment of a spiritual goal.[28] Because this is both a popular and pious story, it is twice removed from the high-brow and subversive *maqāmah*.[29] By setting Tamīm al-Dārī's story side-by-side with the tale of the Yemeni false claimant of Ṣaᶜṣaᶜah, we glean quite pointedly the fact that closely identical narrative epitomes (though different in the details they contain) may undergird both edifying texts and ones that are a- (or anti-) moralistic. The antonymy between the edifying and the morally disquieting or dispiriting comes across in the following two short anecdotes, which, within a much closer span of text, can be viewed as a diptych of contrast:

> The great Sufi Sheikh al-Junayd (d. 908 AD) departed on his walkabout. During his journey he was taken by thirst; he found a well, but it was so deep that he could not drink from its water. So he took off his waistband, dangled it into the well until it reached the water. He then lifted it out and pressed the water into his mouth. A Faqir now appeared and said to him, 'Why are you doing it like this? Just say to the water "rise" and drink from your hands.' The Faqir then approached the edge of the well and said to the water, 'Rise, God willing!' It rose, and both the Sheikh and the Faqir drank from it. The Sheikh then turned to him and asked, 'Where are you from?' He said, 'I am one of God's servants.' So he asked, 'Who is your Sheikh?' He replied, 'My Sheikh is al-Junayd, but I have yet to see him.' So he asked, 'How did you come to this [knowledge].' He replied, 'By thinking well of my Sheikh.'[30]

The second anecdote is less edifying – they are poles apart:

> It is told . . . that Harim b. Hayyan (d. 46 of the Hijra) – the same of whom it is related that his mother carried him for four years – met a storyteller in a mosque who told religious tales quoting him [Harim] as authority. When Harim revealed his identity and it became obvious that the story-teller had never seen him, the latter answered there and then, 'I have always heard that you were a strange fellow; what you are saying is very odd indeed. In this mosque alone there are fifteen people praying with us who are called Harim b. Hayyan and you appear to flatter yourself with the thought that you are the only one bearing this name.'[31]

These anecdotes, in which recognition is designed for the reader or listener to register, as much as the narrative players themselves, are quite patently antithetical to each other. The first leaves one on a spiritual ascent, the other on a moral tumble. Now, the *maqāmāt* as a genre may sometimes be disposed to hint at the first type, but they are invariably in the end akin to the latter – turning on the kind of recognition that casts everything into doubt, and creating for the reader the epistemological conundrum of the unreliable witness. Such is the case in the *Maqāmah* of Kufa, a tale in which, as we have seen even in synopsis, the revelation of a moving truth that turns on kinship is discovered to be a scandalous deception.

I gave a précis of the *Maqāmah* of Kufa above; I now provide the whole *maqāmah*, in an adaptation of Thomas Chenery's translation. I follow the format adopted by the thirteenth-century AD commentator al-Sharīshī of breaking up the narrative into short paragraph-length sections and providing commentary. My aim is to show that a broad hermeneutics of cultural background contributes to the dynamic of reading and discovery that gives recognition its force, and is necessary to both understanding and explaining narrative – or these particular narratives – fully.

Al-Ḥarīrī's *Maqāmah* of Kufa: The Non-existent Revenant[32]

Setting the Scene and the Arrival of the Stranger

> Al-Ḥārith ibn Hammām related: I was conversing at Kufa, in a night whose complexion was of a twofold hue, whose moon was an amulet of silver—With companions who had been nourished on the milk of eloquence, who might draw the train of oblivion over Saḥbān.[33]—Each was a man to remember from, and not to guard against; each was one whom his friend would incline to, and not avoid.—And the night talk fascinated us until the moon had set, and the watching overcame us.—Now when night's unmingled dark had spread its awning, and there was nought but nodding among us—We heard from the gate the faint sound of a wayfarer, rousing the dogs; then followed the knock of one bidding to open.—We said, 'Who is it that comes in the dark night? (*mani l-mulimm fī l-layli l-mudlahimm*)'[34]

The time, the location, the players: all are introduced. On the location, Kufa, al-Sharīshī departs in his detailed commentary on a long initial excursus of detail, ruing the old garrison town's latter-day melancholy of dilapidation (as remembered after him by Ibn Jubayr (d. 1217 AD) in his travelogue, or *Riḥlah*, which al-Sharīshī evokes)[35]. The particular setting and scene of this *maqāmah* is either distinct from this civic and urban history, and thus represents a time before decline, or it harbours itself some insidious facet of that decline as reflected in its inhabitants. This latter notion is at most latent, and the resonance of the lamenting note – if that is what it is – stems from al-Sharīshī's habit of overindulging the relevance of an entire tradition in his detailed commentary; he is a marvellous curator of cultural and literary curios to the same degree that he is an interpreter. The notion (and the threat) at which we intimate comes across much more in the ambiguities about the time and the players that are both, ostensibly, unequivocally good things. The night is one of twin aspect, with a bright sliver of moon hanging as a pendant in the dark surrounding sky. The contrast between light and darkness is significant in so far as it winds its way through the narrative as a symbolic theme. A related dichotomy is conveyed in the image of the moon's shape as an 'amulet', as something that both embellishes and protects. But what is there to be protected from? The game of scandal and deception? The shameless story-hawker and eloquent trickster? In the *maqāmah* generally an image – which has a sense, a value, a meaning, a connotation – will tend to provoke its opposite in ways that are initially beyond grasp and subsequently beyond control. Thus, where there is comfort in the sense of light or ornamentation, there is also risk of darkness and need for protection. Al-Sharīshī, for his part, demonstrates with sundry materials that the association of the moon and silver is an old one in poetry, citing examples. The attractiveness of the image is cajoling. It evokes a sense of beauty and, with that, of security. However, one example cited by al-Sharīshī beckons us to pause: 'The moon appearing in the dark recesses of the night is like a trap of silver set up to snare the stars' (*mithlu fakhkhi l-lujayni ṣī / -gha li-ṣaydi l-kawākibī*). Does al-Sharīshī, in his retrospective reading, alert us to the snare of some hermeneutic game?

The qualities of the night companions are markworthy, too: they have bred on the milk of eloquence and drawn the cloak of oblivion over the memory of Saḥbān. Ostensibly, they are pinnacles of sociable grandiloquence, deft masters of culturally enriched conversation. But there seems to lurk a warning about rash inadvertence in that they have drawn a veil of forgetfulness over a paragon of eloquence, the legendary Saḥbān; within the micro-realm of this locution, they are bamboozled into forgetting what they should always remember. Covering up evokes exposure. The fact that one notion can lead one to think of its converse is a potential warning: eloquence might in the end be exposed as its obtuse opposite. The idea of drawing a veil across a subject and forgetting it thus harbours a warning about possibly mistaken and highly insouciant perception. Understood in this light, the image is certainly double-edged, even paradoxical. Equally significant, and in a similar vein, is the phrase that they are each 'a man to remember from [as an authority], and not to guard against [with suspicions of deceit]'. There is paronomasia here in Arabic creating a semantic link (which may itself have symbolic consequence) between what is preserved from these companions as cultural authorities, on one hand, and caution about a delusion that may transpire on their account, on the other. Might they be sources of what is untrustworthy in fact? The way the story transpires will suggest so and provides us with an entertaining instance of this. If they command something to be set down in writing to preserve it for posterity, yet that very thing turns out to be false, then the phrase '*yuḥfaẓu ᶜan-hu*' ('one whose learning should be put to memory') – which was intended to celebrate the truth-purveying authority of each individual among their company – is forever compromised.

The companions were fascinated by night talk until, that is, 'the moon had set, and the watching overcame them.' Two things should be noted: first, the idea of being overcome and its relationship, semantically and symbolically, with defeat such as might inhere in, for example, their wit being outshone; second, that the Arabic for the setting moon is *gharaba*, which has the same root as the *gharīb* (stranger) who now appears at the door. Kilito first suggested that the moon and Abū Zayd are one and the same in the *maqāmah*'s figurative realm and the narrative will go on to tell us as much again. So the word *gharaba* evokes the stranger as well as the *gharāʾib* (strange stories) he will later tell, and the verb is associated here with its rhyme word *ghalaba* (overcoming); in this light, we read the evocations of the Arabic word *mustaftiḥin*. The stranger knocks at the door 'to seek its opening'. *Fataḥa* is the root for opening; clearly that is also the primary meaning. The secondary meaning is that of seeking a conquest (a '*fatḥ*') and seeking to open something else; to open purse strings would be apt in the scheme of Abū Zayd's puckish antics. The opening of purse strings, in turn, would itself constitute its own, and the rogue's own, victory. There is one more detail relating to *mustaftiḥ* worth assessing, to wit, the implications of the phrase that comes immediately before it, where the stranger Abū Zayd arrives as 'a wayfarer rousing the dogs [*mustanbiḥin*]'. *Mustaftiḥin* and *mustanbiḥin* rhyme elegantly, but the morphological verbal link highlights also an ironic semantic dissonance, hiding an agenda. For in the Arabic tradition, a stranger who causes dogs to bark is effectively arriving at the home of an ungenerous man. A truly generous man's dog will not bark, inured as the creature is to the constant visits of people. With the barking of the dogs in the opening scene of this *maqāmah* comes a challenge for Abū Zayd to have the door opened to welcome him, first of all, and, thereafter, to have the purse strings of the company in attendance opened also. These details, which easily go unrecognised, are a challenge to reading and readerly perception.

The Bid to Enter

Then the traveller answered:

> People of this house, be guarded from ill!
> Be shielded from harm so long as you live!
> Harken! The night-gloom has driven to you
> A dishevelled journey-man, grime-laden,
> A brother of journeying, lengthy and extended,
> He stands now bent and yellowed by dust
> Like the new moon on the horizon when it smiles.
> He approaches your courtyard, begging boldly,
> Repairing to you before all other people,
> Seeking food and a billet
> In him you'll find a gladdened guest, ingenuous,
> Gratified with all, sweet or bitter;
> He'll quit your company to announce your charity abroad.[36]

Threatening, negative images combine harmoniously in the first couplet: evil, harm and the dark night. They are then contrasted in the third verse in which the stranger introduces himself as 'bent and yellow like the new moon of the horizon when it smiles' – a comforting, positive image. So much for one dichotomy. The stranger then projects the dichotomy of good and evil, or sweet and bitter fortune, onto the world around him. But neither the narrator nor his companions realise that his sweet tongue might also in fact hide a bitter lesson.

'The Best Suppers are those that are Cleary Seen'

> Said Al Ḥārith, son of Hammām: Now when we were caught by the sweetness of his utterance, and knew what was behind his lighting, We hastened to open the gate, and met him with welcome; And said to the boy 'Quick, quick! Bring what is ready!' / Then said our guest, 'Now, by Him who has set me down at your abode, I will not roll my tongue over your food,

> Unless you pledge me that you will not make me a burden, that you will not, for my sake, task yourselves with a meal. / For sometimes a morsel aches the eater, and forbids him his repasts. / And the worst of guests is he who imposes trouble and annoys his host, And especially with a harm that affects the body and tends to sickness. / For, by that proverb, which is widely current, "The best suppers are those that are clearly seen." / Is meant that supper-time should be hastened, and eating by night, which dims the sight, avoided. / Unless, by Allah, the fire of hunger kindle and stand in the way of sleep.'[37]

In this dark night, light keeps shining forth: the lightning bolts of the stranger's eloquent wit. He casts his disingenuously restrained request for food in a significant image: 'The best suppers are those that are clearly seen [*sawāfir*].' On the word *sawāfir*, al-Sharīshī provides a long note; it is one of several excursuses that key in well, in fact, with the layered epistemology of the narrative. *Sawāfir* is the plural of *sāfirah*, 'a woman who has removed the veil from her face and exposed it; it is as if when you can see the food you eat [in the evening] the food has shed the darkness from itself.'[38] That one should be able to see what one eats is another veiled warning from (and about) a man who tells tall tales. Here, hunger kindles the light that the stranger will eat from – but Abū Zayd in any case can see, and knows, what he is doing and what he drives at with his loaded words, however frugal the morsel he pretends to be satisfied with.

There is a further detail to note in the phrase 'Now when we were caught by the sweetness of his utterance, and knew what was behind his lighting.' The Arabic for 'we were caught' is *khalaba*, which means to bewitch or beguile on its own, but coupled with *barq* gives the expression *barqun khullabun*, signifying 'lightning without rain' or a 'delusion'. So what is this knowledge that the men have? What is it that they *know* exactly? In Hava's dictionary, *khullab* is defined as a 'rainless cloud', and of *barqun khullab* Hava writes that it is 'Said of a promise without effect'. That the signs of eloquence should be delusional, like clouds that promise rain when lit by lightning but fail to deliver, suggests the company's dimness of wit; perhaps they are dissipated and eat late into the night. There is more than a hint of mockery in mention of that which 'dims the sight'.

The Recognition of Zayd (Part 1)

> Said al-Ḥārith: Now it was as though he had got sight of our conviction. / Accordingly we gratified him by agreeing to the condition, and commended him for his easy temper. / And when the boy brought what was to be had, and lighted the candle in the midst of us, I looked close at him, and lo! It was Abū Zayd. / So I said to my company, 'Joy to you of the guest has come! Nay, but the spoil is lightly won! / For if the moon of Sirius has gone down, truly the moon of poetry has risen: / Or if the full moon of the Lion has waned, the full moon of eloquence shines forth.' / Then ran through them the wine-glow of joy, and sleep flew away from their eye-corners. / And they refused the rest which they had purposed, and returned to the spreading out of pleasantry, after they had folded it. / But Abū Zayd kept intent upon plying his hands; however, when what was before him might be removed / I said to him, 'Present us with one of the rare stories from your night talkings, or some wonder from among the wonders of your journeys.'[39]

The first recognition is a surprise both to the narrator and the reader. The narrator is, of course, always surprised when he realises he is in the presence of Abū Zayd, but the readership in this instance may also be incredulous that the protagonist has been identified so soon, before any apparent trickery has taken place and long before the end of the *maqāmah*.[40] This is a variation upon a theme, yet in and of itself it is part of the conning that will lead to other more real anagnorises, since the reader's defences are lowered and her credulity is heightened before the ensuing narrative in which true deception supervenes. The *maqāmah* thus far is a virtual tribute to al-Hamadhānī's short *Maqāmah Kūfiyyah*, which should be considered briefly. It is inconceivable that al-Ḥarīrī in his own fifth *maqāmah* was doing anything but paying a literary homage to the earlier anecdote, its namesake, while simultaneously toying with and expanding upon it; enough details of the short original are reworked into al-Harīrī's sequel. In al-Hamadhānī's tale, the narrator travels to Kufa with a man about whom ᶜIsā b. Hishām relates,

> I saw nothing wrong to make me repudiate him (*lam unkirhu ᶜalā sūʾin*).[41] Now, when we had exchanged confessions and confidences, the story revealed that he was a Kufan by principle and Sufi by profession . . .

This will not turn out to be Abū al-Fatḥ, for

> When the eye of the night had drooped, and the dawn on its lip had sprouted, there was a knock at the door. We asked, 'What wanderer is knocking?'[42]

The stranger then recounts his suffering: harmful and bitter experiences; being chased from human settlements by barking dogs; hounded by ungenerous people; separation from his children – all of which lead to the narrator grabbing his own purse 'as a lion snatches at something and handing it over to the man' (who is then allowed in, *sic*). When the door is opened to him, he is revealed to be Abū al-Fatḥ al-Iskandarī; in Arabic the simple paronomasia is that *fataḥnā* leads to Abū al-Fatḥ. It is another conquest. The narrator's surprise provokes a smile and an explanation in doggerel to the tune of: 'I am a rich man, do not be deceived!' The essential semantic game of this *maqāmah* is that the stranger's figurative qualities of *ᶜarf al-ᶜūd* ('wafting fragrance [of character] from sweet burning sandalwood') lead to thanks and recognition for generosity (*al-ᶜurf*), which provoke the anagnorisis of Abū al-Fatḥ and, with it, his galling lesson that one should not be deceived by the appearance of indigence. In al-Hamadhānī one kind of recognition is married to another and misrecognition leads to disabused misprision. Even within its exceedingly short span, the *maqāmah* plays a subtle variation upon a semantic theme.

Returning to al-Ḥarīrī, as Kilito has observed, the light of the moon is a borrowed light, for the moon's beam is simply the reflection of the light of the sun. The stress on the selenic aspect of Abū Zayd might alert one to the fact that there is no real or satisfactory light there at all; after all, it requires 'a lighted candle' for the narrator to recognise him. This is a far cry from the coruscating light of the sun and, what is more, the artificial man-made light of the *sirāj* evokes the *nisbah* of the man it reveals, Abū Zayd al-Sarūjī, a man who shows his very *kunyah* to be unfounded in the tale he concocts about himself with consummate fakery. The light he will shed on the underlying nature of human experience through the *gharāʾib* he is asked to relate will have all the edifying force of the flickering light of a candle. We will return to the root and significance of *ᶜajībah* – the pendant of *gharībah* – presently.

The Request for a Story

> He said, 'Of wonders I have met with such as no seers have seen, no tellers have told.—But among the most wondrous was that which I beheld tonight, a little before my visit to you and my coming to your gate.'—Then we bade him tell us of this new thing which he had seen in the field of his night-faring.—He said, 'Truly the hurlings of exile have thrown me to this land: And I was in hunger and distress, with a scrip like the heart of the mother of Moses.—Now, as soon as the dark had settled, I arose, in spite of all my footsoreness, to seek a host or to gain a loaf.—Then the driver hunger, and Fate, which is bye-named the Father of Wonders, urged me on, till I stood at the door of a house, and spoke, improvising.[43]

Most Arabic anecdotes that pretend to have truth-value and authority would ultimately shy away from the claim 'such as no seers have seen, no tellers have told'. The phrase holds up a paradox to the canny reader: on the one hand, this is the ultimate enthralling scoop of showing and telling; on the other, what no one has seen or told by definition has no *isnād*, no verifying authority. According to certain textual protocols, it cannot by definition be true at all. Perhaps it is the obsession with the protocol that is being jibed at. What is more, there is no temporal or spatial depth to the tale Abū Zayd tells: it has happened practically there and then, not, like most tales of wonder, in a distant land and in a far off time. It is almost as if it is happening before their very eyes, which is the case since the wonder of the *maqāmah* is Abū Zayd's deception of his audience by means of a shallow tale.

What does have authority is the image of the empty 'heart of the mother of Moses'. It is a short but powerful Qur'anic image fraught with background. In his detailed and allusive commentary, al-Sharīshī brings that religious lore to the fore and tells an emotionally charged story of family recognition. He writes:

> Pharaoh had taken on the Israelites as slaves; half of them were used for building, the other half for tilling the land. Those who had no such work were nevertheless taxed the *jizyah*.[44] The sovereign saw in a dream fire appearing from the holy land to destroy the Egyptians but sparing the Israelites. He consulted about the meaning of this vision and was told: 'A

man will emerge from this country that the Israelites came from and at his hands Egypt will be destroyed.' So he ordered the killing of every child born to the Israelites. He gathered together the tribes and imposed this upon them, killing the children and torturing the pregnant women until they had miscarriages. They almost all perished, so he was told: 'They are your servants; if you kill all the newborn they will have no progeny and perish.' So he ordered all the male newborn children to be killed on alternate years. Aaron was born on a year when the newborn were spared, Moses was born in a year when they were to be killed.

When his mother gave birth to him, she despaired about him, and thus God inspired her with the following: 'Keep him and suckle him, but when you fear for him cast him into the river. Do not fear or despair.' So she made him a basket and placed him into it and cast it upon the river. She said to his sister, 'Follow it.' The water carried him to some bushes outside Pharaoh's palace where his servant women were cleaning the laundry. They found the basket and brought it into Asiya, Pharaoh's wife . . . She opened the basket and discovered him inside. She took pity on him; she took him and informed Pharaoh. He wanted to kill the child, fearing that he was the newborn about whom he had been warned. But Asiya clung to him and he let her keep him. Thus God spoke in the Qurʾan: 'So the family of Pharaoh took him so that he would become their enemy and source of sadness' (Q Al-Qaṣaṣ 28:9) . . . Pharaoh had no child so he adopted him as a son and gave him over to the care of wet nurses. He refused all their breasts. His mother missed him and was sad in her heart, so she sent his sister to offer to suckle the child. When she saw how desperate they were about his rejection of all the wet nurses . . . she said, 'Can I show you a family who will take care of him?' They agreed and she came back with her mother.

When she saw the infant, so intense was her love and joy that she almost said 'He is my son!' risking exposure of the whole affair, but God prevented her.[45] She gave him her breast and he began to feed. She brought him up in Pharaoh's palace; when he began to walk she brought him to Pharaoh; when he held him Moses reached out with his hand to touch Pharaoh's beard and plucked at it. Pharaoh called out, 'Bring the executioners – *He is the one*!' Asiya said, 'He is your darling and mine; do not kill him, for he is a child and doesn't understand what he is doing.' . . . So the child was reared in his care.

> When he reached puberty Pharaoh adopted him as a son; he would ride in his cortege and dress in his royal attire, and was called the 'son of Pharaoh'.[46]

The story of Pharaoh and Moses is, then, a story of recognition – of falsely understood paternity that, as anyone who knows the Qurʾan even vaguely is aware, comes to light in a terrifying disclosure of condign punishment meted out upon the unbelieving Egyptians. By alluding to this particular Qurʾanic verse ('the heart of the mother of Moses was so empty *that she almost exposed him*'), Abū Zayd is looking to expose himself, toying with his company in a rich verbal game of allusion. Although the stories have something in common, there could hardly be more bathos than in the sheer contrast between Abū Zayd's somewhat comic story of deluded paternity side-by-side with that of the Pharaoh. It is not just that the picaresque peddles stories of delusion, but the picaresque can feed on the authority of other stories, purveying allusions held in words, atavistic images and patterns of events.

A Request for Alms

> Greetings people of this dwelling,
> May you live an easy and plentiful life!
> What can you offer a son of the road, one crushed to the sand,
> Worn with journeys, stumbling in the pitch-dark night,
> Aching in entrails [ᶜalā l-ṭawā], which enclose only hunger?
> For two days he has not tasted the savour of a meal:
> He finds no refuge in your country.
> And already the van of the drooping darkness has gloomed;
> And through bewilderment he is restless.
> Now in this home is there any one, sweet of spring,
> Who will say to me, 'Throw away your staff and enter:
> Rejoice in a cheerful welcome and a ready meal?'[47]

Allusions to Mosaic lore are sustained. In the third verse, the Arabic *ᶜalā l-ṭawā* ('in entrails') reminds one of the valley of Ṭuwā where God spoke to Moses.[48] The meanings of words do not have to be related for acoustic echoes to work. The Arabic phrase for 'Throw away thy staff!' is *alqi ᶜaṣāka*; as Kilito has shown us, this command used in a hospitable way, with a sense of 'make yourself at home', reminds one of Moses' challenge to the sorcerers of Pharaoh who cast down their staffs and watch with horror as the inanimate objects come to life as snakes. The Qurʾan also characterises what the sorcerers peddle in their actions as 'lies'; this is clear in Surah 26 before their conversion where Moses's staff-turned-snake devours the serpents they have deceitfully concocted (*mā yaʾfikūna*). There is thus much mendacity plied into Abū Zayd's phrase *alqi ʿaṣāka*: it conjures a false sense of security while having some scriptural force. This is darkly allusive antiphrasis.

A Son's Account of Misery

Then appeared a lad in a tunic, and answered:

Now by the sanctity of the Shaykh who ordained hospitality,
And founded the House of Pilgrimage in the Mother of cities,
We can offer the night-farer nothing
But conversation and a lodging in our hall.
For how can one who is hungry to the bone and sleepless
Provide hospitable entertainment to the visitor?
Now what say you of my tale? What do you think?[49]

The shaykh evoked here is the Patriarch Abraham/Ibrāhīm and the mother of cities is Mecca. We begin to notice in this *maqāmah* how a variegated lexical and narrative stress is laid on fathers, mothers and relationships of kin. We have already encountered in different contexts: the Mother of Moses; the Mother of Cities; the Father of Wonders; the Son of the Road and Brother of Journeying. The whole *maqāmah* is a web of family relations; but the true paternity will belong to the father of a fabulous and fictitious story. Regarding Ibrāhīm, it is perhaps significant that al-Sharīshī tells another short story of adoption in his commentary: 'Sarah gave birth to Isaac [when Ibrāhīm was a hundred and fifty years old] and the Canaanites said, "The old man and the old woman have found a boy and adopted him; so God made him in the image of Ibrāhīm."' True paternity in religious material is underlined in a contrarian way by evocation of the unstable, temporary state of adoption.

Fictional Anagnorisis

I said, to myself at first, 'What shall I do with a hollow household languishing in indigence?—But tell me, youth, what is your name, for your

> intelligence has charmed me.'—he said, 'My name is Zayd, and my birth place Fayd: and I came to this city yesterday with my mother's relatives of the Banū ᶜAbs.'—I said to him, 'Tell me more, may you live and be raised when you fall!'—He said, 'My mother Barrah told me (and she is like her name, "pious") that she married in the year of the campaign on Māwān a nobleman of Sarūj and Ghassān; But when he was aware of her pregnancy (for he was a crafty bird, it is said) he made off from her by stealth, and away he has stayed, Nor is it known whether he is alive and to be looked for, or whether he has been laid in the lonely tomb.'—Said Abū Zayd, 'Now I knew by sure signs that he was my child; but my penury turned me from making myself known to him, So I parted from him with a heart crushed and tears flowing.—Now, you gentlemen of understanding, have you heard anything more wondrous than this?'—We said, 'No, by Him who has knowledge of the Book.'—He said, 'Record it among the wonders of chance; bid it abide for ever in the hearts of scrolls; for nothing like it has been told abroad in the world.'—Then we bade bring the ink-flask, and its snake-like reeds, and we wrote the story elegantly as he worded it.[50]

This is the recognition scene that Abū Zayd concocts brilliantly as the narrative crux of his *maqāmah*. It shows masterful understanding that this kind of anagnorisis may be – and commonly is – the signature of a story; it also hints to us that he knows, at the obtuse company's expense, that it is also the very signature of a fiction. It has tokens (*ᶜalāmāt*) but invests names with the significance of the particular semiotics of the text, as we suspect the man from Sarūj harks back to his initial discovery under the artificial light of a lamp (*sirāj*). It conjures life and death, and tension is generated between expectation and uncertainty. It limns an emotionally fraught recognition, and then, in a brilliant narrative move, suppresses it. Al-Harīrī knows exactly what he is doing. The point comes across in the Qurᵓanic evocation: 'And now, you men of understanding, have you heard anything more wondrous than this?' The Joseph story is prefaced at verse 3 with the following: 'In the telling of their story is a lesson (*ᶜibrah*) for those "men of understanding (*ūlī l-albāb*)."' In the Qurᵓan, the archetypal story of family recognition is clearly presented as one on which to heed for what it teaches. So it is here: the story of Abū Zayd is intended by him for men of understanding; yet it is not an *ᶜibrah* it will offer, rather a sense of the marvellous (*ᶜujāb*). This word is problematic. These are the words that paint the scepticism and sarcasm of the Kāfirūn: 'Has he [Muḥammad] rendered many gods into one? / that is a marvellous thing (*a-jaᶜala l-ālihata ilāhan wāḥidan in hādhā la-shayᵓun ᶜujāb*)!' There is a dissonance, therefore, in al-Harīrī's phrase *hal-samiᶜtum yā ūlī l-albābi bi-aᶜjaba min hādhā l-ᶜujāb?* ('Have you heard, intelligent people, of a something more extraordinary than this wonder?') Are the religiously intelligent meant to gape in wonder, like Kāfirūn? Surely the tension between the *ūlī l-albāb* and the *ᶜujāb* that they thirst for draws one close to a point of scenic and textual rupture; this is a conjunction of the good and the unseemly that should blow the cover off Abū Zayd's story. It is not so much a slip of the tongue on Abū Zayd's part as another symptom of his manipulative verbal antics. He is almost challenging his company to hear, see and sense the disjunctive moral cacophony of what he is saying.

When Abū Zayd says gallingly 'nothing like it has been told abroad in the world!' he mocks the witless, coaxing them to see that this is in fact the belabored essence of story – of family separation and recognition between father and son. In the Qurᵓan, the phrase *aḥsan al-qaṣaṣ* suggests that such a story is the most perfect model of human narrative (see Chapter 1). At this point in the *maqāmah* comes the rub: the company call for snake-like reeds in order to write out the story in an elegant hand. But the elegance does not erase the fact that snakes in the Moses story, in whose allusive wake we are reading, are the product of the lying fabrications of sorcery (*mā yaᵓfikūn*). The company should have taken their cue from Abū Zayd when he suppressed acknowledgement of his son, instead they do something diametrically opposed: they record on paper something which, from a moral perspective, should be silenced and laid to rest.

In *S/Z*, Roland Barthes develops an open-ended model of narrative codes that yields some insight when applied to this *maqāmah*. In this poststructuralist theory of narrative, a text is understood to be invested with five 'codes'. Through the shifting emphases they can be perceived to have, the text becomes 'infinitely transcribable'. That is, no code is invested with more inherent meaning than any other, and it is hard to fix or determine without equivocation the interpretation of a text. Two of these 'codes' are of particular relevance here: the 'hermeneutic' (the deciphering of events in the narrative as one might decipher a riddle) and the symbolic (a transcendent and effectively hypostasised realm of meaning and value, on the level of, say, 'good and evil'). Barthes avers,

> The key point . . . is that the hermeneutic code in *Sarrasine* is embodied in the theme of castration. The answer to the riddle, the thing we've been waiting for, is the unveiling of a monstrous excision. To make *being-castrated*, an anecdotal condition, coincide with *castration*, a symbolic structure, is the task successfully carried out by [Balzac] . . . This success hinges on a structural artifice: . . . making the search for truth (hermeneutic structure) into the search for castration (symbolic structure), making the truth be *anecdotally* (and no longer symbolically) the absent phallus.[51]

According to Terence Cave, 'Barthes encapsulates [in this gloss] the condition of anagnorisis, which – potentially at least – always entails the projection of a thematic or symbolic structure onto an enigmatic narrative structure.'[52]

The symbolic order in al-Ḥarīrī's *Maqāmah* might be construed as medieval Islamic society's veneration of religious and edifying truth preserved and conveyed to posterity in the form of recorded anecdotes (*akhbār*); the pedestal on which this truth came eventually to be placed and revered after the ninth century – though one should perhaps argue the point, historically – was the written word. When Abu Zayd's story is ceremoniously commissioned to be set on paper by his gullible audience (*raqashnā l-ḥikāyah ᶜalā mā sarada-hā*), an effective endorsement of perceived factual truth is enacted. But it is one that sits uncomfortably with the subsequent emergence of his outrageous deceit. Recognition unmasks the crisis of imposture. The following phrase captures the poetics of what is afoot: 'Recognition . . . is not the recovery for good or ill of certain knowledge, nor the reassuring restoration of the co-ordinates of kinship and social position. It unmasks a crisis, a perpetual threat of imposture.'[53]

The Final Recognition

> After which we sought to draw from him his wish about receiving his boy.—He said, 'If my purse were heavy, then to take charge of my son would be light.'—We said, 'if a *niṣāb* of money would suffice you, we will collect it for you at once.'—He said, 'And how should a *niṣāb* not content me? Would

any but a madman despise such a sum?'—Said the narrator, Then each of us undertook a share of it, and wrote for him an order for it.—Whereupon he gave thanks for the kindness, and exhausted the stock of praise; until we thought his speech long, or our merit little.—And then he spread out such a bright mantle of talk as might shame the stuffs of Yemen, Until the dawn appeared and the light-bearing morn went forth.—So we spent a night of which the mixed hues had departed, until its hind-locks grew gray in the dawn; And whose lucky stars were sovereign until its branch budded into light.—But when the limb of the sun peeped forth, he leaped up as leaps the gazelle, And said, 'Rise up, that we may take hold on the gifts and draw payment of the cheques:—For the clefts of my heart are widening from yearning after my child.'—So I went with him, hand in hand, to make easy his success.—But as soon as he had secured the coin in his purse the marks of his joy flashed forth, —And he said, 'Be you rewarded for the steps of thy feet! Be God my substitute towards you!'—I said, 'I wish to follow you that I may behold thy noble child, and speak with him that he may answer eloquently.'—Then he looked at me as looks the deceiver on the deceived, and laughed till his eyeballs gushed with tears; and he recited:—

> So you who did fancy the mirage to be water when I recounted what I did!
> I didn't think my guile would be hidden, or that what I meant would be doubted.
> By Allah, I have no Barrah for a spouse; I have no son from whom to take a bye-name.
> Nothing is mine but divers kinds of magic, in which I am original and copy no one:
> They are such as al-Aṣmaᶜī tells not of in what he has told; such as al-Kumayt never wove.
> These I use when I will to reach whatever my hand would pluck:
> And were I to abandon them, my state would be quite altered, nor should I gain what I now gain.
> So allow my excuse; nay, pardon me, if I have done wrong or crime.

Then he took leave of me and passed away, and set the coals of *ghaḍa* in my chest.[54]

There is a close resemblance in Arabic between the word *niṣāb* – the quantity of money, twenty dinars (according to al-Sharīshī) promised to Abū Zayd – and *naṣṣāb,* which means a 'swindler or trickster' and describes his role to perfection. This may be coincidence. What we should observe is the deliberate choreography of diurnal time and the related light it sheds in the closing scene: night has given way to day, the moon to the sun, and with it comes the piercing primal solar light. What other light 'sheds light' on the sense of the ending? When Abū Zayd receives the narrator's purse in the morning, 'his joy *flashed* forth' (*baraqat asārīru masarrati-hi*). This echoes the figurative lightning flash that had deluded the company the night before. This is still therefore a *barqun khullab* that promises rain but has nothing to give, and now shows that it gives nothing even while it takes from others. Furthermore, the liquid substrate of the metaphor of the empty promise is sustained in the first line of the closing poem of Abū Zayd: 'O you who did fancy the mirage to be water.' It is significant that this image of a 'dry' deception should gain strength from the fact that, when he comes clean about his ruse, Abū Zayd's mocking eyes laugh 'till his eyeballs gushed tears'. Just as his light deludes the gullible, so the only water he produces for the thirsty are tears of derision. The force of the metaphor is carried in the pun with which this verse of poetry ends: 'you thought the mirage to be water *when I related what I related*'. In Arabic the phrase italicised here plays on the verbal root of *rawā*, meaning 'to relate': the very same verb means 'to give to drink'. What Abū Zayd relates cannot quench the thirst for knowledge, as the mirage cannot quench a real thirst. The pun is simple but quite brilliant, and captures as well as anything in this *maqāmah* the engaging verbal duplicity of Abū Zayd. He has the charm to convey polyvalent meaning; indeed, if it were not for the polyvalence of language and rhetoric, Abū Zayd would not be the conning trickster that he is.

Three other tropes or figures, both persons and metaphors, further inform the allusive way Abū Zayd reveals himself in his valedictory poem. Although he is Abū Zayd, he has 'no son from whom to take a bye-name' (*wa-lā liya bnun bi-hi ktanaytu*). Bye-name in Arabic is *kunyah* (the root contained in the verbal form used here, *iktanaytu*). It smacks of *kināyah* (allusion), which is the characterising rhetorical figure of the *maqāmah* as a whole and defines Abū Zayd's identity as one in which outer meaning hints at inner (or other) meaning. There is also allusion when he describes in the following line the fact that, in eloquence, he has 'all types of sorcery'. Mention of sorcery caps the earlier allusion to the Moses story: it resolves, in the full context of this *maqāmah*, the allusion to the mendacious sorcery of Pharaoh's magicians. 'Mine is a perjuring magic of language' might be the full way to read this confession. As we carry on through the poem, we gather further that this is an original magic of eloquence, unlike anything related by the great Abbasid philologist al-Aṣma^{c}ī or composed by the Shi^{c}ite poet, al-Kumayt. For al-Sharīshī, even mention of al-Kumayt hides a story of recognition. But whereas Abū Zayd has confessed that he is a rum gagger, having pretended that his story of anagnorisis is unique[55] when it is anything but, al-Kumayt comes through as a figure of authenticity. Not even Abū Zayd, it transpires, reading from the capacious material relayed by al-Sharīshī, controls the connotations and allusions of all that he says:

> Ibn Zayd al-Asadī was the name of al-Kumayt. He was a fine poet and composed prodigiously; his *dīwān* is cited often. After he had composed his Hāshimiyyāt he made for Baṣrah and approached al-Farazdaq. He said, 'Abū Fāris! I am your nephew.' On being asked who he was, al-Kumayt detailed his *nisbah*. Al-Farazdaq said, 'This is all true, so what is it you need?' He replied, 'You are the Sheikh of Muḍar, doyen of their poets, so I wanted to recite to you some of the verses I have composed. If it is any good you will order me to broadcast it widely, if not you will order me to hide it away.' Al-Farazdaq then said, 'Nephew! I consider your poetry to be as good as you are intelligent; recite, for you are an upright man.' . . .
>
> On account of his poems in praise of Banū Hāshim and allusions against Banū Umayyah, he was pursued by the Umayyad caliphs. For twenty years he kept on the run from them. Hishām ibn ^{c}Abd al-Malik was one of those serious in tracking him down but he never found him. Fearful for his life al-Kumayt determined never to settle in one place. Maslamah ibn ^{c}Abd al-Malik needed something from Hishām. He went hunting one day and people came up to him to greet him. Al-Kumayt was among the retinue but Hishām did not recognize him. Al-Kumayt said, 'Peace be upon you and God's mercy and blessings. Now I shall recite:
>
> > Stop at the abandoned home as a visitor stops . . .
> > [And he recited until he reached the verses]

Muslim ibn Abī l-Walīd, you who can raise the dead at will,
My ropes of friendship have become attached to yours; I pledge myself to you as a dutiful neighbour;
I have now come over to the Banū Umayyah: things take their destined course;
Now my actions augur well – I'm now a righteous man who yesterday was lost.'

Maslamah asked: My God! Who is that man who came among the group of stragglers, greeted us then recited poetry? He was told, al-Kumayt. He then marvelled at his eloquence and then inquired about what he had done during his long absence and mentioned to him Hishām's anger against him. But Maslamah guaranteed al-Kumayt's safety, travelled with him and brought him into the presence of Hishām. Hishām did not know or recognize him. Al-Kumayt said, Peace be upon you, Prince of the Faithful and God's mercy and blessings. Hishām then replied, Yes, Thank God! Who is this? Al-Kumayt said: The One Who began [his scripture] with thanksgiving and created it; the One Who privileged Himself for gratitude; Who ordered the angels to show it and made it the opening of his book . . . as well as the speech of the people of Jannah. I give Him thanks as one who knows with certainty and who sees clearly and I give testimony according to the way He gave testimony regarding Himself who has no like or partner; and I testify that Muhammad is His Arab servant and His illiterate prophetic messenger whom he sent to the people who had languished in perplexity, error and darkness; the one who conveyed from God what he was ordered to convey until knowledge of the certain came to him. I myself, O Prince of the Faithful, was lost in perplexity and intoxication. I was distracted and went astray, steadily deviating from the right path, preaching other than the truth. However, this now is a man who stands before you seeking your protection, a repentant, who now sees the path of guidance after lengthy blindness. O Prince of the Faithful, how many a one who has stumbled over have you picked up after his stumbling, and how many a transgressor have you forgiven his transgressions. Hisham then asked, having realized that this was al-Kumayt: Who set you out on your errant path and led you on in blindness?[56]

This is a recognition that carries the force of repentance and forgiveness, both in human and religious terms; the emphasis simply depends on how one elects to read. In the final section on al-Kumayt, al-Sharīshī conveys two important details. First, he shows that al-Kumayt praised the caliph Hishām ibn ᶜAbd al-Malik as someone whose intellect could dispense with the counsel of the *dhawū l-albāb*. It is significant, once one sees the connection, in so far as the company of men whom Abū Zayd swindles during the course of the *maqāmah* are addressed wryly by him as *ūlī l-albāb* or 'men of intelligence capable of discerning the truth' when, in fact, the affair in which they are embroiled shows precisely that they are not. Secondly, al-Sharīshī presents the whole section about al-Kumayt as a vindication of the poet: he was a truly authentic and eloquent poet, and not merely a name inserted into Al-Harīrī's *maqāmah* because it fit the rhyme. Al-Sharīshī has a sense – perhaps his own very deep and interpretive sense – that al-Ḥarīrī is aware of the background and contextual details of his narrative, and how they reflect on each other. On this view, then, the recognition of al-Kumayt by Hishām ibn ᶜAbd al-Malik is in stark contrast, as an act of authentication, with the dispiriting anagnorisis that Abū Zayd unfolds for the bemused al-Ḥārith ibn Hammām and his dull-minded cronies.

Allusion: 'The Lightning Flash' and Tropes of Filial Discovery

Several thematic tropes run as leitmotifs through al-Ḥarīrī's *maqāmāt*. They exist on two levels: (1) as circumscribed metaphors used for their own sake to enrich the eloquence of the narratives with rhetorically bamboozling effect; and (2) as themes essential to the unfolding of the plot of deception, sometimes veneered with literary allusion, thus embellishing the 'séance' and adding depth to discrete *maqamāt* within their familiar, iterative model. On one occasion, in *Maqāmah* 25 'of Kerej', an article of clothing provides the answer to a riddle and is the very object of anagnorisis. However, the two dominant tropes are variations on the lightning flash and filial relations.

In an adroitly crafted combination, lightning, rain and varieties of attire run through *Maqāmah* 2 and provide its structure as a game of antithesis.[57] Let us follow first the trail of clothing. The text begins with al-Ḥārith stating (p. 113) 'ever since my amulets (*al-tamāʾim*) were doffed and my turbans (*al-ᶜamāʾim*) were donned, I was eager to visit learning's seat . . . and to robe myself in its raiment (*fī taqammuṣi libāsih*).' In Ḥulwān, encountering the prodigious Abū Zayd, 'adorned with grace and information . . . I clung to his skirts for the sake of his peculiar accomplishments (*taᶜallaqtu bi-ahdābih li-khaṣāʾiṣi ādābih*).' After Abū Zayd's disappearance at the end of a season and his subsequent return, his companions, though still in thrall to him, doubt his authorship of verses by which they are enchanted; he answers their skepticism so: 'the hand of truth rends the cloak of doubt (*inna . . . yada l-ḥaqq taṣdaᶜu ridāʾa l-shakk*) . . . I now expose my hidden store to the proving.' Among the verses he now declaims is the following erotic line: 'I asked her when she met me to put off her crimson veil, and to endow my hearing with the sweetest tidings . . .' The erotic subject will be key, as we shall see, to reading both themes together. Finally, in reward for his eloquent *divertimento*, he is given 'goodly clothing'. This series of images contains the subtext of exposure and concealment (and vice versa) that runs through the collection. But the dynamic within this *maqāmah* comes across much more effectively woven as it is in parallel with the other sustained, unfolding leitmotif – of light, lightning and rain. We must show how the two tropes are related; in fact, there is a naturalistic synesthesia at play here.

The critical idea is that lightning may augur imminent rain, but the metaphorical meaning associated with rain varies in the *maqāmāt*: it may be truth, or astonishing eloquence, or lucre. The first and third elements are of course antithetical, since lucre is associated with the verbal scams of Abū Zayd; and so the *maqāmāt* achieve their alloy of paradox and ambivalence. The other critical point, of course, is that lightning clouds may disappoint in that they fail to discharge rain. This too is associated with the notion of the promise of truth being fulfilled by the realisation of deception – of a horrible emptiness: verbal, monetary and moral fraud.

Continuing our précis of *Maqāmah* 2, in a metaphor styling his eagerness to seek knowledge and eloquent learning al-Ḥārith describes himself at the outset of the séance as keen for 'my draught both of the rain-flood and the dew'. Knowledge, little or large in its offering, is conveyed in a liquid image. When he then first encounters Abū Zayd, he tells in verse: 'I looked upon his nearness to me as kinship . . . his life as rain', modulating the liquid image, 'the hand of want [then] mixed for him the cup of parting'. When Abū Zayd, still incognito, reappears after a season and is tested again for his qualities as a poet, he recites the following amorous line about an imaginary darling (we have already encountered her crimson veil): 'She rained pearls from the daffodil, and watered the rose, and bit upon the grapes with hailstone.' The figure of water is sustained: pearly raindrops (her tears) water her rosy cheeks while she bites into grapes with teeth as white as hailstones. It pours from the figurative clouds as he describes his imaginary loved-one. There is no drought now that Abū Zayd has returned. Or so it seems. And yet the recognition will bring with it the threat that this is all but a mirage; al-Ḥārith goes on (p. 116): 'when I saw the blazing of his firebrand, and the gleam of his unveiled brightness . . . And lo! He was our Sheikh of Seruj.' Inquiring why it was that al-Ḥārith had not been able to recognise him, Abū Zayd recites verses that include this line about changing fortune: 'Trust not the gleam of its lightning, for it is a deceitful gleam.' He then rose and departed, like the passing clouds, having applied to fortune an image that really applies to himself. The gleam of Abū Zayd's lightning is deceitful too – it brings no rain of truth, as we learn from other *maqāmāt*. This is how he and his audience are exposed, in discrete senses. The promises contained in the liquescent images, both in the narrative itself as well as the erotic verse, are false promises. Understanding this gives metaphorical richness – as well as that emptiness – to the anagnorisis of Abū Zayd.

Al-Ḥarīrī's Maqāmah 7 'of Barqa^{c}īd' (or 'The Lightning Flash of the Feast')[58]

In his analysis of al-Ḥarīrī's *Maqāmah* of Barqa^{c}īd, Daniel Beaumont[59] sensitises us further to the reading of signs, showing how images of light and clothing as specific codes weave a tissue of apparent and latent meaning. The latent meaning becomes apparent as a facet of anagnorisis.

> Ḥarīrī's *al-Maqāma al-Barqa^{c}īdiyya* . . . begins with the narrator al-Ḥārith saying:
> I had determined to travel from Barqa^{c}īd but now I noticed the lightning flash of the *^{c}īd* (or festival) and I loathed to quit that city before I had witnessed in it the day of adornment . . .
> . . . Both the adornment of clothing and the brilliance of lightning relate in the same way to the general theme of appearance versus reality or, to be more precise, to the theme of appearance masking reality. The phrase

'flash of the festival' (*wa-qad shumtu barqa ᶜīdin,*) puns on the name of the town Barqaᶜīd. The verb *shumtu*, from *shāma,* is also noteworthy with regard to this theme. The nineteenth-century translator of Ḥarīrī, Theodore Preston, says in his note that it peculiarly signifies 'to observe clouds and the lightning flashing from them in order to detect the possibility of rain.' . . . Thus the colorful clothing worn by the locals betokens the approaching feast, even as lightning does approaching rain; and as the rainstorm renews life in a physical way, so too the feast is meant to ensure the renewal of life through prayer and sacrifice . . .

While al-Ḥārith observes . . . from a distance, Abū Zayd orders [an] old woman [who escorts him] to go about in the crowd, circulating scraps of paper that bear verses written in colored ink. His hope is that someone will make a donation when they have read the poetry describing the pair's poverty. Al-Ḥārith takes one of the scraps, reads the clever verses on it, and then guesses the identity of the old man. Just as it is not the religious significance of the festival that attracts al-Ḥārith, but rather its pomp and color, so, too, it is the 'garb of the verse' that attracts him to Abū Zayd. He misses, however, the ruse of the old man's blindness . . .

In the attempt by al-Ḥārith to learn the identity of Abū Zayd, the themes of vision and blindness come to the fore. Al-Ḥārith says that he wishes to see the old man in order 'that I may test the quality of my discernment upon him'. Al-Ḥārith, then, seems to doubt his own powers of vision. He goes on to say that 'I made him the fetter of my sight.'

Al-Ḥārith follows the 'blind' man home and scolds him, but before he gets far into his reprimand

Abū Zayd sends him in search of a toothpick whose qualities he describes in a series of metaphors.

Abū Zayd's speech is a rhetorical set piece, . . . It recalls a topos of classical rhetoric, the squandering of rhetorical devices on some trivial subject . . . At the same time, it must be remembered that the use of a toothpick is a subject treated by *ḥadīth.* The Prophet prescribed the use of the toothpick after eating, and the fastidiousness of Islamic law on such points of hygiene might weigh against the conclusion that it is a parodic exercise . . . When [al-Ḥārith] returns with the toothpick, Abū Zayd and the old woman have

> vanished . . . al-Ḥārith misreads the text because he tries to read Abū Zayd's speech as pure mimesis, and he ignores the rhetorical or semiotic dimension. It is al-Ḥārith himself, now, who is the unwanted remnant. He is the bone that Abū Zayd has picked clean: and it is Abū Zayd's description of the toothpick, the speech itself, which acts as a toothpick to get rid of him.[60]

Beaumont's account of the use of clothing and lightning as loaded tropes, and the way their semiotics emerge in step with the events of the hero's deceptive play, are compelling. We should reiterate and stress: the trope of lightning in Barqaᶜīd is similar to that of lightning in the *Maqāmah* of Kufa – in both, lightning seems to be the potential augurer of rain (of something positive) but it disappoints; it marks the potential instability and indeterminacy of signs generally. The *barq* of Barqaᶜīd is similar, therefore, to the *barqun khullab* of the *Maqāmah* of Kufa.

Three further aspects of the Barqaᶜīdiyya should be accentuated as they relate to other *maqāmāt*: (1) the theme of blindess; (2) the challenge of the riddle; and (3) the subject of paternity. As Beaumont notes, there is something familiar about the 'ironic reversal where the seeing are blind and the blind are seeing'. Tiresias is the archetypical blind seer; whereas Oedipus – while he can see – is blind, and when he does 'see' what he has been blind to, he blinds himself with the weight of the burden. It is, more particularly, a standard theme in other *maqāmāt*; and this is also what Beaumont alludes to. We have seen how the blind man who is not blind features in one story of al-Tanūkhī,[61] which is just one of a number of *faraj* anecdotes redolent of (and possibly providing a model for) the picaresque *maqāmah*. Al-Ḥarīrī would surely have been influenced more tangibly by the *Maqāmah Makfūfiyyah* of al-Hamadhānī, which shows how the presence of a recognition scene can influence the language and imagery of a given text. The blind rogue of al-Hamadhānī, who deceives the crowd to collect lucre, first says of himself to curry sympathy: 'no flowing robes conceal my state' (*yā qawmu qad ᶜīla li-faqrī ṣabrī wa-nkashafat ᶜannī dhuyūlu l-sitri*). The figurative description of being cloaked in the disguise of material exposure to the cruel elements is inherently paradoxical; the figurative image is borrowed by the narrator when he threatens the rogue with another kind of exposure: 'by God, you will reveal your secret to me or else I shall expose you from behind your cover!' (*wa-llāhi la-turiyannī sirra-ka aw la-akshifanna sitra-ka*). The threat of exposure thus borrows the language of the disguise. This lexical feature is a variation upon the fact that the *maqāmāt* play with cognates of a dominant cognitive language and, as here, with a language of concealment and disclosure.[62] The running pun of the *maqāmāt* is that *ᶜarafa* (recognition) is coterminous with *inkār*: the narrator recognises (*ᶜarafa*) Abū al-Fatḥ or Abū Zayd but rejects (*yunkir*) the immorality of the ruses perpetrated in search of a living. But the resonance of *inkār* lingers, and invites a hermeneutics of reading that cannot in fact settle answers in an unequivocal way. It is noteworthy that the *Makfūfiyyah* (The *Maqāmah* of Blindness) troubles the normally moral and positive sense of *sitr* (cover). *Sitr* can be the protective veil offered by God and providence, hence the adjective *mastūr* meaning 'sheltered'. Here it is more ambiguous: can there really be any sense at all that the rogue hero's disguise is divinely sanctioned? This requires us to consider the ambiguity of the *maqāmāt* in general. Because the justifications of the rogue hero make sense, they have a lingering effect that muddies the clear waters separating the good and the reprehensible.

A striking moral conundrum occurs in the *Maqāmah Wabariyyah* of al-Ḥarīrī (see below). The deciphering of riddles upon which some *maqāmāt* are constructed can chime in with the disclosure of identity, this being the way they are emplotted for the most part. In the *Barqaᶜīdiyyah*, as Beaumont shows, the request for the toothpick will lead al-Ḥārith to understand that he has been picked clean. Other *maqāmāt* of this kind in al-Ḥarīrī alone include the third (in which the description of a dinar hides the semi-concealed Janus-like image of the two-faced Abū Zayd); the ninth (in which a wife hauls her husband before a judge to plead that he had married her under false pretenses by claiming to her father that he had an excellent trade as a pearl merchant; but 'he denies that he had deceived her in calling himself a "pearl-stringer", for the pearls that he meant were the pearls of thought, by stringing which into elegant poems he had been accustomed to make large income from the liberality of the rich and noble'); the most striking case in which runaway description turns out to be an enigmatic metaphor alluding to something other than its surface meaning – and in a way that provides anecdotal coherence in the game of deception – exists in al-Ḥarīrī's *maqāmah* of Shiraz.

Fathers and Sons and Other Ties of Kinship

In the *Barqaᶜīdiyyah* Abū Zayd justifies his capers with a statement that toys with a kind of anagnorisis; he discloses that he is the son of time, the latter being 'the father of mortals' who is blind to guidance. In his sardonic scheme of speaking, this explains the 'son's' – Abū Zayd's – pretence to being blind. As we gather from *Maqāmah* 5, al-Ḥarīrī's narratives, in particular, are highly inflected by this theme in tales of recognition: the discovery of kinship. It shores up the parodic nature of the genre and reflects the self-conscious poetics of storytelling, playing as it does with one of the standard tropes in romance and tales of deliverance.

On both the level of local detail and the broader structural level, the theme of discovered kinship is key to the *maqamāt* of al-Ḥarīrī, much more than is the case for al-Hamadhānī – the anti-hero's very name somehow beckons at us to glean this fact. Abū Zayd, by his very *kunyah*, is identified as the father of an emblematic name in grammar (the foundation of rhetoric). In the *Maqāmah* of Kufa, as we have seen, he is the father of a complex fiction and a brilliant fabricator of tales, cognisant that quintessential features of a good story are separation and reunion through the recovery of lost family ties. In addition to the fifth *Maqāmah*, there is another narrative in which a boy is invented for the purpose of gaining lucre: this is *Maqāmah* 43, in which Abū Zayd reports a lengthy debate with a youth who condemns the institution of marriage.[63] It turns out that the young boy is a fiction – a mouthpiece for a game of words and ideas, and a vehicle for deception. What is interesting, though, is that the charade of the boy's existence somehow parallels the theme of celibacy that he extolls, since in normative society it requires marriage to sire a child. Indeed, the youth is a figure for Abū Zayd's conning games, for the texts they result in are in a palpable sense the children of his invention.[64]

The Real and Treacherous Son of Abū Zayd

> I am the Sarūjī and this is my son (*Maqāmah* 8)[65]

> 'Were you pleased with the sharpness of that fawn?' I said: 'He is the youngster of the Seruji, by Him who brings the pearl from the deep.' Then I said:

> 'I dare testify that you are the tree on which his fruit has grown, and the fire from which his spark has sprung.' (*Maqāmah* 41)[66]

Maqāmah 4 evinces the complicitous partnership that can exist between Abū Zayd and his young offspring. They form an engaging pair. In the morning,

> when the sun shone forth and robed the sky with light . . . I caught sight of Abū Zayd and his son, and upon them were two worn mantles . . . so I approached them as one enamoured of their refinement, pitying their shabbiness . . . now we were in a night camp whence we could discern . . . the fires of hospitality then [they] coursed away . . . [But they had promised to return]. So we stayed and watched for him as men watch for the new moons of feasts . . . until the sunlight was weak with age, and the wasted bank of day had nigh crumbled . . . then when the term of waiting had been prolonged and the sun showed in faded garb . . . I said to my companions it is plain the man was lying.'[67]

They find verses left by Abū Zayd on their host's saddle pack alluding to the Qur'anic verse: When you have eaten separate[68] (Q Al-Aḥzāb 33:53) (p. 126). Other than revealing the potential implications of a Qur'anic phrase, this narrative has no anagnorisis in its commonest form. Typically, we tend to discover, as a séance unfolds, the identity of Abū Zayd and then his son. In this way the son – or, in some cases, an issue pertaining to the son – becomes a figure for the ingenuity of deception.

Such is the case in *Maqāmah* 15 in which a legal issue of family and paternity comes to light, reconfiguring the more usual anagnorisis of the son.[69] Abū Zayd is recognised early and solves a riddle about family and inheritance. In Chenery's essential summary (adapted):

> Abū Zayd explains his want of appetite by relating the adventures of the day. He had been as usual destitute, and his hunger had been further excited by the sight of the dates and milk that were displayed in the market. At last, when almost exhausted, he had seen a man weeping. He had inquired the cause and found that the stranger was deploring the decay of learning, inasmuch as no one was able to solve for him a puzzle which had come into his possession. This was to explain how a man, dying childless, could leave a brother perfectly competent to inherit, and yet that his property

> should go to his wife's brother. Abū Zayd at once perceives the answer, but demands a supper before revealing it. The stranger takes him home and treats him to dates and cream, which he eats greedily, and then explains that the deceased man in the puzzle had had a son by a former wife, who had married the mother of his, the father's second wife, and then died, leaving a son who would be the brother of the second wife, and the grandson of the deceased whose property was in question. This child would therefore inherit in preference to the deceased's brother.[70]

Abū Zayd is then adjured to remember his family and 'be beforehand with the raincloud' that looms and threatens. He strides out and is drenched by rain, an unusual turn of events, yet one that is figuratively consistent with his provision of the answer to the conundrum. The son, or in this case, grandson, is in effect discovered as the child of Abū Zayd's ingenious (pluvial) invention.

Issues of family can modulate in other ways. In *Maqāmah* 19, Abū Zayd is found to be ill and housebound; he is visited by friends while convalescing and orders his son to prepare a meal for his guests. The repast is described entirely using the cant of the Banū Sasān in which each dish is the 'father' of a certain quality: 'Father of Pleasantness', for instance, is white bread, but the list is long and detailed. The *maqāmah* ends with advice: 'Be patient when fear assails, for time is the father of wonders.'[71] These, then, are the displaced discoveries of kinship in a *maqāmah* otherwise devoid of picaresque deceit.

Modulation: The Father in League with his Son

In most cases, when a young boy plays a part in a partnership of deception he turns out to be the son of Abū Zayd. The two characters form a father-son duo, and what becomes apparent is that, just as Abū Zayd has raised or fostered a child, he has educated him in the art of rhetorical guile; Abū Zayd has reared an incarnation of deception. The son represents the second generation of cycles of verbal deceit, treachery and duplicity.[72] Both motifs of clothing and lightning suffuse such tales.

Upon arriving in Saᶜdah in the thirty-seventh *maqāmah* al-Ḥārith relates, 'I inquired from the most knowing town-folk, whom of lordly persons and mines of excellence it contained, so that I might take him for a beacon-light (ember) in times of darkness.'[73] Abū Zayd makes his appearance in anonymity: 'There entered an old man, in plumage worse for wear, of shaky appearance.' He is accompanied by a youth about whom he tells the Qadi, 'Behold, this is my son.' The Son complains to the Qadi, 'ever since his substance has gone, and he has been visited with penury, he urges me to roll about my tongue in begging, and to ask rain from the clouds' bounty.' (p. 84) Father rebukes son and the latter carps: Where is he to find the generous folk his father alludes to? The Qadi at this point is moved to intervene, piqued in his sense of tribal (Tamīmī) pride to reveal his own munificence, thus taking the bait which father and son have laid for him. 'Stop,' says the judge, 'for among arrows that stray from their target is one that hits, and not every lightning deceives, so distinguish between flashes if you watch the clouds [for rain], and testify not but what you know.' By evoking the figurative language of Abū Zayd's deception – lightning that deceives – it is clear that this is indeed the snare the Qadi has been trapped by. Al-Ḥārith follows the father and son to learn their identities. But the anagnorisis is fleeting. They abandon him, high and dry.

In *Maqāmah* 47 'of the cupping', Abū Zayd's precocious son is his tenacious sparring partner.[74] Watched by al-Ḥārith, the son asks to be cupped, but Abū Zayd asks first that his fee be paid, refusing to work on credit. At this, the son, whose identity is as yet unrevealed, rails violently: 'None breaks faith, save the mean, the contemptible, and none resorts to the pond of treachery but the worthless, and if you knew who I am, you would not let me hear ribald talk.' Abū Zayd replies angrily in a diatribe against lineage and bloodlines: 'Bane of your father! . . . are you of a status to brag about, and is your heritage one to be blazed forth? . . . Boast when you boast of your belongings not of your forefathers, and of your gatherings, not of the roots from which you spring, and of your own qualities, not of your rotten bones, and of your valuables, not of your pedigree.' The two men quarrel and wrestle, as a result of which the boy's garment is torn. The act evokes *Sūrat al-Inshiqāq*, which alludes itself to the earning of one's just desserts. Abū Zayd is at his wit's end before collecting money from the gathered crowd to recompense the boy for his damaged clothing. He then tells the boy bluntly, warning his audience in a familiar motif, that he is not what he seems: 'Spy for another's lightning than mine!'

He caps this all with an oath made in verse: 'If I had food for but one day I would never touch the lancet or cupping-cup.' Despite this, when at the end al-Ḥārith asks rashly to be cupped, Abū Zayd comes clean: 'What do you think of my cunning and guile, and what occurred between my kid and myself? Any shoe suits the barefooted who walks on flint.' Father and son then run off, eluding their chasers, like two race horses. It is clear: Abū Zayd has inculcated in his son the fleet, ephemeral pedigree of deception.

Joseph, Discovery and the Allusive Game of Kinship

There are several references to Joseph, the archetypal figure for the lost son, in al-Ḥarīrī; most are essentially of Qurʾanic origin but others come from the related exegetical-cum-apocryphal tradition of prophetic lore.[75] Some are fleeting cultural details within the wider scope of the entire narrative.[76] Others, on two, arguably three occasions, underscore the sustained parodic nature of the *maqāmāt*, simultaneously borrowing the Joseph story's cognitive structure in their unfolding recognitions (and turning deliverance on its head).

The Slaves of Zabīd[77]

Maqāmah 34 is one of the deftly assembled treasures of al-Ḥarīrī's collection. Al-Sharīshī himself wrote in his commentary that the text is built upon the Joseph narrative of the Qurʾan; in a long note, he provides account of the prophet's turbulent story of enslavement and transfiguration. This alerts one to a sustained use of allusive imagery. However, even though al-Sharīshī has a global sense of the relevance of Joseph in structuring the story, he says nothing about how this construction upon the Qurʾanic narrative works to undergird the unfolding epistemology of this layered tale. Surah 12 is a kind of hypotext of *Maqāmah* 34; the latter's relationship to the former is one of allusion, parody, antiphrasis and subversion. The pleasure to be had from al-Ḥarīrī's text is to glean perceptively how this unfolds in a game of semiotic reading. All references to Joseph in the *Maqāmāt* of al-Ḥarīrī are in fact associated with a move towards discovery and recognition.

In Steingass' translation, the third line of English describes al-Ḥārith's young slave with whom he crossed the deserts to arrive at Zabīd in the Yemen as someone 'he had reared up to full age': deserts, *bīd*, rhymes with Zabīd

– which is not mentioned idly as a setting as it was a slave market in medieval times; in the Dār al-Kutub al-ᶜIlmiyyah edition of al-Sharīshī's commentary, volume 2, the second line of the Arabic original has *rabbaytu-hu ilā an balagha ashuddahu*. The English only scantly alerts the reader to the fact that the Arabic phrase (*balagha ashuddahu*) cites Qurᵓanic descriptions from two different Surahs (viz. 12 and 26) of both Joseph and Moses, respectively, reaching their maturity. At this point, the reader of Arabic might wonder which of the two prophets evoked is more relevant to the unfolding story. It is soon clear, in any event, that the young slave is not himself the figural incarnation of either Moses or Joseph, for he promptly dies upon arrival in Zabīd, to the intense chagrin of al-Ḥārith. The Qurᵓanic evocation early on in the narrative simply strikes a note that will chime in with subsequent imagery and the cognitive development of the entire piece.

In Surah 12, when Joseph reached 'his full age' (*balagha ashuddahu*), God gave him wisdom and knowledge. This iconic Qurᵓanic moment is in marked contrast with the sorry demise of al-Ḥārith's servant. This notion of an ideal being rendered dystopian winds its way through the *maqāmah* and is part of the game of parody.

Grief-stricken, al-Ḥārith was for months incapable of touching food. Eventually, to acquire a youth of like quality to the deceased, he sought the aid of a local slave merchant: 'I want a lad who gives satisfaction when he is probed [tried] and who is approved when he is tested, and let him be one of those whom the intelligent have educated, and poverty alone has thrown into the market.'[78] These are prophetic words in large part, though the wish they articulate will turn against al-Ḥārith, for it is the latter who is unwittingly probed and tested – made a fool of, no less – at his own expense.

Time went by: 'new moons completed their round' with 'their increase and wane, but there came to pass [the fulfilment of] none of their promises, and no thunder cloud yielded rain in response thereto'. Although superficially these metaphors refer to the slave merchants who disappoint their client, they evoke and foreshadow the person of Abū Zayd, as we have alluded to in several places above; his association with the moon, that rises and sets, waxes and wanes – unstable and always changing – runs throughout the *maqāmāt*, as does the image of the thunder and lightning cloud with which he is so often associated, pouring rains of eloquence upon his listeners but also – just as often, and conversely – bearing false promises as a harbinger of pluvial (in the sense of blessed) truths. In any event, at this stage of the narrative, the evocations are really only fore-rumblings of the devious agencies that will play their hands.

Eventually, al-Ḥārith recounts 'lo! There accosted me a man who had the face-veil drawn over his nostril, and who held a boy by his forearm.' This man lapses into descriptive verse about the boy he is angling to sell. The latter is said to be wondrously eloquent in both poetry and prose: *ṭālamā ʾabdaʿa fīmā ṣanaʿā / wa-fāqa fī l-nathri wa-fī l-naẓmi maʿā* ('he has long been verbally inventive, excelling in both poetry and prose together'). Al-Ḥārith's reaction to seeing the boy is telling and significant: 'This is not a man, but for sooth an honored angel' (p. 64). Even in English, these are clearly recognisable as the words uttered by the women of Memphis when Joseph is brought before them by his master's wife. In Arabic, the phrase *mā hādhā basharun in hādhā illā malakun karīm* ('this is no human: he must be a gracious angel!') is unmistakably Qurʾanic, and the figure of Joseph is now palpably reified in the mind of the reader, following hard upon the earlier Qurʾanic phrase *balagha ashuddahu*. (But one would be wrong to determine as a consequence that Moses is now entirely out of the picture; the *maqāmah* is bookended in interesting ways by Qurʾanic allusions, as we will see.)

By his reaction, citing the women of Memphis, al-Ḥārith may have triggered the crucial Qurʾanic detail in the continuing exchange between himself and the young slave. The former inquires after the boy's name and identity in order to test his eloquence but 'he uttered not a sound of the son of slave-woman or a woman of free birth' (p. 65). When this dogged reticence enrages al-Ḥārith, the boy recites three verses, which include the following crucial element: 'But if you are not pleased unless [my name] be revealed, then listen: *Joseph I am, am Joseph, hear!* (*Anā yūsufun anā yūsufū*).[79]

The final verse of the tercet uses the language of recognition. Steingass translates it more or less thus: 'Now I have lifted the veil for you and your wits are sharp, you know, but I fancy you know not.' This is antiquated English and does not capture the full resonance of the Arabic phrase which I gloss, 'If you're intellectually sharp you will have recognised who I am and the allusions I have made but I do not imagine you have recognised a thing!' (*in takun faṭinan ʿarafta wa-mā ʾikhāluka taʿrifū*). Al-Ḥārith had not especially wanted to 'have knowledge' of the boy's name (*lā li-raghbatin fī ᶜilmihi*), but rather intended to probe the quality of his speech. That quality, however, as it transpires, is precisely to be able to manipulate language in a game of deception, and the boy has now, as a consequence, embroiled al-Ḥārith in a challenge not simply to know generally but to recognise what and whom he already should know; to make him fully aware of what he appears to be, as yet, either only semi-consciously sentient or obtusely quite ignorant. The continuing narrative contains a significant juxtaposition of allusions, sustaining the notion that al-Ḥārith is in fact only half conscious of the cultural memory with which he flirts – or rather, which flirts tantalisingly with him: 'I was too bewildered to perceive the truth, and made oblivious of the story of Joseph the faithful (*al-Ṣiddīq*), and I concerned myself only with asking his master's charge for him, and inquiring after the amount of his price, so that I might pay it in full.' Bartering the cost of a slave is precisely what should put al-Ḥārith in mind of Joseph and the significance of that story. Furthermore, the boy's master offers him up at a low cost (*nazura thamanuhu*). This idea is not so very different from the fact that in Surah 12, Joseph was sold into Egypt for a paltry sum (*thamanun bakhs*); those who traded for him, failed to recognise his true worth.

The youth complains about the contract of sale with compelling detail and force: 'Is it right to sell one such as me to fill the empty bellies?' (*hal mithlī yubāᶜu likaymā tashbaᶜa l-karishu l-jiyāᶜu?*) (p. 66). The young lad cares nothing for feeding the hungry as Joseph did during the famine in Egypt, and is aware of justice and legal rights (he speaks of *shirᶜatu l-ᵓinṣāfi*). Joseph too would see justice done before accepting to become Pharaoh's plenipotentiary in the land of Egypt, but, earlier, when he was younger and in Potiphar's house, he meekly accepted incarceration 'for a time' even after his innocence was established by his master (that is, after the accusation that he tried to seduce his master's wife). The youth further indicates that he is often used as a snare to capture game: 'in my nets are wild prey'. In the Joseph story, by contrast, it is he, in his brothers' baleful game of perjury, who is falsely claimed before Jacob of being the fatal victim of a fictitious wolf.

The merchant's tearful response to the lad's complaint is to say that he holds the boy 'in the place of [a] son'. He quotes a hadith (*fī l-āthāri l-muntaqāt*) in support of a bargain that would allow him to rescind on his sale in the future. Al-Sharīshī, revealing the source of al-Ḥarīrī's thought, quotes the hadith *ma^c^rūf* from Abū Hurayrah: *man aqāla nādiman bay^c^atahu aqālahu llāhu bay^c^atahu* ('whosoever regrets and rescinds his sale, so too does God rescind his sale'). So, the sale is on shaky ground even by the merchant's admission. To the youngster, the merchant now says in cloying verse, further undermining the permanence of the sale: 'Bear patiently . . . May not for long the time of parting last, nor flag the mounts that bring us reunion (*talāqī*)!'

When the youth departs with his new master, who is still deluded, he sobs, but his tears are effusions of derision and mockery. He tells his 'master': 'Do you know for what I have wailed and why?' A chain of disclosures now begins through to the end of the *maqāmah*; it is prefaced by a saying of the Prophet Muḥammad, underlining the cluelessness of al-Ḥārith as it will come to be known: 'You are in one valley, and I am in another.' Now the youth comes clean, again in verse, with the shocking news about which al-Ḥārith had been forewarned by allusion: 'have not those subtle words warned you enough that I was free, rendering my sale unlawful?' What 'Joseph meant was clear as daylight' (*idh kāna fī yūsufa ma^c^nan qad waḍaḥ*). The shocking facts divulged lead to jostling between the two men – altercation, fisticuffs, and an eventual appeal to a judge. As in so many *maqāmāt,* the truth emerges from an act (or charade) of litigation. The Qadi pronounces a judgement that resonates significantly with the way the *maqāmāt* in general toy with the reader – prodding it to galvanise awareness: 'he who has put one on his guard is like one who has given information, he who has made one see the state of affairs, has done no damage' (p. 68). It is clear: the lad had warned al-Ḥārith but he failed to grasp the allusion. Thus the judge advises him to keep his obtuseness suppressed, hidden from public view. (In litigious *maqāmāt,* it is often the judge himself who pleads for the suppression of the fact that he has been duped by the rogue, Abū Zayd. A judge cannot be seen to be the target and victim of deception. Indeed, generally, it is the flawed readiness to judge others mistakenly that is held up to farce and facetious scrutiny in al-Ḥarīrī's collection of stories.)

Having accepted the fact that he has been fooled, al-Ḥārith asks to know the identity of the lad's father. Here the anagnorisis of Abū Zayd comes bursting forth. To al-Ḥārith's question 'And do you know his father?' comes the answer: 'How should Abū Zayd be unknown for whose wounds there is no retaliation, and of whom every judge has stories to tell and proclamations to make.' Al-Ḥārith now knows for certain (*ayqantu*) that it was Abū Zayd's face veil that was the cause of his being deceived. But this seems to be a superficial way of understanding the root meaning of *yaqīn*, which in the Qur'an conveys certain truth. The Qadi enjoins al-Ḥārith now to have *ṣabr* (forbearance) and to learn the lesson offered by his misadventure: to note the meaning of the *ᶜibrah* it contains: of the *ṣabr* which is such a significant object of didacticism in Surah 12.

Al-Ḥārith is still in denial, in a sense: when, at the very tail of the story, he comes upon Abū Zayd 'in a narrow path', he frowns and keeps his silence. Abū Zayd inquires what 'ails' him, to which al-Ḥārith replies 'Have you forgotten the thing which you have done?' (p. 70). The allusion contained in the question comes across only in the original Arabic: *a-nasīta innaka . . . faᶜalta fiᶜlataka llatī faᶜalta* ('Have you forgotten the deed that you committed?'). In Surah 26, this phrase – 'the deed which you committed' – refers to Moses's killing of the Egyptian. In prophetic history, it was a necessary evil; here it sustains the dystopian and fractured reenactment of prophetic lore. Abū Zayd justifies his action in verse with further reference to the dominant Joseph narrative of the *maqāmah*: 'Heretofore the tribes sold Joseph, though they were what people know they were.' In Surah 12, Joseph exonerates his brothers, effectively on God's behalf: (*lā tathrība ᶜalaykum al-yawm*: 'no blame is to be directed towards you today'). Abū Zayd requests, for his part, less momentously, that al-Ḥārith 'forgive his brother' (*fa-ᶜdhar ᵓakhāka*). The latter, indeed, ends up excusing his friend – the one he had failed to recognise, just as Joseph's brothers failed to recognise Joseph – for he is taken in by the eloquent sorcery (*siḥr*) of his words. *Siḥr,* of course, against the backdrop of the scriptural allusions of the narrative, places Abū Zayd more in league with Pharaoh's magicians than the blameless Moses. But this wrinkle in the note of reconciliation is utterly in keeping with the ambivalent moral world of the story – this antiphonal Joseph narrative, inflected with surfeit reference to Mosaic lore, and structured like, and because of, the original archetype of revelation towards a series of dispiriting recognitions.

The Innocent and Non-existent Wolf of Raḥbah[80]

Maqāmah 10 – 'of Raḥbah' – has significant elements in common with that of Zabīd. Its rich, internally consistent imagery is built up in several ways:

upon the figures of day and night, light and dark, of a diurnal cycle of deceit that becomes clear with the dawning of the second day. Just as purposefully, it weaves a tissue of images for the hunt as a metaphor for captivating a victim in an erotic game or chase. It has a litigious setting, but here it is a judge who, in thrall to the snare of *eros*, shows poor judgement and is tricked – ensnared. It is a *maqāmah* in which kinship plays its customary hand: when Abū Zayd is recognised by al-Ḥārith, the identity of the former's son is also made apparent together with the shabby deception they have played upon the judge. Most significant is the use of a telling image taken from the Joseph narrative. In this case, the judge himself utters words that should put him in mind of the truth to which he is blinded by his lust.

In the opening scene, al-Ḥārith 'saw a boy cast in the mould of comeliness, and clothed by beauty in the garb of perfection; – and an old man was holding onto his sleeve, asserting that he had slain his son.' Using the language of recognition, the boy denied knowledge of him (*ʾankara ʿirfatahu*). In the language of its beginning, the *maqāmah* is primed for a scene of recognition relating to the father and this young boy.

Brought before the judge, the old man insists that the youth he has accused of murder swear an oath testifying to his innocence. But the oath is a snare designed to captivate the judge, for it focuses on the overwhelming beauty that the boy incarnates. Easily swayed by his desires, the governor now offers to provide money that will satisfy the father's claim; blood-money of a kind. The governor, in the idiom of *adab* and classical poetry, is effectively 'killed off by his passion': he is *ṣarīʿ al-hawā*. Abū Zayd, who dictates the detailed oath that the youth is to swear, rounds it off with elements of clear self-reference: 'If it be otherwise [i.e. that I turn out to be guilty of the murder], may God strike my full moon with waning, and my silver with tarnishing, and my rays with dark.' These foreshadow the dawning – the concomitant disappearance of the moon, i.e. of Abū Zayd himself – at the end of the *maqāmah*.

The most significant image in the *maqāmah* comes when the judge states that, once Abū Zayd has collected all the blood money put up by the judge himself in the morning, the young boy 'may go guiltless as the wolf went guiltless of the blood of the son of Jacob'. He unwittingly alludes to the kind of perjury that has been committed at his own expense. There never existed a wolf that murdered Joseph, for there was no murder but rather an appalling family perjury. However, as in the apocryphal exegetical tradition of commentary, the judge reifies a wolf in his mind to establish its innocence. It is, paradoxically, a way of incarnating innocence and the fact that a murder did not take place. In his commentary, al-Sharīshī tells a version of the apocryphal story, not bothering to doubt the existence of the wolf, simply stating that it was a victim of calumny. Interestingly, the story of the wolf, which speaks eloquently of its innocence before Jacob, serves the dynamic of disclosure: it conjures a magical conversation in which felonious, surreal and, in the end, sublime truth comes to light.

Just as the killing of Joseph was a fiction conceived by his brothers, so too the killing of Zayd by Abū Zayd is a fiction. Reference to the Joseph story simply parallels the principal idea of this *maqāmah*, and, shores up its dynamic of disclosure. When Abū Zayd tells al-Ḥārith that 'I have resolved to slip away at dawn', al-Ḥarīrī makes a point of describing the intended hour of departure as 'the tale of the wolf' (*dhayl al-sirḥān*) which traditionally described the early light of dawn on the horizon. This image resolves the underlying lupine metaphor of the Joseph story at the time of Abū Zayd's customary disappearance, once his identity is known.

The *Maqāmah* of Raḥbah is inscribed with other suggestive cultural references. Taking leave of al-Ḥārith, Abū Zayd gives him a letter intended for the judge to explain his ruse. But al-Ḥārith opens the letter, just as the pre-Islamic poet al-Mutalammis opened the letter he was carrying to the governor of Bahrain with a warrant for his own execution. Thus he saved himself, unlike the tragic Ṭarafah (who refused, on principle, to open his letter). Al-Mutalammis avoids his own murder. The story resonates with treacherous deception. But, having read the note, al-Ḥārith tears it into pieces. There will be no physical trace of the wily conning Abū Zayd has performed. The significance of this is analogous with his habitual disappearances at the end of so many *maqāmāt*; acts of departure, of evaporated truth, that always promise a return – the return of what al-Ḥārith so consistently represses.

The recognition scene in the *maqāmah* is quintessentially about the instability of truth, hence the function of the disappearances and departures of Abū Zayd at the end of each episode (or so it seems). The narrator can never grasp him stably. In *Maqāmah* 21 the relationship between the following two phrases, the first uttered by Abū Zayd to al-Ḥārith, the second voicing al-Ḥārith's despair at the end of the narrative, is deeply symptomatic of the way knowledge is so ephemeral in the series and therefore susceptible of recurrence and return: 'I am he whom you know, Harith . . .'; but, by the end of the narrative, 'there was none of us who knew his abode, or could learn what locust had gone off with him.' In *Maqāmah* 41 (p. 113), al-Ḥārith enounces, 'I burnt with grief at his departure and fain would not have met him.' In *Maqāmah* 15, al-Ḥārith receives Abū Zayd as a guest, but the latter stays only one night, for the 'new moon' is seen only once. Again the promise of return is immanent in the image. At the end of *Maqāmah* 37, of Sa^{c}dah, al-Ḥārith has this final exchange with Abū Zayd: the latter says, 'Here is the dutiful son of your brother at hand (i.e. let him tell you what you want to know).' He then left, passing his way. Al-Ḥārith continues: 'The youth, however, did but laugh, then he fled, as yonder had fled. So I went back after I had ascertained their identity, but where was I to find the twain of them?'

Discovering the Literary Code

In discussion of the riddles and enigmas upon which many *maqāmāt* are constructed, we have referred once already to the *maqāmah* of Shiraz (the thirty-fifth in al-Ḥarīrī's collection).[81] It is, *par excellence*, the *maqāmah* that shows most plainly how literary codes can be toyed with in this genre generally, providing at times the very touchstone of anecdotal deception. The plots of most *maqāmāt* are quite transparent and divinable: a sham is uncovered and the protagonist of the fraud is recognised as Abū Zayd. Sometimes, as a variation upon a theme (and as we have seen in the *Maqāmah* of Kufa), Abū Zayd is recognised early in the sequence of events, and thus another kind of deception supervenes, one which revolves even more densely around the duplicities of language and rhetoric. In the *Shīrāziyyah*, Abū Zayd asks for money to pay for the wedding preparations of his young daughter whom he decribes in detail; it transpires, however, that she – the object of description – is no woman at all but rather a choice wine which he seeks to buy at the tavern. The metaphors and metonymic language of *adab* (and poetry, more specifically) are the semiotic code that cloak the real intent of the protagonist. His game is discovered with shock and surprise. Withal – and with great irony – the author enacts the classic anagnorisis of kinship where a relationship of paternity is in question and comes into focus: in this case, '*this* is my daughter: not human flesh and blood but the spiritual daughter of the vine.' The *Shīrāziyyah* is, indeed, a feat of sustained metonymic displacement.

The opening paragraph contains the signature – the DNA, one might say – of the entire anecdote. It is cast in a series of antitheses and contains some clues to the game of deception that the narrator fails to see even though he is seemingly primed, in his own use of language, to detect it. He arrives in Shiraz, a town known for its grape and its wine; he accepts the invitation to join a company of men in order to 'discover the secret of their inner essence, to distinguish between the fruit and the blossom.' This is loaded; the idea that the surface hides an inner reality is the fundamental idea upon which the anecdote builds its literary game. The narrator thus detects a warning – a syndrome of disjunctive meaning – which he himself ignores in the ensuing discourse. Once ensconced among his company he describes the merriment he enjoys as more pleasant than the 'milk of the grape'. In retrospect this too will have a resonance he should not have ignored – it introduces the bacchic theme that hoodwinks him and others.

The opening scene contains an unusual number of grammatical dual forms. Abū Zayd's first appearance is described thus: 'there entered our midst a man in two tattered pieces of clothing who well-nigh reached the two terms of life . . . Now the people made little of him, on account of his ragged attire, forgetting that they would have to reckon with the two things smallest in him (his tongue and his heart).' The two terms of life are the first forty years of life and the last forty years, respectively – the prime of life followed by decline. The sense conveyed is that of contrast, which inheres most pointedly in the dual image of the heart and the tongue: the tongue can speak but hide the true content of the heart. Chiming with this, when Abū Zayd initially addresses the company, he says reprovingly: 'O you people, if you had known that behind the protective cloth there is pure wine you would not have slighted a bearer of tattered garments.' The image adumbrates the very nature (that is, both the theme and the cognitive dynamic) of his ensuing swindle. He begins his performance: 'exploding forth from the springs of *adab* and the inner points (*nukat)* of choice subjects . . .' This language too seems to foreshadow the deception that ensues. In al-Sharīshī's commentary we note the gloss on the word *nuktah*: 'it is the core of something which differs from its exterior hue'; '*nukat* are the hidden meanings'.

Having recognised Abū Zayd, al-Ḥārith nevertheless keeps his identity hidden from the company ('just as an inner ailment is kept hidden'), though he is a fool if he thinks this privileged knowledge makes him immune from the rhetoric of the rogue. Abū Zayd now declaims his poem:

> I crave Allah's forgiveness, humbling myself, for all the sins whose heavy load burdens me.
> Folks! how many old maids kept at home, though in assemblies were their virtues praised about
> Have I cut down not fearing from any heir that might revenge them on me or claim a fine.
> And when the sin was laid at my door, I boldly cleared myself and said: it was fate.
> And never stopped my soul its headlong career in cutting damsels down, and kept going stray,
> Till grey locks shone on the crown of my head and checked me from performing such evil deeds.
> So since my temples have turned grey I shed no more the blood of maidens, old or young,
> But now I rear, in spite of what may seem of my condition and my slacking trade,
> A lass who for a long time has stayed at home, sheltered, and veiled carefully from air itself.
> And she in spite of being thus kept recluse, has wooers for her comeliness and pleasingness.
> But for her outfit, at the least, I can't do without a hundred, though I try as I may,
> While in my hand there is not one silver coin, the ground is empty and the sky yields no rain.
> Now is one here to help me that I may wed her amidst the singing-girls' cheering strain,
> Then let him wash my grief with its proper soap and cleanse my heart from sorrows that worry me,

That he may cull my praises, whose fragrance will only cease to waft when man prays in vain.

The poem is ostensibly about two things: (1) Abū Zayd's erstwhile murderous treatment of women, young and old – crimes he committed fearing no vengeance or retribution; and (2) his rearing of a young girl who has many suitors but whom he cannot afford to dress for her wedding. The reality is quite different; the verses in fact contrive two related metaphors: (1) the mixing of wine and water, and (2) the limning of a young wine which Abū Zayd simply cannot afford to buy. The plea that his heart be 'cleansed from sorrows' more or less gives away the fact that wine is the latent subject alluded to.

There is some striking imagery in this poem, and the force of equivocation in interpretation becomes thus quite marked. The killing of the women evokes the practice of *waʾd*, the killing of female infants in pre-Islamic Arabia. Al-Sharīshī draws our attention to this in his commentary, anecdotally, in a way that has some relevance to the epistemology of the *maqāmah*:

> The killing of young girls, which he mentions, is the *waʾd* practice of the Jāhiliyyah (the burial alive of infant females). In the Qurʾan, God says [referring to this]: 'When the young infant is asked for what crime was she killed' [at the Eschaton] . . . Qays ibn ʿĀṣim al-Minqarī came to the Prophet; some of the Ansar told him that Qays practiced the burial of infant girls. He said to the Prophet, 'I have buried alive all my female infants; I spared only one whose mother bore her while I was travelling. She gave her over to her brothers (the child's uncles). When I returned, I asked about the pregnancy and my wife told me that the child had been stillborn. Years passed by and the girl grew into an adolescent and visited her mother. I entered my wife's tent one day and saw her: she had plaited her daughter's hair and perfumed her and decked her out in a necklace and a sea-shell amulet. I asked, Who is this young girl? I find her beauty attractive. She then burst into tears and said, This is your daughter; I had told you that I gave birth to a stillborn child, but this is the girl who was born. I placed her in her uncle's care and now she has grown up. I restrained myself until her mother was distracted one day then took her out, dug a ditch and placed her in it. She called out, Father, are you covering me in sand!? I carried on until she could not be seen and her voice

> faded out.' . . . The Prophet's eyes filled with tears and he said, 'Whosoever shows no mercy will not have mercy shown to him!'[82]

The nature of this tragic recognition between father and child may act inversely as a palliative and have some mitigating force upon the way Abū Zayd is judged when he confesses to the obtuse al-Ḥārith what he has truly meant by his poem:

> 'Cutting down' means . . . 'thinning the wine' not, friend, killing a man with lance or sword.
>
> And the maid, kept at home with me, means the daughter of the grape-tree, not the virgin of high descent.
>
> And to wed her to cup and flask was the errand, which you saw me intent upon when I joined you.
>
> Understand then what I have said, and decide on kind forbearance, if so you will, or to rebuke me.[83]

If, like al-Sharīshī, one reads with the anagnostic design of a literary tradition stacked up as a backdrop – as one is clearly meant to, reading from the 'well spring of *adab*' as al-Ḥarīrī states of Abū Zayd's initial discourse – disclosures pile heavily upon each other. In such a comparative scheme, the relatively paltry confession of Abū Zayd seems quite tolerable. It is not a woman or a child he has killed, so he deserves forbearance. The power of disclosure feeds the emergence of an ambiguous, equivocal and relativist statement about the morality that inheres in words and actions.

Such relativism and ambiguity is nowhere more apparent than in the *Maqāmah Wabariyyah* ('The Tent Dwellers').

The Rustler and the Saviour: The *Maqāmah Wabariyyah* ('The Tent Dwellers')[84]

The *Wabariyyah*, al-Ḥarīrī's twenty-seventh *Maqāmah*, is part of that genre of tales that transports its audience out into the desert. It is akin to the *Iblīsiyyah* of al-Hamadhānī; both are related specifically to the story genus about men who lose their mounts and meet with strange encounters while wandering abroad to track them down. The outset of the *Wabariyyah* establishes an idealistic view of the Bedouin; in this respect the text is similar to the *Aswadiyyah* of al-Hamadhānī.[85] It celebrates a cultural ideal: al-Ḥārith searches out the Bedouin Arabs to experience their proud spirits and to learn from their 'Arab tongues'. To this end, he travels far and wide, high (through the Najd plateau) and low (the Ghawr), to gather up a herd in order to partake of their lifestyle. The contrast between the Najd and the Ghawr establishes a basic scheme for a whole series of antitheses that end up undermining the clear, quite fabled idyll. At the outset, he takes refuge among Arab herders who follow noble chieftains and are sources of paragonistic sayings; the irony of this is that the *maqāmah* itself ends up being something of a cautionary tale rather than an exemplum about Bedouin comportment (we in fact never meet any Bedouin paragons, except ones that turn out to be more like Pharaoh than Moses, as the Arab saying goes). Most of the exempla (the sayings or *aqwāl*) in the *maqāmah* are themselves undermined by the bathos of the picaresque themes that come instead to the fore. Indeed, the pristine ideal of the *maqāmah*'s opening is broken in a way that ends up stirring up a dilemma of moral judgement. The quandary will emerge in the person of Abū Zayd: for the question this *maqāmah* asks is not so much who is Abū Zayd, as what is he – hero or villain?

The initial equilibrium is upset when, from the herd he has gathered, al-Ḥārith loses a choice she-camel that produces copious milk. In search of her, he follows 'every trace he comes upon', through mountain and vale; this is clear cut, unequivocal determination. But al-Ḥārith's fortitude is blunted when he fails in his quest and becomes, the way he coins it loadedly, as a Ghaylān distracted from Mayy. According to the intense cultural archetype, the amorous poet Ghaylān (also known as Dhū al-Rummah, d. *c.*735 AD) should not be distracted from the Mayy to whom he is utterly devoted in love. This faltering stirs and muddies the waters; it introduces a note that modulates into the ambiguity of ensuing events, contorting and skewing an otherwise straight and pristine sense of cultural values.

When al-Ḥārith rests from his exhausting search, he observes a figure appear, ominously (*sāniḥ*). He fears its approach and appeals to God to protect him from harm. As readers our curiosity is pricked to see what will transpire. Al-Ḥārith recognises then the figure of Abū Zayd. Though he knows him, he is wary and attempts to stay awake when Abū Zayd dozes off after they share a meal. He succumbs to exhaustion, however; when he awakes, Abū Zayd has disappeared and with him al-Ḥārith's horse. This is rendered in a playful pun: 'There was neither the man from Sarūj nor the saddled (*musarraj*) mount' (*wa-lā l-sarūjīya wa-lā l-musarraj*). Al-Ḥārith now claims to suffer sorrows like those of Jacob, articulating an abuse of the cultural code; it is an exaggeration and an emptying out of the meaning contained in an exemplary figure. He then espies a man riding some distance off. He hopes that the stranger will this time come towards him. Instead, al-Ḥārith has to give chase and when he finally reaches him, he finds the stranger to be riding the very camel he had lost at the tale's outset, the original object of his quest. The words here in Arabic are significant (*wajadtu nāqatī maṭiyyata-hu wa-ḍāllatī luqṭata-hu*); taken on its own, this locution comes close to suggesting 'he has found the lost object of his quest', almost as if the matter of the original search had issued in a triumph. But that conclusion is possible only if we focus on this pronouncement; in reality the issue is of course much messier. When he demands his camel back, he bids the stranger 'do the right thing' by evoking a cultural figure of notoriety: 'Do not be like Ashᶜath', an infamously mean and miserly man. An anecdote about him told in al-Sharīshī's commentary seems relevant: ᶜĀᵓishah bint ᶜUthmān (daughter of the third caliph) had charged him with taking care of the linen [of the palace], and after a year she inquired after his progress; he replied, 'I have learnt half the job and one half remains; I have learnt how to unfurl the linen, I still need to learn how to gather it in.' It is this rendering of matters into dichotomous halves such as to colour the way they are to be interpreted, problematically, that reflects on the *maqāmah* itself, which is about a good deed being offset by a bad one. The idea that a good thing may be the pendant complement of something unseemly invests this *maqāmah* with its moral dilemma. This impulse of opposition is evident in the way the stranger who has taken the camel vacillates with contrary attitudes: 'and while he assaulted and relented in turns, now acting the lion, now cowering, behold, there came upon us Abū Zayd, clad in the leopard's skin, rushing along with the rush of the furious torrent.' At this second arrival, more unexpected even than the rogue's first appearance, al-Ḥārith is choked with fear, expressed, again, through locutions of complementarity and contrast: 'I feared that his feat today might be like his performance of yesterday, that the brightness of his full moon would equal that of his sun . . . after which I would become a mere tale after the substance' (*aṣīra khabaran ba^{c}da ^{c}ayn*).[86]

The Arabic of al-Ḥārith's question to Abū Zayd – had he come 'to make good [his] wrong or to encompass [his] utter ruin?' – is cast in a deft pun, the words for 'making good' and 'ruination' being virtually homonyms: *talāfī* and *itlāfī*. These pendant words are acoustically and morphologically almost identical, yet antithetical in meaning, just as Abū Zayd means both, perhaps even simultaneously, someone unscrupulous and someone good (or at least occasionally helpful), as we soon see. For he now chases off the other rustler and reunites al-Ḥārith with his prize camel. He keeps the horse, however, with the advice that an act of villainy has been followed by an obvious boon, and that one calamity is in any case better than two. Al-Ḥārith does not know whether to revile Abū Zayd or thank him, but the latter of course ends up showing us the extent of – indeed being the very incarnation of – the dichotomous scheme of this *maqāmah*, undermining the pristine ethos of the Bedouin context where values are imagined to be unequivocal and noble. The search for the *ḍāllah* – the lost beast – is successful in the end, but along the way the narrator loses moral clarity and the Bedouin milieu now seems quite distant, if not utterly forgotten. He himself becomes the object lesson of a cautionary tale, 'the *khabar* having been the ^{c}*ayn*'. This *khabar* (which also means 'predicate' in Arabic, fortuitously) is the predicate of all recognition including, and indeed essentially, that of the paragonistically mercurial Abū Zayd.[87]

Al-Ḥarīrī's 'Penitent': Recognition and Return

The fiftieth and final *maqāmah* of Al-Harīrī's series is quite different;[88] it is apparently pious and staid. The series, which Al-Harīrī himself established in a fixed and standard sequence, begins with Abū Zayd as a homilist; every tenth *maqāmah* thereafter has a religious theme (thus the eleventh, the twenty-first, the thirty-first, etc.). In most cases, while the theme is religious, Abū Zayd is nevertheless unmasked as a rum and dishonest preacher. The collection is bookended naturally with the fiftieth narrative, which also has a strongly religious theme about Abū Zayd's ostensibly sincere repentance. Steingass' précis of the *maqāmah* gives one a strong sense of this: '[Abu Zayd] is now represented as redeeming, under the touch of divine grace, his life of venturesome expedients, frequently bordering on crime, by sincere repentance and transports of pure and unremitting devotion.'[89] What is crucial to add about this *maqāmah* is that it is all about Abū Zayd – not about his cunning antics but his very person. Partly at his own instigation, his complicated persona is probed relentlessly, as if the whole piece is the detailed unveiling of a now true Abū Zayd. By providing a sort of confession of who and what he has been, it – or he – now tries to convince his entourage that the present turn toward repentance is sincere. Most commentaries acquiesce in this sincerity. It seems rash that they should.

The *maqāmah* is in two parts. In the first, al-Ḥārith ibn Hammām arrives in Basra and finds a crowd gathered around a preacher:

> I hastened in his direction and sought access to him, hoping to find the cure from my disease, and I ceased not shifting places, heedless of knocks and blows, until I was seated opposite to him, where I was safe of mistaking him, when, lo, it was our Shaykh the Serûji, no doubt in him, nor any disguise to conceal him. Then at his sight my grief subsided, and the hosts of my cares scattered.[90]

Abū Zayd now launches into a moving and detailed eulogy of Basra, praising it as the gateway to Mecca, a haven of religiosity, the site of a long tradition of culture and learning. At the end of his eulogy, he begins to disclose details about himself:

> to one who knows me not, I will now disclose truly my character . . . Ask of me the East and the West, the hoofs (of camels) and (their) humps, assemblies and hosts, tribes and squadrons, and gather clear tidings of me from the reporters of traditions and the story-tellers at night-talks, from the drivers of caravans, and the sharp-sighted diviners, that you may know how many mountain-passes I have threaded and veils I have rent, . . . how often I have beguiled the minds of men, . . . how many a hidden one I have brought out by my spells . . .

After this speech al-Ḥārith follows Abū Zayd to probe his new found repentance. Abū Zayd says: 'I swear by Him who knows all hidden things and forgives transgressions, my case is indeed a miracle and the prayers of your fellow-people have been answered.' He departs, leaving the narrator 'tormenting

[his] thoughts on his account, and looking out for means of testing the truth of what he had stated.'

Now the second part of the *maqāmah* begins, pursuing further the essence of what Abū Zayd has become. After a period of time, al-Ḥārith is informed by some travellers that they have seen Abū Zayd settled in Sarūj 'leading the rows of prayer and . . . become a famous devotee'. Al-Ḥārith travels there to verify the truth of this and there he finds that Abū Zayd

> had joined the seven saints, and that his heart was imbued with the love of seclusion. So I formed within me the resolution to depart and to leave him all by himself in this state. Then it was as if he had read my purpose or had revealed to him that which I kept concealed, for he sighed like one grief-stricken, after which he quoted (from the Koran): 'If you make a resolution, put your trust in God.' Thereupon I testified to the truthfulness of my informants, and knew for certain that in our dispensation inspired ones are found. So I went nigh to him, to put my hand in his, and said: 'Give me your bequest, servant of sincere counsel,' when he said: 'Keep an eye on death, and this is the parting between me and you.' With this he bade me farewell, while tears streamed from the corners of his eyes, and my sighs rose from within my entrails, this being the last of our meetings.[91]

Two things should be underlined in any commentary of this concluding episode. First, it lays great stress on who Abū Zayd is, acknowledging his past in a partial register of confession and warranting the sincerity of the devout man he has become. The language of revelation is inscribed in several ways into this protracted statement of repentance: Abū Zayd unveils himself and al-Ḥārith insists on chasing down the truth of his contrition. There is great cumulative force to what unfolds; it contrives a weighty argument that appears unassailably conclusive. Second, and herein may lie the rub, Abū Zayd's very last words, while enunciating what strains to be an apothegmatic finale before death may in fact be something quite the opposite. For the phrase 'this is the parting between you and me' are the words Khiḍr utters to Moses in Surah 18 (verse 78) just before the gnostic paragon disabuses the prophet of his misapprehensions about a series of appalling actions whose significance Moses has misunderstood. In the Qur'anic narrative, apparently baleful and wicked acts are shown by Khiḍr to have an ulterior significance, quite the converse of their appearance. Do these words of Abū Zayd then collapse the verbal edifice of personal reform that he has constructed ostensibly about himself? It is impossible to determine for sure. But, given the amount of verbal play that has preceded this encounter, there is a distinct possibility that this may indeed be the case. Most moments of recognition in the *maqāmah* genre are problematic and unstable in their on-going context, and warrant a continuing cycle of deceit. As Malcolm Lyons has written about this genre:

> It is the recurrent theme of anagnôrisis that supplies the Maqamat with their characteristic pattern. What cannot be doubted is that the repeated patterns of disguise and recognition underline the importance to their audience of the simple point that things are not what they seem and that the world cannot be taken at face value.[92]

Neither can a word or a text be trusted superficially. The irony of the *maqāmāt* is that the path from ignorance to knowledge – the path traced in the very semantics of anagnorisis – the unveiling of a name and an identity, is instantiated in an antithetical progression: the truth is incessantly discovered to be a pack of lies. It is perhaps apt, however, that the first self-avowed fictional genre in high Arabic literature involving anecdotes with human characters should be about lies, delusion and deceit.

Notes

1. For a guide and introduction to the themes and bibliography of this literature, see Philip F. Kennedy, 'The *Maqāmāt* as a Nexus of Interests', in Julia Bray (ed.), *Writing and Representation in Medieval Islam – Muslim Horizons* (London: Routledge, 2006). The most detailed literary history of the genre is Jaakko Hämeen-Anttila's *Maqama: A History of a Genre* (Wiesbaden: Harrassowitz Verlag, 2002); he engages little with anagnorisis, except as it features in the *maqāmāt* of the Andalusian, al-Ashtarkūwī (pp. 258–9). While he identifies the figure, Hämeen-Anttila does not explicitly connect it with a hermeneutics of reading; cf. James T. Monroe, *The Art of Badī*ᶜ *az-Zamān al-Hamadhānī as Picaresque Narrative* (Beirut: American University of Beirut, 1983), pp. 21–4, and Monroe's enlightening readings and analysis of al-Ashtarkūwī, in *Al-Maqāmāt al-Luzūmīya by Abū Ṭāhir Muḥammad ibn Yūsuf al-Tamīmī*

al-Saraqustī ibn al-Aštarkūwī (Leiden: Brill, 2002), especially the section 'Doubling and Duplicity', pp. 80–100.

2. This is especially true of the various ways one can interpret the literary dispositions of 'The Two Viziers' and '[c]Alā al-Dīn Abū al-Shāmāt'.
3. This aspect of the genre, which is an important symptom of the way I understand anagnorisis in this kind of narrative, is captured in James Monroe's comments about *tawriyah*, discussed by Kennedy ('The *Maqāmāt* as a Nexus', p. 195) as follows: 'To describe language as a "veil of obscurity" surely captures well an aspect of at least some of the *maqāmāt*. In this context, he quotes Kilito, who evokes the rhetorical concept of *tawriyah* (double-entendre), in which the primary sense of the word is intended to mislead, and it is the secondary sense which carries the true meaning, just as, in many of the *maqāmāt*, the purpose of appearances is to deceive. *Tawriyah* is just one aspect of the allusiveness and intertextuality of the *maqāmāt*, and in this connection, Monroe points out the multiple resonances of al-Iskandarī's *kunyah* (agnomen), Abū al-Fatḥ.'
4. Terence Cave, *Recognitions: A Study in Poetics* (Oxford: Clarendon Press, 1988), p. 46.
5. See Sheila Murnaghan, *Disguise and Recognition in the Odyssey* (Princeton: Princeton University Press, 1987).
6. Luīs [c]Awad made use of the figure of Penelope in his love poem '*al-Ḥubb fī Sān Lazār*' ('Love at Saint Lazare Station'), published in the collection *Plutoland* (Cairo: Maṭba[c]at al-Karnak, 1948), pp. 59–71. He meets on a train journey a woman whom he recognises as the ideal image of Penelope he has been waiting for, weaving his own loom of patience. Their encounter is short lived, the length of a train journey from London to Paris, and ends in a melancholy uncertainty. It is as if the intensity of ideal love can only be experienced physically in a fleeting recognition, despite the constancy of the image that might haunt us.
7. On the relationship between the texts of the *maqāmāt* of al-Ḥarīrī and their various manuscript illuminations, see Oleg Grabar, *The Illustrations of the Maqāmāt* (Chicago: University of Chicago Press, 1984), and his 'Pictures or Commentaries: The Illustrations of the *Maqāmāt* of al-Ḥarīrī', in Peter J. Chelkowski (ed.), *Studies in Art and Literature of the Near East* (Salt Lake City: Middle East Center, University of Utah, 1974), pp. 85–104.
8. To borrow Kilito's title for the fifth *Maqāmah* of al-Ḥarīrī.
9. Cave, *Recognitions*, p. 4.
10. Ibid., p. 273.
11. See Kennedy, 'The *Maqāmāt* as a Nexus', *passim*.

12. See Muḥammad b. al-Ḥasan al-Ṭūsī, *Kitāb al-Ghaybah*, ed. Muḥammad Ṣādiq al-Mūsawī (Najaf: Maktabat al-Ṣādiq, 1385/1965), pp. 152–3.
13. This detail itself toys with convention, for marvellous tales happen in distant lands during some time well in the past.
14. Precisely stories like al-Tanūkhī's earnest family romance of deliverance, '*Anā Abū-ka*' ('I am your father') (F 342, in *Al-Faraj ba*ᶜ*d al-shiddah*, ed. ᶜAbbūd al-Shāljī (Beirut: Dār Ṣādir, 1978), III, pp. 314–20), with which I juxtapose it by design – it ends Chapter 4.
15. Abū Zayd was for a time logically the *kunyah* of the Prophet Muḥammad until the repudiation of Zayd b. al-Ḥārithah; having been the adoptive father of Zayd, Muḥammad then became the Seal of the Prophets and adoption was proscribed by the Qurᵓan in Surah 33 (al-Aḥzāb). In Chapter 3 above, I read this as a recognition story. It would be tendentious, however, to argue that al-Ḥarīrī had this narrative in mind when he named his rogue hero Abū Zayd al-Sarūjī.
16. Bernard Haykel, 'Dissembling Descent, or How the Barber Lost his Turban: Identity and Evidence in Eighteenth Century Zaydī Yemen', *Islamic Law and Society* 9:2 (2002), pp. 194–230.
17. The irony of the use of this phrase in this context is delightful; see the discussion of *ma*ᶜ*rūf* and *munkar* in the Introduction.
18. Natalie Zemon Davies, *The Return of Martin Guerre* (Cambridge, MA: Harvard University Press, 1983). Cf. *Le Retour de Martin Guerre* (dir. Daniel Vigne, 1983).
19. Cave, *Recognitions*, p. 15.
20. Ibid., p. 15.
21. A version of this story is told in English rhyming couplets by Thomas Moore in 'The Veiled Prophet of Khorassan': see *Lalla Rookh: An Oriental Romance* (London: Longman *et al.*, 1849), pp. 11–103. What is fascinating is the way the story is positioned to chime with the epistemology of an overarching tale; Robert Irwin gives a detailed but succinct account of this in *The Arabian Nights. A Companion* (London: Penguin, 1995), p. 264. Quite transparently, and according to a pattern of construction we see in much literature, one recognition story is set within the wider arch of another; the one – the embedded – foreshadows the later one, gives it a human depth and engages the reader to make what is effectively a hermeneutic connection.
22. Borges, 'Tom Castro, the Implausible Impostor', in Norman Thomas di Giovanni (trans.), *Universal History of Infamy* (New York: E. P. Dutton, 1972), pp. 34–5.

23. Michael Cooperson, 'Baghdad in Rhetoric and Narrative', *Muqarnas: An annual on the visual culture of the Islamic world* 13 (1996), p. 107. The Arabic source is al-Khaṭīb al-Baghdādī, *Tārīkh Baghdād* (Beirut: Dār al-Kutub al-ᶜArabī, 1931), vol. 7, pp. 70ff.
24. As in the different versions of the Demon Ṣakhr's imposture as King Solomon. For a readable version of this tale in English, drawing generally on the Islamic tradition, see W. A. Clouston, *Popular Tales and Fictions: Their Migrations and Transformations* (Whitefish: Kessinger Publishing, 2003), pp. 191–2.
25. Richard Burton, *The Book of the Thousand Nights and a Night*, vol. V (London, 1885–8), pp. 74–5; in Arabic this corresponds with Būlāq edition, vol. I, p. 566.
26. H. T. Norris' 'Fables and Legends', *CHALUP* (*Arabic Literature to the End of the Umayyad Period*), eds A. F. L. Beeston *et al.* (Cambridge: Cambridge University Press, 1983), pp. 139–41. Norris points out that this is a story about love and adventure but also about edification. For a detailed analysis of the legend of Tamīm al-Dārī and its sources, see Francesca Bellino, 'Tamīm al-Dārī the Intrepid Traveller: Emergence, Growth and Making of a Legend in Arabic Literature' available at http://arabistica.academia.edu/FrancescaOdiliaBellino/Papers/1265608/Islamic_legends_OM_Tamim_al-Dari_the_Intrepid_traveller.
27. Norris, 'Fables and Legends'.
28. Burton tells this similar tale of Khiḍr from a Turkish source in his supplementary volumes (supplementary vol. II, Appendix: pp. 325–7), but does not identify the source.
29. The *Maqāmah Iblīsiyyah* of al-Hamadhānī toys by allusion with the mysterious appearances of Khiḍr and ends up unveiling to the reader the figure of Iblīs instead. See Philip F. Kennedy, 'Some Demon Muse: structure and allusion in Al-Hamadhānī's *Maqāma Iblīsiyya*', *Arabic and Middle Eastern Literatures* 2:1 (1999), pp. 115–35.
30. Epigraph to Elias Khoury's *Gate of the Sun*, trans. Humphrey Davis (New York: Archipelago Books, 2006).
31. Ignaz Goldziher, *Muslim Studies*, ed. S. M. Stern, trans. C. R. Barber (Piscataway: Aldine Transaction, 2006), vol. I, pp. 151–2.
32. The following discussion of the *Maqāmah* of Kufa was inspired largely by Abdelfattah Kilito's *Al-Ghāʾib* (Casablanca: Dār Tūbqāl li-l-Nashr, 1987). My reading is distinct in its precise detail since driven by a perspective that focuses on anagnorisis; nevertheless, there is palpable influence in my reading which is intended as a homage to Kilito's much cited work.

33. A legendary paragon of rhetorical excellence.
34. Cf. al-Sharīshī, *Sharḥ Maqāmāt al-Ḥarīrī*, ed. Ibrāhīm Shams al-Dīn (Beirut: Dār al-Kutub al-ᶜIlmiyyah, 1419/1998), vol. 1, p. 133.
35. Al-Sharīshī died in 122 AD.
36. Cf. al-Sharīshī, *Sharḥ*, 1, p. 137
37. Ibid., 1, p. 138.
38. Ibid., 1, p. 139.
39. Ibid., 1, pp. 140–1.
40. For a detailed and full taxonomy of the way the recognition scenes are built into al-Ḥarīrī's *maqāmāt*, see Katia Zakharia, *Abū Zayd al-Sarūǧī, imposteur et mystique* (Damascus: IFEAD, 2000), pp. 193–212.
41. Another way of translating this would be: 'to make me refuse to recognise him on account of any bad or evil quality'.
42. Al-Hamadhānī, *The Maqamat of Badi' al-Zaman al-Hamadhani: with Introduction and Notes*, trans. W. J. Prendergast (Lexington: Forgotten Books, 2008), p. 38.
43. Cf. al-Sharīshī, *Sharḥ*, 1, p. 142.
44. The poll tax for foreigners, followers of non-state religions.
45. This is referred to in the Qurᵓan: 'The heart (*fuᵓād*) of the mother of Moses was so empty that *she almost exposed him*, were it not for the fact that We bound up her heart (*qalba-hā*).'"
46. Cf. al-Sharīshī, *Sharḥ*, 1, pp. 142–3.
47. Ibid., 1, p. 144.
48. As in Surah 79.
49. Cf. al-Sharīshī, *Sharḥ*, 1, p. 145.
50. Ibid., 1, pp. 146, 150.
51. Cave, *Recognitions*, pp. 208–9.
52. Ibid., pp. 208–9.
53. Ibid., pp. 14–15.
54. Cf. al-Sharīshī, *Sharḥ*, 1, pp. 151–3.
55. 'I have innovated, not following a model' (*abdaᶜtu fī-hā wa-mā qtadaytu*).
56. Cf. al-Sharīshī, *Sharḥ*, 1, pp. 153–6.
57. For the Arabic of this text, see al-Sharīshī, *Sharḥ*, 1, pp. 56–91. Following English translation from Thomas Chenery (trans.), *The Assemblies of al-Harīrī*, vol. 1 (London: Williams and Norgate, 1867).
58. Al-Sharīshī, *Sharḥ*, 1, pp. 190–214.
59. 'The Trickster and Rhetoric in the *Maqāmāt*', *Edebiyât* 5 (1994), pp. 1–14.

60. Ibid., pp. 1–14.
61. F 454 (see Chapter 4).
62. For an example of this feature in another author, see van Gelder's analysis of the second *maqāmah* of Ibn Nāqiyā in 'Fools and Rogues in Discourse and Disguise: Two Studies', in Robin Ostle (ed.), *Sensibilities of the Islamic Mediterranean* (London: I. B. Tauris, 2008.), pp. 39–42.
63. Al-Sharīshī, *Sharḥ*, 3, pp. 273–313.
64. Cf. *Maqāmah* 14: Abū Zayd's son recites in the last line of a poem, 'and mine are young offspring of the wit which put to shame every poem'. See al-Sharīshī, *Sharḥ*, 1, p. 400: *wa-lī natāʾiju fikrin / yafḍaḥna kulla qaṣīdah.*
65. Al-Sharīshī, *Sharḥ*, 1, p. 228: *anā l-sarūjī wa-hādhā waladī.*
66. Al-Sharīshī, *Sharḥ*, 3, p. 239: *innaka la-shajaratu thamratihi.*
67. Thomas Chenery (trans.), *The Assemblies of al-Harīrī*, vol. 1 (London: Williams and Norgate, 1867), pp. 124–5; al-Sharīshī, *Sharḥ*, 1, pp. 111–32.
68. *Idhā ṭaʿimtum fa-ntashirū* . . . – the Qurʾanic phrase is adapted only slightly by al-Ḥarīrī to *idhā ṭaʿima ntashar.*
69. Al-Sharīshī, *Sharḥ*, 1, pp. 407–32.
70. Chenery, *Assemblies*, pp. 184–6.
71. Al-Sharīshī, *Sharḥ*, 2, pp. 79–80.
72. There is perhaps no better example of the genre's duplicity than *Maqāmah* 28, which one might label 'The sermons on death', in which Abū Zayd, in the guise of a devout preacher, at first declaims the inevitability of death and urges mankind to a life of dedicated worship. Wonderment ensues in the *Maqāmah* when Abū Zayd is found toping wine in a bar. There follows a bacchanalian justification, with death as its driving rationale: 'How can you hope to escape from a net, from which neither Kisra escaped, nor Darius . . .?' Notions of death cut in two clear, didactic but contradictory ways. (And Abū Zayd now solicits an oath from al-Ḥārith to 'screen his repute'.)
73. Al-Sharīshī, *Sharḥ*, 3, pp. 81–102.
74. This piece builds upon a model established by al-Hamadhani ('The Barber of Ḥulwān') and outdoes it in its detail, structure and verbal intricacy. See al-Sharīshī, *Sharḥ*, 3, pp. 398–421.
75. See the discussion of the *Maqāmah* of Raḥbah, no. 10, in which the story of the wolf that did not kill Joseph – and which in fact never existed – is given a role establishing its innocence before Jacob. This element is not Qurʾanic but apocryphal, although it finds its way into the traditions of exegesis.
76. For example, in *Maqāmah* 14, al-Ḥārith asks the old man – Abū Zayd, still

incognito – after he has received quittance for his customary display of eloquence: 'Has our promise been like the promise of ᶜOrqoub or does there remain a need in the mind of Jacob?'

77. Al-Sharīshī, *Sharḥ*, 3, pp. 15–42.
78. F. W. Steingass (trans.), *The Assemblies of al-Harīrī*, vol. 2 (London: Williams and Norgate, 1898), p. 63.
79. The difference in vocalisation of the name reminds one of the fullness of philological exegesis.
80. Al-Sharīshī, *Sharḥ*, 1, pp. 261–310.
81. Al-Sharīshī, *Sharḥ*, 3, pp. 43–61.
82. Ibid., 3, pp. 50–1.
83. Ibid., 3, p. 74.
84. Al-Sharīshī, *Sharḥ*, 2, pp. 309–30.
85. The *Aswadiyyah*, named after the historically real al-Aswad b. Qinān, sets its two players, the fugitive urban narrator (ᶜĪsā b. Hishām) and the anti-hero (Abū al-Fatḥ), against the backcloth of some idealised Bedouin location.
86. Al-Sharīshī, *Sharḥ*, 2, p. 6.
87. The ambiguous morality of this story is analogous to that of a story in al-Tanūkhī's *Faraj* (F 292).
88. Al-Sharīshī, *Sharḥ*, 3, pp. 457–83.
89. Steingass, *Assemblies*, 2, pp. 174–5.
90. Ibid., p. 176.
91. Ibid., p. 185.
92. M. C. Lyons, 'A Note on the *Maqāma* Form', *Pembroke Papers* 1 (1990), pp. 115–22.

Conclusion

It is tempting to contrive a conclusion for a book on anagnorisis with a recognition scene: to declare, somehow, 'this is what anagnorisis tells us, against expectation, or this is what it all turns out to be about.' Such a conclusion would be possible if this study were exhaustive, but it is not.[1] That is to say, both the generic and temporal range of this first book on anagnorisis in Arabic literature is delimited in its perspective. There are other chapters of medieval literature that could be added; and of course modern and contemporary materials provide a study by themselves, relating anagnorisis in the burgeoning present-day Arabic corpus to world literature, as well as film, the most common medium in which we experience it.

Similarly, this study could have confined itself to showing, or confirming expressly, that in Arabic literature anagnorisis comes about in the six ways outlined by Aristotle in chapter 16 of the *Poetics*. By means of *tokens or signs*, as in the Prophet's *khātam al-nubuwwah*, the seal of prophecy; or the details of a long lost purse in a story by al-Tanūkhī. By means of *contrivance*, as in Surah 12 which is crafted by the hand of God; or the conversion of Salmān al-Fārisī, a tale teleologically – and folklorically – structured towards the recognition of Muḥammad; or the picaresque tales told by al-Ḥarīrī with masterful tacit allusion to narrative poetics, often giving the brush of narrative creation to Abū Zayd, the teller of fictions within fictions. By means of *memory and the telling of stories*, as in the case of Joseph's brothers, who are prompted by him to remember their evil past and thus know who he is; or the account of the Damascene prisoner of al-Maʾmūn who tells his story, summoning the past into the present so that he can be recognised by his jailer and saviour; or the sons of the Pious Israelite who tell their discrete stories years after their separation thus recognising each other and being recognised by their mother who chances to be within earshot (there is measured contrivance here too, in the construction of this short tale). By means of *true inference* and *false inference*, as illustrated by the two shirts of Joseph, the first whose lying blood troubles Jacob, and the second whose fabric torn from behind established Joseph's innocence in Potiphar's house. Or by means of *logically unfolding events developed through a story in naturalistic fashion*: to some extent this is true of the calumny told about ᶜĀᵓishah, all the events of which complement each other in a natural way (God, the ultimate *deus ex machina*, is absent for the longest part of the narrative, and this troubles the Prophet), though in the end it is a story contrived by revelation to end as it does, clearing the young wife of the Prophet of any guilt, by means of Qurᵓanic 'signs'.

Studying recognition simply to show how Aristotle's sketchy taxonomy can be applied to non-Western literatures is not rewarding in itself. The onus instead has been to accept Aristotle as a foundation of common sense, and to build upon this to highlight other traits. And these traits do in fact relate to Aristotle's preference for the recognition of identity or truth to come from the events themselves, unfolding naturalistically, organically, logically, causally and spatially as time unfolds, for this category of recognition demands, or places stress on the story or drama being conceived of as an integral whole, as far as possible, by the author and the reader or audience. Indeed, reading stories in their fullness has been a methodological mainstay of my approach. It has allowed us to see the significance of recognition within a narrative; to gauge its ethical and moral importance; to probe the idea that recognition is so often a synecdoche (thus carrying the importance of the narrative, as a story built on surprise, say, or as one that carries moral import as anagnorisis unfolds the truth); to focus on the point in a tale where structure and theme (or *muthos* and *ethos*, in Aristotle's terminology) are hard to prise apart, thus suggesting that hermeneutics can in fact be derivative of structure – of the temporal and spatial fashioning of a story; to determine the element of parody that may be invested in recognition when instantiated in examples that are excessively implausible or easily read as facetious comedy; to examine, further, the fact that whilst being the feature that so often resolves a fractured narrative (one could say this of Shakespeare's comedies and romances) it is a problem moment, failing to put to bed thoughts that are provoked by and survive recognition, and cannot be solved by it; to analyse where relevant the way intertextuality, by being imbedded in allusion, is so often an enriching readerly device in stories of recognition – intertextuality may be functional and mechanistic or interpretive and thematic. Joseph is the archetype here – certainly of this study. In his own scriptural story (or stories) he is a person transfigured; in intertextually related stories it may simply be the structure of his story that is borrowed; he modulates variously; and he – or details borrowed from the textual archetype – may be sublimated subtly and obliquely or affect the very heart and soul of a story.[2]

My close scrutiny of integral texts has shown that angnorisis in Arabic literature – as in other literatures, to be sure – unveils transcendent truths as well as material incertitudes, sometimes discretely and sometimes in a kind of epistemological alloy of the human condition. The Damascene's story from the Introduction prefigures the providential affect of Surah 12: the discovery of the Damascene's identity saves him in the nick of time and is transformative – the audience watching or hearing this pattern of events cannot but be affected within the story and outside of it. Recognition is the fulcrum of the account: the part that stands for the whole, the subject that modulates and refracts through to the conclusion as an alternate ethical theme of gratitude and mercy. In the recognition scene, where the Damascene declares, 'I am that man!' the recursive nature of storytelling becomes apparent: it tells the reader that the past has been reprised and brought into the present to influence events, and, simultaneously, memory has been restored as a blessing. Recognition of a moral lesson is incarnated in the identities that are disclosed to each other – that is the semantic, hermeneutic energy that can be sensed in anagnorisis.

When it exists, anagnorisis lies by definition at the heart of any narrative's epistemology. No text evinces this more clearly than the Qur᾿anic version of the Joseph story, which includes a majestic recognition scene. Recognition is instantiated as revelation both for Joseph and for Muslim posterity – but what is also significant is the way knowledge, threaded in and out of ignorance, unfolds through the entire text. From this process a theology of divine omniscience, judgement and determinism (and its relationship to mankind's temporal development) is articulated, and for some Muslim exegetes this constituted an essential part of the narrative's self-vaunted beauty. That the theology and the beauty emerge from the integrity of the text has had an important influence on the way I have read other narratives in my study: that is, where possible, I scrutinised recognition with the entirety of a text in mind. Such is the case with my analyses of the stories about Zayd ibn Ḥārithah, Salmān al-Fārisī and ᶜĀʾishah. All three are inflected by significant elements of the Joseph narrative; in the case of ᶜĀʾishah scriptural revelation of her innocence is bolstered through her own clumsy yet canny citation of Surah 12. All three stories show recognition working through the Prophet's developing role within his community. Muḥammad emerged as a prophet through cycles of recognition and authentication, and since no single one of the recognition scenes examined in our study resolves his role with certainty we come to see how recognition can be understood as a problem moment, preserving a surplus of doubt for events that unfold beyond it. Taken to the *n*-th degree this allows us to glimpse how and why recognition is inexhaustible in literature.

Intertextuality and parody can be inextricable from each other, depending on whether or not what is parodied is as broad as a genre or as demarcated as a single text. *Maqāmah* 5 of al-Ḥarīrī clearly satirises pretentious literary fools and does so through parody, probably of a genre, and in this case maybe even of himself. In the *Maqāmah* of Zabīd again fools are ridiculed and the means of doing this, in a well-honed narrative, is the borrowing of elements of the Joseph story. The figure of the prophet is evoked and the story of his life is aped in the structure of recognition. No chapter of this study is devoid of Joseph and intertextual relationships. Other examples of intertextuality in these chapters evince how reading is involved in such literary manipulations: recognition of the allusive game afoot.

Let me close with a reflection that links the most uplifting text of this study with the most dispiriting genre (for the excessively po-faced reader). The recognition scene between Joseph and his brothers in the Qurʾan evokes the fact that they were morally flawed, and in that sense ignorant, in their past when they sold Joseph into slavery (or allowed the felony to happen). They were *munkirūn*, which here must mean at once that they were tainted by *munkar* (evil) as well as being incapable of recognising the qualities of their brother; in the latter sense *munkirūn* suggests the antonym of recognition: being ignorant in both cognitive and moral senses. The Joseph story thus transcends *inkār* (denial and rejection), or promises that such transcendence is a possibility (in the life of Muḥammad it was still to come). It is curious and remarkable, therefore, that the corpus of texts that mocks providence by eschewing it totally is the *maqāmah*: these texts, especially those of the great al-Ḥarīrī, end with a running thematic conflict whereby anagnorisis (the recognition of the rogue, Abū Zayd) is coterminous with the narrator's (and possibly the reader's) *inkār*: 'rejection', 'refusal', 'denial', 'rebuff'. . .; in short, with the malaise of lurking and attendant ignorance.

Notes

1. Nor can it be – not out of choice but for fundamental literary reasons: it would otherwise be like producing an exhaustive study of beginnings, and anagnorisis is anything but stable.
2. Several contemporary Arabic novels play intertextually – and are largely at deliberate odds – with the Joseph story, e.g. *Qamīṣ Yūsuf* by Sultan Fayṣal, and *Yūsuf al-Inglīzī* by Rabīᶜ Jābir.

Appendix: Anagnorisis in Arabic *Falsafah*

The Arabic translation for anagnorisis varies in two fundamentally distinct contexts: (1) medieval Arab translators and commentators on the *Poetics*, writing within the philosophical tradition of Aristotelian *falsafah*, used the term *istidlāl* (occasionally also *dalālah*); (2) contemporary Arab scholars of literature discussing recognition as a device in narrative or drama tend to translate anagnorisis, where it has become a general concept of the epistemology of narrative, as *ta^{c}arruf* (see, e.g. Kilito's discussion of anagnorisis in al-Ḥarīrī's fifth *maqāmah* and ^{c}Ayyād's eloquent rendering into contemporary Arabic of Abū Bishr Mattā ibn Yūnus's earliest surviving tenth-century AD Arabic translation of the *Poetics*); in some cases, where 'recognition' is understood in a distended sense as 'discovery', either *kashf* or the more temporally specific *laḥẓat al-iktishāf* (moment of discovery), may convey the basic sense of anagnorisis (see al-Zayyāt).[1]

Thus a full technical account of anagnorisis in Arabo-Islamic culture should address both:

1. the understanding of anagnorisis among the *falāsifah* who were working under the erroneous impression, inherited from Simplicius (fl. 533 AD) or earlier, that the *Poetics* were, like the *Rhetoric*, part of the *Organon* and thus one of the instrumental sciences – (a move that contextualises the *Poetics* within a broadened field of logic in which the purpose of poetry is to produce artful representations through the imaginative syllogism); and,
2. the intuitive use of anagnorisis in its true or proximate Aristotelian sense among Arab authors showing that as a narrative device it is intrinsic to all literary traditions.

Aristotle discussed anagnorisis chiefly in chapters 6, 11, and 16 of the *Poetics.* Chapter 6 states tersely: 'the most important devices by which tragedy sways emotion are parts of the plot, i.e. reversals and recognitions'.[2] It is not until chapter 11 that Aristotle defines what he means in this critical phrase: 'as the term indicates, [anagnorisis] is a change from ignorance to knowledge, disclosing either a close relationship or enmity, on the part of the people marked out for good or bad fortune. Recognition is best when it occurs simultaneously with a reversal, like the one in the *Oedipus.*' This part of the definition restricts anagnorisis largely to the recognition of persons, but the possibility of broadening the predicates of recognition is understood clearly from the added gloss that: 'it is also possible to recognize whether someone has or has not performed some action.'[3] This terse and concise comment opens up immeasurably how anagnorisis can be understood, making it the key moment, both in the action itself and according to a hermeneutics of reading, when knowledge is revealed in narrative.

A typology of the mechanisms that trigger recognition is provided in Aristotle's chapter 16; it is said to occur:

1. by means of tokens, congenital or acquired (e.g. scars or necklaces);
2. by contrivance 'for example, . . . in the *Iphigenia* . . . Orestes declares in person what the poet (instead of the plot) requires';
3. by means of memory, as when Odysseus listens to the tale told to Alcinous in the *Odyssey*, is reminded of his past, and weeps;
4. through inference: 'someone similar has come; no one is similar except Orestes; so he has come';
5. by false inference.

But the best recognition of all (6) is that which arises out of the actual events, where the emotional impact is achieved through actions that unfold plausibly, as in Sophocles' *Oedipus.* Only this kind does without the contrivance of tokens and necklaces.[4]

The Earliest Arabic Translation of the *Poetics*[5]

Abū Bishr Mattā ibn Yūnus (*c.*932 AD), whose earliest surviving translation into Arabic of the *Poetics* was made from Isḥāq ibn Ḥunayn's earlier

Syriac version, renders the relevant part of chapter 6 faithfully: 'the parts of plot (*khurāfah*) are turning/reversal (*al-dawarān*) and recognition (*istidlāl*)'. The definition of recognition in chapter 11 also hews closely to the Greek original, though the Arabic locution is a touch cumbersome: 'recognition (*al-istidlāl*) is the movement (*al-ᶜubūr*) from ignorance (*lā maᶜrifah*) to knowledge (*maᶜrifah*) in respect of things which are determined for success and good fortune or bad fortune and enmity'. His rendering of the typology of Aristotle's chapter 16 contains some misunderstanding: recognition occurs: (1) by means of tokens (*bi-tawassuṭi l-ᶜalāmat*); it is (2) 'invented by the poet (*ᶜamala-hā l-shāᶜiru*) . . . without craft (*bi-lā ṣināᶜah*)'; it is (3) 'that a person should succeed in perceiving when he sees (*yanālu l-insāna an yuḥissa ᶜinda-mā yarā*) . . .' (a clumsy or incomplete rendering of Aristotle's original since the essential idea of memory stirring recognition is omitted from the crucial part of the definition); it occurs (4) by means of thought (*bi-l-fikr*); or (5) by false inference (*mughālaṭat al-qiyās*); and (6) it arises from the matters of the deliberate action, i.e. from the events themselves.[6]

Ibn Sīnā (Avicenna)[7]

Ibn Sīnā (d. 1020 AD) later commented significantly upon the *Poetics*, basing himself on Abū Bishr's translation (and at least one other, now apparently lost). Anagnorisis is construed by him as a rhetorical device of poetic embellishment in a discourse of persuasion. In that part of his commentary which corresponds with chapter 6, he writes

> the parts of plot (*khurāfah*) are two . . . reversal (*al-ishtimāl*) is the transition from one state to its opposite; it resembles what we now call antithesis (*muṭābaqah*). But in their (i.e., the Greeks') tragedies, it was used as a gradual transition from an ugly state to a beautiful state by depreciating the ugly state and embellishing the beautiful, in the manner of the rhetorical devices refutation, adjuration and proof

the point here being that the truth or meaning of an image becomes apparent by means of the enhanced contrast between the bad and the good;

> the second part [of plot] is recognition [here rendered *al-dalālah*] which is the intent [to depict] the beautiful state by means of embellishment (*bi-l-taḥsīn*) and not by depreciation of its opposite.[8]

Ibn Sīnā's understanding of both concepts is suborned to the idea that the *Poetics* are fundamentally about the art of persuasion, hence his comments a little further on that 'in general, the ancients had used poetic representation for the fixation of beliefs in the mind. Then, afterwards, rhetoric came into being and, consequently, they pursued the fixation of beliefs by persuasion' (*bi-l-iqnā*ᶜ; Dahiyat trans., p. 94); Greek poetry was intended according to this view either to induce or prevent an action.

From Ibn Sīnā's comments on the typology of chapter 16, it becomes apparent that for him recognition was tantamount to the enhanced perception of ideas, qualities and characteristics; it occurs:

1. 'by artifical means (*bi-ṣināᶜah*)': '[This type includes] either things that are probable but non-existent – and hence deceive in that they do not exist but are imaginative in that their deception is accepted – or personal belongings that do exist and whose appearance bring to mind certain evident ideas, such as a necklace (which signifies grace) or a sword in the hand (which signifies eloquence)' (Dahiyat trans., p. 109). This is sheer misunderstanding. Tokens, according to Aristotle, convey truth in that they warrant and trigger the disclosure of identity. But here, rather, tokens unveil truths that inhere in basic qualities or ideas – such as grace or eloquence. Nevertheless, Ibn Sīnā shows he was at pains to make sense of Aristotle according to a consistent semantic scheme. As Dahiyat puts it (p. 109): 'We have here a glimpse of the position taken by Avicenna with regard to the relation between poetic representation and logical demonstration: the devices of poetry "create an image" which is pleasant to the soul and is thus accepted, but one who acknowledges such an image does not accept the rigorous scrutiny of logical demonstration, i.e., is not ratiocinatively convinced.' Rather he or she is poetically convinced, one might say. Tokens (of recognition) are understood as figures of speech in a creative discourse;
2. by contrived and inartistic means (*sādhijatun lā ṣīghata shiᶜriyyata fī-hā*);
3. by recollection (*al-tadhkīr*): 'to bring up something that evokes the image of another (*yutakhayyalu maᶜa-hu shayʾun ākhar*)' (Dahiyat trans., p. 109);

4. 'by presenting a likeness to the mind by bringing up a similarity of kind or species (*ikhṭāru l-shabīhi bi-l-bāli bi-iyrādi l-shabīh*)'; this is the essence of the imaginative syllogism and a far cry from Aristotle's idea of recognition by inference, of the kind 'so-and-so's likeness has come therefore so-and-so has come';
5. by false exaggeration 'such as their saying that so-and-so strung a bow which no human can string' – Aristotle's notion of false inference is entirely missed;
6. by the imitation of a deed – 'which is the best sort of recognition'; again, this is remote from Aristotle's idea that the best recognition emerges naturally and plausibly from the actions of a plot.

The crux of Ibn Sīnā's interpretation of recognition is carried in his notion of *taḥsīn* – embellishment. Recognition, in antithetical contrast with reversal, comes when the good is rendered better by means of embellishment such that the essential quality being conveyed in an image can be perceived. This is what he intends, referring to enhanced action described in poetry, in saying that 'amelioration and the revealment (*sic*) of happiness as well as depreciation and the revealment (*sic*) of unhappiness are evidently connected with the actions of some persons whom others emulate and imitate by following their example in deed' (Dahiyat trans., pp. 102–3).

In his very brief discussion of comedy Ibn Sīnā complicates the Aristotelian original by talking about particulars rather than individuals. The original point was that individuals can represent universal qualities. This notwithstanding the comment that 'particulars are hypothetically conceived, but they indicate a universal meaning in a manner resembling what is called synecdoche' is an important symptom of Ibn Sīnā's entire way of reading the *Poetics*; his garbled – but highly intelligent – view of recognition is precisely an aspect of this scheme of reading and perception.

Ibn Rushd

Ibn Rushd (d. 1198 AD) later rendered certain Aristotelian concepts in an Arabic vocabulary distinct from Ibn Sīnā: thus he used *madīḥ* for tragedy (whereas Ibn Sīnā transliterated the Greek original into Arabic: *traghudiyya*) and *hijāʾ* for comedy (whereas Ibn Sīnā transliterated the Greek original:

qumidhiyya); in this Ibn Rushd followed the precedent of Abū Bishr's translation which he consulted. To a greater extent than anyone before him Ibn Rushd actually attempted to construct from the *Poetics* a practical system applicable to Arabic poetry and this fact both mitigates and complicates the misunderstandings inherent in the use of terms borrowed from Arab genres that are quite unlike any of the literary forms Aristotle wrote about. His misapprehension of anagnorisis was almost exclusively conceptual for, like Abū Bishr and Ibn Sīnā, he used the term *istidlāl.*

His overall view of the function of poetry was similar to Ibn Sīnā's: the representation of actions in poetry seeks to move the audience to act or not to act; in this conceptual scheme where poetry is an instrumental discourse, albeit artistic and creative, anagnorisis is a rhetorical device that enhances the perception of what is conveyed in the representation of an action. In his commentary on chapter 6, Ibn Rushd treats *istidlāl* three times; the first two instances of this are linked with spectacle, which is an awkward conflation on Ibn Rushd's part since Aristotle meant recognition in chapter 6 simply as an ingredient of plot not spectacle: 'There are three things compared in eulogy: character, beliefs, and spectacle – I mean, discovery [*istidlāl*] of the correctness of a belief' (Butterworth trans., p. 76).[9] The third instance is closer to Aristotle's description of the two principal ingredients of plot, reversal and recognition:

> the mythic plot has two parts. That is, every representation is prepared either by starting with a representation of its contrary and then passing to its proper representation – and this was known as reversal – or the object itself is represented without the representation of the opposite taking place – and this is what they used to call discovery (Butterworth trans., p. 77).

Here quite clearly *istidlāl* is a rhetorical device reminiscent of antithetical figures of *badī*ᶜ; Ibn Rushd is close in his understanding of this point to Ibn Sīnā, as we have seen, for whom 'discovery' is a movement from good to better the better to perceive the good. In both instances the philosophers gave to their understanding of anagnorisis an essentially thematic gloss rather than a structural one: that is, anagnorisis is a way of emphasising an underlying theme rather than a structural point where the truth comes dramatically to light.

These views are essentially reiterated and explained further by example in his comments on chapter 11; the meaning of *istidlāl* becomes clear by virtue of its contrast with reversal:

> by reversal, I mean first representing the contrary of what is intended to be praised by something that the soul dislikes and then turning to a representation of the praised thing itself – as when one wants to represent happiness and happy people one begins by first representing misery and miserable people, then turns to a representation of happy people and does so by means of the contrary of that by which he represented miserable people (Butterworth trans., p. 87).

From this he states more tersely about anagnorisis/discovery that it is 'simply the representation of something'; in this last statement mimesis and anagnorisis are virtually commensurate with each other. It would in fact be hard to gauge what exactly Ibn Rushd meant, and how distant he is from Aristotle, if he didn't furnish examples from the mainstream canon of Arabic poetry; thus to illustrate the combination of reversal and recognition (i.e. Aristotle's complex dramatic plot) he quotes two lines from al-Mutanabbī:

> Many a stealthy visit shrewder than the wolf's
> Did I make to you among the Bedouins as
> They slumbered;
>
> I slip among them while night's blackness
> Intercedes for me,
> And I turn back as dawn's whiteness tempts me away[10] (Butterworth trans., p. 88).

Discovery/recognition is contained in the first verse, Ibn Rushd tells us; reversal in the second. How *istidlāl* inheres in the first is not entirely clear, other than by virtue of the fact that there is no negative contrast – no reversal. There is simply a shrewd visit (like the wolf's) and a comparatively even shrewder one (like the poet's). The effect of contrast that discovery requires is positive rather than negative. Reversal is evident in the second verse from the contrast between the black night and the white dawn which turns the poet's visit into a flight. The two verses conjure images, not movements in a narrative plot, and show that reversal and discovery were conceived by Ibn Rushd as devices to enhance cognitive perception in a process of imaginative representation: thus broadly operating within a conception of *muḥākāt* (mimesis of reality) and more particularly within the related subfacet of *takhyīl* (poetic imagination).

The misunderstandings outlined above lead to further misconstrual in the six-part typology of chapter 16. According to Ibn Rushd recognition happens:

1. by the imitation of 'sense-perceptible things' through other sense-perceptible things;
2. by the imitation of abstract concepts using sense-perceptible things;
3. through memory;
4. comparing one person to another in terms of physical constitution or natural temperament;
5. false exaggeration: here Ibn Rushd gives a splendid example from al-Nābighah al-Dhubyāni: 'The swords cut through the double-knit coat of mail and ignite on the plate-armor the fire of the firefly';
6. personification.

Ibn Rushd then effectively adds a seventh category: 'the best recognition and reversal comes in respect of willed actions', that is, happen in respect of desirable or reprehensible actions such as are often lauded or censured in the Qurʾan. This idea is very vaguely related, insofar as actions are involved in the definition, to Aristotle's sixth category: that the best recognition should emerge naturally from the events or actions of a plot.

The predominant meaning of *istidlāl* as understood by Ibn Sīnā and Ibn Rushd where the underlying truth of poetic meaning is conveyed – 'discovered' – variously through illustrative comparison between two actions or things, is summed up by Lane's entry for *istadalla*:[11] 'he desired, or sought, to be directed, or guided, by a thing, to another thing'. One lexicographical gloss suggests the meaning 'to discover something that is signified by a thing'; the adjectival form *istidlālī* is used to connote knowledge that is 'inferential, illustrative, or seductive'.

If the Aristotelian concept of anagnorisis in Arabic *falsafah* was essentially pre-determined to be misconstrued (at least in its textual application), this was because the *falāsifah* had only scant, if any, knowledge of the genres of literature – the dramas and epics – for which Aristotle was providing an anatomy. But one should remember: Aristotle himself was not so much prescribing this anatomy as describing what had already evolved innately. While some aspects of what he discusses are certainly limited to the Greek canon (e.g. formal elements such as the metrics of the iambic in lampoon, etc.), the most significant elements (mimesis, catharsis, pathos, ethos and anagnorisis) are staples of most narrative traditions – and thus in various ways, which can be coloured by cultural context, are essential and universal features of all narrative. The irony that emerges, when one considers the *falāsifah* who were striving to cleave to Aristotle conceptually but largely missed the mark regarding some essentials of the *Poetics*, is that medieval authors and storytellers (high and low brow; celebrated and anonymous) knew or reworked instinctively what Aristotle meant by anagnorisis; and of course in the modern period Arab literary critics are both familiar with Aristotle's models, a fact that may nourish their understanding of all literature generally (e.g. Kilito and al-Zayyāt), and may use his concepts aptly in discussion of their own literature without being either consciously or exclusively Aristotelian. In either case, anagnorisis tends to be rendered by the terms *taᶜarruf* or *iᶜtirāf*.

Notes

1. Al-Zayyāt, Laṭīfah, *Ḥawl al-iltizām al-siyāsī wa-l-kitābah al-nisāʾiyyah*, *Alif* 10 (1990). For a discussion of *iᶜtirāf* as an ethical, cognitive and philosophical subject in contemporary Arabic thought, see Ali Benmakhlouf's (ed.), *Al-Iᶜtirāf: ḥiwārāt falsafiyyah* (Casablanca: Editions Le Fennec, 2011). It has little relevance to the study of narrative other than showing that 'confession' may be the form anagnorisis takes, as it does often in Rabīᶜ Jābir's short and powerful novel *al-Iᶜtirāfāt* – a title which can be translated into English either as 'The Recognitions' or 'The Confessions' (the novel is indeed about both).
2. Aristotle's *Poetics*, trans. Malcolm Heath (London: Penguin, 1996), p. 12.
3. Heath, *Poetics*, p. 14.
4. Cf. Stephen Halliwell, *Aristotle's* Poetics (Chicago, University of Chicago Press, 1998), pp. 143–4, on the interpretive problems of chapter 16. Aristotle makes further reference to recognition in chapter 17 in a brief synopsis of the *Odyssey* which he observed was integrated as a story around the return of Odysseus, and in a significant remark that 'recognition pervades' this particular epic (chapter

23; Heath, *Poetics*, p. 39). The distinct structural implications of this are not explored.

5. See D. S. Margoliouth, *Analecta Orientalia ad poeticam Aristoteleam* (New York: Georg Olms Verlag, 2000), pp. 1–76.
6. See now Kilito's facetious critique of Mattā ibn Yūnus's mistranslations of tragedy and comedy in *Lan tatakallam lughatī*. It has been translated by Waïl Hassan as *Thou Shalt Not Speak My Language* (Syracuse: State University of New York Press, 2008).
7. See Margoliouth, *Analecta,* pp. 80–113.
8. Ibid., p. 96.
9. Charles E. Butterworth (trans.), *Averroes' Middle Commentary on Aristotle's* Poetics (Princeton: Princeton University Press: 1985).
10. *Kam zawratan laka fī l-a*[c]*rābi khāfiyatin / adhā wa-qad raqadū min zawrati l-dhībī. Azūruhum wa-sawādu l-layli yashfa*[c]*u lī / wa-anthanī wa-bayāḍu l-ṣubḥi yughrī bī.*
11. Edward Lane, *Arabic-English Lexicon*, 2 vols (Cambridge: Islamic Texts Society, 1984).

Glossary

Abraham	Ibrāhīm in Arabic, the biblical prophet often mentioned in Islamic genealogies that include Abraham, Isaac and Jacob
Abū Ṭālib	the father of ᶜAlī b. Abī Ṭālib and uncle of the Prophet Muḥammmad
Abū Zayd	the roguish protagonist of al-Harīrī's *maqāmāt*
adab	Arabic belles-lettres; the root contains the meaning of edification
agnoia	biblical greek for 'ignorance', 'inadvertence', sometimes with the sense of 'willfull blindness'
aḥsan al-qaṣaṣ	'the most beautiful of storytelling': verse 3 of Surah 12, referring to the ensuing story of Joseph
ᶜĀᵓishah	according to the Muslim tradition she was the favourite (and young) wife of the Prophet in his latter years; she was the daughter of his close ally Abū Bakr
akhbār (sing. *khabar*)	anecdotes and stories typically occuring in early Arabic prose collections, both religious and edifying
allusion (Ar. *kināyah*)	this can be considered the principal trope, used with great deftness, in the *maqāmāt* of al-Ḥarīrī
Arabian Nights	a title used in English for *The Thousand and One Nights*
Arabian Nights' Entertainments	the original English title of *The Thousand and One Nights* in the earliest eighteenth-century translation; the title was commonly abbreviated to the *Arabian Nights* by the nineteenth century
asbāb al-nuzūl	'the causes of revelation'; the body of writing describing the real life occasions of revelation for particular Qurᵓanic verses or passages
Avicenna	the medieval European name for Ibn Sīnā (d. 1037 AD); he was a philosopher, medical doctor, polymath and wrote an eccentric commentary on Aristotle's *Poetics*

ayah	a verse of the Qurʾan; it is invested with the meaning of both 'sign' and 'miracle'
āyāt	'signs' – verses of the Qurʾan
bathos	a figure of speech, referring to a comic drop in register of language or speech
Children of Israel	the Qurʾanic way of referring to the Jews of Arabia
ḍalāl	'error'; the original meaning is of 'being lost', of 'wandering off the right track'; its antonym is *rushd*, which came to mean 'right guidance'
deus ex machina	the resolving of plot over-hastily by improbable, and originally mechanical, means (a player being lifted magically into proceedings)
eloquence vs. *ʿajama*	the latter is the Arabic root for speaking in a foreign tongue; Arabic is associated with clarity and eloquence
faraj baʿd al-shiddah	'deliverance after hardship'; there is a genre of medieval Arabic stories that illustrate the subject according to a providential plan; the most famous collection is by al-Tanūkhī (d. 994 AD)
al-Hamadhānī (d. 1007 AD)	a man of letters and the creator of the *maqāmāt* which provided the basic model of those composed by al-Ḥarīrī a century later
ḥamiyyat al-jāhiliyyah	'the blind zeal of the Age of Ignorance', i.e. pre-Islamic times
al-Ḥarīrī (d. 1122 AD)	Arab scholar, man of letters and high ranking official in the Saljūq bureaucracy, he is best know for his collection of fictional *maqāmāt*, developing the model he inherited from al-Hamadhānī
al-Ḥaqq	'the Truth'; in Sufi (mystical) circles the noun was often used simply to refer to God
ḥattā ḥīn	a phrase used strategically in Surah 12 meaning 'until a certain period of time'; though quite prosaic it implies a divine, providential scheme of narrative
Heliodorus's *Aethiopica*	the most complex of the Greek novels or romances of the Hellenistic period; Heliodorus was from Emesa and lived in the third or fourth century AD
Ibn Hishām (d. 833 AD)	editor and redactor of the most commonly read Sunni Life of the Prophet (or *Sīrah*) based largely on the earlier redaction of Ibn Isḥāq (d. *c.*770 AD)

Ibn Isḥāq (d. *c.*770 AD)	collector of oral traditions that formed the basis of a biography of the prophet Muḥammad; his work does not survive in a full, integral text but can be largely reconstituted from the work of subsequent scholars, primarily Ibn Hishām but also later historians, such as al-Ṭabarī (d. 923 AD)
ʿibrah (pl. *ʿibar*)	a Qurʾanic term meaning a 'didactic lesson'; the stories of the biblical and Arabian prophets are often told as *ʿibar* for the nascent Muslim community
iḥsān	lit. 'doing good or doing things well'; an ethical substrate informed the verbal noun which can also mean '(pious-minded) generosity'
ʿilm	'knowledge'; it is also the word used for science and can be considered equivalent to the French 'savoir'; the French 'connaître' is captured more by the Arabic root *ʿa-ra-fa*
īmān	'faith or religious belief'
inkār	'denial', 'rejection', 'the inability to recognise'; the verbal form has both cognitive and ethical connotations, depending on context; it is the antonym of *maʿrifah*
al-Jāḥiẓ (d. *c.*869 AD)	polymath, intellectual and prodigious essayists; considered among the fathers of Arabic prose literature
jahl	'ignorance'; it has more than a mere cognitive sense: it can refer to the absence of any or all the qualities and virtues that marked the late pre-Islamic and early Islamic tribal code
jinn	the Arabic plural for 'genies' (sing. *jinnīyun*)
Kaʿbah	the rectangular sanctuary built in Mecca by Abraham according to Muslim belief; it constitutes the geographical centre-point of the Islamic faith
maghāzī	the battles and raids fought by the Prophet Muḥammad and his companions after his migration to Medina; the earliest biographies of the Prophet are referred to as *maghāzī*
majlis	a place in someone's home where people congregate and sit to take part in conversation
maqāmāt (or sing. *maqāmah*, 'séances' or 'assemblies')	a genre of picaresque narratives that was given its recognisable form by Badīʿ al-Zamān al-Hamadhānī (d. 1008 AD) but which was perfected as a form in the work of al-Ḥarīrī
maʿrifah and *maʿrūf*	'knowledge, recognition' and 'right, goodness, generosity (lit. what is known as right practice: the antonym of *inkār* and *munkar*)'

Maryam	the mother of Jesus; Surah 19 of the Qur$^{\circ}$an, commonly named after her, tells the story of the annunciation according to Muslim belief
méconnaissance	the French for *inkār* (qv)
Medina	known as Yathrib in pre-Islamic times, it came to be known as Medina, short for Medinat al-Nabī (City of the Prophet), early in Islamic times
Muḥammad	the Prophet Muḥammad ibn ^{c}Abdallah of the Meccan tribe of the Quraysh who preached Islam based on the revelation of the Qur$^{\circ}$an to him by the angel Gabriel between *c.* 610 and his death in 632 AD
munkar	that which is 'unknown, to be rejected or denied, unworthy, wicked, evil', the antonym of *ma^{c}rūf*
paronomasia	punning on verbal roots, known in Arabic as *jinās*, it became a prominent trope among the poets of the Muḥdath period, from the end of the eighth century AD onwards
peripeteia	'reversal of action' in the plot of a tragedy or comedy, first identified as a constituent of plot in Aristotle's *Poetics*; the best reversals come together with anagnorisis
Potiphar	the name given in Genesis for the Egyptian notable who bought Joseph as a slave; in the Qur$^{\circ}$an he is referred to simply as 'al-^{c}Azīz' ('the nobleman')
pre-Islamic Arabia	this phrase refers to the Arabian peninsula during the century before the coming of Islam; many features of Islamic culture were prefigured in this period
qaṣaṣ	'storytelling'
qiblah	the direction of prayer in Islam; originally Jerusalem it was changed in the early Medinese period, as referred to in Surah 2, to Mecca
qiṣaṣ	'stories, tales' (Surah 12 uses the verbal noun of this root to describe 'the best of storytelling': *aḥsan al-qaṣaṣ*)
Quraysh	the powerful Meccan tribal group to which the Prophet Muḥammad belonged
romance	a story type which has a strong providential veneer, and features a plot of separation and adventure followed by eventual reunion (of family members or lovers)
ṣadaqah	alms (noteworthy is that the word is formed from the verbal root, *ṣidq*, meaning 'truth, sincerity')

Salmān al-Fārisī	the first Zoroastrian convert to Islam whose journey in search of Muḥammad is told at length and accorded great significance in Ibn Hishām's redaction of the *Sīrah*
shiddah	'distress, misadventure, evil', the antonym of *faraj* ('deliverance, relief'); it is used in the definition of an important genre of *adab* literature: *faraj baʿd al-shiddah* ('deliverance from evil')
ṣidq	'truth, sincerity'
siḥr	'magic'; it has a negative connotation in the Qurʾan especially evident in the description of the magicians at Pharaoh's court in accounts of Moses in Egypt
sīrah	'biography'; the most important biography in Sunni Islam is the *Sīrah* of the Prophet Muḥammad redacted by Ibn Hishām (d. 833 AD), which draws principally on the earlier authority of Ibn Isḥāq and Ibn Shihāb al-Zuhrī
surah	a chapter of the Qurʾan; there are 114 in total, varying in length, style and content
tafsīr	Qurʾanic exegesis and commentary; largely synonymous with *taʾwīl*, though the latter came to be identified more with hermetic or mystical commentary
al-Tanūkhī	Abū ʿAlī al-Muḥassin ibn ʿAlī al-Tanūkhī (d. 994 AD), one of the most significant men of letters in tenth-century AD Arabic belles-lettristic culture; he is the collector of two of the most significant story collections in Abbasid culture, the *Nishwār al-muḥāḍarah* and the *Faraj baʿd al-shiddah*
tawḥīd	'the unity of God'; the term defines the strict theological concept that underpins Islamic belief; it is effectively the antonym of *shirk* ('associating deities with God's divinity')
taʾwīl/*taʾwīl al-aḥādīth*	'interpretation, exegesis', 'the interpretation of events (as sometimes related in dreams)'
waḥy	'inspiration'
ẓanna	'to think, conjecture'; in the Qurʾan and related literature the root often has a negative connotation that contrasts it with 'certain knowledge' (*ʿilm al-yaqīn*)
Zulaykha	the name given in the Qurʾanic exegesis and the Islamic apocryphal tradition of prophetic stories to the wife of Potiphar (qv); she remains nameless in the Qurʾan, referred to simply as *imraʾat al-ʿAzīz* (qv)

Bibliography

Adams, Barry B., *Coming-to-Know: Recognition and the Complex Plot in Shakespeare* (New York: Peter Lang, 2000).

Alf laylah wa-laylah (*The Thousand and One Nights, a.k.a. The Arabian Nights*)

———'Būlāq edition', 2 vols (Cairo: Būlāq, 1835).

———'Calcutta II', *Alif Laila or Book of the Thousand Nights and One Night (commonly known as The Arabian Nights' Entertainment)*, ed. W. H. Macnaghten, 4 vols (Calcutta, 1839–42).

———'Breslau edition', *Tausend und eine Nacht*, ed. Christian Maximillian Habicht, 12 vols (Breslau, 1825–43).

———'Syrian recension', *The Thousand and One Nights* (Alf Layla wa-layla) *From the Earliest Known Sources*, Arabic text, ed. and notes by Muhsin Mahdi, 2 vols (Leiden: Brill, 1984).

Alter, Robert, *The Art of Biblical Narrative* (New York: Basic Books, 1981).

———*Genesis*, translation and commentary (New York: Norton, 1996).

Alter, Robert, and Frank Kermode (eds), *The Literary Guide to the Bible* (Cambridge: Harvard University Press, 1987).

Anon., *al-Siyāsah wa-l-ḥīlah ʿinda l-ʿarab: Raqāʾiq al-ḥilal fī daqāʾiq al-ḥiyal*, ed. Renée Khawam, revised by Nāzik Sābā Yārid (London: al-Sāqī, 1988).

Arberry, Arthur J. (trans.), *The Koran Interpreted* (Oxford: Oxford University Press, 1983).

Aristotle, *Poetics*, Greek and English texts, trans. Stephen Halliwell (Cambridge, MA: Loeb Classical Library, 1995).

———*Poetics*, trans. Malcolm Heath (London: Penguin, 1996).

———*Analecta Orientalia ad poeticam Aristoteleam*, ed. David Samuel Margoliouth (Hildesheim, Zurich, New York: Georg Olms Verlag, 2000).

Ashtiany Bray, Julia, '*Isnāds* and Models of Heroes', *Arabic and Middle Eastern Literatures* 1:1 (1998). [See also Bray]

Attar, Farid ud-Din, *The Conference of the Birds*, trans. Afkham Darbandi and Dick Davis (London: Penguin, 1984).

Ayoub, Mahmoud M., *The Interpretation of the Qurʾān* (Albany: State University of New York Press, 1984).

ᶜAwad, Luīs, '*al-Ḥubb fī Sān Lazār*' ('Love at Saint Lazare Station'), in *Plutoland* (Cairo: Maṭbaᶜat al-Karnak, 1948).

ᶜAyyād, Shukrī (ed.) *Kitāb Arisṭūṭālīs fī l-Shiᶜr (naql Abī Bishr Mattā ibn Yūnus al-Qunnāᶜī min al-Suryānī ilā al-ᶜArabī* (Cairo: Dār al-Kitāb al-ᶜArabī li-l-Ṭibāᶜah wa-l-Nashr, 1967).

Badawī, A., *Arisṭūṭālīs: Fann al-Shiᶜr, maᶜa al-tarjamah al-ᶜarabiyyah al-qadīmah wa-shurūḥ al-Farābī wa-Ibn Sīnā wa-Ibn Rushd* (Cairo, 1952).

al-Baghdādī, Abū Bakr Aḥmad ibn ᶜAlī al-Khaṭīb, *Tārīkh Baghdād*, vol. 7 (Beirut: Dār al-Kutub al-ᶜArabī, 1931).

Barnes, Julian, *The Sense of an Ending* (London: Vintage Books, 2012).

Barthes, Roland, *S/Z* (Paris: Le Seuil, 1970).

Bayḍāwī, *Bayḍāwī's Commentary of Surah 12 of the Qur'ān: Text, Accompanied by an Interpretative Rendering and Notes*, trans. A. F. L. Beeston (Oxford: Oxford University Press, 1963).

Beaumont, Daniel, '"Peut-on . . .": Intertextual Relations in the *Arabian Nights* and Genesis', *Comparative Literature* 50:2 (Spring 1998), pp. 120–35.

———'Trickster and Rhetoric in the *Maqāmāt*', *Edebiyât* 5 (1994), pp. 1–14.

Beeston, A. F. L., 'The Genesis of the *Maqāmāt* Genre', *Journal of Arabic Literature* 2 (1971).

Bellino, Francesca, 'Tamīm al-Dārī the Intrepid Traveller: Emergence, Growth and Making of a Legend in Arabic Literature'. Available at: http://arabistica.academia.edu/FrancescaOdiliaBellino/Papers/1265608/Islamic_legends_OM_Tamim_al-Dari_the_Intrepid_traveller.

Benmakhlouf, Ali (ed.), *Al-Iᶜtirāf: ḥiwārāt falsafiyyah/La Reconnaissance* (Casablanca: Editions Le Fennec, 2011).

The Bible, *The Oxford Study Bible* (Oxford: Oxford University Press, 1992).

Boitani, Piero, *The Tragic and the Sublime in Medieval Literature* (Cambridge: Cambridge University Press, 1989).

———*The Bible and its Rewritings*, trans. Anita Weston (Oxford: Oxford University Press, 1999).

———*The Genius to Improve an Invention: Literary Transitions* (Notre Dame, IN: Notre Dame University Press, 2002).

Borges, Jorge Luis, 'Tom Castro, the Implausible Impostor' and 'The Masked Dyer,

Hakim of Merv', in Norman Thomas di Giovanni (trans.), *Universal History of Infamy* (New York: E. P. Dutton, 1972).

Boulhol, Pascal, *Anagnorismos: la scène de reconnaissance dans l'hagiographie antique et médiévale* (Aix-en-Provence: Université de Provence, 1996).

Bray, Julia, 'ᶜAbbasid Myth and the Human Act: Ibn ᶜAbd Rabbih and Others', in Philip F. Kennedy (ed.), *On Fiction and* Adab *in Medieval Arabic Literature* (Wiesbaden: Harrassowitz Verlag, 2006).

———(ed.), *Writing and Representation in Medieval Islam – Muslim Horizons* (London: Routledge, 2006).

———'Place and self-image: the Buhlūlids and Tanūḫids and their family traditions', in Antonella Ghersetti (ed.), *Quaderni di Studi Arabi* 3: *Luoghi e immaginario nella letteratura araba* (Rome: IPOCAN, 2008), pp. 39–66.

———'Christian King, Muslim Apostate: Depictions of Jabala ibn al-Ayham in Early Arabic Sources', in Arietta Papaconstantinou (ed.), *Writing 'True Stories'* (Turnhout: Brepols, 2010), pp. 175–203.

Brockopp, Jonathan E. (ed.), *The Cambridge Companion to Muḥammad* (Cambridge: Cambridge University Press, 2010).

al-Bukhārī, *Saḥīḥ al-Bukhārī*, eds Ahmad Zahwah and Ahmad ᶜInayah (Beirut: Dar al-Kitāb al-ᶜArabi, 2011). [for *Ḥadīth al-Ifk*, see pp. 533–6]

Burton, Sir Richard F., *The Book of the Thousand Nights and a Night: A Plain and Literal Translation of the Arabian Nights Entertainments*, 10 vols (London, 1885–8).

Butterworth, Charles E. (trans.), *Averroes' Middle Commentary on Aristotle's* Poetics (Princeton: Princeton University Press: 1985).

———'Translation and Philosophy: The Case of Averroes' Commentaries', *International Journal of Middle East Studies* 26:1 (February 1994).

Calder, Norman, '*Tafsīr* from Ṭabarī to Ibn Kathīr: Problems in the Description of a Genre, Illustrated with References to the Story of Abraham', in G. R. Hawting and A.-K. A. Shareef (eds), *Approaches to the Qurᵓān* (London: Routledge, 1993).

Carter, Angela, *Nights at the Circus* (London: Chatto & Windus, 1984).

Castelvetro, Lodovico, *Castelvetro on the Art of Poetry: An Abridged Translation of Lodovico Castelvetro's* Poetica d'Aristotele Vulgarizzata et Sposta, ed. and trans. Andrew Bongiorno (Binghamton: Medieval and Renaissance Texts and Studies, 1984).

Cave, Terence, *Recognitions: A Study in Poetics* (Oxford: Clarendon Press, 1988).

CHALUP, *Cambridge History of Arabic Literature to the End of the Umayyad Period*, eds A. F. L. Beeston, T. M. Johnstone, R. B. Serjeant and G. R. Smith (Cambridge: Cambridge University Press, 1983).

Cheikho, Luwīs (ed.), *Majānī al-adab fī ḥadāʾiq al-ʿarab*, 6 vols (Beirut: Jesuit Fathers' Press, 1910–13).

Chenery, Thomas, and F. W. Steingass (trans.), *The Assemblies of al-Harīrī*, 2 vols (London: Williams and Norgate, 1867/1898): vol. 1, *The First Twenty-six Assemblies*, trans. T. Chenery (1867); vol. 2, *The Last Twenty-four Assemblies*, trans. F. W. Steingass (1898).

Clouston, W. A., *Popular Tales and Fictions. Their Migrations and Transformations* (Whitefish: Kessinger Publishing, 2003).

Conrad, Joseph, *Under Western Eyes* (New York: Harper & Brothers, 1911).

Cook, Michael, *Commanding Right and Forbidding Wrong in Islamic Thought* (Cambridge: Cambridge University Press, 2000).

Cooperson, Michael, 'Baghdad in Rhetoric and Narrative', *Muqarnas: An annual on the visual culture of the Islamic world* 13 (1996), pp. 99–113.

Corbin, Henry, *Avicenna and the Visionary Recital*, trans. Willard R. Trask, Bollingen Series LXVI (New York: Pantheon Books, 1960).

Culbertson, Diane, *The Poetics of Revelation: Recognition and the Narrative Tradition* (Macon: Mercer University Press, 1989).

Cuypers, Michel, 'Structures rhétoriques dans le Coran. Une analyse structurelle de la sourate "Joseph" et de quelques sourates brèves', *Midéo* 22 (1995).

Dahiyat, Ismail M. (trans.), *Avicenna's Commentary on the* Poetics *of Aristotle: a critical study with an annotated translation of the text* (Brill: Leiden, 1974).

Al-Dārimī, ʿAbdullāh ibn ʿAbd al-Raḥmān, *Sunan al-Dārimī*, eds ʿAlī Sayyid Ibrāhīm and Muṣṭafā al-Dhahabī (Cairo: Dār al-Ḥadīth, 2000).

Davis, Natalie Zemon, *The Return of Martin Guerre* (Cambridge, MA: Harvard University Press, 1983).

Diʿbil ibn ʿAlī al-Khuzāʿī, *Dīwān*, ed. ʿAbd al-Ṣaḥib ʿImrān al-Dujaylī (Beirut: Dār al-Kitāb al-Lubnānī, 1972).

Dols, Michael, *Majnūn: The Madman in Medieval Islamic Society*, ed. Diana E. Immisch (Oxford: Clarendon Press, 1992).

Doniger, Wendy, *The Bedtrick: Tales of Sex and Masquerade* (Chicago: University of Chicago Press, 2000).

———*The Woman Who Pretended To Be Who She Was: Myths of Self-Imitation* (Oxford: Oxford University Press, 2005).

———'Narrative Conventions and Rings of Recognition', in Philip F. Kennedy and

Marilyn Lawrence (eds), *Recognition: The Poetics of Narrative. Interdisciplinary Studies on Anagnorisis* (New York: Peter Lang, 2008).

Fahd, Toufiq, *La Divination arabe: études religieuses, sociologiques et folkloriques sur le milieu natif de l'Islam* (Paris: Sindbad, 1987).

Fielding, Henry, *The History of Tom Jones, A Foundling* (first published by Andrew Millar, 1749).

Fowden, Garth, *Empire to Commonwealth: Consequences of Monotheism in Late Antiquity* (Princeton: Princeton University Press, 1993).

Frye, Northrop, *Anatomy of Criticism: Four Essays* (Princeton, Princeton University Press, [1957] 1971).

———*The Secular Scripture: A Study of the Structure of Romance* (Cambridge, MA: Harvard University Press, 1976).

———*Fables of Identity: Studies in Poetic Mythology* (San Diego: Harcourt Brace, 1989).

Galford, Hugh, 'Sayyid Qutb and the Qur'anic Story of Joseph: A Commentary for Today', in Ronald L. Nettler and Suha Taji-Farouki (eds), *Muslim-Jewish Encounters, Intellectual Traditions and Muslim Politics* (Amsterdam: Harwood Academic Publishers, 1998).

Galland, Antoine, *Les Mille et une Nuits* (Paris: GF-Flammarion, 1965).

van Gelder, Geert Jan, 'Slave-girl lost and regained: transformations of a story', in Ulrich Marzolph (ed.), *The Arabian Nights in Transnational Perspective* (Detroit: Wayne State University Press, 2007).

———'Fools and Rogues in Discourse and Disguise: Two Studies', in Robin Ostle (ed.), *Sensibilities of the Islamic Mediterranean: Self-Expression in Muslim Culture from Classical Times to the Present Day* (London: I. B. Tauris, 2008), pp. 27–58.

———*Classical Arabic Literature: A Library of Arabic Literature Anthology* (New York: New York University Press, 2012).

Ginzberg, Louis, *The Legends of the Jews* (Philadelphia: Jewish Publication Society, 2003).

Goldziher, Ignaz, *Muslim Studies*, 2 vols, ed. S. M. Stern, trans. C. R. Barber (Piscataway: Aldine Transaction, 2006).

Goodman, L. E., 'Hamadhānī, Schadenfreude, and Salvation Through Sin', *Journal of Arabic Literature* 19 (1988).

Grabar, Oleg, 'Pictures or Commentaries: The Illustrations of the *Maqāmāt* of al-Ḥarīrī', in Peter J. Chelkowski (ed.), *Studies in Art and Literature of the Near East* (Salt Lake City: Middle Eastern Center, University of Utah, 1974).

———*The Illustrations of the Maqāmāt* (Chicago: University of Chicago Press, 1984).

Guillaume, Alfred, *The Life of Muhammad: A Translation of Ibn Isḥāq's* Sīrat Rasūl Allāh (Oxford: Oxford University Press, 1955).

Haase, Fee-Alexandra, 'Comparison of the Hebrew Writings and Bible (Genesis 37–42) with Quranic Sura Yusuf as Example for Cultural Adaption. A Study of a Cross-Cultural Differentiation Process of Textual and Oral Traditions for Religious Writings under the Historical Conditions of Middle East Societies', *Journal of Religious Culture* 105 (2008).

Habicht, Christian Maximilian, *Tausend und eine Nacht: Arabische erzählungen* (Leipzig: F. W. Hendel, 1926).

Haddawy, Husain, *The Arabian Nights* (New York: Norton, 1988).

Halliwell, Stephen, *Aristotle's* Poetics (Chicago, University of Chicago Press, 1998).

Halm, Heinz, *The Empire of the Mahdi: The Rise of the Fatimids*, trans. M. Bonner (Leiden: Brill, 1991).

al-Hamadhānī, Badī[c] al-Zamān, *Al-Maqāmāt*, ed. and comm. by Muḥammad [c]Abduh (Beirut: Dār al-Mashriq, [1889] 1973).

———*The Maqamat of Badi' al-Zaman al-Hamadhani*, trans. from the Arabic, with introduction and notes by W. J. Prendergast (London: Curzon, [1915] 1973; Lexington: Forgotten Books, 2008).

Hamarneh, Walid, 'The Reception of Aristotle's Theory of Poetry in Arab-Islamic Medieval Thought', in Milena Dolezelova-Velingerova (ed.), *Poetics East and West* (Toronto: Toronto Semiotic Circle, 1989). [see herein for a detailed general bibliography on the subject of Aristotelian poetics and Islamic philosophy/Arabic poetry]

Hämeen-Anttila, Jaakko, '"We Will Tell You the Best of Stories": A Study of Surah XII', *Studia Orientalia* 67 (1991), pp. 7–32.

———'The Author and his Sources: An Analysis of al-Maqāma al-Bishrīya', *Wiener Zeitschrift für die Kunde des Morgenlandes* 88 (1998).

———*Maqama: A History of a Genre* (Wiesbaden: Harrassowitz Verlag, 2002).

Hamori, Andras, 'The Magian and the Whore: Readings of Qamar al-Zaman', in Kay Hardy Campbell *et al.* (eds), *The 1001 Nights: Critical Essays and Annotated Bibliography* (Cambridge, MA: Dar Mahjar, 1985).

——— 'The House of Brotherly Love: A Story in *al-Tanūḫī's Nišwār al-muḥādara* and in *The Thousand and One Nights*', in Miklós Maróth (ed.), *Problems in Arabic Literature* (Piliscsaba: The Avicenna Institute of Middle Eastern Studies, 2004), pp. 15–26.

Hardison, O. B., 'The Place of Averroes' Commentary on the *Poetics* in the History of Medieval Criticism', *Medieval and Renaissance Studies* 4 (1968) (Proceedings of the Southeastern Institute of Medieval and Renaissance Studies, ed. John L. Lievsay).

al-Ḥarīrī, Abū Muḥammad al-Qāsim ibn ᶜAlī b. Muḥammad ibn ᶜUthmān, *Maqāmāt al Ḥarīrī*. See al-Sharīshī.

———*The Assemblies of al-Harīrī*, 2 vols (London: Williams and Norgate, 1867/1898): vol. 1, *The First Twenty-six Assemblies*, trans. Chenery (1867); vol. 2, *The Last Twenty-four Assemblies*, trans. Steingass (1898).

Hava, J. G., *Arabic-English Dictionary* (Beirut: Catholic Press, 1951).

Haykel, Bernard, 'Dissembling Descent, or How the Barber Lost his Turban: Identity and Evidence in Eighteenth Century Zaydī Yemen', *Islamic Law and Society* 9:2 (2002), pp. 194–230.

Heath, Malcolm (trans.), *Aristotle's* Poetics (London: Penguin, 1996).

Heath, Peter, 'Romance as Genre in the *Thousand and One Nights*' parts I and II, *Journal of Arabic Literature* 18 and 19 (1987).

Heliodorus, *The Aethiopica*, trans. Sir Walter Lamb, ed. with new introduction and notes by J. R. Morgan (London: Everyman, 1997).

Hertz, J. H., *The Pentateuch and Haftorahs: Hebrew Text, English Translation and Commentary* (London: Soncino Press, 1960).

Horovitz, Joseph, 'Salmān al-Fārisī', *Der Islam* 12 (1922), pp. 178–80.

Hoyland, Robert G., 'The Islamic Background to Polemon's Treatise', in Simon Swain (ed.), *Seeing the Face, Seeing the Soul: Polemon's Physiognomy from Classical Antiquity to Medieval Islam (*Oxford: Oxford University Press, 2007).

Humphreys, W. Lee, *Joseph and His Family: A Literary Study* (Columbia: University of South Carolina Press, 1988).

al-Ḥuṣrī, Abū Isḥāq Ibrāhīm ibn ᶜAlī, *Zahr al-ādāb wa-thamar al-albāb*, eds Zakī Mubārak and Muḥammad Muḥyī l-Dīn ᶜAbd al-Ḥamīd, 4 vols in 2 (Beirut: Dār al-Jīl, 1972).

Huxley, Aldous, see http://www.brainyquote.com/quotes/authors/a/aldous_huxley_4.html.

Ibn ᶜAbd Rabbih, *Al-ᶜIqd al-farīd*, 7 vols (Cairo, 1948–1953; repr. Beirut: Dār al-Kitāb al-ᶜArabī, 1983).

Ibn ᶜAsākir, *Tārīkh Dimashq*, ed. ᶜAbd al-Qādir Badran, vol. 3, (Damascus: 1911).

Ibn Ḥabīb, Muḥammad, *Al-Muhabbar*, ed. Ilse Lichstenstädter (Hyderabad: Dāᵓirat al-Maᶜārif al-ᶜUthmāniyyah, 1942).

Ibn Hishām, *Al-Sīrah al-nabawiyyah*, ed. Muḥammad Fahmy al-Sirjānī, 4 vols (Cairo: al-Maktabah al-Tawfīqiyyah, 1978).

———*Al-Sīrah al-nabawiyyah*, eds Muṣṭafā al-Saqqā, Ibrāhīm al-Abyārī and ᶜAbd al-Ḥafīẓ Shalabī, 2 vols (Cairo: Muṣṭafā al-Bābī al-Ḥalabī, 1955).

Ibn Isḥāq, *The Life of Muhammad: A Translation of Ishāq's* [*sic*] Sīrat Rasūl Allāh, trans. Alfred Guillaume (Oxford: Oxford University Press, 1955).

Ibn Kathīr, Abū l-Fidāʾ Ismāᶜīl, *Tafsīr al-Qurʾān al-ᶜAẓīm*, ed. Yūsuf ᶜAbd al-Raḥmān al-Marᶜashlī (Beirut: Dār al-Maᶜrifah, 1986).

Ibn Sīnā, Abū ᶜAlī l-Ḥusayn, *Ithbāt al-nubuwwah li-Ibn Sīnā*, ed. Michael E. Marmura (Beirut: Dār al-Nahār li-l-Nashr, 1968).

Ibn Taymiyya, Aḥmad ibn ᶜAbd al-Ḥalīm, *Muqaddimah fī uṣūl al-tafsīr* (Cairo: Maktabat al-Turāth al-Islāmiyyah, 1988).

———*Al-Tafsīr al-kabīr* (Beirut: Dār al-Kutub al-ᶜIlmiyyah, 1988).

Ibn Ṭufayl, *Taʾwīlāt (Taʾwīl al-Qurʾān)* [published as *Tafsīr al-Qurʾān al-karīm* and attributed incorrectly to Ibn ᶜArabī] (Beirut: Dār al-Yaqẓah al-ᶜArabiyyah, 1968).

———*Ḥayy b. Yaqẓān: a Philosophical Tale,* trans. Lenn Evan Goodman (Chicago: University of Chicago Press, 2009).

Ibrāhīm, Muḥammad Abū l-Faḍl, *et al.* (eds), *Qiṣaṣ al-ᶜarab*, 4 vols (Beirut: al-Maktabah al-ᶜAṣriyyah, 2011).

al-Ibshīhī, *Al-Mustaṭraf fī kull fann mustaẓraf*, 2 vols (Cairo: Muṣṭafā al-Bābī al-Ḥalabī, 1952).

Irwin, Robert, *The Arabian Nights: A Companion* (London: Penguin, 1995).

———*Night and Horses and the Desert: An Anthology of Classical Arabic Literature* (London: Penguin, 1999) [reprinted as *The Penguin Anthology of Classical Arabic Literature* (London: Penguin, 2006)].

al-Iṣfahānī, Abū al-Faraj, *Kitāb al-Aghānī*, 24 vols (Cairo: Dār al-Kutub – al-Hayʾah al-Miṣriyyah al-ᶜĀmmah, 1927–74).

al-Iṣfahānī, Imam Abu Nuᶜaym, *The Beauty of the Righteous and Ranks of the Elite* (*Ḥilyat al-Awliyāʾ wa-Ṭabaqāt al-Aṣfiyāʾ*), trans. Muhammad Al-Akili (Philadelphia: Pearl Publishing House, 1996).

Jābir, Rabīᶜ, *Al-Iᶜtirāfāt* (Beirut/Casablanca: Markaz al-Thaqāfah al-ᶜArabī, 2008).

Jaᶜfar al-Ṣādiq, 'Le Tafsir Mystique attribué à Gaᶜfar Sadiq' (recension al-Sulamī), ed. Paul Nwyia, *Mélanges de l'Université Saint Joseph* 43 (1968), pp. 179–230.

Jaffer, Tariq, *Rāzī: Master of Qurʾānic Interpretation and Theological Reasoning* (Oxford: Oxford University Press, 2015).

al-Jāḥiẓ, *Al-Bukhalāʾ*, ed. Ṭāhā al-Ḥājirī (Cairo: Dār al-Maᶜārif, n.d.).

———*The Book of Misers (al-Bukhalāʾ)*, trans. R. B. Serjeant (Reading: Garnet, 1997).

Jankélévitch, Vladimir, *Le je-ne-sais-quoi et le presque-rien, vol. 2: La méconnaissance, le malentendu* (Paris: Seuil, 1980).

Jayyusi, Salma Khadra (ed.), *Classical Arabic Stories: An Anthology* (New York: Columbia University Press, 2010).

Johns, A. H., 'Quranic Presentation of the Joseph Story', in G. R. Hawting and A.-K. A. Shareef (eds), *Approaches to the Qur᾽ān* (London: Routledge, 1993).

Jones, Alan (trans.), *The Qur᾽ān* (Exeter: Gibb Memorial Trust, 2007).

Jones, J. M. B., 'The Chronology of the Maghāzī – A Textual Survey', *Bulletin of the School of Oriental and African Studies* 19:2 (June 1957), pp. 245–80.

Kemal, Selim, *The Poetics of Alfarabi and Avicenna* (Leiden: Brill, 1991).

Kennedy, Philip F., 'Some Demon Muse: structure and allusion in al-Hamadhānī's *Maqāma Iblīsiyya*', *Arabic and Middle Eastern Literatures* 2:1 (1999), pp. 115–35.

———'Reason and Revelation or A Philosopher's Squib (The Sixth Maqāma of Ibn Nāqiyā)', *Journal of Arabic and Islamic Studies* 3 (2000), pp. 84–113.

———'Recognition and Metonymy in Early Ismāᶜīlī Memoirs – the case of Ibn Ḥawshab, "Manṣūr al-Yaman" (d. 302/914)', in Robert G. Hoyland and Philip F. Kennedy (eds), *Islamic Reflections Arabic Musings. Studies in Honour of Alan Jones*. (Oxford: E. J. W. Gibb Memorial Trust Series, 2004).

———'The *Maqāmāt* as a Nexus of Interests', in Julia Bray (ed.), *Writing and Representation in Medieval Islam – Muslim Horizons* (London: Routledge, 2006).

———'Islamic Recognitions: An Overview', in Philip F. Kennedy and Marilyn Lawrence (eds), *Recognition: The Poetics of Narrative* (New York: Peter Lang, 2008).

——— and Marilyn Lawrence (eds), *Recognition: The Poetics of Narrative. Interdisciplinary Studies of Anagnorisis* (New York: Peter Lang, 2008).

——— and Marina Warner (eds), *Scheherazade's Children: Global Encounters with the* Arabian Nights (New York: New York University Press, 2013).

Kermode, Frank, *The Art of Telling: Essays on Fiction* (Cambridge, MA: Harvard University Press, 1983).

Khalidi, Tarif, 'Review of Robert Irwin's anthology of medieval Arabic literature, *Night and Horses and the Desert*', *Times Literary Supplement* 5061 (31 March 2000), p. 8.

Khoury, Elias, *Gate of the Sun*, trans. Humphrey Davies (New York: Archipelago Books, 2006).

Kilito, Abdelfattah, *al-Ghā᾽ib. Dirāsah fī maqāmah li-l-Ḥarīrī* (Casablanca: Dār Tūbqāl li-l-Nashr, 1987).

———*L'oeil et l'aiguille: essais sur 'les mille et une nuits'* (Paris: La Découverte, 1992).

———*Thou Shalt Not Speak My Language*, trans. Waïl Hassan (Syracuse: State University of New York Press, 2008).

al-Kisāʾī, Muḥammad b. ʿAbd Allāh, *The Tales of the Prophets of al-Kisaʾi*, trans. with notes by W. M. Thackston (Boston: Twayne Publishers, 1978).

Kruk, Remke, *The Warrior Women of Islam: Female Empowerment in Islamic Popular Literature* (London: I. B. Tauris, 2014).

Kugel, James L., *The God of Old: Inside the Lost World of the Bible* (New York: Free Press, 2003).

Lamoreaux, John C., *The Early Muslim Tradition of Dream Interpretation* (Albany: State University of New York Press, 2002).

Lane, Edward William (trans. and ed.), *A New Translation of the Tales of the Thousands and One Nights; Known in England as the Arabian Nights' Entertainments*, 32 parts (London: Charles Knight & Co., 1838–40).

———Lane, Edward, *Arabic-English Lexicon*, 2 vols (Cambridge: Islamic Texts Society, 1984).

Larsen, Kasper Bro, *Recognizing the Stranger: Recognition Scenes in the Gospel of John* (Leiden and Boston: Brill, 2008).

Leder, Stefan (ed.), *Storytelling in the Framework of Non-Fictional Arabic Literature* (Wiesbaden: Harrassowitz Verlag, 1998).

Leibowitz, Nehama, *Studies in Bereshit (Genesis): in the context of ancient and modern Jewish Bible commentary* (Jerusalem: World Zionist Organization, 1976).

Leites, Adrien, '*Sīra* and the Question of Tradition', in Harald Motzki (ed.), *The Biography of Muḥammad: The Issue of Sources* (Leiden: Brill, 2000).

Lowenthal, Eric I., *The Joseph Narrative in Genesis* (New York: Ktav, 1973).

Lyons, M. C., 'A Note on the *Maqāma* Form', *Pembroke Papers* 1 (1990), pp. 115–22.

MacDonald, John, 'Joseph in the Qurʾān and Muslim Commentary. A Comparative Study' *The Muslim World* 46:2 (April 1956).

Mack, Robert L. (ed.) *Arabian Nights' Entertainments* (Oxford: Oxford University Press, 1995).

Madelung, Wilfred, 'al-Mahdī', in *Encyclopaedia of Islam*, 2nd edn, vol. 5 (Leiden: Brill, 1960–2005).

Mahdi, Muhsin (ed.), *The Thousand and One Nights* (Alf Layla wa Layla), 2 vols (Leiden: Brill, 1984).

Maʿmar ibn Rāshid, *The Expeditions: An Early Biography of Muhammad*, trans. and ed. Sean Anthony (New York: New York University Press, 2014).

Mann, Thomas, *Joseph and His Brothers* [Originally published as *Joseph und Seine Brueder* in 4 vols: 1. *Die Geschichten Jakobs* (Berlin: S. Fischer, 1933); 2. *Der*

Junge Joseph (Berlin: S. Fischer, 1934); 3. *Joseph in Aegypten* (Vienna: Bermann-Fischer, 1936); 4. *Joseph, Der Ernahrer* (Vienna: Bermann-Fischer, 1943).]

Margoliouth, D. S., *Lectures on Arabic Historians* (Calcutta: University of Calcutta, 1930).

———(trans.), *The Table-Talk of a Mesopotamian Judge*, from the original Arabic (*Nishwār al-muḥāḍarah* by al-Tanūkhī), *Islamic Culture* 3–6 (Hyderabad, 1929–33).

———*Analecta Orientalia ad poeticam Aristoteleam* ([London: D. Nutt, 1887] New York: Georg Olms Verlag, 2000) [see also Aristotle]

Marzolph, Ulrich (ed.), *The Arabian Nights in Transnational Perspective* (Detroit: Wayne State University Press, 2007).

al-Marzubāni, Muḥammad ibn ᶜImrān, *Nūr al-qabas al-mukhtaṣar min al-Muqtabas fī akhbār al-nuḥāt wa-l-ᵓudabāᵓ wa-l-shuᶜarāᵓ wa-l-ᶜulamāᵓ (Die Gelehrtenbiographien)*, ed. Rudolf Sellheim (Wiesbaden: Franz Steiner, 1964).

al-Masᶜūdī, *Les prairies d'or*, trans. Barbier de Meynard and Pavet de Courteille, rev. Charles Pellat, 5 vols (Paris: Société Asiatique, 1962–97).

———*Murūj al-dhahab*, ed. Barbier de Meynard and Pavet de Courteille, rev. C. Pellat, 7 vols (Beirut: al-Jāmiᶜah al-Lubnāniyyah, 1966–79).

———*The Meadows of Gold: The Abbasids*, trans. Paul Lunde and Caroline Stone (London: Kegan Paul International, 1989).

al-Maybudī, Rashīd al-Dīn, *Kashf al-asrār wa ᶜuddat al-abrār*, ed. ᶜA. A. Ḥikmat (Tehran: Amīr Kabīr, 1982–3).

Meisami, Julie Scott, 'Writing Medieval Women: representations and misrepresentations', in Julia Bray (ed.), *Muslim Horizons* (London: Routledge, 2006).

Mir, Mustansir, 'The Quranic Story of Joseph: Plot, Themes, and Characters', *The Muslim World* 76: 1 (1986), pp. 1–15.

Mleynek, Sherryll S., *Knowledge and Mortality: Anagnorisis in Genesis and Narrative Fiction* (New York: Peter Lang, 1999).

Mohamed, Adel Hamed, *Ajāᵓib wa-asrār Sūrat Yūsuf* (Cairo: Dār al-Kitāb al-Maṣrī, 2009–2010).

Monroe, James T., *The Art of Badīᶜ az-Zamān al-Hamadhānī as Picaresque Narrative* (Beirut: American University of Beirut, 1983).

———*al-Maqāmāt al-Luzūmīya by Abū Ṭāhir Muḥammad ibn Yūsuf al-Tamīmī al-Saraqustī ibn al-Aštarkūwī* (Leiden: Brill, 2002).

Moore, Thomas, *Lalla Rookh: An Oriental Romance* (London: Longman, Brown, Green and Longman's, 1849).

Motzki, Harald, *The Biography of Muḥammad: The Issue of Sources* (Leiden: Brill, 2000).

Murnaghan, Sheila, *Disguise and Recognition in the Odyssey* (Princeton: Princeton University Press, 1987).

al-Nadīm, al-Raqīq, *Quṭb al-Surūr fī Awṣāf al-Khumūr*, ed. Aḥmad Jundī (Damascus: Majmaᶜ al-lughah al-ᶜarabiyyah, 1969).

al-Nahrawānī al-Jarīrī, Abū al-Faraj Muᶜāfā ibn Zakariyyā, *al-Jalīs al-Ṣāliḥ Wa-l-Īnās al-Shāfī*, ed. Muḥammad Mursī al-Khūlī (Beirut: ᶜĀlam al-Kutub, 1981), vol. 1.

al-Naysābūrī, Niẓām al-Dīn, *Gharāʾib al-Qurʾān wa-raghāʾib al-furqān*, ed. Ibrāhīm ᶜAṭwah ᶜIwaḍ (Cairo: Muṣṭafā al-Bābī al-Ḥalabī, 1962–70).

Newby, Gordon D., An Example of Coptic Literary Influence on Ibn Isḥāq's *Sīrah*, *Journal of Near Eastern Studies* 31 (1972), pp. 22–8.

———*The Making of the Last Prophet: A Reconstruction of the Earliest Biography of Muhammad* (Columbia: University of South Carolina Press, 1989).

Nizami, Ganjavi, *Iskandarname*, trans. and ed. E. E. Bertels and A. K. Arends (Baku: Elm, 1983).

———*The Haft Paykar: a Medieval Persian Romance* [1197], trans. Charles Edward Wilson (London: Probsthain, 1924).

———*The Haft Paykar: a Medieval Persian Romance*, trans. Julie Scott Meisami (Oxford: Oxford University Press, 1995).

Nöldeke, Theodor, *The History of the Qur'an* (Leiden: Brill, 2012).

Norris, H. T., 'Fables and Legends', in A. F. L. Beeston *et al.* (eds), *Arabic Literature to the End of the Umayyad Period* [*CHALUP*] (Cambridge: Cambridge University Press, 1983), pp. 139–41.

Omri, Mohamed-Salah, '*There is a Jāhiz for Every Age*: narrative construction and intertextuality in al-Hamadhānī's *Maqāmāt*', *Arabic and Middle Eastern Literatures*, 1:1 (1998).

Powers, David, *Muḥammad is not the Father of any of Your Men: The Making of the Last Prophet* (Philadelphia: University of Pennsylvania Press, 2009).

———*Zayd* (Philadelphia: University of Pennsylvania Press, 2014).

de Prémare, Alfred-Louis, *Joseph et Muhammad. Le chapitre 12 du Coran* (Aix-en-Provence: Publications de l'Université de Provence, 1989).

Prendergast, Christopher, *The Order of Mimesis: Balzac, Stendhal, Nerval, Flaubert* (Cambridge: Cambridge University Press, 1986).

Prendergast, W. J., *The Maqamat of Badī al-Zamān al-Hamadhānī* (London: Luzac, 1915); reprinted, with an introduction by C. E. Bosworth (London: Curzon Press, 1973).

Propp, Vladimir, *Morphology of the Folktale*, rev. and ed. Louis A. Wagner (Austin: University of Texas Press, 1968).

Pynchon, Thomas, *The Crying of Lot 49* (New York: Harper Perennial, 1999).

al-Qurṭubī, Muḥammad ibn Aḥmad Abū ᶜAbd Allāh al-Anṣārī, *Al-Jāmiᶜ li-aḥkām al-Qurʾān* (Beirut: Dār al-Kutub al-ᶜArabī, 1980).

al-Qushayrī, Abū l-Qāsim, *Laṭāʾif al-ishārāt*, ed. Ibrāhīm Basyūnī (Cairo: Dār al-Kutub al-ᶜArabī, 1968–71).

al-Rabzūghī, Nāṣir al-Dīn, *The Stories of the Prophets:* Qiṣaṣ al-Anbiyāʾ*: An Eastern Turkish Version*, vol. 2, trans. H. E. Boeschoten, J. O'Kane and M. Vandamme (Leiden: Brill, 1995).

Raphael, Frederic, 'After Pity and Terror, Knowledge', (Review of Aristotle's *Poetics* by Kenneth McLeish) *Times Literary Supplement* (14 May 1999), p. 14.

Raven, Wim, 'The biography of the Prophet and its scriptural basis', in Stefan Leder (ed.), *Storytelling in the Framework of Non-Fictional Arabic Literature* (Wiesbaden: Harrassowitz, 1998), pp. 421–32.

al-Rāzī, Muḥammad b. ᶜUmar Fakhr al-Dīn, *Sharḥ asmāʾ Allāh taᶜālā wa-l-ṣifāt* (Cairo: Maktabat al-kulliyāt al-azhariyyah, 1976).

———*Mafātīḥ al-ghayb (al-Tafsīr al-kabīr)* (Beirut: Dār Iḥyāʾ al-Turāth al-ᶜArabī, 1980).

Richards, D. S., 'The *Maqāmāt* of al-Hamadhānī: General remarks and a consideration of the manuscripts', *Journal of Arabic Literature* 22 (1991).

Rubin, Uri, 'The Seal of the Prophets and the Finality of Prophecy: On the Interpretation of Sūrat al-Aḥzāb (33)', *Zeitschrift der Deutschen Morgenländischen Gesellschaft* 164:1 (2014), pp. 65–96.

Rūzbihān al-Baqlī, Abū Muḥammad ibn Abī Naṣr, *ᶜArāʾis al-bayān fī ḥaqāʾiq al-Qurʾān* (Lucknow, 1898).

Sadan, Joseph, 'An Admirable and Ridiculous Hero: Some Notes on the Bedouin in Medieval Arabic Belles Lettres, on a Chapter of *Adab* by al-Râghib al-Iṣfahânî, and on a Literary Model in Which Admiration and Mockery Coexist', *Poetics Today* 10:3 (1989).

Saleh, Walid A., 'The Arabian Context of Muḥammad's Life', in Jonathan E. Brockopp (ed.), *The Cambridge Companion to Muḥammad* (Cambridge: Cambridge University Press, 2010).

Sallis, Eva, *Sheherazade through the Looking Glass: The Metamorphosis of the Thousand and One Nights* (London: Curzon Press, 1999).

Salmāwī, Muḥammad, *Ajniḥat al-farrāshah* (Cairo: Dār al-Shurūq, 2011).

Sarna, Nahum M., *Understanding Genesis (Heritage of Biblical Israel)* (New York: Jewish Theological Seminary of America, 1966).

Schoeler, Gregor, *Charakter und Authentie der muslimischen Überlieferung über das Leben Mohammeds* (Berlin: W. de Gruyter, 1996).

———*The Oral and the Written in Early Islam*, trans. Uwe Vegelpohl, ed. James E. Montgomery (London: Routledge, 2006).

Sells, Michael, *Approaching the Qurʾān. The Early Revelations* (Ashland: White Cloud Press, 1999).

El-Shamy, Hasan, *Folk Traditions of the Arab World: A Guide to Motif Classifications*, vol. 1 (Bloomington: Indiana University Press, 1995).

al-Sharīshī, Abū l-ᶜAbbās, *Sharḥ Maqāmāt al-Ḥarīrī*, 3 vols, ed. Ibrāhīm Shams al-Dīn (Beirut: Dār al-Kutub al-ᶜIlmiyyah, 1998).

Shoshan, Boaz, *Popular Culture in Medieval Cairo* (Cambridge: Cambridge University Press, 2002).

da Silva, Aldina, *La Symbolique des Rêves et des Vêtements* (Anjou: Fides, 1995).

Spellberg, Denise A., *Politics, Gender and the Islamic Past* (New York: Columbia University Press, 1996).

Steingass, F. W. [See Thomas Chenery].

Stetkevych, Jaroslav, *Muhammad and the Golden Bough* (Bloomington: Indiana University Press, 1996).

Stowasser, Barbara, *Women in the Qurʾān, Traditions, and Interpretation* (New York: Oxford University Press, 1994).

Stroumsa, Sarah, 'Avicenna's Philosophical Stories: Aristotle's *Poetics* Reinterpreted', *Arabica* 39:2 (1992).

al-Sulamī, Abū ᶜAbd Al-Raḥmān Muḥammad ibn al-Ḥusayn, *Ziyādāt ḥaqāʾiq al-tafsīr*, ed. Gerhard Böwering (Beirut: Dār al-Mashriq, 1995).

al-Ṭabarī, Abū Jaᶜfar, *Jāmiᶜ al-bayān ᶜan taʾwīl āy al-Qurʾān* (Egypt, 1954–7).

Tabbaa, Yasser, *Constructions of Power and Piety in Medieval Aleppo* (University Park: Pennsylvania State University Press, 1997).

al-Tanūkhī, al-Muḥassin, *The Table-Talk of a Mesopotamian Judge*, partial trans. from the original Arabic (*Nishwār al-muḥāḍarah*) by D. S. Margoliouth [repr. from *Islamic Culture* 3–6, Hyderabad, 1929–1933].

———*Al-Faraj baᶜd al-shiddah* (Cairo: Maktabat al-Khānjī, 1955).

———*Nishwār al-muḥāḍarah*, 8 vols, ed. ᶜAbbūd al-Shāljī (Beirut: Dār Ṣādir, 1972).

———*Al-Faraj baᶜd al-shiddah*, 5 vols, ed. ᶜAbbūd al-Shāljī (Beirut: Dār Ṣādir, 1978).

———*Ende Gut, Alles Gut: Das Buch der Erleichterung nach der Bedrängnis*, trans. Arnold Hottinger (Zurich: Manesse, 1979).

al-Thaᶜlabī, Ibn Isḥāq Aḥmad ibn Muḥammad Ibrāhīm, *Qiṣaṣ al-anbiyāʾ (ᶜArūs al-majālis)* (Beirut: Dār al-Maᶜrifah, n.d.).

———*Qiṣaṣ al-anbiyāʾ (= ᶜArāʾis al-majālis)* (Egypt: Maktabat al-jumhūriyyah al-ᶜarabiyyah, 1954).

———*ᶜArāʾis al-majālis fī qiṣaṣ al-anbiyāʾ, or 'Lives of the Prophets'*, trans. and annotated by William M. Brinner (Leiden: Brill, 2002).

Toorawa, Shawkat M. (ed. and trans.), *Consorts of the Caliphs: Women and the Court of Baghdad* by Ibn al-Sāᶜī (New York: New York University Press, 2015).

al-Ṭūsī, Abū Jaᶜfar Muḥammad ibn al-Ḥasan, *Kitāb al-Ghaybah*, ed. Muḥammad Ṣādiq al-Mūsawī (Najaf: Maktabat al-Ṣādiq, 1965).

Tustarī, Abū Muḥammad Sahl ibn ᶜAbd Allāh, *Tafsīr al-Qurʾān al-ᶜaẓīm* (Cairo, 1911).

ᶜUmar b. Abī Rabīᶜah, *Dīwān* (Beirut: Dār Ṣādir, 1971).

Voltaire, *Zadig* (First published in 1747).

al-Wāḥidī, Abū al-Ḥasan ᶜAlī ibn Aḥmad, *Asbāb al-nuzūl* (Beirut: ᶜĀlam al-Kutub, n.d.).

Waldoff, Jessica, *Recognition in Mozart's Operas* (Oxford: Oxford University Press, 2006).

Walker, Ashley Manjarrez, and Michael Sells, 'The Wiles of Women and Performative Intertextuality: ᶜĀʾisha, the Hadith of the Slander, and the Sura of Yusuf', *Journal of Arabic Literature* 31 (1999).

al-Wāqidī, Muḥammad ibn ᶜUmar, *Kitāb al-Maghāzī*, ed. Marsden Jones (Oxford: Oxford University Press, 1966).

Weber, Edgard, *L'Imaginaire arabe et contes érotiques* (Paris: L'Harmatton, 1990).

Wehr, Hans, *Kitāb al-ḥikāyāt al-ᶜajībah wal-akhbār al-gharībah/Das Buch der wunderbaren Erzaehlungen und seltsamen Geschichten* (Wiesbaden: Franz Steiner, 1956).

Wensinck, A. J., *Handbook of Early Muhammadan Traditions* (Leiden: Brill, 1927).

Westermann, Claus, *Joseph: Studies of the Joseph Stories in Genesis* (London: Bloomsbury, 1996).

White, Hugh C., *Narration and Discourse in the Book of Genesis* (Cambridge: Cambridge University Press, 1991).

Wild, Stefan, 'Die zehnte Maqāma des Ibn Nāqiyā: eine Burleske aus Baghdad', in W. Heinrichs and G. Schoeler (eds), *Festschrift Ewald Wagner zum 65.*

Geburtstag. Band 2: Studien zur Arabischen Dichtung (Beirut: Franz Steiner, 1994), pp. 427–38.

———(ed.), 'Self-referentiality in the Qurʾān', *Diskurse der Arabistik*, vol. 11 (Wiesbaden: Harrassowitz Verlag, 2006).

Wilde, Oscar, *The Importance of Being Earnest* [First performed in 1895].

Wright, W., *A Grammar of the Arabic Language* (Cambridge: Cambridge University Press, 1979).

Zakharia, Katia, *Abū Zayd al-Sarūǧī, imposteur et mystique* (Damascus: IFEAD, 2000).

Zamaksharī, Maḥmūd ibn ʿUmar Abū l-Qāsim, *Al-Kashshāf ʿan ḥaqāʾiq al-tanzīl* (Egypt, 1966).

al-Zayyāt, Laṭīfah, *Ḥawl al-iltizām al-siyāsī wa-l-kitābah al-nisāʾiyyah*, *Alif* 10 (1990).

Index